CHINA
TRANSFORMED

CHINA TRANSFORMED

Historical Change and the Limits of European Experience

R. BIN WONG

Cornell University Press
Ithaca and London

First published 1997 by Cornell University Press.
First printing, Cornell Paperbacks, 1997.

Printed in the United States of America

Library of Congress Cataloging-in-Publication Data

Wong, Roy Bin.
    China transformed : historical change and the limits of European
experience / R. Bin Wong.
        p. cm.
    Includes bibliographical references and index.
    ISBN 0-8014-3254-5 (alk. paper). — ISBN 0-8014-8327-1 (pbk. :
alk. paper)
    1. China—History. 2. Europe—History. 3. China—Economic
conditions. 4. China—Social conditions. 5. Europe—Economic
conditions. 6. Europe—Social conditions. I. Title.
DS735.W76 1997
951—dc21   97-23232

Cornell University Press strives to utilize environmentally responsible suppliers
and materials to the fullest extent possible in the publishing of its books. Such
materials include vegetable-based, low-VOC inks and acid-free papers that are
also either recycled, totally chlorine-free, or partly composed of nonwood fibers.

Cloth printing   10 9 8 7 6 5 4 3 2 1

Paperback printing 10 9 8 7 6 5 4 3 2 1

CONTENTS

v

ACKNOWLEDGMENTS

Parts of this book were first drafted some years ago as discrete exercises in comparative history. I didn't plan to make them part of a single volume until I found myself repeatedly surprised by what Western scholars said about Chinese history, often basing their arguments on just a few items of English-language scholarship. I became convinced that those of us who spend most of our time laboring on so-called non-Western parts of the world should make greater efforts to offer analyses that engage arguments about historical change in European history systematically—not simply to distinguish the times and places of our research from the paradigmatic Western cases, but to generate the elements of well-grounded comparative history that can identify issues in European as well as non-European history, contribute to projects in world history, and create a new basis for building social theories to replace the great nineteenth-century efforts limited in large measure to European foundations.

My interest in economic history, political development, and social conflicts goes back many years to undergraduate reading courses on Europe with Charles Tilly at the University of Michigan. In graduate school at Harvard University in the mid-1970s, I was unable to answer a question posed by David Landes about what he, as a historian of Europe, could learn by studying China—a failure I remember quite vividly because it occurred on my Ph.D. oral examination. This book is a belated response. During those student years the late Joseph Fletcher Jr. offered his guidance, support, and friendship, all of which helped me keep the goal of doing comparative history firmly in my mind.

The opportunity to think more systematically about topics in this book came when I spent three and a half years of intellectual stimulation and enjoyment as a Junior Fellow at the University of Michigan's Society of Fellows. Toward the end of my tenure there, Charles Tilly, then at the New School for Social Research, suggested that I write a short book about states that included the Chinese case, since it was so obviously different from many others and never quite accounted for. His proposal prompted me to think more about what has become Part II of this book.

Several years later, some conversations with James Lee helped push me to bring together this book comparing Chinese and European patterns of historical change. Three colleagues at the University of California at Irvine helped in different ways. Teaching with Ping-ti Ho and engaging in many long conversations with him afforded me a rare opportunity to be inspired by one of the most learned historians of China in the United States. Kenneth Pomeranz, who read multiple drafts of this book, not only flagged numerous problems but helped solve many of them. Dorothy

Solinger repeatedly responded to my queries about contemporary politics with materials that always helped me understand a period outside my area of expertise.

I'm grateful for the efforts of scholars who have read one version or another and offered important criticisms and advice: Timothy Brook, Bozhong Li, Jean-Laurent Rosenthal, Julia C. Strauss, Charles Tilly, Ernest P. Young, and an anonymous reader for Cornell University Press. Others read sections of the manuscript and made valuable suggestions; I thank François Godement, Linda Grove, Mio Kishimoto, James Lee, Robert Moeller, Yoshinobu Shiba, Ann Waltner, and Pierre-Etienne Will.

Various versions of the material in this book have been delivered at seminars and conferences. I am especially grateful to the Academia Sinica in Taipei, the Ecole des Hautes Etudes en Sciences Sociales in Paris, and the University of Tokyo and International Christian University in Tokyo for hosting research stays and providing venues to discuss many parts of this book. In the United States, I have benefited repeatedly from the collegiality of the All UC Group in Economic History, an organization that affirms the best kind of intellectual exchange that the University of California system can promote.

Some material in chapter 5 appears in "Confucian Agendas for Material and Ideological Control in Modern China," in *Culture and State in Chinese History*, edited by Theodore Huters, R. Bin Wong, and Pauline Yu, and is used by permission of the publishers, Stanford University Press. Copyright © 1997 by the Board of Trustees of the Leland Stanford Junior University. Material in chapter 10 was initially prepared for a 1987 conference on Chinese local elites organized by Joseph W. Esherick and Mary Backus Rankin. Earlier versions of chapter 2 appeared in *Zhongguo shehui jingji shi yanjiu* and *Kindai Chūgoku shi kenkyū*, and an earlier version of Chapter 9 appeared in *Annales ESC*. At Cornell University Press it was my good fortune to work with Roger Haydon and Barbara Salazar, who moved the manuscript along, and Carolyn Pouncy, whose copy editing has sharpened the book's prose. Randy Stross, working under time pressure, graciously created the indexing program that allowed me to make my own index.

On the personal side, my wife, Kathy Lazarus, has encouraged me both to finish this book and to keep the effort within some larger perspective. My children, Leilani and Jay, have repeatedly tolerated the spurts of intense work that periodically made me less visible at home than they expected. For their various efforts to prod and push me to get my work done and spend more time with them, I'm grateful to my family.

American customs suggest that the author generously absolve all who have helped him of any errors and cheerfully bear the burdens of his mistakes. I prefer to think (and hope) that this book may become part of various discussions about Chinese history, comparative history, and world history, stimulating other scholars to construct alternatives that amplify, qualify, and even overturn some of the proposals I put forward here. In such a scenario, neither I nor those I've acknowledged need worry too much about what isn't yet "right" in this book, as long as enough has been said to persuade people to ponder these problems and formulate additional solutions.

R. BIN WONG

CHINA
TRANSFORMED

INTRODUCTION
Beyond European Models
of Historical Change

When scholars look for the origins of the contemporary world, many begin with the political expansion of Western states across the globe and the economic transformations brought on by a capitalist system of European origins. Indeed, it has become difficult to imagine the construction of Europe and the expansion of Western power across the world without the seemingly natural and necessary unfolding of national state formation and capitalist development. History often seems to reach non-Western peoples as they come into contact with Europeans. Their modern histories are conventionally constructed along the axis of native responses to Western challenges.

Alternatively, the cultural and historical integrity of non-Western societies may be considered apart from European influences, or as hybrid societies built from a combination of native and Western influences. This distancing of non-Western parts of the world from Western power asserts multidimensional identities for Africa, Asia, and Latin America, distinct from the one-dimensional native–Western axis. The urge to establish distance and separatedness from Western power has led people to create multiple markers of their differences.

Comparing Patterns of Historical Change

Growing recognition of the analytical and interpretive limitations of seeing non-Western history in terms of European national state formation and the development of capitalism has led numerous scholars to focus on such issues as cultural identity, gender formation, race, and nation. This book too aims to dislodge European state making and capitalism from their privileged positions as universalizing themes in world history, but it offers a new approach: comparison with the dynamics of economic and political change in a major non-Western civilization. It seeks to establish how this civilization differed from Europe, but only as part of a larger program of identifying similarities and connections as well.

One conventional way in which comparisons have been made has been to assert some key difference. In the 1950s one common family of explanations for the *failure* of East Asian countries to develop modern industrial economies cited cultural factors, stressing the absence of an aggressive and acquisitive individualism in Confucian societies. Basing their arguments at least loosely on Weberian arguments, some scholars of the post–World War II world claimed that a country such as Japan lacked the entrepreneurial spirit of daring and innovation necessary for a modern industrialized economy.[1] More recently a very different story has been told in which Confucian virtues, such as respect for authority and the submerging of individual desires to group goals in a spirit of self-sacrifice, are promoted to explain the Japanese economic miracle.[2] The juxtaposition of these polar assessments of "culture" suggests a contradiction: how can cultural attitudes simultaneously hinder and promote economic change? The same methodological problem arises in respect to the significance of the ecological and organizational features of rice agriculture, in contrast, at least implicitly, to those of European dry field farming. In 1957 Karl Wittfogel made the irrigation demands of rice agriculture a cornerstone of his theory about hydraulic societies composed of peasants who labored under despotic governments. More recently, however, some scholars have suggested that rice agriculture encourages small-scale family farming because intensive labor demands require supervision costs too high to make large-scale management reasonable. Petty commodity production results from rice agriculture, promoting the social freedom of peasants (Palat 1995). How can rice agriculture be the foundation for both despotism and an independent market-oriented peasantry?

Differences alone cannot create comparability. Without standards for comparison, effective generalization is limited. We are condemned to an extreme relativism without any strategy to replace various forms of Eurocentrism with interpretations that can embrace Western and non-Western experiences on an analytically more equal basis. Unless comparisons and contrasts are made first, assessments of connections between Western and various non-Western countries too readily reflect only the Western view. Creating strategies of comparison that avoid privileging European categories of analysis and dynamics of historical change is one important task for the chapters that follow.

---

[1] Of course even in the 1950s, as the Japanese economy recovered from the catastrophe of World War II, the long-term base of economic development was firmly placed. But this did not resolve the challenge of embracing Japanese cultural traits in a concept of "modernization." See, for example, John W. Hall 1965.

[2] A range of interpretations locate Japan's economic success in the country's particular history and culture. They include works as diverse as Morishima 1982 and Dore 1987.

A second set of problems addressed in this book concerns the nature of historical explanation, in particular the difficulties of explaining long-term processes of change and continuity. Historians generally study examples of change. Somehow change seems to require more explanation than the absence of change. But the absence of apparent change suggests the reproduction of a set of relationships or conditions. Why reproduction or continuity should take place rather than change is important, especially with respect to China and Europe, since we conventionally view the former as experiencing far less change than the latter.

When historians aspire to be scientific, they usually seek to explain some sequence of events. The exercise in formal terms resembles the approach adopted by astronomers, evolutionary biologists, and geologists, whose task is to explain the past. They do not, like physicists or chemists, *predict* certain outcomes from substances with particular properties under specified initial conditions. Geologists, for example, don't predict the Grand Canyon—they explain how it came to be. In all complex historical processes of either the natural or human worlds, there are contingencies and surprises that shape later patterns of activity in new ways, even if historians easily associate what did happen with what "had to happen." This sense of necessity masks the multiple possibilities always open at particular historical moments. The longer the time span covered, the more likely that alternative paths could have been taken at any of several junctures. Long sequences of historical change are neither logically necessary nor organically natural, but some outcomes are more likely than others at any particular point along a specific historical trajectory, because many kinds of historical change are path-dependent— what has happened before shapes what is likely to happen in the future. Scholars who reject the long causal sequences of nineteenth-century social theory have yet to develop modified explanations that recognize path-dependent probabilities of historical changes.

For historical trajectories to matter, there must be more than one. Western social theory has generally analyzed only that created by the twin processes of European state formation and capitalism. Western states and economies have histories that matter to the formation of the modern world. Other parts of the globe, according to the research strategies employed in most social science research, had no histories of comparable significance before Western contacts began to transform them. Their modern fates are generally assumed to be determined more by their connections to a larger system than by their own trajectories of historical change. If we supplement studies that proceed from those assumptions with others that ask more seriously how long-term trajectories of change are shaped, both in China and in Europe, we may more effectively delineate a range of futures. We can replace outmoded teleologies with more restrained suggestions about less-certain possibilities. To do this, we must first reconstruct the dynamics of non-Western trajectories. This book makes such an effort for China. Its first goal is to establish elements of an analysis for long-term historical change in China that accord weight to dynamics distinctive to the Chinese case. A second goal, then, is to account for similarities between Chinese and European dynamics, so that we may grasp what the differences may mean. To pursue these tasks, I propose strategies for avoiding an exclusive reliance on European categories without forsaking them entirely.

One Thousand Years of Chinese History and Western Social Theory

During the last century, expectations about historical change over the past millennium of Chinese history have been based on European history. Beginning in the early twentieth century, Japanese historians have pictured China between the tenth and twelfth centuries as a society with a growing urban culture supported by an expanding commercial economy. The major question then becomes: What derailed China from this promising beginning and kept China from sustaining its developmental lead over Europe? An alternative view stresses the absence of secular change before the nineteenth century. Political ideology, social institutions, and cultural practices are seen to reproduce a constant and permanent order. Change is conceived as cyclical, the most famous formulation being the traditional dynastic cycle, in which a ruling house is vigorous in its youth and rules benevolently, only to become lazy and corrupt in later generations.

These two basic views of China—social change gone wrong and stagnation— are themselves developed out of the Western tradition of social theory as explanatory of modern society. Karl Marx and Max Weber each argued for a distinctive cluster of traits that set Europe off from other parts of the world; these traits account for Western successes and the failures of others. In Marx's account of capitalism and modern society, focused primarily on Europe, Asia was a region of stagnation, and European imperialism there was a brutal but positive force for social and economic change. Weber's study of world religions led him to emphasize European religious and economic change; describing historical development according to a dynamic of economic development and bureaucratic rationality, Weber, like Marx, presented a path of social development defined by Europe's distinctive successes.

Marx and Weber offer particular paths toward modernity. Later scholars universalized these alternative statements of Europe's trajectory of change. For instance, many Chinese and Japanese historians of China have seen the country moving through Marxist stages of development. Chinese historians in particular have identified an "incipient capitalism" in which changes in production and trade argue for China's trajectory along a common economic path to modernity. But expectations for historical change held by Western historians of China as well have their empirical basis in accounts of European historical development. Nearly all scholarship on Chinese social and economic history, whatever its origins, is based on assumptions about social change imported from European experiences.

After World War II, American sociologists promoted European history as the basis for social theory. Talcott Parsons (1966), for example, explicitly derived his general theory from an interpretation of European historical change. Looking back from the mid-twentieth century to reconstruct how Western society, and American society in particular, had reached its present state, Parsons created a structural-functional model of social change in which the differentiation of politics, economics, and religion became the norm for modernity. To generalize his theory beyond the historical path derived from Western experiences, Parsons shifted to an evolutionary model of social change that portrayed the traits of successful societies as functions necessary to become modern. But since these functions were derived from Western experiences, the norms of social development remained resolutely rooted in a particular reading of the European past. Parsons viewed sociocultural developments as a process of social differentiation in which religion separates from secular culture and the economy becomes independent of government interference. The Industrial Revolution and the development of democratic institutions in the wake of the French Revolution powered the process of social change. Parsons's scheme embraced variations within Europe, but what of areas outside the European framework? Are they stagnant, or do they simply parallel Europe for a while before diverging? Neither alternative is particularly helpful.

The radical alternative to reliance on Western categories is to ignore them entirely. Scholars who have labored to reconstruct Chinese historical phenomena without explicit reference to European history or Western social theory have made clear contributions in intellectual history. But reliance on native categories limits us to imagining possibilities within that specific linguistic frame of reference. Problems immediately follow. If, for instance, notions of historical time or secular change do not exist linguistically, do they not exist historically either? Does the failure of participants to observe change mean that outside observers too cannot see change? When we turn to social, political, or economic history, the very categories that participants and later analysts use to examine phenomena raise issues of comparability. Simply to examine kinship, for instance, suggests that kinship ties in China can be compared with those in other societies. To say that the Chinese had a "state" or "government" depends on some general category for which the Chinese and other cases share common characteristics. Similarly, discussions of "markets" presume that commercial exchange has certain qualities found even in widely separated contexts. How scholars today could invent explanations innocent of any assumptions about how things work elsewhere is difficult to imagine. The degree to which our analyses presume common or distinctive terms shapes how "general" or "particular" we consider our research problems to be, but even the most particular are ultimately framed at least implicitly by knowledge beyond the specific case.

Western social theory first developed through disagreements over how to characterize the particular path of change that led to modern society. The contemporary Chinese historian whose world view and perspective on the past is already shaped by influences beyond China faces a particular problem when he or she considers topics involving important connections between China and Europe. Many important traditions of scholarship on the modern world treat such connections as primary. Marx's insight into the disruptive impact of imperialism, for example, becomes the starting point for the Marxist tradition's efforts to build upon the connections forged between Europe and the world to construct a system within which non-Western changes are dictated by European powers. Alternatively, Western impact can be more positively viewed as introducing new opportunities economically as well as politically and socially as society is remade in a modern, that is Western, manner. This intellectual strategy easily associates "traditional" with barriers obstructing the positive dynamics of change.

To invest the native with independent meaning of its own and not just meaning derived from its reaction to the West, American scholars began to turn in the 1980s to the eighteenth century where they analyzed domestic dynamics of historical change preceding Western impact. There they found Japanese scholars looking forward from the sixteenth century.[3] Nonetheless, the search for native dynamics often finds parallels to European dynamics; alternatives to European dynamics are proposed less frequently. In either case Europe looms large as a point of reference for studies of modern China.[4]

How can the agenda for understanding Chinese history not be reduced to either its links to Europe or its parallel evolution? Here is my strategy. First, I compare the two master processes of modern European history—the development of capitalism and the formation of national states—to Chinese economic and political changes. I identify important features of the European processes through comparisons with Chinese dynamics, then consider small-scale and large-scale collective actions that seem surprisingly similar and yet include crucial differences. Regarding economic change, I argue for a cluster of similar dynamics of economic change in early modern Europe and late imperial China followed by a crucial rupture in nineteenth-century Europe. As for state making, I contrast the historical circumstances of Chinese and European political changes before and after Western (and Japanese) military power threatened China with dismemberment between the mid-nineteenth and mid-twentieth centuries. Finally, I explore the rationales, contexts, and significance of small-scale political and economic protests (grain seizures and tax resistance) and large-scale actions (revolutions). The outcomes of this enterprise supply fresh perspectives on major dynamics of change in both Chinese and European history. These comparisons can then be used to extend and revise social theory.

Nineteenth-century social theory has been discredited in many quarters. One way to move beyond the great social theorists of the nineteenth and early twentieth centuries is to incorporate the patterns of historical change found in non-Western societies, a challenge that affects scholars in several disciplines. This book offers

---

[3]For an introduction to the Japanese literature in English, see Grove and Daniels 1984.
[4]For examples of scholars who take European references for Chinese change, see Huang 1990 and Rowe 1993. Rowe consciously looks for Chinese parallels with Europe; Huang claims to be escaping European references in an essay predicated upon European norms. R. B. Wong 1990, 1992, and 1993 discuss their efforts.

one response to this crucial task, a response that seeks both to reduce the aspirations of generalizing in social theory and to expand the range of material that such theory can adequately encompass. I start in Europe, from which so much research on non-Western parts of the world has struggled to escape. To transcend Eurocentric views of the world, I believe we should return to European cases to consider carefully how national state formation and capitalist development actually took place as historical processes rather than as abstract theoretical models. After assessing Chinese dynamics according to European measures of changes I evaluate European possibilities according to Chinese standards in order to introduce comparisons not usually made by contemporary analysts. This strategy allows us to qualify and revise older insights rather than discard them for being deeply flawed. Eurocentric views of the world are inadequate, but they are not necessarily more wrong (or right) than comparisons made from other vantage points.[5] Sustained comparison of Chinese and European patterns of economic development, state formation, and social protest can suggest ways of interpreting historical change in both parts of the world, identify those subjects on which additional historical research may be especially useful, and contribute to the construction of social theory grounded not only in the European historical past but that of other regions as well.

A Disclaimer and a Defense

A book of this scale unavoidably contains descriptions and assessments that some readers will consider incomplete or misleading. Readers with a strong background in either Chinese or European history may find me belaboring the obvious in some situations and being too cryptic in others. Those who wish for a more explicit engagement with traditions of social theory will find the book short on context for some of my arguments. I intend my discussions of Chinese and European history to highlight features that become especially significant when viewed comparatively. My strategies of comparison recognize, whenever possible, the virtues of beginning with similarities in order to establish a clear basis for assessing the nature and importance of differences. Yet much of what has intrigued generations of historians looking across civilizations are the differences that separate various parts of the world. Social theories generally have difficulties explaining large clusters of differences. I intend my analysis to provide one set of strategies to deal with this basic problem in social theory. Solutions alert us to topics in both Chinese and European history that deserve careful scrutiny. When history is written to help develop our more general ideas about social change, we can aspire to improve our explanations of different worlds in the past.

---

[5]Foucault's insight that the production of knowledge is intimately enmeshed with the production of power relationships has provided fertile ground for research in the social sciences and humanities, but it is not adequate to adjudicate among competing interpretations. If we can do no more than recognize differences and attribute them to social and political factors, we significantly limit our ability to generate systematic social science knowledge.

This is primarily a book about Chinese history and secondarily a book about European history. The comparisons I draw allow me to suggest some ideas on how to build better general social theory. When the aim is to reach a variety of readers, no mix of argument and evidence will serve all readers equally.

There are also analytical difficulties in a work embracing long stretches of both Chinese and European history. First, the spatial units of China and Europe are often much larger than the areas being compared in particular ways. Economic and political patterns vary considerably in both China and Europe. Those patterns I present as typical or important for China and Europe do not include all particular situations at either end of Eurasia. Wherever it is useful and feasible to do so, I have tried to remind the reader of the particular spatial units being analyzed. Second, some issues that some specialists deem important receive modest attention, if any. I urge the reader to judge the usefulness of my arguments and evidence on the basis of what they directly help to explain as well as what they suggest about related types of analysis. Noting items not addressed or inadequately treated matters, I think, only when such absences undermine the arguments or qualify the evidence presented.

PART I

ECONOMIC HISTORY
AND THE PROBLEM
OF DEVELOPMENT

Economics as a discipline emerged alongside the development of capitalism. It became the set of analytical tools used to explain the operations of markets, firms, and individual economic actors. Originally tied intimately to the study of politics—the classical economists such as Adam Smith, Thomas Malthus, and David Ricardo engaged in political economy—economics narrowed its focus to a set of issues that have come increasingly to be addressed in the language of formal mathematics. For some economists, the discipline has reached a point of crisis. Its divorce from explanations of real-world behavior is no longer acceptable, but the conventional model remains the testing of theoretical propositions with appropriate data. When data sets do not fit the parameters of a theory, one looks for a set of data that provide a better fit. In this the economist resembles the experimental scientist: both accept a distance from naturally occurring reality as the cost of achieving some control over selected phenomena.

The discipline of economics has invested most of its efforts and reaped its largest rewards in the study of contemporary capitalist economies. When we turn to economic history, economics does best in institutional settings in which its assumptions clearly apply. The further we move from the contemporary West in time and space, the more fragile is the fit between economic assumptions and social conditions. In analyzing economic history in this book, I argue that certain principles, such as trade flows according to supply and demand, price movements according to changes in supply and demand, and spatial specialization of labor (e.g., a cotton producer buying his grain), fit what we know of late imperial China's economy quite comfortably. I further argue that a Chinese peasant's economic undertakings were similar in fundamental and important ways to those of his European counterpart. Before the nineteenth century, peasants across Eurasia aimed to insure their subsistence and expand their incomes. In a world of limited resources and modest opportunities, few could dream of becoming rich, but all could hope to increase their sense of security. Such "rational" purposes say nothing about other kinds of connections people made to either the material or spiritual worlds. Moreover, the larger views of the economy within which these rudimentary principles operated could well be different. To establish a sensible basis of comparison, we need not argue an extreme set of similarities such as the proposition that European bourgeois ideology also flowered on Chinese soil. We can make do with a far less demanding criterion in order to compare the trajectories of economic change in China and Europe. As long as people can be "rational" with regards to material means–ends calculations, we can compare their efforts. They may not enjoy similar successes. Differences can emerge for a wealth of reasons, including the facts that people in different societies develop alternative ways of organizing capital and labor, technologies differ, transport possibilities vary, and the distributions of natural resources are uneven.

Even if Eurasian trajectories of economic change do not trace a single path of development, there are common features to successful expansions of economic production. Increased per capita output results from specialization, higher investments, and technological change. As the factors making for economic development have become better understood, strategies for creating modern economies have been elaborated to achieve the benefits many Europeans came to enjoy without a conscious policy-making process.

Economic development in Europe and the United States was often composed of private-sector changes. Governments played supporting roles, but the initiative and drive rested in entrepreneurial hands. Contemporary efforts to create modern economies in Africa, Asia, and Latin America often require far more of governments, which must choose among alternative paths of development. The possible strategies for creating economic change are far more numerous than those available to European economies in the eighteenth and nineteenth centuries. But the persistent difficulties attending economic progress in parts of Africa, Latin America, and Asia make clear that the expanded horizons of economic possibility have not brought material advances any closer to the lives of millions of people. Economists have not proven uniformly successful in creating development policies that work.

These difficulties appear to be quite different from the problems of explaining change in economic history, particularly since economic historians generally study the American and European past, while development economists work on less developed countries. One group can apply principles known to work while the other is searching for ways to apply those same principles to very different conditions. To span the empirical distance separating economic historians and development economists, the Chinese experience has the virtue of fitting both discourses. It is an economy with both a well-studied history and a carefully examined set of development possibilities.

Chapter 1 sets out some basic economic similarities China and Europe enjoyed before the nineteenth century. Chapter 2 considers the parallel roles of rural handicraft industry before a set of technological changes in Europe created a fundamentally new set of economic possibilities. Chapter 3 makes the journey from economic history to economic development to compare twentieth-century Chinese economic changes with those in the industrial West. The chapters of Part I show that economic principles have a powerful capacity to order diverse economic experiences even as they prove inadequate to explain the multiple paths of Eurasian economic history and development.

1

ECONOMIC CHANGE IN LATE IMPERIAL CHINA AND EARLY MODERN EUROPE

The decades since the early 1960s have seen a wealth of research on Chinese economic history, principally by Chinese and Japanese researchers. Scholars have identified a cluster of major changes beginning in roughly the tenth century, especially in the area of eastern China near modern-day Shanghai known as Jiangnan in the late imperial period. Agricultural land productivity rose because of new seed varieties and technological improvements; cash cropping expanded as increased trade carried goods to growing cities and towns. These changes were supported by improved transportation, the formation of merchant organizations, and government policies that gave freer rein to market exchange.

A broad consensus also exists regarding the general status of China's contemporary economy—as its industries grow, China is only beginning to experience sustained economic growth with rising standards of living; only since the 1980s has the transformation of the agrarian basis of life shared by hundreds of millions of people begun in earnest. Between these two points of general agreement that bracket a millennium of Chinese history, we lack a fully persuasive interpretation of Chinese economic changes.[1]

---

[1]Feuerwerker (1992) identifies some of the analytical problems that confront economic historians of China. My approach to these problems complements his effort to distinguish among sources of growth as a strategy to explain more effectively economic change in Chinese history.

The Problem of Economic Change in Chinese History

Perhaps the central reason for the historians' failure to explain what happened to China's economy in mid- and late imperial times lies in the continued effort to frame the problem in terms of what *didn't* happen. China did not follow any European path of economic development. Studies of Chinese economic practices between 1500 and 1900 usually proceed in one of two ways. They pinpoint a Chinese difference from Europe and label this the key differentiating factor; for example, Nishijima's classic study (1966) of cotton handicrafts shows how production was tied to rural industry. Alternatively, research highlights a small cluster of similarities that promised European-style success for China but did not deliver. Studies of agricultural commercialization, the use of hired labor, the expansion of handicraft production, and urban factory formation, among others, often finger one of three villains to explain the absence of a more cheerful storyline (Liu Yongcheng 1982: Li, Wei, and Jing 1983; Wu and Xu 1985; Zhang Guohui 1986). The first is the Chinese state, which obstructs progress to protect its power. The second is imperialism, which warps economic changes to serve foreign interests. The third group of villains are "feudal" powerholders anxious to defend their elite positions against change. Some studies are framed with a mechanical Marxist perspective. But the attempt to define what went wrong in China according to what went right in Europe informs non-Marxist scholarship as well. Mark Elvin's influential 1973 study, *The Pattern of the Chinese Past,* asks why China did not experience European-style scientific and organizational changes after achieving a "medieval economic revolution." More recently, Philip Huang (1990) explores the divergence of Chinese experiences from European ideal types that the author associates with Smith and Marx. Nor is the search for what Chinese economic history lacks confined to China specialists. John A. Hall (1985:56) speaks of Chinese "institutional blockages to the market" in his wide-ranging assessment of world history from the perspective of European development, whereas E. L. Jones, in the second of his thought-provoking comparative economic histories (1988:141), suggests the Chinese state stifled development through "under-government," the standards for which are European government policies.

What unites almost all assessments of economic change in late-imperial China is an agreement that China possessed ingredients for continued economic change based on the dramatic developments of the Song period. The Marxist analysis looks for villains that blocked what would otherwise have been a natural set of developments toward capitalism. Though resolutely not Marxist, E. L. Jones (1981, 1988) offers a similar perspective on economic growth as a natural phenomenon that once on track continues to reproduce itself unless taken off track by some arbitrary interference. For China, he sees the government as the force that both fails to provide the necessary framework for continued growth and blocks what had been positive developments. He typifies a perspective that simultaneously makes the state too weak to have been positive but strong enough to have been negative.

Although most analysts search for positive obstructions to economic development in China, a smaller group searches for a key ingredient that the Chinese lacked. The most famous of such analyses remains Max Weber's contrast of the Protestant ethic with religious beliefs in other parts of the world. The argument that Protestantism was particularly conducive to the development of capitalism has been qualified in several ways. Within Europe, Catholic areas also achieved economic development. Beyond Europe, arguments have been made for the fit between religion and economic change. For China, Yu Ying-shih (1987) has shown how new concerns in sixteenth- and seventeenth-century Confucianism paralleled the rise of a distinctive merchant point of view as trade expanded in importance. For eighteenth-century Japan, Tetsuo Najita (1987) has shown how a group of Osaka merchants created a respected place for themselves in a Confucian world view. It is difficult to isolate a set of beliefs that proved crucial to social change for two reasons. First, the situations in China and Europe suggest that at least partially parallel kinds of intellectual change can appear in different societies without producing the same dynamics of economic change. Second, economic developments in Catholic and Protestants parts of Europe suggest that both areas in which religion changes and those where it does not can experience the same economic changes. The linkages between intellectual belief and economic change are simply too complex to reduce to simple expectations about the impact of religious belief on economic behavior.

Explaining what happened in Chinese economic history by appeal to what did not happen raises several difficulties. For one, it precludes the assessment of Chinese practices that do not fit neatly into European categories.[2] For another, it makes explanation too easy. The changes that led to European capitalism include numerous elements that were historically distinctive. One can find with little effort any number of differences between China and Europe, but assessing which of these differences mattered is difficult without developing analytical standards of significance.[3] One source of such standards is a baseline of similarities, which can then be used to delineate the arena within which important initial differences occurred. Other differences can then be introduced as we explore further the distinctive paths followed by different parts of Eurasia. Otherwise, all differences compete for our attention. The economic similarities considered here begin with Adam Smith.

---

[2] Eurasian differences in state making and political economy appear to have been partially obscured by an insistent adoption of European standards of state making and political economy. This issue is explored further in Part II.

[3] For instance, if we attribute England's Industrial Revolution to its abundance of resources and skilled mechanics, an appropriate approach to technical problems, a supportive political system and social structure that developed property rights, patent laws, rational taxes, and a laissez-faire approach to economic activity, we end up with a broad-based description rather than an explanation of the Industrial Revolution (Snooks 1994: 14–15).

Early Modern European Dynamics of Growth

The driving force behind economic improvements in Adam Smith's *Wealth of Nations* is productivity gains attending division of labor and specialization. By producing what they are best suited to produce and exchanging their products with others, people capture the benefits of comparative advantage at the market place. Division of labor is limited only by the extent of the market. As the market expands, the opportunities for Smithian growth increase accordingly. A decentralized price system widens the scope of the market and extends the advantages accruing from the division of labor (Blaug 1985:61). These dynamics of expansion were qualified in early modern Europe by the rhythm of demographic change and unpredictable fluctuations in harvests.

The demographic losses associated with the Black Death of 1348–50 decimated populations from the Black Sea through the Mediterranean to northern Europe.[4] Cities and towns were especially hard hit, with a cluster of economic consequences. First, handicraft production was disrupted, and trade between cities declined. Second, urban demand for agricultural goods fell, and farmers shifted from agriculture to livestock rearing in many areas. The gradual demographic and economic recovery of Western Europe from the Black Death led in the sixteenth century to higher levels of total population and aggregate economic output. During the fifteenth and sixteenth centuries a new financial infrastructure emerged to support long-distance trade. The elaboration of banking and marketing institutions made possible increasingly sophisticated patterns of exchange that recognized division of labor and specialization in production. But these new developments rested upon the fragile economic base of agriculture. Harvest conditions determined the annual fluctuations in food prices, which in turn heavily influenced the labor costs of manufacturing. When successive poor harvests lowered real wages, nonagricultural production usually fell, so that harvest shortfalls triggered cyclical declines in industry as well as agriculture. This cycle, made famous by Ernest Labrousse (1990), marked the rhythm of the pre-nineteenth-century European economy through its longer phases of growth and decline.

Amidst the constant fluctuations that marked the gradual recovery and then growth of Europe's economy, significant shifts occurred in the continent's most active economic centers. As new marketing networks developed and changes in textile production and other crafts took place, older centers in the Mediterranean were replaced by northern centers, especially in Holland and England. Economic growth looks especially impressive, therefore, if one focuses only on the regions of greatest growth. If, however, we look at a larger Europe and recognize that some areas declined as others rose, while yet others remained relatively unaffected, economic growth in early modern Europe appears more modest. The success of Venice and Genoa came in part at the expense of Muslim traders. Italian traders

---

[4]The following paragraphs highlight some of the main themes in the economic history of this period. Among the sources consulted are Cipolla 1972–74, 1980; Lopez 1971; Miskimin 1969, 1977.

were in turn overshadowed by the expansion of Dutch, then English, finance and trade across the Atlantic and into Asia. Since agricultural production bulked so large in overall economic activity, economies had little ability to grow much faster than the rates of expansion in agriculture where growth was the product of some combination of the following factors: (1) extended arable; (2) increased inputs of capital and labor; (3) increased specialization; and (4) technological improvements. Each of these factors played a role in expanding economic production. They were also related: for instance, increased capital went to technological improvements, and more labor was expended in response to market opportunities for specialization. Both the economy and population grew in the early modern period, but not without cycles of expansion and contraction. The seventeenth-century "general crisis" of economic, social, and political difficulties has included in some scholarly assessments a crisis of population and resources, a Malthusian crisis.

During the eighteenth century many parts of Western Europe increasingly participated in commerce through their agricultural and industrial production. England had broken free in the eighteenth century from the dire threat of famines, while in France subsistence crises were no longer of the killing magnitudes common a century before (A. Appleby 1969). The Europe Smith analyzed was certainly better off than it had been before, but it had yet to begin its nineteenth-century urban factory industrialization which led to a fundamental transformation of society and economy. The economy of Smith's *Wealth of Nations* remained principally an agricultural economy. No wonder then that Smith stressed agricultural investment, assumed economic growth was finite, and expected real wages ultimately to fall to subsistence levels (Caton 1985, Smith 1937, Blaug 1985:35–66). Malthus and Smith lived in the same world of limited economic possibilities. Smith's world was not Europe of the nineteenth century. In key ways, eighteenth-century Europe shared more with China of the same period than it did with the Europe of the nineteenth and twentieth centuries.

Smithian Dynamics in China

We witness Smithian dynamics across much of China between the sixteenth and nineteenth centuries. The broad features of increased cash cropping, handicrafts, and trade are well known in the Chinese and Japanese literature, even if Smithian propositions are not explicitly identified to explain parts of the process. Most famous are the expanding cotton and silk industries of the Lower Yangzi region near Shanghai, the two principal handicraft industries that joined rice and other cash crops to create China's richest regional economy. To feed the population of this area, rice grown in the upstream provinces of Anhui, Jiangxi, Hubei, and especially Hunan and Sichuan moved down the Yangzi River. Other cash crops and handicrafts, such as cotton, indigo, tobacco, pottery, and paper, emerged in parts of these provinces as market expansion connected an increasing number of locales (Wu and Xu 1985:82–95, 143–55, 272–76).

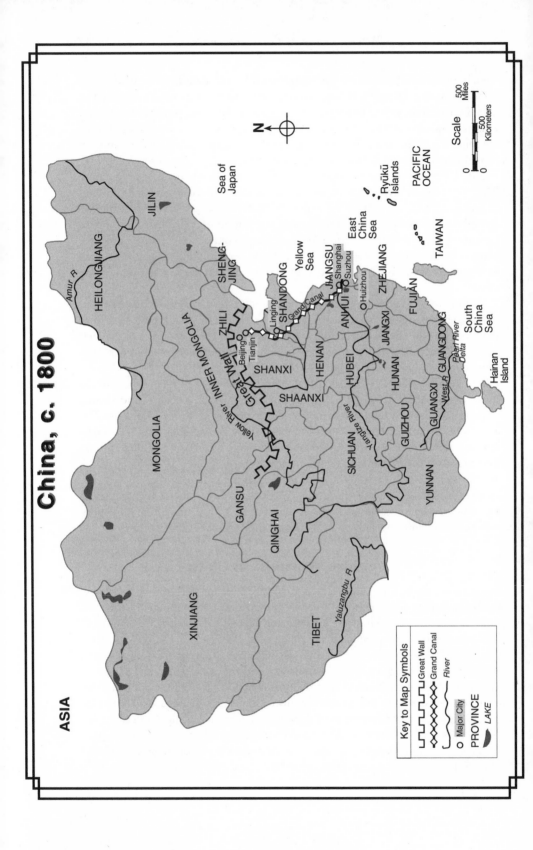

China, c. 1800

ASIA

N

Scale

500 Miles

500 Kilometers

Key to Map Symbols

- Great Wall
- Grand Canal
- River
- ○ Major City
- PROVINCE
- LAKE

ASIA

HEILONGJIANG

Amur R.

JILIN

MONGOLIA

SHENG-JING

INNER MONGOLIA

ZHILI

Yellow River

Beijing

Tianjin

Linqing

Great Wall

Grand Canal

SHANDONG

SHANXI

SHAANXI

HENAN

GANSU

XINJIANG

QINGHAI

TIBET

Yaluzangbu R.

SICHUAN

Yangtze River

HUBEI

ANHUI

JIANGSU

Shanghai

Suzhou

Huizhou

ZHEJIANG

JIANGXI

HUNAN

GUIZHOU

YUNNAN

GUANGXI

West R.

GUANGDONG

Pearl River Delta

FUJIAN

TAIWAN

Hainan Island

South China Sea

East China Sea

Ryūkū Islands

PACIFIC OCEAN

Yellow Sea

Sea of Japan

Market expansion was most salient along the Yangzi River, but hardly limited to this vast area. In south and southeast China, cash crops and handicrafts expanded in several areas. The Pearl River delta in Guangdong produced sugar cane, fruits, silk, cotton, ironware, and oils from sesame and tung plants (Tang and Li 1985; Luo Yixing 1985). Along the southeast coast, sixteenth-century foreign trade ties stimulated cash-crop production in tea and sugar (E. Rawski 1972). The northern half of the empire witnessed less market expansion, in large part because river transportation was more limited. But cash cropping, handicrafts, and trade did develop. Grand Canal towns like Linqing became major commercial centers with merchants who sold cloth, grain, pottery, paper, leather, tea, and salt (Xu Tan 1986). The hinterland of the city Tianjin became a center for fishing and salt, while Shandong province more generally witnessed market development led by the cash crops of cotton and tobacco (Guo 1989; Li Hua 1986).

Commercialization stimulated productivity increases. Studies of land productivity for both the lower Yangzi region and other parts of the Chinese empire show an increase over time after the tenth century. Improvements and extension of irrigation techniques, seed varieties, and farming methods have been documented. In general, land productivity increased with the application of additional fertilizer, the development of weather-resistant seed varieties well suited to local conditions, and more effective cultivation techniques (Li Bozhong 1984a, forthcoming; Min Zongdian 1984; Huang Miantang 1990). Labor productivity in agriculture rose in some cases, but whether there was much sustained increase in per capita income is far from clear. Growth may have been extensive much of the time, leading to an increase in total production, rather than intensive, with an increase in per capita productivity.

Working against the increased benefits derived from spatial divisions of labor and specialized production, a portion of the growing Chinese population in the eighteenth and nineteenth centuries turned to less fertile fields and to marginal economic pursuits. The clearance of hill lands during this period often brought into cultivation inferior food crops in conjunction with some cash crops and handicrafts. The case of southern Shaanxi, in northwest China, is instructive. This area had been the scene of some fighting in the late Ming dynasty (1368–1643); when the Qing dynasty (1644–1911) was established, migration repopulated the area and soon made it grow beyond its Ming population levels. New food crops on hill lands, including corn and sweet potatoes, complement wheat and millet to feed a population that included individuals in the timber trade, paper making, and iron workers (Fang 1979; Tan 1986; Xiao 1988; Chen and Zuo 1988). Development in this rather remote and none too fertile land did nevertheless take place. Market exchange was basic to the successes enjoyed by peasants. But since the basic resource possibilities of this part of China fell short of those in richer ecologies like the Yangzi River delta, labor productivities and standards of living could not match those of more favored regions. The same logic broadly applies to the many other hill land areas of China where land was opened during the Qing dynasty (Fu 1982; Zhang Jianmin 1987).[5]

The development of product markets provides the clearest indications of commercialization in China between 1500 and 1900. The increase in markets created a dense network of exchange. In Jiangnan the markets in some prefectures doubled or tripled in number between the late sixteenth and eighteenth centuries. Product specialization among markets also emerged with the rice trade centered at Suzhou and cotton and silk concentrated at other market sites (Liu Shiji 1987; Fan 1990). In addition to product markets, factor markets also emerged in some areas. For Jiangnan and southeast China, there is considerable evidence of a land market for both rentals and sales, which gave the seller the opportunity to repay the purchase price with interest during a specified number of years. If he failed to do so, he usually became the tenant of the buyer. These arrangements would persist over generations, with a son or grandson attempting to redeem land sold decades earlier (Yang Guozhen 1988).

Labor markets also developed for both short-term and long-term labor. Short-term labor filled two distinct purposes. It was important during the busy agricultural season, especially at harvest time. Conversely, during the winter slack season, peasants could search for off-farm employment. Other people accepted year-long contracts to work in agriculture. During the eighteenth century the inferior legal status of hired laborers tied to their positions as dependents within a household was gradually transformed; hired laborers became legally independent, if economically dependent upon others (Liu Yongcheng 1982:54–72; Li, Wei, and Jing 1983:243–516).

Analysis of China's late imperial credit markets lags behind studies of land and labor markets, not to mention product markets. Critiques of twentieth-century usury have led many to assume that the few late imperial credit markets were geared simply to consumption needs. But peasants in areas where trade was increasing turned to crops and crafts requiring capital to begin production and more modest annual infusions of capital to continue production. As Pan Ming-te (1994) has shown, the late imperial expansion of both cotton and silk textile production in Jiangnan depended on the availability of credit.

The combination of different factor markets meant that many peasant families made multiple adjustments to maximize production. In an ideal scenario, a peasant family could adjust their land by renting in or out and by selling or buying; they could adjust labor through hiring in or out; and they could seek loans to cover capital requirements. The absence of one or more of these markets limited the options available to a peasant. But wherever some of these factors markets existed, peasants had greater flexibility to use their resources efficiently to produce for the market than did peasants without markets.

---

[5]This does not mean, of course, that all migration was to less fertile areas. The repopulation of Sichuan and the opening of Manchuria stand out as the most salient instances of migration to fertile regions. For an overview of Qing migration movements, see Lee and Wong 1991.

Commercialization stimulated peasant efforts to combine land, labor, and capital to yield the greatest benefits. The pursuit of increased incomes did not mean Chinese peasants were any less liable to suffer poor harvests and even subsistence crises than were European peasants of the same period. As in Europe, there were considerable variations in the productivity and poverty of local agrarian economies. Regional economies in China, the equivalent in many cases to national economies in Europe, experienced cycles of expansion. Sixteenth-century expansion was most salient in the lower Yangzi, southeast coast, and South China regions. New groups of merchants organized expanded patterns of exchange that connected China's major cities to one another and to networks of market towns and the countryside around each of them.[6] After the economic decline initiated by the Ming rebellions followed by the disruptions caused by the Manchu invasion, the eighteenth century witnessed the resettlement of deserted land, the opening of new fields, and a renewed commercial expansion spanning even larger portions of the empire. Economic growth in the middle and upper Yangzi regions complemented growth in the lower Yangzi. Parts of North and Northwest China also increased production. The dynamics of Smithian expansion were present throughout.[7]

What then of economic change in the nineteenth century? With fundamentally different interpretations, to be sure, most Chinese and Western analysts of China's economy between 1850 and 1950 assign foreigners a crucial role. For Chinese Marxists, imperialism twisted and distorted China's path of development and blocked the country from replicating the stages of success enjoyed by Europe (Yan 1989). For Western-trained scholars, foreigners created the opportunities and offered the skills and techniques to build a modern economy in China (Hou 1965; Dernberger 1975). What both positions usually obscure is the degree to which the late nineteenth and early twentieth-century economic impact of foreigners was felt by most Chinese in terms of trade opportunities, the principles of which did not differ from those available in previous centuries. New commercial opportunities expanded the spatial scale on which Smithian dynamics worked; they did not fundamentally alter those dynamics. The regional impact of foreign markets was felt most strongly in the areas near transport nodes and along transportation routes. These included the recently opened treaty ports, the cities in which foreigners were allowed to reside and do business, and the new railroad lines that were laid in areas without decent river transport.

Railroads especially stimulated commercialization in northern areas that enjoyed close proximity to the lines; these areas began planting tobacco, peanuts, sesame, and soybeans. Foreign demand for tung oil spurred production in Yangzi

---

[6]The classic works on the two most important merchant groups are Terada 1972 on the Shanxi merchants and Fuji 1953–54 on the Huizhou (or Xin'an) merchants. On merchants groups more generally, see Fu 1956 and Zhang and Zhang 1993.

[7]The Chinese article and journal literature on Ming Qing economic expansion is voluminous. Two good book-length studies are Chen Xuewen 1989 and Zheng 1989.

River provinces and in the south (Liu Kexiang 1988). Per capita incomes in China's most prosperous farming regions which had the best access to international markets may well have risen as a result of international trade.[8] At the same time, there were surely instances where market changes created hardships like those of the early 1930s depression. But despite the positive impacts of international trade and the hardships that markets could cause, larger questions remain. How far could Smithian growth stimulate a modern industrialized economy in early twentieth-century China? Was a Malthusian crisis lurking in the background to threaten economic development?

Population Dynamics: Birth and Death Rates

Adam Smith stressed the limits on Chinese economic growth when he suggested that the country may have reached its height before Marco Polo's arrival. "It [China] had perhaps, even long before his [Polo's] time, acquired that full complement of riches which the nature of its laws and institutions permits it to acquire" (1937:71). Smith shared with Ricardo and Malthus a belief that economic growth itself was limited. All three asserted that subsistence costs and wages were dynamically linked through the economic determination of demographic rates. In Smith's estimation, high wages promoted the survival of children, and as more children survived, population growth drive wages down (1937:64–86). He also held that profit levels and interest rates fall in wealthy countries where opportunities to multiply riches have been exhausted (1937:87–98). Working within the same basic framework, Ricardo anticipated the exhaustion of natural resources (Blaug 1985:88), while Malthus feared the multiplication of populations beyond what their resource bases could support.

Though we conventionally associate Smith with the study of modern economic development, he and other classical economists interpreted a world yet to experience the massive industrial changes of the nineteenth century. As Mark Blaug counsels, "We need to remember that when the book [*The Wealth of Nations*] appeared, the typical water-driven factory held 300–400 workers, and there were only twenty or thirty such establishments in the whole of the British Isles. This helps to account for Adam Smith's neglect of fixed capital and for the convention, which he never really abandoned, that agriculture and not manufacture was the principal source of Britain's wealth" (1985:37). Smith, Ricardo, and Malthus all lived in a world in which agriculture remained the dominant sector of the economy.

---

[8]Loren Brandt unveils some dramatic estimates of growing per capita incomes and rising labor productivity in provinces along the Yangzi River, which he attributes in large measure to the integration of Chinese markets with world commodity markets. Through a variety of indirect evidence Brandt estimates an increase in per capita incomes of 44 percent and a rise in labor productivity in agriculture of 40 percent between the 1890s and 1930s (1989:133). Doubts about the data, estimation techniques, and assumptions Brandt uses suggest we not place too much faith in these conclusions. See R. B. Wong 1992 for a fuller discussion.

The conventional picture of China poised on the brink of Malthusian crisis due to population growth outstripping resources is a powerful one. Its persuasiveness builds upon early twentieth-century perspectives of observers from industrialized countries and more recently upon contemporary perspectives that identify massive populations as a drag on modern economic growth in developing countries. A comparative analysis of China and Europe in early modern times qualifies these perspectives: putative differences in Chinese and European demographic histories are less certain than usually assumed. First, it should be noted that the broad rhythms and rates of population expansion were similar in China and Europe between 1400 and 1800 (Snook 1994:18). In general, the economies of both China and Europe expanded to support growing populations. Certainly there were fluctuations in living standards over time and regional differences as well, but estimates of aggregate population in China and Europe do not reveal fundamentally different population and resource conditions in China and Europe before 1800.

The crux of the matter concerns birth and death rates. In northwest Europe, where preventive checks of late marriage and a relatively large proportion of never-married women kept fertility rates below their biological maxima, high mortality rates were not necessary to hold population growth in check. China is seen as a land of high fertility and high mortality, population stability being achieved through the positive check of high mortality. An examination of the evidence on fertility and mortality does not, however, support this stereotypical contrast between China and Europe.

The only systematic analyses of late imperial fertility in fact show two types of preventive check, although these differ from the types encountered in Europe. Between 1700 and 1840, first births among the Qing nobility came approximately thirty-seven months after marriage, roughly double the interval among European populations. At the other end of the reproductive span, women stopped bearing children at about age 34, in contrast to European women, who did not stop until age 40 (Wang, Lee, Campbell 1995). As a result, China's marital fertility was much lower than people previously assumed.

Similar results were obtained in research on a rural population in northeast China for the century beginning in 1774, where fertility rates were only two-thirds those of comparable European populations. Again, late onset and early cessation of childbearing proved important. In addition, breast feeding appears to lengthen the period of infecundity and hence to increase birth intervals and reduce the total number of children born (Lee and Campbell 1957:93–94). While longer birth intervals due to breast feeding are found in numerous settings, the Chinese preventive checks of late starting and early stopping contrast sharply with European practices.[9] Though the particular preventive checks differed in China

---

[9]An explanation for these differences would take us into the realm of cultural norms and social expectations about marriage and family. Briefly, it appears that the husband–wife relationship was less central to family life in China than in Europe. Regulation of conjugal relations was more possible and desirable in Chinese settings than in European ones.

and Europe, their effects were similar. Both tended to reduce rates of possible population growth.

The mortality component of demographic change is more complex. Certainly China, like Europe, suffered war, famine, and disease, the factors that Malthus considered positive checks on population growth. But China had another kind of positive check, one less often encountered in Europe and the result of deliberate parental action: infanticide. Long birth intervals and skewed sex ratios reflect the practice of female infanticide (Lee and Campbell 1997:65–70; Lee, Wang, and Campbell 1994). A reduction in the supply of women in turn leads to slower population growth in the next generation as the number of marriageable women falls. Together with the late onset and early cessation of births, the Chinese custom of infanticide acted as a sufficiently strong positive check to explain the generally similar patterns of population growth in China and Europe without invoking the positive check of high levels of adult mortality.

Other factors that affect mortality rates are less easily determined. It is difficult, for example, to prove that there is a direct link between mortality levels and availability of resources. Few people die of starvation except in crisis conditions. Many may suffer chronic malnutrition, but the effects of this condition on mortality are unclear, even among contemporary populations (Carmichael 1985, Livi-Bacci 1985, Scrimshaw 1985, Taylor 1985). Still, modern scholars continue to associate food supply conditions with levels of mortality (Simon 1985:218).

The idea that the Chinese suffered a low living standard that exposed them to higher mortality risks is a venerable one. Both Adam Smith and Thomas Malthus deplored the dietary conditions about which they had read in accounts of Chinese society. As Smith said, "The poverty of the lower ranks of people in China far surpasses that of the most beggarly nations in Europe. . . . The subsistence which they find . . . is so scanty that they are eager to fish up the nastiest garbage thrown overboard from any European ship. Any carrion, the carcase of a dead dog or cat, for example, half putrid and stinking, is as welcome to them as the most wholesome food to the people of other countries" (1937:72).

Malthus's assessment echoes Smith's: "If the accounts we have of it [China] are to be trusted, the lower classes of people are in the habit of living almost upon the smallest possible quantity of food, and are glad to get any putrid offals that European laborers would rather starve than eat" (1976:53).

Yet other European writers, including careful first-hand observers, came away with quite different assessments. Witness, for instance, Robert Fortune, a Scotsman who did not hold a very high opinion of Chinese agriculture but nevertheless noted: "for a few cash . . . a Chinese can dine in sumptuous manner upon his rice, fish, vegetables and tea; and I fully believe, that in no country in the world is there less real misery and want than in China" (1847:121, cited by Anderson 1988:96). In another volume he wrote, regarding the diet of tea-picking laborers:

> The food of these people is of the simplest kind—namely rice and vegetables, and a small portion of animal food, such as fish or pork. But the poorest class-

es in China seem to understand the art of preparing their food much better than the same classes at home. With the simple substances I have named, the Chinese labourer contrives to make a number of savoury dishes, upon which he breakfasts or dines most sumptuously. In Scotland, in former days—and I suppose it is much the same now—the harvest labourer's breakfast consisted of porridge and milk, his dinner bread and beer, and porridge and milk again for supper. A Chinaman would starve upon such food (1857:42–43, cited by Anderson 1988:96).

Fortune was observing mid-nineteenth-century China, a land scholars generally view as already subject to a growing crisis. How much truer his assessment may have been for the century preceding. No wonder that at least one modern specialist has asserted confidently that "the Chinese peasant of the Yongzheng [1723–1735] and the first half of the Qianlong [1736–1765] eras was in general better nourished and more comfortable than his French counterpart during the reign of Louis XV."[10] In short, the fragmentary evidence on nutrition and living standards offers little ground for concluding that Chinese standards of living were so low as to make plausible higher mortality rates because of resource limitations. Some foreign observers may have been reacting to food supply issues in cultural terms of taste and convention more than scientific terms of nutritional quality.

Nevertheless, there is no doubt that late imperial China was subject to famine. Particularly in the nineteenth century, crises created by some combination of natural and human factors raised mortality across different regions of China. Beginning at mid-century, rebellions hit the Yangzi River valley and the Huai River to its north, as well as parts of Northwest, Southwest, and South China. The worst natural disasters occurred in North and Northwest China, where years of successive drought between 1876 and 1879 depleted grain reserves and drove peasants to search for food. Where drought failed to wither the crops, armies interrupted the agricultural cycle and extracted much of what was left. We can expect that mortality rose as increased malnutrition made people more vulnerable to disease and as some succumbed to starvation.

Foreign and domestic observers alike recorded their bleak assessments of this period. For Qingzhou in the North China province of Shandong the Dutch minister J. H. Ferguson estimated between 30 and 60 percent of the families in many villages had been wiped out by famine, while the English Baptist missionary Timothy Richard reported a death rate reaching 90 percent in some smaller villages (Bohr 1972:15). To Shandong's west, Shanxi's governor, Zeng Guochuan, reported in late 1879 that some 80 percent of the population had been affected by the recent famine, with 60 to 70 percent suffering from typhoid fever (Bohr 1972:23). Bohr (26) estimates some nine and a half million people may have died in the North and Northwest.

---

[10]Gernet 1972:420–21. The English translation erroneously has "in general, much better and much happier" (1982:481).

As grim as these accounts are, it is uncertain that such crises set China apart from Europe. Early modern Europe also experienced sharp mortality peaks resulting from famines, epidemics, and wars. The plague was a major killer in the fourteenth and fifteenth centuries: wars were less devastating directly but because they interrupted production and trade could lead to subsistence crises (Hohenberg and Lees 1985:79–83). Scholars have discovered that in the aftermath of some mortality crises, fertility rises to accelerate the replacement of lost populations. Thus mortality crises appear to have at most a temporary impact on population and resource issues (Flinn 1981:25–47); Charbonneau and LaRose 1979; Bongaarts and Cain 1980). Subsistence crises continued to be a problem even in nineteenth-century Europe. Such crises were still a serious threat for some populations early in the century, and they continued to cause fear even at mid-century (Post 1976; McPhee 1992:57–61). These problems did not block industrialization. It seems unlikely therefore that population and resource issues, at least as reflected in mortality crises, limited the possibilities of industrialization.

Whatever the impact of crisis mortality on population dynamics, a more basic similarity between Chinese and European mortality patterns is obscured: overall, life expectancy was the same in Europe and in China. This similarity contradicts a growing body of data indicating that Chinese mortality levels rose continuously from the late seventeenth century into the nineteenth century. Ted Telford, for example, argued on the basis of genealogical data for Tongcheng county in Anhui that life expectancies at birth dropped from 39.6 between 1750 and 1769 to 33.4 a half-century later (Telford 1990:133). Liu Ts'ui-jung (1985, 1992) also found dramatic declines in life expectancy during the eighteenth century. There is reason to doubt, however, that such a sharp downward trend in life expectancy occurred. Even the genealogical demographers themselves note problems with their data (Harrell 1987; Telford 1990). As the genealogies become more inclusive of infants and children, for example, as they do over time, mortality rates seem to rise. The parallel declines in life expectancy found by Liu and Telford may be artifacts of changes in the way the genealogies were recorded.[11] Nor do the reported trends match the historical context. It is perplexing to find life expectancy highest during the economic recession of the late seventeenth century, when officials, especially those along the Yangzi River, feared for the poor peasants who received low prices for their crops and for the laborers who could not find employment (Kishimoto 1984). As crop prices rose and employment grew throughout the eighteenth century. Telford reports rising mortality. Of course, the very low levels of life expectancy attained in the mid-nineteenth century could have

---

[11]Telford attributes the early high life expectancies in the Toncheng lineage to this factor. He rejects the estimates of life expectancy at birth (E_0) of over 40 years before 1750, and calls 1750–1769 male life expectancy of 39.6 the likely peak of life expectancy during the Qing (1990:133). However, there is no evidence that reporting of infants and children was complete by 1750. A gradual improvement in completeness would explain why, over a series of cohorts from 1790–1809 to 1860–1879, infant and child mortality rises monotonically, while adult mortality remains basically unchanged (1990:fig. 8).

been influenced by the Taiping Rebellion, but this would have been a temporary phenomenon.

Probably, therefore, life expectancy in China did not decline throughout the eighteenth and nineteenth centuries as the genealogical data suggest. But even if we assume these data are correct, the overall similarity of Chinese and European life expectancies remains. Except in the most prosperous regions of Europe, life expectancy did not surpass the Chinese level until the end of the nineteenth century (see Table 1).[12] Thus it seems quite unlikely that resource shortages affected mortality in China but not in Europe. Malthus's argument that eighteenth-century European populations were freed from positive checks while Chinese populations were not seems to be untenable.

Economic Dynamics and Preconditions of Capitalism

But what of the potential for Smithian growth in China? Several works on China's agrarian economy depict China more in Malthusian terms, seeing in it a dynamic equilibrium between population growth and economic expansion that fits within the classical economists's world of limited possibilities. Most explicitly in discussing the population–resource issue was Dwight Perkins's 1969 study of Chinese agriculture from the fourteenth century forward. Perkins assumed that per capita grain consumption remained roughly constant over a six-hundred-year period, an assumption based on his estimates of rising land productivity, extended arable, and total population. He then addressed various other factors responsible for the continued balance of population and resources—seeds, cropping patterns, new crops, farm implements, water control, fertilizer, and grain marketing.

Ping-ti Ho's classic study of Chinese population also addressed the problem of population and resources in Malthusian terms (Ho 1959). In Ho's opinion, the nineteenth-century rebellions and natural disasters were Malthusian checks on a population that had reached an optimal level in the late eighteenth century. Ho argued that China's population and resources were forced into equilibrium through checks on population growth rather than by a continuing expansion of the resource base. Ho's analysis of these issues is the only major work that explicitly appeals to Malthus's writings, but not the only one to fit within the framework created by European classical economists. Kang Chao (1986), for example, offers a sweeping view of Chinese agricultural history in which Chinese demographic growth matches any and all increases in aggregate production, canceling out any per capita economic growth. Chao suggests that cultural values led Chinese people to have large families. Like the classical economists, Chao describes a situation in which an equilibrium between population and resources brings people close to subsistence.

Even works that are not obviously within the framework of classical economics offer arguments and findings that affirm an equilibrium between population

---

[12]These issues are discussed at greater length in Lavely and Wong 1991.

Table 1. Life expectancy at birth (E_0) for various Chinese and European populations

	Period	Life Expectancy	Source
German villages[a]	Pre–1800	35.1	Knodel 1988:59
	1800–1849	38.7	
	1850+	39.4	
Geneva	1600–1649	32.2	Henry 1956:158
	1650–1699	31.9	
	1700–1749	41.6	
	1750–1799	47.3	
	1800–1849	51.6	
	1850–1899	57.9	
British peeragee (males)	1330–1479	24.0	Hollingsworth 1965:358
	1480–1679	27.0	
	1680–1729	33.0	
	1730–1779	44.8	
	1780–1829	47.8	
	1830–1879	49.8	
	1850–1954	54.6	
French Villages[b]	Pre-1750	25.0	Flynn 1981:130–31
	1740–1790	30.0	
	1780–1820	36.0	
Tongcheng lineages (males)	1690–1709	46.2	Telford 1990:133
	1710–1729	42.1	
	1730–1749	40.7	
	1750–1769	39.6	
	1770–1789	38.2	
	1790–1809	33.4	
	1800–1819	34.9	
	1820–1839	31.1	
	1840–1859	28.2	
	1860–1879	24.5	
Zhejiang Shen[c]	1725–1739	36.0	Liu 1985:52
	1740–1754	38.5	
	1755–1769	38.5	
	1770–1784	38.5	
	1785–1799	36.0	
	1800–1814	36.0	
	1815–1829	31.2	
	1830–1844	31.2	
Liaoning villages[d]	1792–1867	35.9	Lee and Campbell 1997:62

[a]According to Coale-Demeny (1966) model west.

[b]Model west female E(0) implied by mean l(10).

[c]Males, period rates.

[d]Males, ages 1–5 *sui*; *sui* indicates the number of calendar years during which a person has lived. People are one *sui* at birth and two *sui* at the next New Year.

and resources. Philip Huang has argued, first for northern Chinese agriculture, and then for the more productive region of the lower Yangzi, that Chinese cases lacked the kind of market development that led England to industrial capitalism (Huang 1985, 1990). The assumption of European market expansion leading to industrial capitalism misses the economic and demographic similarities of China and Europe before the Industrial Revolution. When Huang argues that population and resources remained in a rough balance to create a persisting subsistence economy in China, he unintentionally echoes assessments made of early modern Europe. Mark Elvin (1973) shares Huang's assumption that market expansion should lead to broader economic changes, but unlike him, Elvin stresses the dramatic ways in which China's commercial economy developed in the Song dynasty and expanded in the Ming and Qing dynasties. Elvin puzzles over why these changes ended in a "high-level equilibrium trap." The mystery is considerably reduced if we recognize that Elvin's assessment of late imperial China's market economy fits within a Smithian framework. This Smithian framework need not mean an end to the Malthusian limitations of population and resources. The view of agrarian China as a massive society in which population and resources broadly stayed in a balance over many centuries remains persuasive, but this balance may have been considerably above a subsistence minimum. James Lee and his associates, for example, that have shown the Chinese demographic system was far more regulated than we previously believed. On the economic side, Smithian dynamics were responsible for much of the economic growth that did take place. As commercial exchange fostered the development of more sophisticated merchant organizations and stimulated market activity, common people in both China and Europe were drawn into market exchange. In China, market demand induced additional investments in water control, the search for higher and more stable yield seed varieties, and shifts to alternative cash crops.

But Smithian dynamics need not necessarily lead to sustained increases in per capita incomes. Outside China, in the heart of Europe's developing capitalism, including England during the centuries of early modern growth, real wages over the long run did not change. The dramatic change in real wages and in the ratio of population to resources did not come until nineteenth-century urban factory industrialization (Levine 1987). Over the long run, pre-nineteenth-century populations generally adjusted to economic conditions. In the short run, however, there were all manner of fluctuations driven by fertility and mortality responses; wages could fall as well as rise. Chinese population and resources probably stayed approximately in balance, with cycles of rising and falling standards of living that remained widely variable across regions over many centuries. Although no radical rupture permitting sustained per capita growth took place, few places have experienced such a break endogenously.

More important perhaps is to explain how the lower Yangzi achieved the considerable economic success that it did. This area was one of Eurasia's most consistently dynamic economies between 1350 and 1750. Chinese commercialization clearly helped make the "long run" in which it became possible for increasing numbers of people to survive on ever-smaller allotments of land.

Jan de Vries (1993, 1994) characterized some of the changes taking place in seventeenth and eighteenth-century Europe as an "industrious revolution." Between 1600 and 1800 increasing numbers of Europeans, including peasants, became dependent upon market purchases. This demand stimulated market expansion at a time when per capita incomes were not rising, and indeed may have even been falling. This seems counterintuitive. Why did people buy and sell more goods if their wages did not increase? De Vries explains that Europeans began to work harder; they became more "industrious." As evidence he cites the reduction of nonworking days for both artisans and peasants, and he suggests that people became more willing to trade leisure for money. Thus de Vries's argument explains the expansion of early modern Europe's commercial economy without requiring rising per capital incomes.

De Vries argues for an "industrious revolution" in order to shift our attention from the supply-side innovations of the Industrial Revolution to an earlier set of demand-side shifts. But is this industrious revolution simply a European phenomenon?[13] The Smithian dynamics of growth found in China share at least some features of the industrious revolution de Vries describes. Increased labor for commercial production also characterized parts of China between the sixteenth and eighteenth centuries. This increase in market-oriented labor produced thriving silk and cotton craft industries in the lower Yangzi region; women's increased labor for market production was especially crucial in the expansion of textiles (Huang 1990:44–57). In agriculture, new crop rotations and clearance of additional land reduced the number of days in the slack season as peasants aimed to produce additional crops for market sale. Labor intensification accompanied Smithian growth in China as it did in Europe.

Philip Huang calls this process of increased market production in which Chinese peasants worked harder "involution," because returns on each workday appear to decline as laborers increase the number of days they work annually. For Huang involution is the centerpiece of how Chinese economic growth differs from European economic development. But how different is Huang's lower Yangzi from de Vries's Dutch Republic and England? In Europe too people worked harder without necessarily experiencing rising per capita incomes. Such similarities between early modern Europe's industrious revolution and what Huang labels "growth without development" in China deserve further analysis. For the moment it appears that de Vries's industrious revolution and Huang's involution share some important features, and these features were part of the Smithian dynamics of market-based growth supported by labor intensification in

---

[13]De Vries (1993:126) acknowledges a prior use of the term "industrious revolution" to describe changes in nineteenth-century Japanese economic history by Akira Hayami. Hayami (1989) proposed the term as an alternative to Europe's "Industrial Revolution" to describe how Japan and Europe differed. Japan, in this argument, relied more on intensification of labor than on capital to achieve growth.

the advanced regions of China and in Europe in the centuries preceding the Industrial Revolution.

The parallels between China and Europe deserve emphasis because they are so deeply obscured in the best analyses of Chinese and European patterns of economic change. Certain caveats, however, are in order. First, more research is needed. Without data on Chinese patterns of consumption in the late imperial period, for example, we cannot determine whether the economic impacts of Chinese and European consumption were fully parallel. Second, the *degrees* to which peasants in various settings can intensify their labor and reduce their slack season unemployment differ. One of the basic issues in twentieth-century peasant societies has been the recalcitrant problem of surplus agricultural labor. Problems that afflicted China in the 1920s and 1930s, however, may not have existed in the 1720s and 1730s. In the earlier period, peasants in some regions may have found constructive ways to work harder more easily: fewer people were searching for ways to be productively employed, and they could exploit techniques that were no longer new in the twentieth century. The industrious revolution that could not occur now, therefore, may have occurred then. Third, the supply-driven Industrial Revolution that followed the demand-led industrious revolution in Europe did not happen in China. De Vries argues for an unbreakable link between the changing consumption patterns of early modern Europe and the Industrial Revolution, but it is by no means clear that such a link is inevitable. We have seen that China too manifested certain Smithian patterns of economic growth, as well as areas where intensified labor did not raise per capita incomes, so these factors alone cannot explain the European Industrial Revolution of the nineteenth century. In studying what set China apart, we may acquire a better understanding of both Chinese and European developments.

Conclusion

Both the early modern English and the late imperial Chinese agrarian economies were subject to the positive and negative forces of change discussed by Adam Smith and Thomas Malthus. This is not to say that England and the lower Yangzi manifested exactly the same economic and demographic behaviors, for certainly there were differences. Some of these differences, however, turn out to have been more apparent than real.[14] China and Western Europe shared a common world

---

[14]For instance, Philip Huang makes much of the many restrictions on the competitive functioning of labor and credit markets (1990:106–11). He implicitly measures Chinese markets against the ideals taught in a first-year economics course. In the real world of early modern Europe, constraints on markets were significant too. Indeed, rural land and credit markets were often far less free than those in China that Huang finds so limited (Goody, Thirsk, and Thompson 1976:25, 126–27, 132–33; Hoffman, Postel-Vinay, and Rosenthal 1992; Rosenthal 1993). European and Chinese markets both diverged from theoretical ideals; the greater challenge is to explain how and where the dynamics in the two cases run parallel and then diverge.

of harvest insecurities and material limitations. Both suffered through cycles of economic expansion and contraction that created gradually larger economies propelled forward by similar Smithian dynamics of spatial divisions of labor and comparative advantage through the market.

China and Europe shared the demographic possibilities sketched out by Malthus. Contrary to stereotypes, before 1800 China was not clearly more vulnerable than Europe to economic and demographic crisis. Even if future scholarship affirms important differences in demographic rates in China and Europe, the presence of a potentially fragile population–resource ratio will remain common to both ends of Eurasia. Even if arguments about a considerable margin of prosperity in early modern Europe demonstrate that a Malthusian danger was not yet near at hand, Smithian dynamics alone could not guarantee that such a danger would remain distant. The economic cores of both China and Europe may have sustained a considerable margin as true Malthusian pressures weighed down on China's ecologically more precarious peripheries by the mid-nineteenth century. Whatever future research suggests with respect to these large issues, the limits of economic possibility within a world defined by classical economists remain relevant for both China and Europe (and the rest of the world) before the nineteenth century. When we turn in the next chapter to industry in China and Europe during the seventeenth and eighteenth centuries, we once again will discover surprising similarities, further narrowing the terrain on which we can expect to locate crucial economic differences.

2

DYNAMICS OF INDUSTRIAL EXPANSION IN EARLY MODERN EUROPE AND LATE IMPERIAL CHINA

Though European industrial production never accounted for a large portion of economic activity before 1800, the dynamics of industrial expansion occupy a privileged place in historiography because of what industry would come to be in the nineteenth and twentieth centuries. Economic historians study industrialization retrospectively in search of the paths leading to modern economies. In particular, the precursors to the Industrial Revolution that burst forth in England in the late eighteenth century are assumed to be more general factors that could promote similar economic change elsewhere. We can identify three periods of European industrial activity beginning in the early modern period: (1) late fifteenth to early sixteenth centuries: urban craft production; (2) mid-sixteenth to mid-eighteenth centuries: rural cottage industry; (3) late eighteenth to late nineteenth centuries: urban factory mechanization. The shift from urban production controlled by craft guilds to rural cottage industry is generally viewed as the liberation of production from the restrictions imposed to protect producer interests; this becomes one sign of the breakdown of "feudal" control. The subsequent shift of industry back into the cities is usually seen as the triumph of the Industrial Revolution, which heralds the ascendancy of the bourgeoisie. In between lies the period of rural industry when neither "feudal" nor "capitalist" elements were clearly in control in Europe.[1]

---

[1] I have expressed the changes within a Marxist set of categories because such a formulation highlights the framework within which many Chinese and Japanese economic historians look at Chinese and European industrialization. But even without the use of "feudalism" and "capitalism" as basic categories, the phenomenon of rural industry is widely recognized as an important precursor to the Industrial Revolution.

A search for the origins of nineteenth-century Europe's industrialization in earlier patterns and practices of economic activity makes good sense as an explanation of what happened in European history. But this exercise may have far less to say about predicting how industrialization occurs in other times and places. Many of the features of European rural industrialization considered by some scholars as the precursor of nineteenth-century factory industrialization can also be found in China. The causal sufficiency of rural industrialization for the Industrial Revolution is therefore called into question by the Chinese experience.

Rural Industry and Demographic Change in Europe

During the 1970s and 1980s, much of the work on early modern rural industries employed the term "proto-industrialization." The concept refers to the increased production of craft goods in a number of European regions by rural households, often located near cities, many of whom remained part-time agriculturalists. Many of the most famous cases concern textiles. But the rural location of important parts of the production process does not mean that urban actors did not play important roles in the expansion of rural production. Some goods made in the countryside were finished in the cities. Moreover, production was often financed by urban merchants, and distribution was always organized by urban merchants who moved the goods over great distances. Finally, dispersed craft production could even take place in cities (Berg, Hudson, and Sonenscher 1983). In general, however, the expansion of industries took place near towns and cities which were simultaneously the nodes of networks that spanned large areas and the central places of urban hierarchies that spatially structured regions.[2]

Where rural industry expanded, populations often grew. Much of the work on European proto-industrialization has focused on the relationship between economic changes and demographic behavior. The general line of argument, stripped of its nuances, has been that populations grew more rapidly because ages at marriage fell and proportions married rose in areas experiencing rural industrialization. The argument has not gone unchallenged. Skeptics have noted cases that lack a coordinated set of economic and demographic changes.[3] But the failure of all potential cases to conform to the general argument does not mean that an important set of economic and demographic changes are not occurring in some areas. To appreciate the significance of these economic and demographic changes, we must consider earlier conditions.

---

[2]The spatial context for viewing European rural industrialization and the importance of cities is brought out persuasively by Hohenberg and Lees 1985. A spatial framework for such matters should be familiar to most students of China, since G. William Skinner's pioneering work (especially 1977) has highlighted these issues.

[3]Proportions ever married and median age at marriage may well have varied independently of economic change. Taking economic factors alone, the precise patterns of demographic change were also influenced by other factors, such as the demand for labor beyond the local economy (Levine 1977). For a critique, see Jeannin 1980.

For the late medieval period, historians of Europe often find growing populations that survive on precarious resource bases. Some stress social and political struggles as causes of problems that others portray as Malthusian demographic crises. After the epidemics of the fourteenth century, the cycle of growing populations that gradually outstripped expanding economies repeated itself in some parts of Europe. But in parts of northwestern Europe, notably much of England and parts of France, a more stable balance between agrarian resources and population was reached. Whereas land had been parceled into increasingly small plots until the fourteenth century, this practice was gradually abandoned in favor of an equal division of stock and gear accompanied by retention of land in one person's hands; the sons who did not receive land received cash payments as their shares of the family estate.[4] These practices permitted agrarian communities to achieve a small-scale economic and demographic equilibrium before the emergence of rural industry.

This kind of European community has been conceived in an idealized form as an ecological environment with a fixed number of niches tied to property. Household formation required access to a niche. Some scholars have noted that the idealized niche system based on land never really existed; instead, a homeostatic balance between resources and population was achieved through a more complex cultural logic that tied marriage rates to economic conditions more generally and wage levels more specifically (Schofield 1989). In one standard scenario, a single son inherited the land, and he married only when his parents were no longer able or willing to work the land. Many of the young men who could not find a niche left to make their livings elsewhere; others who stayed worked as laborers and did not marry. Where strict impartibility of the land did not obtain, successive generations of agriculturalists faced the threat of smaller average land holdings, a threat sometimes relieved by a combination of outmigration and the bringing of new lands under cultivation. The famous European marriage pattern—late age at marriage for men and women and high rates of celibacy for both—was neatly connected to the institutional structures that limited household formation and encouraged a close fit at the community level between demographic and economic reproduction in each generation.

Rural industrialization in Europe basically upset this stable regime. People with little or no land could form households. More people could marry, and they could marry earlier, because they did not have to wait for an agricultural niche to open. As David Levine explains the population growth accompanying rural industry,

It would seem that rural industry played a crucial role in undermining the prudential and restrictive reproductive regime of the preindustrial world. By permitting, one might even say promoting, a multiplication of productive

---

[4]Analyses of the late medieval crises range from those that have been called neo-Malthusian, e.g., Le Roy Ladurie 1976, to self-consciously Marxist interpretations, e.g., Bois 1984. The changes in England have been addressed by Smith 1981. On France, see Moriceau 1994:475–512.

units—each based on a separate household—the old nexus of patriarchal control over marriage was broken. Men and women could contemplate marriage in the knowledge that their "independence" was not granted by a supervening authority. Marriage could be undertaken with reference to a system in which they sold the products of their labor. (Levine 1983:29)

Rural industry was often associated with a cluster of specific social and economic phenomena. Principal among these was partible inheritance. The development of rural industry could even promote a change from impartibility to partibility as Rudolph Braun (1978) has shown for the Zurich highlands. More generally, Franklin Mendels has argued that rural industry had less impact in areas where impartibility was practiced and farm sizes were large enough to supply all residents with labor opportunities than in places where land partibility and small farm size predominated.

> Suppose, however, that the expansion of seasonal crafts was accompanied by the practice of fragmenting the farms through partible inheritance or through sub-leasing, or that new garden-size plots were made available on land previously closed off. As farms were now shrinking, immigrants moving in, and marriages facilitated, the population would expand to fill the new settlement niches while the peasant population now ceased to find enough agricultural work on their own tiny plots, even at harvest-time. . . . So, when a peasant community possessed the combination of a good market outlet for the product of its rural crafts, an on-going process of farm fragmentation or easy settlement opportunities on new land, together with nearby opportunities for summer agricultural employment, this could clearly engage the process of involution that proto-industrialization entailed in the small-farm zone, the area of *petite culture*. (Mendels 1980:182)

Mendels's scenario is part of a larger body of analysis on rural industry that ties basic demographic and economic change together and has reoriented our perspectives on both phenomena. Rural industry had previously been seen as part of the old order that was displaced by the new nineteenth-century urban industrialization, the classic Industrial Revolution. Population growth had earlier been considered as an autonomous and exogenous process explained in terms of demographic variables alone. Now rural industry is being viewed as a set of related antecedents to nineteenth-century economic changes, while studies of demographic changes often stress household decision making about nuptiality and fertility made within specific social and economic contexts.[5] Focusing on the linkages between economic and demographic behavior takes us back to the interests of the classical economists.

In the 1990s, continued research on European proto-industrialization has fur-

---

[5]Other scholars challenge the linkage between economic and demographic change. Richard Smith (1981), for example, sees economic changes without the destruction of fertility controls.

ther undermined the idea of a vast and single tie between the development of rural industry and demographic behavior (Schulmbohm 1996:13–16). Perhaps it should not surprise us that few specific cases actually exhibit all the general characteristics anticipated by the arguments about proto-industrialization. Too many other factors intervene. What may be more unexpected is the degree to which many parts of late imperial China exhibited the conditions associated with European proto-industrialization.

Rural Industry and Demographic Change in China

Historians of China have noted increased cash cropping and handicraft activities in different parts of the Chinese empire between the sixteenth and eighteenth centuries. Many of the most famous handicraft centers were in densely settled areas like the lower Yangzi delta and Pearl River delta. And, as in Europe, textiles formed a major rural craft, especially in the many Jiangsu and Zhejiang province villages where increasing numbers of peasants began to turn to either cotton yarn and cloth production or silk weaving during the sixteenth century. By the eighteenth century cash cropping and handicrafts had spread across much of the empire. Wealthy merchants, many of them either from Huizhou in Anhui or from Shanxi, controlled long-distance trade.[6] The conditions facilitating this expansion paralleled those often associated with rural industries in Europe—good market opportunities, land partibility, and seasonal nonagricultural employment. The expansion of rural industry in regional settings at both ends of Eurasia represented to some degree, at least, similar processes of economic change in which small-scale household production was marketed by merchants over long distances.[7] Certainly, for rural households, the economic possibilities created by rural industries were broadly similar—nonagricultural sources of income became available that did not generally take labor away from village life.

If the economic opportunities created by rural industry were broadly similar for European and Chinese households, were the demographic effects also the same? The Chinese never developed communities composed of stable sets of niches of fixed sizes. Niches were much more flexible in China, because land in many areas was frequently bought and sold and because generational land divisions among sons periodically threatened to reduce family holdings. But the demographic effects were presumably similar; in both China and Europe, rural industry support-

---

[6]Collections of Chinese articles that include discussions of rural industries and trade are Nanjing daxue 1981, Nanjing daxue 1983, and Tian and Song 1987; the bibliographies in each together list other works on the subject published between 1949 and 1985. The standard Chinese source on this period has become Wu and Xu 1985.

[7]This is not to say that the initial conditions for change were closely similar. In fact, industry appears to have grown from an existing rural base in China, whereas it moved from cities to the countryside in Europe.

ed lower ages at marriage and higher proportions of ever married than would have been plausible in its absence. This does not mean that ages at marriages dropped in Europe when rural industry appeared, but the possibility was present. For China, the development of rural industry may not have lowered ages at marriage or raised proportions married as much as it allowed previous practices of relatively low ages at marriage and high proportions of women ever married to continue.

Similar economic changes in China and Western Europe both facilitated or at least accommodated demographic growth, even if the larger economic contexts and the institutional frameworks governing demographic behavior differed. Fertility constraints could be less severe in an economy with rural industry than in one without it. The specific conditions associated with European proto-industrialization—expansion of seasonal crafts, shrinking farm size, and good marketing systems—may have been even more widespread in China than in Europe. Thus the spread of rural industry was a phenomenon common to the Smithian dynamics of economic expansion in both China and Europe. But the sequence from proto-industrialization to industrialization posited by a number of Europeanists as part of the larger industrialization process does not emerge at all clearly in China.

From Proto-Industrialization to Industrialization

Franklin Mendels, who coined the term "proto-industrialization," wrote that the process was a regional one in which peasant, or at least rural, households produced for distant markets (Mendels 1984). He argued that most regions experiencing urban industrialization in the nineteenth century passed through a proto-industrial phase. Other analysts, however, highlight a more contingent relationship between proto-industrialization and nineteenth-century urban industrialization.

David Levine suggests that the expansion of rural industries, which depended on an increased use of cheap labor with low levels of skill, possessed no endogenous dynamic to promote technological change, improve the skills of the workforce, and raise wages. Its dynamics were thus distinct from those that created the technological changes basic to industrialization.

> Much protoindustrial manufacturing, textiles in particular, could be characterized by the notion Clifford Geertz has dubbed "involution". Economic activity transformed demographic conditions, but equally, there was a reciprocal movement as population growth influenced the organization of production. . . . As long as labor was both cheap and plentiful, there was little incentive to undertake capital investments to raise productivity. Low wages meant that primitive techniques were most profitable, while this low level was labor intensive so that cheap labor was of critical importance. . . . The exit from this blind alley was the introduction of powered machines which replaced human skills with enormous productive capacity. But that is another story. (Levine 1977:14)

Precisely, the departure from proto-industrialization to industrialization is a story separate from the expansion of rural industry. If we follow Levine, the stories do not have much in common.

From Peter Kriedte, we gain a third view of proto-industrialization.

> Proto-industrialization did indeed provide certain conditions for a capitalistic industrialization; they were not however sufficient to actually introduce the process of industrialization. For the domestic system of production to be pushed into industrialization, a certain general framework was necessary, in addition to the internal contradictions or an impetus from outside. If that framework was lacking or insufficiently developed, the mechanisms which regulated the protoindustrial system could break down under the combined pressure of its internal contradictions and the outside thrust. The system would collapse altogether, without succeeding at industrialization, or become subject to a succession of severe crises. (Kriedte et al. 1981:145–46)

Like Levine, Kriedte stresses the dangers latent in the proto-industrial dynamic. He also leaves unspecified what "a certain general framework" necessary for industrialization is empirically.

The importance of specifying this framework for industrialization becomes clearer when we consider just how strong the proto-industrialization dynamic was and how slowly the transition to industrialization could sometimes be. Despite his argument about industrialization developing out of proto-industrialization, Mendels has stated the difficulties of this transition clearly.

> The correct match for the fully uprooted proletariat is the type of factory where fixed capital dominates, where the plant must work continuously, and where the higher productivity of labor can also justify its higher cost to the capitalist. When one realizes how difficult it has been to eradicate all traces of seasonal underemployment from the agricultural sector, this should also help to understand the slow rate at which the flow of new best-practice techniques was actually incorporated into production, thus the prolonged co-existence of handicraft methods and modern methods of production in manufacturing. (Mendels 1980:190)

Mendels thus joins Levine and Kriedte in recognizing the often competing rather than simply sequential character of handicraft and factory production. More recent research has qualified depictions of poverty among Europeans engaged in rural industry (Vandenbroeke 1996), but these findings do not make the connections between rural handicrafts and factory production any simpler or clearer.

A final appreciation of the distinction between a proto-industrialization dynamic and the development of urban industry can be gained by following Charles Tilly back to a mid-eighteenth-century point of view, from which the development of nineteenth-century industrialization was by no means obvious.

> If we moved our imaginations back to 1750, blanked out our knowledge of things to come, and projected the future of such a system, we would most

likely predict an increasing division of labor between town and country—but a division of labor in which cities housed Europe's rentiers, officials and large capitalists as they specialized in marketing, administration and services, but not manufacturing. We might well anticipate a countryside with a growing proletariat working in both agriculture and manufacturing. (C. Tilly 1983:133)

Tilly moves on swiftly to remind us that this is not what happened in Europe. Rural proto-industrialization was, after all, followed by urban industrialization. But Mendels, Levine, Kriedte, and Tilly all alert us to the disjuncture between the two. If we look forward from the mid-eighteenth century at the possibilities of the proto-industrial system rather than at the "origins" of nineteenth-century urban industrialization, the absence of a smooth path of natural economic change defining European industrialization becomes obvious.

In China, there is a different story to tell, one that reinforces the absence of a necessary story line from rural industry to urban industry. Chinese rural industries persisted for centuries. Indeed, Tilly's projection of Europe's possible future in 1750 rather neatly fits much of what we know happened in China. What we see in various regions of China between the sixteenth and eighteenth centuries is the growth of rural populations that depended, at least in part, on either wage labor or craft production for the market and an increase in the number of size of urban centers which generally lacked much of a manufacturing base. For Jiangnan, China's most commercially developed area, we have a pretty clear picture of increased handicraft production among peasant households who relied on markets to purchase silk or cotton and sell their finished products to merchants who in some cases supplied capital through a putting-out system.

Japanese scholars were among the first to lay the empirical foundations and to erect intellectual frameworks to interpret these developments. For Nishijima Sadao (1966), the cotton handicraft industry's development was stimulated by the state's demands for taxes; cotton textiles represented a new form of specialized rural industry distinct from the classic combination of farming and handicraft by individual households for their domestic consumption. Tanaka Masatoshi (1973) took issue with Nishijima's stress on land taxation as an "external" stimulus to rural handicraft development; he examined "internal" issues, placing considerable emphasis on the relationship between changes in the "forces of production" (the social and technical arrangements of production) and the "relations of production" (the socially determined allocation of benefits through incentives and expropriation). Though they differ in their explanations of the development of rural industry, each made clear distinctions between the development of rural industry and the "incipient capitalism" (*ziben zhuyi mengya*) studied by Chinese scholars.[8] Both Nishijima and Tanaka recognized important

---

[8] The most impressive Chinese scholarship on "incipient capitalism" is by Wu Chengming and Xu Dixin (1985). In the first of their three volumes on the development of Chinese capitalism they examine commercial development, handicrafts, and cash cropping, with extended investigation of changes in particular regions.

differences between Chinese rural industry and the dynamics of European capitalist development. Much of their work parallels more recent work on European proto-industrialization. But where Nishijima and Tanaka found phenomena that distinguished China from Western Europe, there is now more evidence of similarities when viewed from the perspective of European proto-industrialization. In fact, Mark Elvin's "high-level equilibrium trap," noted earlier for the way its analysis of population and resources can be fitted into a classical economics framework, describes, one might say, a "successful" proto-industrial system. As Elvin (1973) reconstructs the lower Yangzi's late imperial experience, the expansion of markets and rural industries sustained an ever-larger population. But the expansion of rural industry did not contain any stimuli for major capitalization or technological changes. Elvin's efforts to explain why an Industrial Revolution in classic nineteenth-century European terms did not occur in China may be a false labor if in fact the dynamics of proto-industrialization and those of nineteenth-century urban industrialization are analytically distinct. The literature on European economic history reminds us that rural industry was a potential trap. Europeans, of course, escaped the damaging dynamics of rural industrialization in the nineteenth century. Not so the Chinese.

Philip Huang's work on the North China Agrarian economy (1985) shows quite clearly that home craft production was an important source of income in five of thirty-three North China villages in the early twentieth century. Huang rightly warns readers not to overestimate the general importance of handicraft production to all poor households. But in the absence of further evidence about the economic contexts and the demographic behavior of these various villages, we can reasonably hypothesize that a dynamic of rural industrialization broadly similar to the European experience in earlier centuries was taking place in some of the villages Huang studied.[9] Indeed, he suggests as much when he sees wage labor as a possible stimulus to population growth (Huang 1985:303). Another similarity emerges when Huang, inspired by Clifford Geertz's work, sees a kind of involution in twentieth-century North China, represented by the decline in the value produced by family labor on a poor peasant farm below the wage paid to hired labor. This observation parallels to some degree what Mendels has said about involution as part of proto-industrial dynamics. It also resonates with David Levine's claim about a process of involution associated with proto-industrialization similar to Geertz's classic Indonesian case.

> Not only did workers replace themselves at a rapid rate, but any sustained period of prosperity occasioned both an increase in the number of marriages and an influx of new workers. For these reasons, costs were kept low. As long

[9]Huang 1985:194–95; Huang seems to find the proto-industrialization literature less useful for comparison than I do because he refers to those themes in the literature that stress the connections between proto-industrialization and industrialization. I have seized on those parts of the literature that make clear the differences.

as labour was both cheap and plentiful, there was little incentive to undertake capital investments to raise productivity. Low wages meant that primi-
tive techniques were most profitable, and yet this low-level technology was
labor intensive, so that cheap labour was of critical importance. In effect,
these factors created the kind of vicious circle that has been called *involution*.
(Levine 1977:33–34; emphasis in original)

Huang goes on to argue that the economy was increasingly vulnerable to crisis as
populations grew and a major economic transformation was not forthcoming. His
argument resonates strongly with those made by some scholars of European proto-
industrialization. The crisis he perceives in early twentieth-century North China
seems quite close to what other analysts feared would strike Europe in earlier centuries. The broad similarities in demographic situations, however, suggest that
China may not have been as close to a Malthusian margin as Huang and others
have imagined. Rather, a combination of population and economic dynamics
working in the manner understood by Smith and Malthus account for important
similarities among the economic dynamics in China and Europe before the Industrial Revolution.

The parallels between European and Chinese rural industries have been no-
ticed but not taken seriously,[10] partly because many of us have been searching for
something else. We have been looking for the development of capitalism in China. In fact, the European proto-industrial dynamics that most resemble features
of the Chinese case do not lead necessarily to nineteenth-century industrial capitalism.[11] Proto-industrialization can be considered part of the industrious revolution and Smithian dynamics that account for the economic growth and
commercial expansion that took place before the Industrial Revolution. To the
extent that we see even partial parallels between Europe's proto-industrialization,
industrious revolution, and Smithian dynamics on one hand and dynamics of rural industrial expansion and commercial development in China on the other, we
might wonder how effectively these European phenomena can account for the later emergence of an industrial revolution.

---

[10]Chao (1986), for example, has asserted that rural industry was much more common in China than
in Europe. His assessment diverges from mine because he appeals to exogenous demographic changes
to explain the phenomenon. He sidesteps, it seems to me, the implications of the important arguments
about interactions among economic and demographic phenomena that much of the European work
has brought out. He says, "The difference between proto-industrialization in these European rural villages and the ruralization of nonagricultural production in China is only one of degree. Proto-industrialization in Europe took place only in a few rural pockets where population growth was unusually
fast or where land was unusually poor in quality. Ruralization of nonagricultural production in China,
by contrast, was as universal as the overpopulation that caused it" (pp. 24–25).
[11]Distinctions between proto-industrialization and industrialization by Mendels, Levine, and Kriedte
have been mentioned in the text. Among critics, Coleman 1983 and Jeannin 1980 note the uncertain
relationship between proto-industrialization and industrialization.

Proto-Industrialization, Social Mobility, and Economic Change

Even if proto-industrialization did not lead necessarily to urban factory industry, the process did nevertheless help to create a distinct class of proletarians who, according to Charles Tilly (1984), largely reproduced themselves for generations before their marginal ties to the land were broken by the expanded opportunities for urban employment in the nineteenth century. In China, rural industry did not, generally speaking, create a distinct class of people marginally tied to the land and therefore easily recruited into urban life. Partible inheritance, which kept Chinese peasants tied to the land more effectively than European practices, generally reduced average holdings in successive generations, but active land markets meant that some people rebuilt their holdings to equal or even exceed the bequests they had received. Others relied on renting land or hiring out their labor.

Semiproletarians, people who depended in part on the sale of their labor, and those engaged in rural industry more generally, were a doubly unstable group. Mobility could raise them into the ranks of tenants and small holders or drive them down into landless poverty. At present it seems unlikely that Chinese semiproletarians reproduced themselves as a distinct class for at least three reasons: (1) social mobility undermined class stability within generations; (2) the economic constraints on fertility of the poor meant that those who stayed poor were least likely to reproduce themselves and thus create class continuity;[12] and (3) households engaged in rural industries often continued to work in agriculture as well and thus could not develop a social identity sharply distinct from those engaged solely in agriculture. Chinese local social structures rarely produced the increasingly sharp distinction between farmers and rural workers found in some parts of Europe. Thus Chinese people engaged in rural industry did not form a class easily recruitable for migration into cities.

This phenomenon, common in China, could also be found in Europe. Despite the general trend toward proletarianization in the eighteenth century and the movement of rural proletariat into cities during the nineteenth century, not all people engaged in rural industry were destined to become urban industrial proletarians. One example of an alternative comes from the northern French village of Montigny in Cambresis, where Liana Vardi (1993) has reconstructed the eighteenth-century development of a linen industry among male peasants who lacked

---

[12]Indirect evidence of a relationship between wealth and male fertility is suggested in some 1930s survey data on farm households in North China, where the lower the ratio of females aged 20 to 50 to males aged 20 to 60, the less land the household owned; since semiproletarians had little or no land, probably fewer of them than of landowners had wives (Lavely and Wong 1992:451–52). Only 82 percent of some 3,514 men aged 36 to 40 in the years 1774–1873 were ever registered as married in a northeastern Chinese population analyzed by James Lee and Cameron Campbell (1997:85). While we don't know the economic status of the unmarried men, in general the more distantly the man was related to the household head, the more likely he was to have been unmarried.

adequate land to survive as farmers. As a land market developed and agriculture became concentrated in the hands of a few larger farms, peasants became weavers buying, selling, and mortgaging their property in order to raise funds for engaging in linen weaving. The more successful weavers became merchants and prospered through the production and sale of cloth. Both in the 1780s the linen trade faced a crisis of overproduction stimulated by easy credit. The subsequent contraction of commerce on the eve of the French Revolution led the richer merchant-weavers to turn back to land investments. Poorer weavers who were unable to secure land lost out while others became peasants again.

The French Revolution led to some nationalized property being sold to peasants, thereby reinforcing the deindustrialization of this part of this part of the northern French countryside. Towns and cities became the centers of commercial and industrial expansion, while villages lost the rural industrial dynamics basic to eighteenth-century changes. Where rural industry persisted past the French Revolution it was not a simple continuity from earlier times. In the Mauges of western France, Tessie Liu (1994) shows an eighteenth-century development and decline of linen broadly similar to Vardi's account of linen in northern France. But while Montigny began to deindustrialize in the nineteenth century, Cholet and surrounding villages in the Mauges become the site of new forms of rural industry. First cotton replaced linen; merchants exercised greater control over the product because they advanced the raw materials which were brought into the region. But the handloom weavers avoided becoming proletarians through organized resistance to merchant efforts to reduce them to wage labor status. Cotton cloth production remained small scale and dispersed as entrepreneurs abandoned their efforts to form new mills to which weavers would be recruited.

Liu's account highlights the struggles and negotiations between different groups to specify relations of social control and property rights. Whether or not people who engaged in rural industry became proletarians depended at least in part on the battles joined by producers and merchants or would-be mill owners. The outcomes also depended on plain economics: when could dispersed rural industry compete with concentrated manufacturing? When rural industry is economically viable, it can become politically successful. Alternatively, handloom-weaver protests might drive merchants to establish mills elsewhere. In this case the area where weavers have "won" then deindustrializes.

In economic terms, rural industry proves more viable than the dominant European dynamics suggest. There are cases in which rural industry persists within highly industrialized economies. Indeed, some analyses of European and American industrialization have stressed the ways in which a textbook view of industrialization fails to capture the multiple forms that industrial production takes in the nineteenth and twentieth centuries. Rather than imagining a swift, sharp, and total shift from handicraft to industrial manufacture, we might better consider a continuum of organizational formats in which different technologies are combined in varying ways.[13] Indeed, the most recent evaluations suggest that European pro-to-industrialization sometimes developed into industrialization, sometimes led to de-industrialization, and in yet other cases persisted alongside industrialized production. Sheilagh Ogilvie (1996) has argued that differences in social institutions help to explain the multiple possibilities.

A brief look at the contrasting institutional situations in China and Europe helps make clear that rural industry and commercialization in China were situated in different social structures than those found in Europe. The social implications of commercialization subsequently differed in China and Europe. In some parts of Europe the development of long-distance commerce was associated with the destruction of peasant communities and their rights to commons and communally based resources. In some cases, landlords enclosed lands and privatized resources to reap profits on the market; more generally, the commercialization of crop production where there were economies of scale promoted class differentiation in the countryside.[14] As a result, a process of rural proletarianization took place in which a growing stratum of the population was no longer tied to the land. In China peasants had few communal resources that they shared; crop production with economies of scale were rare in Chinese agriculture. Many peasants owned at least some of their own property, and many also rented some land. Virtually all land was worked at the household level of production; landlords who expanded their bases of direct production in response to market opportunities were few.

The expansion of Chinese commerce over longer distances drew peasants as well as landlords into the market. While some social differentiation took place in certain Chinese areas, there wasn't the sharp sort of class division that emerged in parts of Europe. Thus rural social structures during commercialization, called within a Marxist scheme the "relations of production" in the agrarian economy, clearly differed in Europe and China. In Europe landlords became more powerful with the expansion of commerce; in western Europe a few did so through enclosures and more generally in response to market opportunities; in eastern Europe they did so through the imposition of serfdom, in part stimulated by market opportunities. Neither was the norm in China, where peasants became active participants in market exchange. But these differences of social structure do not mean that the markets themselves operated in different ways economically. Rather they alert us to differences in the distribution of benefits from commercialization.

Some class differentiation certainly took place in many parts of the Chinese countryside between the nineteenth and early twentieth centuries. The elaboration of complex tenurial systems and the expansion of commercial production cre-

---

[13]On England, see Bythell 1978 and Berg 1986; on France, see Gullickson 1986 and Liu 1994. More generally, see Sabel and Zeitlin 1985. For Japanese examples, see Saito Osamu 1985 and Yasuba and Saito 1983. A leader in highlighting multiple possibilities is Philip Scranton (1991).
[14]For an example of social differentiation amidst commercialization in France, see Baehrel 1961:395–431.

ated new types of relationships among people. We find managerial landlords who used hired labor, as well as peasants who turned to specialized market production.[15] Scholars expecting changes in social relations to follow commercial change tend to downplay the persistence of small-scale peasant farming among people who could change their tenurial statuses and labor allocations several times during a lifetime and move modestly up as well as irrevocably fall down the social hierarchy.

Scholars of China have invested much effort in examining tenurial distinctions among farming households as structural differences. But these may matter less to the overall dynamics of economic change than the persistence of farming households. These households certainly experienced social mobility amidst class differentiation. In many cases they turned to handicraft industries for a modest or major part of their income. Yet most of them remained close to the land, if not rooted in the soil. The Chinese combination of household farming and handicraft industry may sometimes have been transformed by commercial penetration, but was rarely destroyed completely. Property relations, working through partibility and land markets, facilitated the reproduction of a social system in which class differentiation was not a crucial process. The social and economic implications of rural industry in China and Europe therefore differed in important ways.

Chinese rural industry was strongly rooted in a particular cluster of institutions constructed upon a distinctive cultural logic. But a linkage between farming and handicrafts was common across Asia. Francesca Bray (1986:135) offers support for a close connection between small-scale farming and handicraft industry in rice-based agrarian economies; she observes the intensification of wet-rice agriculture and the growth of part-time petty commodity production proceeding together. This observation, common to the rice economies of China, Japan, and parts of Southeast Asia, spans economies that followed sharply distinct trajectories of economic change in the nineteenth and twentieth centuries. Though Bray does not develop the contrast, its presence should alert us to the inability of rural industry itself to "cause" any particular pattern of industrialization in Asia.

Osamu Saito (1985) has directly compared the Japanese trajectory of industrialization with that found in parts of Europe, showing the basic similarities among changes in parts of England, Flanders, and Japan. As Saito shows, the Japanese case fits European expectations more closely than does the Chinese. Taken together, Bray and Saito show us that the association of a certain agrarian regime (its technologies and social organization) with domestic industry should not lead us to expect any particular sequence of economic change such as a shift from rural industry to urban factory industry. This East Asian contrast complements the earlier contrast made between China and Western Europe. Beyond East Asia one can go to other non-European areas such as India where during the Mughal period domestic industry remained basic amidst numerous economic

---

[15]Important works on the organization of agricultural production include Philip Huang 1985, Li Wenzhi et al. 1983, and Liu Yongcheng 1982.

changes (Habib 1969). Frank Perlin (1983) has extended the concept of proto-industrialization to South Asian cases, though, in contrast to my arguments about China, he takes the phenomenon as evidence for the potential for European-like changes there. In general, Eurasian evidence collectively confirms that rural industries can fit within numerous patterns of economic change.

In the European case, agrarian class differentiation is central to the formation of regional and national markets, on the one hand, and the creation of rural industry, on the other. Class differentiation is basic to the shift from a feudal social order to a capitalist one. In China, both commerce and rural industry developed without a comparable set of changes in social relations and social structure. Capitalism, conceived as a particular constellation of market relationships and social relationships to the means of production, developed in many parts of early modern Europe, but not in China. The formation of labor forces for rural industries in Europe and China reveals certain contrasts: Chinese peasants became semiproletarian because they often retained their ties to the land; and semiproletarians in China were less likely to reproduce themselves than were proletarians in Europe because of China's shortage of women, caused by female infanticide. Chinese semiproletarian ranks were renewed through the arrival of downwardly mobile peasants who in turn failed to reproduce themselves.

Social relations can influence the tenacity of rural industry. the contrast between raw-materials availability and control in Tessie Liu's linen and cotton textile cases is instructive: where producers had access to the raw materials to make linen without relying on a few rich merchants, they could sustain themselves far more easily as independent producers than could producers who had to buy raw cotton imported to the area by wealthy merchants. Social relations can also affect the ease with which an urban industrial proletariat is formed. But the forces that drove the shift away from rural industry in both eighteenth-century China and Europe were technological changes, changes that raised productivity beyond the levels previously achieved in the countryside. These changes generally favored large-scale concentrated production in urban-based factories.

Technological changes, however, need not necessarily deindustrialize the countryside. Indeed, some changes such as new looms and the use of machine-spun thread did enter the countryside. Moreover, since labor costs were lower in the countryside, because rural workers had lower food costs and could gain part of their income from agriculture, rural industries could remain competitive even using less efficient technologies. In parts of the French countryside, for example, rural industries persisted through the second half of the nineteenth century; workers went to the fields at harvest time (Postel-Vinay 1994). Until increased specialization and efficiency made it advantageous for labor to relocate to cities, some workers remained in the countryside. Until labor markets were integrated, supply and demand for labor in urban industry and the countryside were not subject to the same set of factors; wage differentials therefore appeared between town and country.

Rural industry persists under these conditions even if the producers are far less productive than those in urban factory industry. The most important factor favoring urban over rural locations for industrial production in the second half of the nineteenth century and into the early twentieth century was the lack of energy and power sources in the countryside. But as electrical power grids began to span the European countryside, the advantages of urban industrial location were reduced. In China, the expansion of a new round of rural industry beginning in the 1970s is in part made possible by the increasing diffusion and increase of electrical power sources.

In the century or two before the Industrial Revolution, Eurasian industry was largely a craft activity located in small towns and in the countryside. I do not mean to suggest that rural industry's characteristics were the same all across Eurasia, only that a cluster of common social conditions in agrarian economies favored the emergence of household-based rural industries. The comparison cannot predict additional similarities in the dynamics of economic change, because the character of rural industries was shaped by a combination of those commonly shared conditions and other contextual factors that varied dramatically across Eurasia. As a consequence, scholars should not expect Chinese rural industry to develop in exactly the same way as European industry.

The development of rural industry was a salient feature of Smithian expansion. Rural households specialized to some degree in the production of goods for the market according to their resource endowments and commercial opportunities. The elaboration of trade patterns that linked rural production more closely with urban centers and spanned long distances were significant changes experienced by people at both ends of Eurasia. Different parts of China and Europe experienced periods of Smithian growth bracketed by periods of equilibrium or stagnation. Scholarship on Europe that has reconstructed dynamics of economic expansion before the Industrial Revolution has been important for rectifying the error of believing that economies did not experience growth or expansion before modern dynamics of industrialization became possible. One basic message of research on European proto-industrialization has been to affirm any array of complex connections between the forms of industrial production before and after the Industrial Revolution (Ogilvie and Cerman 1996). In a similar vein, I suggest in later chapters some particular linkages between China's late imperial rural industries and twentieth-century developments.[16] These long-term perspectives encourage parallel insights into dynamics distinctive to each set of cases. In the European literature there has also been a tendency to diminish the impact and significance of the Industrial Revolution, and, as a result, to argue that the dynamics of economic growth have been a long-term gradual process without any sharp rupture. In the Chinese literature there isn't a single case in which modern factory industry emerges from rural industrial activity *before* the arrival of European models and methods. With our improved understanding of the multiple outcomes in differ-

---

[16]The persistence of rural industry in the twentieth century is addressed in chapter 3. The logic of rural industry within late imperial Chinese political economy is considered in chapter 6. Finally, the nature of rural industries since the early 1980s is considered in chapter 8.

ent rural industry scenarios, Chinese cases encourage us to consider the links between pre-industrial and industrial economic dynamics not only as complex and particular but as contingent and therefore difficult to predict. The ability of industrialization dynamics in 1900 to make possible the creation of material wealth unimaginable in 1800 makes it difficult to believe that industrialization grew naturally out of pre-industrial dynamics. The Industrial Revolution therefore retains a significance that some research on proto-industrialization has tended to obscure, if not erase, through a stress on gradual change. What, then, happened in Europe to encourage a shift from proto-industry to industrialization that did not occur in late imperial China?

There certainly were some obvious economic differences between China and Europe. Europe enjoyed several advantages that postponed the classical economist's end of growth. Central to Europe's early success were the discoveries in the New World, which offered what E. L. Jones (1981:84) has called an "unprecedented ecological windfall."[17] Certainly the resource base Europeans created through their expansion was superior to that created by the Chinese in their land-based frontier expansion which brought large amounts of new land under cultivation, but not always of top quality. Worse yet, resource depletion and land exhaustion became a serious problem in some Chinese areas. Returning to the example of southern Shaanxi, after an eighteenth-century phase of expansion, the production of foodstuffs on mountain lands became increasingly precarious and the timber industry greatly curtailed in the nineteenth century (Fang 1979; Tan 1986; Chen and Zuo 1988; Xiao 1988).

This kind of cycle bears some resemblance to early modern cycles in Languedoc and other parts of France studied by Le Roy Ladurie. But European dynamics of economic expansion transcended the immediate limits present in such situations. Europeans increased their resource base by exploiting new lands, sometimes with slave labor, and competing for lucrative items of trade like spices, silks, tea, coffee, and sugar. None of these activities, however, ultimately transcended the limitations of the classical economist's world. Future research may be able to produce more precise quantitative comparisons of Smithian dynamics in China and Europe. It may be discovered that Smithian dynamics were in fact stronger in parts of Europe than in any part of China. But whatever the differences future research may establish in regard to Smithian dynamics, those contrasts alone are unlikely to be adequate to explain the persistence of the constraints of the classical economist's world in China and their destruction in Europe.

Many analysts, including economists, tend to ignore those aspects of the classical economists' view of the world that do not accord with our understanding of more recent times. We anoint Adam Smith the father of modern economics even though he was not prepared to analyze the implications of the Industrial Revolu-

---

[17]The contrast between China and European powers that aggressively participated in commerce and agricultural production in Africa, the Americas, and Asia—an important aspect of European political economy—is considered more closely in chapter 6.

tion that was about to take place in England—perhaps because the changes of the Industrial Revolution were of a form and significance foreign to the economic world within which Smith and other classical economists lived. Furthermore, the economic world Smith, Ricardo, Malthus, and others understood was in some important ways similar to the Chinese economy, which they themselves misunderstood because of the severe limitations of European knowledge about China at that time. Economic growth could take place in the world analyzed by classical economists, as contemporary scholars, especially E. L. Jones (1988), have stressed. But the point Smith and others made that is less commonly acknowledged today is that there were limits to the growth that they could imagine taking place, largely because they could not anticipate the unprecedented technological change that occurred in Europe. Even Europe and China's most advanced regions in the eighteenth century, England and the lower Yangzi, had not escaped the limits of the economically possible scenarios envisioned by classical economists of the period.

Europe broke free of the intrinsic limitations of Smithian growth not merely by capturing additional resources through its overseas discoveries or even increasing production through institutional innovations. E. A. Wrigley (1988, 1989) has argued that the English escaped the limits of Smithian growth by tapping mineral sources of energy on a scale unprecedented in world history. Productivity increases based on coal as a new source of heat and steam as a new form of mechanical energy were the key features of the initial industrialization process that set parts of Europe off from the rest of Eurasia for much of the nineteenth century. The persistence of what he calls the organic economy, in contrast to the mineral-based economy, leads Wrigley to argue not merely for a shift in the timing of crucial economic changes leading to modern growth, but for a logical separation between the dynamics producing economic growth for Smith and the logic of expansion based on new sources of fuel and energy. "The world of the classical economists was a bounded world where the growth path traced out by a successful economy might at best be asymptotic; it could never assume the exponential form that became the hallmark of economies that had experienced an industrial revolution" (Wrigley 1989:34).

The contingent linkage between the economic growth of the classical economists and modern economic growth is obscured by the concept of "capitalism," which has been used to describe Europe's economic system both before and after the Industrial Revolution. First the term must be distinguished from commerce more generally. Fernand Braudel (1979, 1982, 1984) makes this distinction within his three-tier analysis of the early modern economy. At the bottom level is Braudel's material life where food, clothing, and shelter are the prime objects of attention; people across the world in 1500 shared similar possibilities and limitations materially. For many people, most items of daily use were produced near at hand within the family, village, or locale. But some of these items also entered a market economy, Braudel's second level of economic activity, where many buyers and sellers exchanged goods at prices set by supply and demand. This market economy was quite distinct in Braudel's mind from the rarefied world of capitalism in which wealthy merchants built their fortunes through monopoly control over valuable goods. He makes a basic distinction between market economy, which he finds in many parts of the early modern world, and capitalism, which he finds primarily in Europe. For Braudel, market economies exist wherever buyers and sellers get together to exchange goods at prices that both parties find sensible. There are no mysteries about supply and demand since the transactions are usually conducted between people who both know the market situation well. Capitalism, however, is largely based, for Braudel, upon a combination of monopoly and force; capitalists are merchants who reap huge profits from their control over the supply of a scarce commodity; producer and consumer are usually distant from each other.

Other scholars have argued for a kind of commercial capitalism in South Asia, and still others for a kind of incipient capitalism in China. Despite terminological and empirical uncertainties, we can assert a range of exchange relations that span from local market barter to overseas trade. Braudel's schematic may make too much of the gap among his levels of economic activity, for certainly there is evidence of how some goods—sugar, tea, and coffee for instance—moved all the way from capitalist networks spanning the oceans into the consumption patterns of at least some quite ordinary people. The distinctions among the three levels of the economy may also exaggerate the gap between market exchange and capitalism; the market for some goods has many buyers and sellers, but it also spans great distances.

Even allowing for connections among the levels of economic activity and recognizing that capitalism existed in some areas beyond Europe, the distinction between a Braudelian commercial capitalism and the operation of Smithian dynamics of economic expansion remains important. Institutions matter. China certainly had market institutions, but it did not have some of the organizational forms and financial institutions of early modern Europe that promoted the creation of commercial capitalism. The importance of these institutional differences will become clearer when we look at commercial capitalism as a kind of political economy in chapter 6.

While the distinction between commercial capitalism and Smithian dynamics of economic expansion is important, even more crucial for present purposes is the distinction between the commercial capitalism that could exist in the classical economists' world of limited possibilities and the industrial capitalism that only became possible with the shift from Wrigley's organic economy to his mineral-based economy. He argues,

> To succeed in breaking free from the limitations experienced by all organic economies, a country needed not only to be capitalist in the conventional sense, to have become modernized, but also to be capitalist in the sense that its raw materials were drawn increasingly from mineral stocks rather than from the annual flow of agricultural production, and above all, in the sense that it could tap great stores of energy rather than depend upon the kinds of renewable energy sources that had always previously provided any heat or power needed for production. The English economy was capitalist in both

senses of the word, but the connection between the two was initially casual rather than causal. (Wrigley 1988:115)

The Chinese case supports Wrigley's crucial distinction between a Smithian world and the capitalist world of nineteenth- and twentieth-century Western Europe and North America. Energy use is but the clearest indicator of a larger cluster of changes that took place in Europe but did not take place in China. Wrigley makes clear the logical independence of the economic system analyzed by the classical economists and the new economic system that emerged after the rupture represented by the radical shift to mineral sources of energy. Once this fundamental break took place, Europe headed off along a new economic trajectory. Rural industry's varied transformations were part of this larger set of changes.

The distinction Wrigley makes between two kinds of "capitalist," one he calls conventional and a second that refers to use of mineral stocks, is similar to the distinction in the Marxist tradition between "relations of production" and "forces of production." In many Marxist accounts depending on this distinction, including Chinese analyses of the late imperial economy, it is changes in the forces of production that compel changes in the relations of production. Forces of production then become essentially the exogenous variable that drives other economic changes. Basically technologies of production through which people transform nature, the forces of production do not change according to any simple and direct economic logic.

The argument I have made so far suggests that fundamentally similar dynamics of economic expansion via the market took place across Eurasia and that the development of rural industry was also similar in important ways. Despite differences in social relations of agrarian production typical of Europe and China, these differences existed within the same world of economic possibilities bounded by constraints recognized by classical economists. To discover how Europe escaped those constraints, we need to consider issues of technology or forces of production. If an unprecedented set of technological changes had not taken place, there might well have been increased pressure of population on resources—the sort of possibility we label Malthusian because of his articulate expression of the danger.

Through the eighteenth century there is, in fact, little evidence that the demographic dynamics in China and Europe were very different. Populations outstripping resources was not a serious problem in either China or Europe. By the end of the nineteenth century, however, Europe had clearly escaped those potential problems because of a combination of economic and demographic changes. China, in contrast, appears to have entered the twentieth century with the specter of Malthusian crisis ever more likely, at least in some regions. But what had changed was less the dynamics to which China was subject than the dynamics driving European economic growth. How did Europe escape the limits of growth identified by classical economists? To answer this question we turn in chapter 3 to reconsider the importance of the Industrial Revolution and explore further its analytical separation from much of the dynamics producing growth in earlier centuries.

3

MAKING MODERN ECONOMIES

Making an analytical separation between the organic economies analyzed by classical economists and the mineral economies of more recent times suggests that we cannot predict the development of industrial production from the patterns of handicraft production that preceded it. Industrial capitalism is not the necessary and obvious development out of commercial capitalism unless certain necessary technological changes occur. There are at least two kinds of situations where a market economy clearly makes a difference or is even necessary to foster technological change. First, when pre-existing demand is crucial to stimulate industrialization, an active market economy promotes industrial development; demand for farm implements in the United States and Europe is one example. Second, where market returns to technological change are established, as happened with patent regulations in both England and parts of the United States, market institutions can be used to predict where technological innovations are most likely to be attempted and to succeed. But in neither of these instances is the presence of a market economy or commercial capitalism *sufficient* to create industrialization: the technological changes that went into the Industrial Revolution were not simply a response to economic stimuli.

Logics of Technological Change: Contingent Possibilities

The causal linkages to explain technological change have proven difficult to pinpoint precisely because they are very diverse. The multiplicity of possibilities precludes any simple model as Joel Mokyr (1990) has shown in his study of technological change. Sweeping across European history while making an explicit comparison to China, he begins by stressing the rare occurrence of intensive bursts of technological change. He then reviews those factors that appear to in-

53

fluence the rate at which technological changes occur. Cultural values—for instance, the orientation of religion to the material world and the social status and material rewards accorded tinkerers—loom large; in general, cultures vary in the importance they assign to efforts made to improve people's relation to the material world. Mokyr also believes that technological change is most likely to take place in countries lacking a strong government capable of suppressing this kind of change. Where political power is weak and technological innovations are directed to processes with market values, change is most likely to take place.[1] These conditions broadly define key characteristics of late medieval and early modern Europe. From Mokyr's presentation we see the Industrial Revolution emerging from the gathering momentum leading to the eighteenth- and nineteenth-century explosion of inventions featuring the steam engine and textile machinery.

In part, Mokyr's presentation offers descriptive generalizations rather than a causal argument. To create greater explanatory potential, Mokyr contrasts the early modern European situation with both classical Europe and late imperial China. For classical Europe, most technology was directed to public works under state control; technological change did not become enmeshed within an expanding private economy. These differences support the importance he assigns to technology directed to goods with market-exchange value in a politically open environment.

For China, Mokyr has a larger challenge—he must explain why China, once a great innovator with many technologies, became after 1400 far less creative. Mokyr advances two reasons for an apparent decline in Chinese technological innovation. First, he suggests that the Chinese experienced changes in their philosophical outlooks toward the material world; second, he argues that the state became increasingly hostile to technological advances and projects that supported such changes. Both claims are problematic conceptually and difficult to support empirically. Whether or not changes in philosophical discourse were detrimental to study of the material world is by no means certain. Chinese scholars sustained and even developed further a tradition of empirical investigation directed both toward the natural world and Chinese history after 1400, especially from the late seventeenth through the early nineteenth centuries (Elman 1984). Moreover, whether such changes in philosophical discourse, if they existed, had much impact on the minds of those responsible for technological change remains unclear, since, just as in Europe, most technological change before the nineteenth century came from practical people tinkering. As for the notion that the state actively suppressed technological change, it seems a bit farfetched, since this was not a state with the infrastructural capacity to monitor such activities effectively, let alone any clear incentives to do so. The state heard of such changes only if people produced something to challenge Confucian sensibilities. Technological

---

[1]Mokyr also recognizes that government in more recent times has been able to promote technological change. Historically, however, he suggests that diffuse rather than centralized power facilitates technological progress. "It seems that as a general rule, then, the weaker the government, the better it is for innovation" (Mokyr 1990:180).

changes in general produced nothing that would arouse the government's anxiety since the state's definition of orthodoxy concerned a moral political and social order. To the degree that the state was aware of technological changes with economic benefits, it became a advocate, not a critic.[2] In brief, a search for changes in philosophical climate and government attitudes to explain differences in rates of technological change seems unlikely to be very productive. Why should these factors even matter?

The case for state antipathy to technological change and for change in intellectual attitudes toward the material world is motivated by a desire to find out why technological change stopped. The need to find an explanation for the apparent slowdown in Chinese technological change assumes that unless technological change is impeded, it will continue on. Yet such an assumption contradicts Mokyr's initial insight that bursts of technological change are relatively rare in world history. Before the second half of the twentieth century, when progress in high-tech fields became virtually programmed by strategies of research and development, technological change could not be considered predictable. To apply, even implicitly, an expectation that technological advances would continue at similar rates over time may simply be anachronistic for periods before 1950.

The explosion of changes in Europe was far more surprising than the absence of continued change in China. Social constraints may affect the rate of what Mokyr calls "micro-inventions" but cannot explain "macro-inventions." When we consider that Smith and other classical economists assumed that technological change had fixed limits beyond which it would not go, the finite boundaries of the classical economist's universe again become apparent; they did not expect bursts of technological changes. We should therefore be less perplexed by the apparent slowdown of Chinese technological change and more puzzled by Europe's technological innovations, the scale and duration of which were unexpected by the keenest eighteenth-century economic observers.

As Mokyr and others have shown, technological change is the product of many factors. Thus it is difficult to say such change is absent simply because a particular feature of change is missing, and difficult to predict dramatic technological changes, because major changes come far less often than minor improvements. The degree to which technological change will swiftly affect the economy depends in part upon how responsive technology is to market conditions. When people think about improving production because they can expect to reap rewards from the improvements, then institutions promote technological change. European institutions of property rights, especially patents, for example helped to channel people's inventiveness and curiosity into activities with technological and economic returns. Making technological change responsive to Smithian dynamics was a feature of Europe's Smithian expansion absent in China. But the demand for technological change can go only so far in creating a supply of technological

---

[2]Chinese officials wrote agricultural treatises and promoted the dissemination of agricultural knowledge as part of their larger responsibility to promote production (Deng Gang 1993:126–30).

changes, since many other factors influence the supply side of technological change. Only huge research and development budgets of the post-World War II world have made technological advance become more predictable.

The relationship between markets and technology in Europe suggests a corollary to our assessment of markets and economic growth. the dynamics of Smithian expansion follow from the implementation of market principles and institutions. Smithian growth in this simple model takes place within the space bounded by the production possibilities frontier. This frontier in the short-run is fixed, but over time technological change can move its limits outward. The European case suggests that Smithian dynamics can even help to move the frontier over time. Thus, Smithian dynamics can stimulate other sources of growth and create the possibility of escaping the limitations of the classical economist's world. But Smithian dynamics alone cannot account for the profound rupture in possibilities initiated by the development of mineral sources of energy.

The technological changes that began with the turn to coal as a key source of energy continued through the nineteenth century—from coal to steam to chemicals and electricity, nineteenth-century industrialization created production possibilities unimagined a century earlier. Technological changes, especially those centered on the exploitation of mineral sources of energy, were crucial to the successful escape from a classical economist's world of limited growth. But recent accounts of European economic change that stress quantitative measures of growth downplay the significance of technological change, because there was no sudden shift in the growth rates to reflect the importance of technological change. The set of changes in economic possibilities is swift only when we set aside calculations of annual quantitative growth and consider instead how different technological capacities were in 1880 compared to 1780. Then it becomes clear that a major technological shift in production possibilities lies at the base of the economic gains made after industry rapidly expanded in a largely urban framework. Nothing in this shift from rural to urban bases of production was necessary either to the general Smithian dynamics of economic expansion or to the specific logic of rural industry's development. Nor could commercial capitalism on its own escape the limits of the classical economist's world. We look back from the late twentieth century and clearly see the development of European capitalism and its global spread through commercial and industrial phases. We easily naturalize these changes and assume them to be necessary simply because they took place. As a result, we miss changes that were startling and unanticipated.

The sequence of technological changes, at the center of which was the shift to mineral sources of energy, made possible unprecedented levels of productivity. Economic institutions were invented to take advantage of these technologies. New financial networks mobilized and moved the increasing amounts of capital necessary for larger-scale industrial production, as previous reliance on family or friendship networks failed to yield the scales of capital needed to build steel mills or railroad lines. Conversely, new technologies supported the expansion and improvement of transportation networks composed of railroads and steamships; expanding the effective size of markets by lowering transaction costs made possible greater economic integration within countries and across national borders.

A new type of firm emerged at the forefront of economic expansion. Gustavus Swift revolutionized the meat-packing business in the 1890s and Henry Ford created the assembly line for automobile production in the 1910s. The modern business enterprise began to take shape in the United States and Europe. Resources and products previously allocated through markets became subject to decision making by business enterprises. Internalizing decision making made possible a more intensive application of the capital and labor used to produce and distribute goods in the industries where administrative control proved more profitable than market transactions. The new stratum of managers that staffed the expanding bureaucracies of business enterprises led Alfred Chandler to label this economic system "managerial capitalism."[3] The market continued to play the crucial role of setting the demand conditions to which firms responded. Of course, firms sought to shape the market and to create demand, but the system remained driven by market principles which set basic incentives for enterprise behavior.

By the end of the nineteenth century, new institutions in finance, transportation, and production formed key features of Euro-American industrial capitalism. Heavy industrial development in steel, railroads, and machinery were joined by changes in the petrochemical industries, further taking advantage of mineral sources of energy (Landes 1969; North, Anderson, and Hill 1983). Industrial capitalism created economic integration across ever-larger spatial areas with different spatial patterns of specialization and diversification on regional and national levels. Market economies in Western Europe and North America were now dominated by capitalist firms and financial institutions. In some sectors of production, a handful of big companies exerted oligopoly control as they competed for monopoly powers. In other sectors, small-scale production with multiple buyers and sellers fulfilled Smith's ideal form of market exchange.

Despite its inability to create a radically more productive economy which depended crucially on technological changes, commercial capitalism mattered to the formation of industrial capitalism in Europe in at least three ways. First, and most importantly, the decision to shift to factory production of textiles was a decision taken by capitalists; the principles of market exchange do not dictate the formation of factories. Second, commercial capitalism supplied the raw materials for Europe's expanding textile industry; and third, the stimulus for European textile development was the influx of Indian cotton cloth, which had expanded its sales on European and African markets. Capitalism's institutions became more important to heavy industry, which required larger amounts of capital and scales of pro-

---

[3]Chandler 1977:11. The most influential analyses of these changes are Chandler's. His work on business enterprises in the United States and Europe has achieved great acclaim as well as critique. See the symposium devoted to Chandler's *Scale and Scope* (Chandler et al. 1990). Differences between Chandler and his critics matter little to the argument proposed here because the appearance of a new kind of business enterprise is recognized by all parties.

duction. Commercial capitalism developed ways of mobilizing capital; industrial capitalism concentrated this capital along with labor to create a new kind of industrial production that depended upon inorganic sources of energy and other forms of new technology. Industrial capitalism became a coherent system of production and distribution once the shift to inorganic energy sources and the construction of large firms with capital raised through banks and by governments became major features of the economy.

The nineteenth-century European economy experienced increasing integration. First, there were multiple forms of market integration through which growing volumes of capital, labor, and finished goods passed within national borders and across them. Second, there was an increasing integration of commercial capitalism and the market economy, which had proceeded more independently of each other in earlier centuries, a result of the demands and desires of industrialization that transformed commercial capitalism into industrial capitalism. Industry devoured resources and labor with a power and passion unimagined in earlier times. The Industrial Revolution created a new set of ways for capitalism and the market economy to become joined. Only in the second half of the nineteenth century did railway lines link much of Europe to integrate larger amounts of production and consumption. The confluence of a market economy driven by Smithian dynamics, processes of technological change centered on an energy revolution, and the institutions of commercial capitalism came together to form late nineteenth-century industrial capitalism.

Each of the elements that became the compound of industrial capitalism was logically independent of the others despite their empirical connections. Technological change, in particular, was not caused in any simple and direct manner by either Smithian dynamics or commercial capitalism. The particular combinations of economic change creating industrial capitalism in Europe were historically specific. But from these experiences we can discern more general reasons for how and why economies can grow.

Sources of Economic Growth and China's Prewar Industrialization

Economies can grow for at least five reasons.[4] First, a process of commercial expansion according to division of labor and comparative advantage allows people to specialize in activities for which they can become more productive; we have seen this process, highlighted in Adam Smith's *Wealth of Nations,* at work in both late imperial China and early modern Europe. Second, growth can result from increased investment; if people consume less in order to invest in enlarged capaci-

---

[4]My list is a modification of one by Joel Mokyr (1990:4–7). His four types of growth include Smithian growth, growth due to increased investment, and growth due to scale or size; his fourth type, growth due to increases in stocks of human knowledge, I divide into the separate categories of technological change and changes in organization of production.

ties for future production, the economy will grow. Some types of production in both China and Europe involved larger investments than others; in China both paddy agriculture and silk production required more capital and labor than dry field grains. As people specialized in these kinds of production and increased their investments, the economy expanded. Third, an increased scale or size of an economy can lead to growth by making feasible types of production specialization or infrastructural investment like roads that would otherwise be unlikely. Some writers have therefore argued that population growth, by increasing the size of the economy, can lead to economic growth (Boserup 1981). Fourth, technological progress leads to economic growth by making the resources used more productive. The Industrial Revolution represents a period of major technological changes with important growth results. Fifth, people can become organized more efficiently to expand output without increasing inputs; the modern business enterprise is an example of this kind of change.

Some of these sources of growth existed before the Industrial Revolution; Smithian dynamics of growth were particularly important as the major source of economic expansion before the Industrial Revolution. To the extent that scale factors in the form of population growth stimulated economic growth, this could occur both before and after the Industrial Revolution. Smithian dynamics remained important after the Industrial Revolution; in combination with increased investment, technological change, and organizational change, they formed the sources of modern economic growth.

In China, a modern industrial sector developed rapidly during the first third of the twentieth century. It grew as new financial networks amassed larger sums of money, in part drawing funds out of China's older, traditional banking system and in part through mobilizing new funds both domestically and overseas. Industrial growth also depended crucially upon the introduction of new technologies from abroad. Improvements in transportation, railroads and steamships in particular, meant that trade opportunities reached more people. The legal basis for modern firms developed in China by 1904 with the recognition of limited liability firms, laying the foundation for Chinese firms to compete successfully with foreign businesses in succeeding decades (Faure 1994:28–53). Estimated industrial growth rates for the years 1914/1918 to 1933/1936 range from 7.7 to 8.8 percent (T. Rawski 1989:272–74). Growth was concentrated in a few urban areas, especially Shanghai and northeast China. Shanghai became the major center of China's financial network and light industries. With its seaport capabilities it also became a major transportation node between China and the larger world. In northeast China, industrialization gathered momentum in the early 1930s, as a product of Japanese colonial policies in the puppet state of Manchukuo. Other urban areas of China experienced more modest degrees of modern economic growth; in Canton, Tianjin, and Wuhan, for example, a variety of industries were formed in the early twentieth century. China's industrialization during the 1910s–1930s is certain, but two questions about the process remain difficult to answer: (1) to what extent did industrialization processes link up with and affect economic activities in rural China; and (2) would industrialization have become a self-sustaining economic process in the absence of the 1937 Japanese invasion? How we answer these questions shapes how we understand economic change in twentieth-century China more generally.

Let's begin with textiles because this was the major Chinese handicraft industry. How was urban economic growth of a new kind linked to older forms of agrarian economic activity? For textiles, there are some parallels with and differences from European experiences. In both Europe and China, there was an initial expansion of weaving in rural households with the introduction of factory-produced machine-spun yarn. In England, handloom weavers grew from 90,000 in 1795 to 270,000 in 1811 and 300,000 in 1833 (Pollard 1981:25). In China, the linkage between factory yarn and handicraft weaving shows up in Gaoyang, for instance, where a boom in textile production in 1915–20 was occasioned by the new availability of factory yarn and iron-gear looms (Chao 1975:188).

Technological advances in weaving increased labor productivity in both China and Europe. But European textile production became increasingly an urban phenomenon during the nineteenth century. In China, peasant households successfully competed with modern factories in cloth weaving through the first half of the twentieth century. Kang Chao (1977:174–79) has argued that labor productivity for factory-produced cloth was four times that of handicraft producers, but because, he suspects, handicraft producers worked for lower wages and because production costs were lower in peasant households, handicraft products were competitive. Factory industry expanded the supply of machine-spun yarn which displaced homespun yarn in both handicraft and factory weaving. Nonetheless, as the protoindustrialization literature for Europe would predict, it was extremely difficult in China for modern factory production to displace handicraft production. Indeed, amidst cyclical fluctuations, both handicraft and factory textiles grew in the two decades preceding the Japanese invasion of 1937. Only then did modern textile production definitely displace handicraft weaving.

Beyond textiles, the expansion of industrial production in the 1920s and 1930s included a considerable amount of small-scale production outside major cities. In the eastern coastal province of Jiangsu, for instance, many of the rice mills, oil-pressing factories, and printing firms averaged less than ten workers per firm in many counties (Nanjing tushuguan tecangbu and Jiangsu sheng shehui kexue yuan jingji shi keti zu, eds., 1987:229–33, 292–308). This wide spatial dispersion of small-scale industries was also found within the most commercially advanced areas, such as Suzhou, where even after the formation of the People's Republic the value of handicraft output remained at 50 to 60 percent of total industrial output each year between 1949 and 1957 (Duan and Zhang 1986:576).

The combination of modern and traditional sector growth in prewar China led Thomas Rawski (1989) to argue that a sequence of modern economic growth had been begun that would have continued in the absence of the massive disruptions caused by the Japanese invasion of 1937. Rawski bases his anticipation of economic growth on future structural changes in the economy with the modern sector absorbing labor and capital from the traditional sector in the manner proposed by Simon Kuznets (1966). The fact that Rawski's analysis of China's growth before 1937 identifies a crucial role for growth in traditional economic activities suggests that the transformative potential of modern sector production is less than certain.[5] At the same time, however, the dynamics of early industrialization in England also show that modern sector changes initiate and stimulate broader developments in traditional sectors. Berg and Hudson (1992:31) go so far as to argue: "In reality, it is impossible to make clear-cut divisions between the traditional and the modern as there were rarely separate organizational forms, technologies, locations, or firms to be ascribed to either." At issue is the degree to which changes in a new modern sector stimulated changes in the traditional sector to promote broadly based and sustainable economic growth. Only future research will prepare us to make a clearer assessment of the actual changes. For the moment, let us review some of the possibilities.

Handicraft industries offered work to rural people who would otherwise have been more seriously underemployed as part of a population without significant employment in agriculture. The presence of this labor surplus makes the China of the 1920s and 1930s a good candidate for analysis as a "dual economy." A dual-economy model, broadly speaking, is one in which there are organizational asymmetries in manufacturing and agriculture. The institutional mechanisms to channel factors of production between manufacturing and agriculture are absent, so that the marginal product of each factor cannot be equalized across the two sectors (Kanbur and McIntosh 1989). Since W. Arthur Lewis (1954) combined this structural scenario with labor surplus so that the marginal product of labor in agriculture is close to zero, even as wages in industry are much higher, the problems of transforming agriculture amidst modern industrial growth have become widely recognized. A dual-economy approach makes sense only if we think there is a gap between the industrial and agricultural sectors. A standard neoclassical approach assumes that factor markets will emerge across industrial and agricultural sectors to equalize returns to capital and labor. Even labor economists who do not adopt a dual-economy approach recognize that labor markets are less than the ideal posited by neoclassical economists (Grantham 1994). A cluster of simplifying assumptions in neoclassical economics posits processes of change that in fact apply only to certain cases—those in which economic growth or development takes place. The gradual integration of factor and product markets is not logically necessary, but it is found in some places at certain junctures in history. In any number of other instances these assumptions of change will not hold. The danger lies in assuming that economic growth is natural and that if it does not take place, arbitrary human actions (usually thought of as politics) must be interfering. By closely identifying a theoretical ideal with a "natural" state of affairs, neoclassical economic theory loses its potential to explain how economic change is in fact historically created through the building of economic institutions. These institu-

---

[5]For a fuller discussion of this argument, see Wong 1992:608–9.

tions—both markets and firms—are what make it possible for economies to become integrated, to seize upon comparative advantage and the division of labor, to diffuse new technologies, and to move capital and labor to those projects yielding the highest returns.

China in the 1930s was only beginning to develop financial institutions and labor-recruitment strategies for modern industry. Much of China had long enjoyed the benefits of product markets for commodities produced in the countryside, as well as factor markets for capital and labor in the countryside. But urban markets for capital and labor were only beginning to be formed. Transportation outside of major waterways and railways was lacking. The government was not in a position to take a strong lead in developing infrastructure or promoting economic change. The inability of the institutions of industrial capitalism to penetrate broadly throughout agrarian China meant that a considerable portion of the economy still functioned within the classical economist's world marked by Smithian dynamics and Malthusian dangers.

Industrial capitalism in China possessed neither the institutional structures nor the capital to transform large parts of the country. China in the 1920s and 1930s was not about to achieve what had only been accomplished a few decades earlier in late nineteenth-century Europe. Chinese and European economies that exhibited parallels in the two or three centuries before 1800 began to appear crucially different in the early 1900s. As increasing proportions of European and American labor forces moved from agriculture to industry and in the process urbanized their societies, the economies of Western Europe and North America shared fewer obvious parallels with China, even as the economies themselves became increasingly connected through international factor and product markets. China remained, for much of the twentieth century, an agrarian society where Smithian dynamics continued to account for positive change and Malthusian realities of poverty and the presence of surplus labor qualified the extent to which such changes would become significant.

Smithian and Malthusian Dynamics in China's Agrarian Economy

The extension of production coupled with the gains of Smithian development allowed the Chinese economy to expand through the eighteenth and nineteenth centuries. But regional variations were pronounced. Limits to the extension of arable in China were clearly serious. Even with the successes of land reclamation companies, only marginal additions to cultivated land were made in the early twentieth century (Huang and Zhang 1988; Dai 1985). Increasing land productivity usually meant the application of ever-greater amounts of labor to carefully designed crop rotation schemes that would maximize the value of the land's production, but none of these efforts could radically raise labor productivity. In Wrigley's terms, the absence of technological inputs in the form of mineral sources of energy precluded dramatic increases in the productivity of either land or labor.

The problem was not a new one. Difficulties of amassing sources of energy have been identified by Li Bozhong (1984b) as a key constraint on lower Yangzi economic developments from the sixteenth century forward. He has shown the limitations on coal resources and the consequent small size of metals industries; the most common fuel sources for peasant households were firewood and threshing stalks. Outside the relatively rich Yangzi delta, early twentieth-century Chinese agriculture showed signs of suffering severe organic energy shortages. Kenneth Pomeranz (1993:123–37) shows that the most generous estimates of fuel supply for a part of inland North China still yield a total per capita figure less than one-third of the level researchers today consider the bare minimum for subsistence— a figure lower than that for poor areas in Bangladesh, rivaled in the late twentieth century only by parts of Sahelian Africa. Even if this part of North China was worse off than many other areas, it hardly stands out as significantly poorer than many other parts of northern and northwest China at this time. The grim energy situation in parts of rural China does not mean that China failed entirely to tap mineral sources of energy. In the prewar period, both traditional and modern methods of mining coal were practiced. Modern coal mines principally fueled the industries of Manchuria in the northeast and the lower Yangzi area of Shanghai. Small-scale, seasonally operated coal mines were found in many parts of China; these supplied fuel for handicraft industries and to peasants and urban dwellers for consumption as well (Wright 1984). Handicraft industries included ironworks which produced farm implements throughout the country. Indeed, China had a considerable iron industry in late imperial times; the techniques of these small-scale works not only persisted in the early twentieth century but became celebrated and indeed caricatured by the late 1950s effort of the Great Leap Forward to expand dramatically the number of small blast furnaces throughout the country (Wagner 1985). What China lacked was convenient access to mineral sources of energy that could be harnessed for technologically more efficient forms of production in the most advanced parts of the country.

Despite energy constraints which show that Wrigley's break from an organic economy had yet to take place in agrarian China, market exchange continued to introduce benefits in North China as well as elsewhere. In a perhaps unexpected way, Smithian dynamics could be at work even as local ecologies and resource situations deteriorated. The overall economic outcome was uncertain, since it depended upon both positive Smithian dynamics and the resource constraints of a local area. These contingencies allowed for the mixed evaluations of the agrarian economy found in many studies, from fieldwork done in the 1930s to the most recent scholarship. Smithian dynamics could persist, but they could not by themselves surmount the limitations of increasingly scarce resources.

Much debate surrounds Chinese agriculture in the 1920s and 1930s. Analysts at the time found much to worry about—gross inequities in the social structure, a poverty of resources, low standards of living. Prescriptions for change ranged from broad calls for social revolution to more focused proposals for institutional changes to create credit and marketing cooperatives for farmers. Individuals expressed uncertainty over the most important elements. In his famous *Land and Labor in China,* first published in 1932, R. H. Tawney (1966) called for improvements in credit, marketing, supplies, and insurance; he believed these basic institutional changes would promote positive changes. By the late 1930s, Tawney doubted that institutional changes were possible under the current social structure: "The improvement of agricultural methods is, no doubt, indispensable; but it is idle to preach that doctrine to cultivators so impoverished by the exactions of parasitic interests that they do not possess the resources needed to apply it" (Institute of Pacific Relations 1938:xviii). Most observers shared Tawney's view that China's peasantry was very poor. The most negative assessments suggest an agrarian world haunted by Malthusian fears of population growth outstripping resources.

Although China's population and resources in the late imperial period broadly resembled those in early modern Europe, Europe escaped the limits of the classical economist's world with the Industrial Revolution. China, however, faced what many observers saw as the threat that population would outstrip resources. More accurately, population and resources continued to be in rough balance, but the poverty of both became increasingly stark in relation to Europe's material advances. The possibility of industrial advance in China meant that some people were given an opportunity to earn higher incomes. Difficult and exhausting as factory labor was, the wages earned by workers generally exceeded what they could earn in the countryside. Industrialization introduced a disequilibrium between population and resources; it created a gap in production possibilities between a relatively small number of people and the vast majority of the population.

Despite its relatively rapid growth, the ability of China's modern industrial sector to transform the agrarian economy is open to doubt. At present we have no clear and systematic picture of the ways in which urban industrial changes were connected to and separate from economic activities in the countryside. It seems reasonable to expect that peasants in periurban areas did benefit from urban industrialization, since demand for industrial raw materials and food supplies must both have risen. But complete integration of capital, labor, and product markets seems unlikely. Reality probably lies somewhere between Philip Huang's dismissal of important economic links connecting the cities to the countryside and Thomas Rawski's assumption that markets were integrated.[6] In contrast with European capitalist development, in which large-scale markets formed by commercial capitalists were then used by industrial capitalists, a sophisticated market economy in

---

[6]Huang (1990) argues that rural areas surrounding Shanghai remained at a subsistence standard of living despite urban industrialization; he sees economic development in the lower Yangzi countryside only after 1978 when economic reforms facilitated the absorption of rural labor into industries. Rawski, in contrast, sees no barriers between urban and rural economic activities in prewar China. Rawski assembles a large number of data to document many important changes in production and to estimate the scale of other changes such as labor productivity. The basic argument begins with a modern manufacturing sector which develops through increased investment in new forms of production, supported by improved transport and communications and new financial and banking institutions (T. Rawski 1989: 65–238).

China was constructed without a strong capitalist thrust; when twentieth-century industrial capitalists emerged in Chinese cities, they had more modest contact with the agrarian economy's vast commercial networks.

When China's prewar twentieth-century economy is viewed from the perspective of urban–rural relationships, we can see evidence of economic change linking urban and rural areas as well as indicators that much of rural China may have been only marginally affected by urban industrial changes. Our empirical uncertainties suggest a need for additional research on economic change during the Republican period. As this future work is formulated, the problem of China's great size deserves particular attention. What are the appropriate units within which to envision economic change? What relations among these units seem most plausible? In Rawski's effort to examine national aggregates, the lower Yangzi region looms large. Rawski estimates that Jiangsu together with Manchuria, accounted for two-thirds of China's industrial output with only one-seventh of the country's population in 1933 (T. Rawski 1989:73). Rawski stresses the regional locus of economic growth. Since changes in Jiangsu, especially the Shanghai region, and Manchuria drive Rawski's estimated per capita output increase of 1.2 to 1.3 percent annually and per capita consumption increase of 0.5 percent annually, "other regions experienced below average, and possibly negative, growth" (T. Rawski 1989:271).

It is easy to underestimate industrial change in China by thinking in conventional national terms. China dwarfs any particular European country; many of China's provinces are themselves larger than the smaller European countries. To make more meaningful comparisons, we might want to look at regions of China and compare them with European countries. Were we to do so, China's most advanced regions might look little different in their growth profiles from European regions. Certainly we could expect the Shanghai region to continue its industrialization, and if we assume that Chinese–Japanese economic relations continued to develop peacefully, the Northeast as well.

Less clear is the manner and degree to which other areas would have been affected by regionally concentrated dynamics of industrialization. Two different "integration" scenarios would have been plausible. The first involves the development of additional industrial regions, such as had happened a few decades before in Europe, where "the industrial revolution jumped, as it were, from one industrial region to another, though in a general direction outward from the North-West, while the country in between remained to be industrialized, or at least modernized, much later, if at all" (Pollard 1981:45). In this scenario, industrialization spreads the possibilities of modern growth to larger numbers of people across greater stretches of territory. For a second scenario the spread of economic opportunities is far less important. In this second scenario, the wealthy and productive regions attract raw materials, labor, and capital from other parts of China, because these advanced areas are the places where capital, labor, and resources can be most efficiently used. These places have the institutional structures to achieve optimal levels of production and people with the incomes to purchase the new products. Under this second scenario there is little spread of industrialization; rather a concentration of capital, labor, and resources in wealthy areas takes place.

These opposing scenarios are both created through processes of market integration, but with the flows of factors of production and commodities obeying different principles. The historical record outside China includes both kinds of market integration. West European and North American patterns of economic development represent the broader-based dynamics of industrialization, while the nineteenth- and early twentieth-century integration of much of Southeast Asia and South America into global markets represents the limited positive transformative impact of industrialization.

The formation of a modern industrial sector suggests that at least part of the economy was moving beyond Smithian dynamics of expansion, even as classical fears of a population and resource crisis in agriculture echoed in the pronouncements of twentieth-century Chinese and foreign observers. But the uncertain linkages between modern industrial and traditional agricultural sectors makes the impact of twentieth-century industrial change difficult to assess. What needs to be determined is whether or not the economic linkages among different regions and within them were adequate to judge the economy to be an integrated one, a network of only loosely connected economies, or an economy segmented into separate spheres bearing traits of a dual economy.

At present we need to learn more about credit, labor, and product markets in prewar China. While urban-based credit networks through modern banking clearly existed, it remains unclear how systematically, if at all, urban credit was integrated with rural credit. Similarly, for labor, migration patterns were limited, as were labor markets in their spatial dimensions, but the degree to which these institutional limitations created disparities in regional economic performance in the Republican period has not yet been analyzed. Certainly, striking regional differences are known to have existed between standards of living in China's remote northwest and southwest and those of the lower Yangzi region, Canton, and Manchuria. Should we expect these differences to disappear "naturally" over time had the Republican period economy's development not been interrupted by the Japanese invasion? Integration could have meant an increased concentration of resources in core areas rather than the diminishing of economic differences.[7] The prewar Chinese economy pos-

---

[7]In his work on a portion of inland North China between 1853 and 1937, Kenneth Pomeranz (1993) argues for a shift of resources from peripheries to cores. Ming-te Pan's (1994) research on credit markets in the Qing and Republican periods suggests that funds previously available for rural credit increasingly were drawn into urban financial networks. For their parts, Brandt (1989:106–37) and Rawski (1989:285–329) either assume or assert with spotty evidence a neoclassical world in which wage rates equilibrate across sectors; labor and capital move easily across urban and rural sectors to achieve optimal returns; and integration, if not present in a particular area, is expected to develop in the future. Huang (1990:93–114), to the contrary, essentially argues that Chinese land, labor, and credit markets fell far short of the neoclassical ideals that he assumes to be at work in England. Only a concrete comparison of economic institutions, however, could demonstrate how similar and different real world cases truly are. Kenneth Pomeranz (1993:27–68) analyzes credit markets in a manner that helps to establish

sessed both a vital agrarian commercial economy, the basic institutions of which had existed for several centuries, and a growing industrial economy constructed in the twentieth century by native and foreign capitalists. Growth certainly took place in the capitalist economy, and some growth appears to have taken place in some parts of the agrarian commercial economy. The defeat of the Japanese did not mean a return to the logic of a market-based agrarian economy and capitalist-driven industrialization. After 1949, neither markets nor capitalist institutions played much role in socialist China's first three decades of economic change.

Perspectives on Development in China since 1949

Following a Soviet model of centralized government planning and control over development that stressed heavy industry, Chinese leaders aimed to expand China's industrial base beyond the regional concentrations present in 1949. Industry grew during the first three decades of Communist rule. Increased levels of investment and the development and spread of industrial technologies were the principal economic sources of growth. As a centrally planned economy, socialist China relied little on market dynamics and thoroughly rejected capitalist financial institutions and bourgeois business practices. At the enterprise level, the locus of control and management varied from the 1950s through the late 1970s between technically trained managers and politically correct party members; market pricing played virtually no role in allocating resources or shaping product mixes. There was no market economy for industrial goods. Socialism meant economic planning for industrialization. The government severed the problematic relationship between China's earlier market economy and capitalism by making industrialization a process promoted outside both the market and capitalism.

Rural China was kept institutionally separate from urban industrial developments. Strict controls over migration effectively created distinct economic worlds in China's cities and the far vaster countryside. Villages were radically restructured, first through collectivization, then in the late 1950s through the formation of communes, which further centralized political and economic decision making. In socialist China a conscious decision was taken by government leaders to limit the connections between urban and rural economies. Peasants supplied through taxes much of the capital used to develop industry. Because much of the capital-intensive industrial change was in heavy industry without direct consumer benefits, socialist industrialization promoted a strong government more than a wealthy society. Commercial relations that had once connected peasants across many regions were broken as the peasants' economic horizons shrank. Throughout the 1950s and 1960s, efforts were made to reduce wealth disparities in the countryside as overall

---

a baseline for assessing economic possibilities based on changes in credit markets. His careful reconstruction of the institutional structure of Shandong credit markets is an exemplary alternative to the diametrically opposed lines of reasoning Brandt and Rawski, on one side, and Huang, on the other, employ to address the general issue of economic institutions and economic growth.

production increases were gained through infrastructural developments and some modern inputs. While local disparities could be leveled, it proved far more difficult to reduce the differentials between wealthy and poor regions. Spatial differences persisted despite some efforts by planners to direct resources to poorer areas.[8]

In some ways, post-1949 economic development dynamics mark a sharp departure from earlier dynamics. Soviet-style centralized planning in the 1950s mobilized capital for industrial development and promoted technological developments without product or factor markets playing any important role. The collectivization of agriculture and the subjection of peasant households to higher levels of economic decision-making authority represented a radical alternative to the organization of agrarian production in earlier times. In other ways, however, post-1949 economic change followed patterns clearly linked to earlier practices. The economy remained primarily agrarian. Rural industry, which had been important since late imperial times, continued to be important. Moreover, rural industry was separate institutionally from centralized heavy industrial planning. The uncertain connections between urban and rural China that had led to what was probably a dual-economy situation before 1949 were further undermined after 1949. Finally, the regional disparities that developed in late imperial times and were subsequently exacerbated by a regionally concentrated industrialization process in the early twentieth century persisted after 1949 despite efforts to reduce the gaps.

How do these Chinese changes fit within a global context? Throughout the world, economic decision making has had an increasingly explicit political component which defines preferences among different methods for creating economic change. As a consequence, political strategies for economic development can vary dramatically. Governments of late-developing countries can use various macroeconomic policy tools such as monetary supplies and interest rates, import tariffs and domestic production subsidies, and promotion of foreign trade and "open" markets. Chinese development strategies in the 1950s began with a program for heavy industry and a strategy of collectivization in agriculture. The pursuit of any particular policy sets in motion changes that can move an economy forward; but where "forward" leads is not everywhere the same. Pursuing an export strategy based on natural resources, for instance, may lead in a very different direction from the building of import-substituting industries. But success with any strategy can make possible other changes, such as a more efficient and productive agriculture or a sophisticated banking system, that may eventually bring economies that adopted different strategies closer to one another.

There are no guarantees for success. But failure with one strategy does not represent global failure. Much depends on the linkages that develop between one set of changes and other parts of the economy. The presence of alternative policies to promote economic growth in late-developing economies reflects the uncertainty

---

[8]On marketing, see Skinner's classic articles (1964–65). Regional differentials exist nationally (Lardy 1978) and within provinces, such as Guangdong (Parrish and Whyte 1978).

planners feel regarding any particular policy choices. The inability of planners and policy makers to predict accurately the results of specific initiatives means that economic change is a combination of intended and unintended results. This has led many analysts in the closing decades of the twentieth century to argue that political efforts at creating economic development have not worked well.

Much economic policy making in the late twentieth century has been centered on market reforms. Such efforts have been accompanied by enthusiastic announcements in some quarters that socialism and communism have failed and that capitalism has triumphed. Within capitalism, the virtues of the free market are held up as the essential cure for the vices of planned economies. What such pronouncements often obscure is the degree to which many economic decisions are not made by markets, even in economies where markets are key institutions. Many economic choices are in fact made administratively within large and complex business enterprises and by governments setting policy and establishing rules within which private (or public) economic actors make their decisions. Thus economic change in the late twentieth century clearly and obviously involves politics. In fact, politics mattered to economic change in earlier periods as well. The answer to the question of why China didn't develop capitalism is in part a political one. But before moving on to consider political aspects of economic change more closely, let's review where our questions about economic change as distinct from political economy have taken us so far.

The economic question is not why China didn't develop capitalism, but rather what were the dynamics and limitations of economic expansion in China and how were they similar to and different from those at work in Europe? In addressing this question I have argued that the economic contrast between China and Europe before 1800 is not between a Malthusian China and a Smithian Europe. When we consider what did in fact happen in China between the sixteenth and nineteenth centuries, we discover that important Smithian dynamics of expansion were shared by both early modern Europe and late imperial China. A sharp economic divergence did not emerge until after the Industrial Revolution. Europe's nineteenth-century creation of industrial capitalism led to the formation of a global economy in which other regions of the world have also begun processes of industrialization.

In the first half of the twentieth century, Chinese industrial capitalism made sizable advances in the Shanghai region and Northeast China, but did not remake the entire economy. The abrupt and crucial changes created by the Japanese invasion, followed by civil war and the triumph of the Chinese Communist Party, alert us to politically determined changes for the Chinese economy. For Europe, however, reconstructions of economic change often lead us to expect each step to follow naturally. We tend to think of European economic changes as largely market-centered, with private economic actors making all the relevant decisions. While the institutional forms in which politics mattered in early modern Europe differed from those in mid- and late twentieth-century China, economic change in both cases has political components we often ignore. Furthermore, when we stress the gradual and cumulative character of economic growth in Europe, the Industrial Revolution loses its salience as an extraordinary cluster of changes.

In China, in contrast, scholars rarely see continuities or even connections between development possibilities since 1949 and the country's economic history. We tend to see China's economic past largely as a set of problems or failures to change in certain ways. We furthermore assume, when we don't assert, that economic change is largely the imposing of foreign models and methods on a Chinese system in need of changes that can only come from outside the country. Armed with these expectations there is little point to examining the possible connections between Chinese economic history and its development possibilities. To claim that there might be such connections is part of a larger proposal to take seriously a Chinese trajectory of economic and political changes that shares some but not all elements in common with the trajectories of change found in Europe. To understand better the Chinese historical dynamics and to place them within broader patterns of historical change, we need to shift our focus from economic change to politics and state making. Once we have an initial sense of how patterns of state formation and transformation differed between late imperial China and early modern Europe, we will be able to reconsider economic changes as changes in political economy and then follow Chinese and European state-making processes into the twentieth century.

PART II

STATE FORMATION AND TRANSFORMATION IN EURASIA

In 1100, most of sedentary Eurasia lived in rural areas and depended upon agriculture. Peasants relied upon timely spring rains and the warmth of long summer days to nurture the crops for an autumn harvest. Over the next four centuries, increasing numbers of goods entered expanding trade networks. Regional economic systems developed in China and Europe in broadly parallel fashion. In sharp contrast to these important similarities, Eurasian politics were organized in a myriad of ways. Within Europe a host of rather small political units included city-states, bishoprics, duchies, and kingdoms. China, however, was a vast empire in which European-style nobilities, religious institutions, and political traditions were largely absent. If we were to start a discussion of Eurasian state making in 1100, we would anticipate distinctive paths of change for China and Europe, if for no other reason than the different initial conditions.

For all their differences, China and northwestern Europe are relatively easy to contrast, because their trajectories of political change were largely independent of one another before the mid-nineteenth century. Comparing patterns of state formation, however, encounters the same difficulty that afflicts studies of economic change: we conventionally begin with standards of political development abstracted from European experiences. Analysts differ greatly regarding the features of Western experiences they choose to stress, but the collective weight of different traditions often crushes the Chinese experience into a form that fits Western expectations more closely than Chinese realities. Analysts of China habitually see Chinese divergences from European practices as signs of failure or incompleteness. I address the limitations of a solely Eurocentric view of Eurasian politics by positing analytical categories intended to capture both similarities and

71

differences between China and Europe. But because political ideologies and institutions differ far more than economic principles and market institutions, it is
necessary to examine more closely both political ideologies and institutions in order to create a procedure for evaluation that escapes the limitations imposed by
Eurocentric vantage points.

Despite the difficulties of comparing political dynamics in China and Europe,
understanding processes of state formation and transformation demand that we
make such an effort. The spread of European power to Africa, Asia, and Latin
America gave Europeans increasing influence on political developments there.
These contacts of Westerners and others gave rise to important asymmetries in
politics that paralleled those in economics. Their existence complicates our task
of making comparisons. In order to analyze the process of Chinese grappling with
Western political power, it will help to create a larger context in which domestic
dynamics of state making are also reconstructed. If we search for the persistence
of concerns on China's political agenda that cannot be derived from European
practices at the same time as we strive to explain how certain practices of Western
origin came to be Chinese ones over time, we can aim for a more comprehensive
understanding of Chinese state transformation from late imperial times forward.

Chapter 4 lays out a framework for comparing the formations and transformations of Chinese and European states with the aim of identifying the importance of both the similarities and differences in these dynamics of political change.
Chapter 5 explores the issues of domestic rule more closely to show the presence
of Chinese strategies in an agrarian empire that, not surprisingly, find little parallel in European experiences; the significance of those differences for understanding the dynamics of political change in the twentieth century are examined in later
chapters. Chapter 6 combines analyses of political and economic change to consider the different dynamics of Chinese and European political economies before
industrialization; while no government could escape the limits of the preindustrial world, some became better equipped to take advantage of the new industrial
possibilities than others, though not necessarily intentionally. Chapter 7 carries
forward the analysis of state transformation into China's postimperial period with
the fall of the final dynasty in 1911 to discover how twentieth-century dynamics
moved amid possibilities in part determined by late imperial sensibilities and practices. Chapter 8 concludes this section with consideration of post-1949 Chinese
state transformations in Eurasian perspective; since this period is conventionally
considered in terms of how China's situation resembles that of other twentieth-
century countries, the chapter stresses those features that are more clearly connected to the trajectory of changes begun centuries before. If the analysis is
successful, the reader should gain new perspectives on state formation and transformation in China and Europe and be able to place both in a framework that accounts equally for their common and their distinctive features.

4

CHINESE AND EUROPEAN PERSPECTIVES ON STATE FORMATION AND TRANSFORMATION

European national state making is the historical experience that conventionally defines expectations for modern state formation on a global scale. Yet general definitions of the state lack any specific historical context. Thus, when Charles Tilly offers a broad definition of the term, he says: "Let us define states as coercion-wielding organizations that are distinct from households and kinship groups and exercise clear priority in some respects over all other organizations within substantial territories" (1990:1). The late imperial Chinese state meets Tilly's criteria. But the process by which it achieved these traits does not fit among the paths taken by European national states. To appreciate the differences in Chinese and European state making, we need to consider the historical trajectories that made different parts of Eurasia into components of distinct political systems in 1100.

If we reach back into the period of empire formation by the Romans in Europe and the Qin and Han emperors in China, we arrive at a point when the basic political forms at either end of Eurasia were more closely parallel than at any later time before the twentieth century. After the fall of the Roman Empire, political authority remained fragmented for many centuries and was never again wielded on an imperial scale. Napoleon's early nineteenth-century successes marked the largest territorial achievements by a post–Roman-empire West European state; modest by Chinese standards, Napoleon's conquests lasted but a moment.

The Chinese, however, sustained the vision and repeatedly recreated the reality of unified empire. At the end of the first millennium C.E., China's mid-imperial period and Europe's Middle Ages have few obvious political parallels. Politics appeared to be headed in different directions after the tenth and eleventh centuries, with the Chinese enjoying the far more stable and integrated political order. But by the nineteenth and twentieth centuries, the superior power of European states had remade the world's map, subjugating China and many other countries as parts of a larger interstate system. Once-parallel, and later apparently skewed, lines of political development became interconnected pieces of a larger political system.

State Formation: Expectations and Perspectives

The challenge of creating distinct Chinese and European perspectives on state formation and transformation involves several discrete components. First, there is the issue of selecting sets of conditions in each that can be taken to represent comparable initial conditions. Second, given a set of similarities, we must account for distinct trajectories of political change before the nineteenth century, when international relations brought them together. Third, to give these differences a common theoretical framework, it will not do simply to invoke some notion of "culture" as the source of differences. That would make sense only if we succeeded in demonstrating that all other types of influence on state formation were the same. Since material conditions differ as well as ideas about political rule and social order, we can afford to ignore none of them.

The theoretical framework I propose begins with the simple proposition that political power depends on the mobilization of resources and the exertion of control. The notion of "resources" is straightforward enough. A ruling group must be able to bring together the material wealth needed to sustain itself and its chosen activities if it is to stand a change of success. When circumstances change and resource demands increase, a ruling group will fail if its members prove unable to expand their resource base. "Control" is more difficult to describe, because it can take different forms. Coercive control is perhaps most obvious and usually most deadly. It is also very expensive, labor intensive, and sometimes capital intensive; it requires large armies or police forces to be exercised broadly. Cheaper ways to assert control include some forms of exchange mechanism. Exchange may take the form of services for taxes; taxes without services represent coercion, while services or goods without taxation indicate a payoff to avoid trouble—a form of insurance or bribe, like the presentations sometimes made by the Chinese state to various groups along its northern borders. When control is achieved through exchange of services or goods for taxes, the levels of taxation and services differ in the amounts that states and the people they tax find acceptable or desirable. Finally, control can be gained through acts of persuasion, such as the creation of beliefs in the morality, sensibility, necessity, or desirability of a certain kind of social order; when persuasion is successful, states gain a resource-cheap means of asserting control in a form some analysts call legitimacy.

Would-be rulers seeking to mobilize resources and exert control face other individuals and groups who seek either to compete for resources and control or to limit the ruler's access to resources and his span of control. Would-be state makers must engage in various kinds of negotiations with individuals and groups who have their own resource bases and control mechanisms over other people. The formation of states represents but one, very important to be sure, kind of political power. Tensions exist in many systems between the elites' efforts to create flows of influence or even to limit central state authority, to channel and delimit state initiatives and expectations, and the state's efforts to impose its power through broad resource mobilization and multiple forms of control.

Beyond the realms of resources and control, state makers competed with other territorial powers to delineate their respective arenas of authority. Similar episodes of competition among would-be state makers took place in China and Europe nearly two millennia apart. In China, the fighting among states during the Warring States period (403–221 B.C.E.) led to the emergence of a single victor, the Qin emperor. In Europe, the competition among would-be state rulers beginning around 1500 created a system of centralized states that by the twentieth century remapped the entire globe. To broaden our perspective on these similar episodes of state formation leading to dramatically different political systems, let's consider briefly the early empires in China and the West.

The Formation of Early Empires and Their Legacies

The Roman empire was an impressive creation. Within the ancient world, it was for a time an exemplar of success, incorporating conquered elites, creating symbolic capital for its political authority, and asserting its cultural order. Built upon military conquest, the empire's political powers were gradually frustrated by bureaucratic and fiscal limitations. Uneven political control generally grew weaker toward the peripheries where strong local elites exercised de facto control. After the collapse of the Roman Empire, the West never again had an imperial political formation of any great size with the capacity to exercise centralized control over its territories. Political authority devolved to multiple small units ruled by noble, clerical, and urban elites. The image of empire remained powerful, however, through the late medieval period. Indeed, the empire itself continued to exist, though it encompassed considerable political diversity.[1]

The process of imperial formation in China was not swift in developing, nor was the endpoint of unified empire an obvious and necessary one. The tenth-century B.C.E. Zhou state lacked the bureaucratic capacities to sustain effective central control over its lands. By the eighth century B.C.E. the ruling house enjoyed only symbolic authority. Initiative lay in the hands of local and regional officials bent on developing their bases of power through expanding their territories. The

---

[1]As Bernard Guenée declares, "The Empire was perhaps not a State of the same kind as England or France, but it was a State just as the countries within the Empire (the kingdom of Bohemia, the Swiss Confederation, the principalities and the imperial towns) were States very different from imperial Germany and very unlike each other" (1985:17).

political aggressiveness of statesmen in the Warring States Period between the fifth and third centuries B.C.E. complemented and partially created major social and economic changes, including the improvement of agricultural technologies, the expansion of commerce, and the emergence of new military and political elites (Hsu 1965).

Some two millennia later, strikingly similar dynamics in Europe transformed a mosaic of small, fragmented political units into a few national states engaged in serious competition, first for territories within Europe and later for large parts of the world beyond Europe. What similarities and differences can we find in these two situations? Both can be described as competition among states, some of which succeed in expanding their power through warfare, which in turn created demands for resources and men that were organized through the development of formal state capacities. But, as I noted already, the two cases have very different end points. In Europe, a state system was established with a chronically fragile equilibrium of power persistently punctuated by war. In China, by contrast, an empire was forged. Indeed, Europe never lost its state system after its early modern political competition, while China never really experienced permanent fragmentation after its period of intense interstate competition ending in the third century B.C.E. What explains these divergent paths from similar dynamics in widely separated historical periods?

Part of the answer lies in the bases of competition, specifically the varying abilities of political powers to extract and concentrate resources. In the early modern European case, several centers of economic wealth permitted the expansion of intensive extraction which could raise sums adequate to the tasks of warfare. In what would become China, more than fifteen hundred years earlier, there were not yet the scales of resources or their multiple concentrations to sustain interstate competition. The Qin conquest was a military success that destroyed contenders for power and thereby established Qin power over a vast territory. The limitations of the Qin state, however, swiftly became problematic. A ruthless and coercive state, as traditional historiography characterized it, the Qin caused suffering among its people, who could not bear their burdens and therefore welcomed the righteous founder of the Han dynasty. The conventional account alerts us to the crucial task of achieving domestic control over a population of peasants and local power holders. Consolidation of the empire was less a military challenge than a civilian challenge of rule. The weakness of the Qin lay in its inability to create a stable set of relations among groups in Chinese society. This dynasty failed to develop bureaucratic capacities of government and lacked the political imagination to create an ideology to guide political practice, social beliefs, and personal expectations. The succeeding Han dynasty developed both.

A key feature of the Han dynasty's formal political structure was its penetration of the local level and integration of local elites into government service. But organizational structure is only the framework for political action. It provides the potential for effective rule rather than the actuality of political control. Unless the people appointed are loyal to the system's leaders rather than ready to act on their own interests, the structure will not serve the purposes for which it was created. The Chinese did not permanently solve this problem until the second millennium of imperial rule. The Han state nevertheless enjoyed some success at limiting the independent power of magnate families by incorporating them into the bureaucratic system. The Han state also sought to limit its dependence on magnates by creating a peasantry under its own direct control. The more successful the state proved at securing tax payments directly from the peasants, the less crucial would government reliance upon magnate elites for resources prove to be. The Han state therefore developed a strong interest in peasant welfare, not from an altruistic sense of charity or benevolence but because an economically viable peasantry was understood to be the social base for a politically successful government.[2]

Though the Han state did fall and magnate power proved a hindrance to reunification efforts over the next several centuries, the basic political logic linking peasant welfare to imperial state success had been clearly articulated. Reunification was propelled by the concentration of military resources in the hands of northern power holders who fought among themselves, the victor then moving to incorporate south China in the early seventh century. The initial stability of imperial rule was made possible through the use of bureaucratic instruments of rule kept alive in China's historical memory from the early empire, which had ended some four centuries before. With the successful formation of China's middle empire, issues of popular welfare became central to constructions of legitimacy and political ideology.[3]

China's early empire left an institutional and ideological legacy upon the basis of which another empire was created which could claim legitimate succession from the earlier governments. The Roman empire left behind an important institutional and ideological legacy from which could be drawn ideas about law and social order, but no successor imperial system. The Holy Roman Empire kept alive the idea of universal empire and assigned the Church a central role in establishing a civilizational unity, but there was no administrative infrastructure to sustain empire as a political reality. The idea of empire in Europe created a frame of reference within which numerous small-scale political units could be superficially ordered. But once relations among small units became more common and competition created drives for the formation of larger units, the rubric of empire became increasingly a poor fit for the political possibilities of the late medieval European world.

China and Europe represent two extremes among political formations in the Eurasian world. China's equilibrium political form came to be a unified agrarian empire. Europe's was for centuries a conglomeration of small units with sometimes overlapping jurisdictions before the dynamics of warfare spurred the formation of larger territorial units that became the first set of what we recognize as

---

[2]A systematic review of Han fiscal policies can be found in Ma Daying 1983.
[3]The importance of welfare issues beginning with the middle empire of the Sui and Tang dynasties is suggested by Hoshi's (1988) study of welfare policies.

European states today. Between China's unified empire and Europe's extreme fragmentation lies a range of shorter-lived empires, including the Roman, Byzantine, Ottoman, Safavid, and Mughal, as well as systems of smaller states such as those in Southeast Asia. My focus is on the two end points of this political spectrum and on the dynamics of change at each of these points toward twentieth-century state formation.

One of the basic differences between the political dynamics at either end of Eurasia was the relative importance of military force. European challenges to political fragmentation included military force as one basic means to extend claims over locales previously independent or under another power's rule. The technologies of warfare focused on local and defensive strategies. Siege warfare and castle defense were basic components of European military competition that were relatively inconsequential in China. More generally, what we see in China and Europe are the constructions of two ranges of political possibility created out of at least partially common conditions of early agrarian empire. In the Chinese case, the early empire of the Qin-Han period became the basis for the formation of later political powers that expanded the Chinese empire southward. The dominant axis of political change became one of unity versus fragmentation. An early imperial ideology was buttressed by institutions that created the possibility of unified political order. Sustaining this order was never easy or certain, but the *possibility* of achieving this kind of order became a political norm.

In Europe, early imperial systems failed to create a legacy of institutions and ideologies that could be called upon to order society in ways similar to those of the past. An imperial legacy was involved in a variety of guises and influenced political institution building in later centuries as well, but the reproduction and elaboration of political institutions and ideologies to establish rule, extract resources, and assert control as an agrarian empire did not become a likely outcome. Instead, political order was created on more limited spatial scales.

One important reason for the early fragmentation of political authority in Europe was the partibility of political domains. Political power in terms of control over resources from various lands was a family attribute. For example, between the ninth and eleventh centuries partibility benefited the Norman invaders, who were constantly expanding their territorial domains through violent conquest. To avoid the increasingly obvious difficulties of fragmenting political power through partibility, families began to recognize only one son as heir. Coordinated territorial control was expanded through alliances built upon kinship ties which exemplified the principles of coordination employed by the Norse when they settled Normandy (Searle 1988). The formation of European aristocracies, noble houses with their own landed resources and military men under their control, precluded the easy establishment of larger-scale centers of political power. Multiple and fragmentary forms of political control between the seventh and twelfth centuries left uncertain what kinds of state formation would in the end shape European history.

The ranges of political possibility differed in China and Europe. These ranges overlapped but were not the same. The political problems common to Chinese and European states, of gaining resources and establishing control, were not solved in the same ways. Explaining these solutions within a common theoretical framework is difficult for several reasons. First, the framework must include explanatory categories that can account for the very different ranges of political possibility China and Europe faced. Second, the explanations must work *equally* for both cases. It won't do simply to argue that an explanation of one set of cases, the European, can also guide us in accounting for the Chinese experiences, because such an approach, like parallel attempts to explain the absence of capitalism in late imperial China, offer us explanations of what *didn't* happen. Thus scholarly efforts to explain why China didn't develop democracy, for instance, tend to examine less carefully and explain less directly the political dynamics that existed independently of the absent democratic practices. To solve these analytical and interpretive challenges, we need to consider more carefully why they are so difficult.

A Eurasian Perspective on Modern State Making

When we look forward from 1100 to compare the political possibilities that China and the myriad of European polities could envision, it is difficult not to be more confident about China's future as a unified and stable political order than about the chances that European duchies, principalities, free cities, and the like will transcend their extreme fragmentation. In China, a state staffed by a civil service bureaucracy ruled a vast society according to rules and regulations created by a policy-making process that limited the arbitrary actions of the ruler. Strategies of rule changed in response to opportunities created by major changes in agriculture, commerce, and urbanization—new commercial taxes, relaxation of control over markets, and efforts to create new wealth on the frontiers (Elvin 1973, Hartwell 1982, Shiba 1968). When we consider Europe, we are at best uncertain about its possibilities for future development. Hundreds of small political units ruled limited agrarian areas and modest urban centers, usually separated from each other. Economic life rarely connected areas very closely. Yet our sense of what should have happened—namely, China's continued prominence as a great power with a developing economy sustaining its lead over the fragmented political units of Europe with their economically simpler societies—did not, in fact, occur.

China continued to be an agrarian empire, but Europe was transformed politically from a patchwork of little units into a region dominated by several strong states. The process of rapid change in Europe is usually seen to be the product of particular causes, in sharp contrast to expectations about economic change in which growth and development are seen as natural. Political continuities, like China's, are instead considered "natural." We therefore lack much scholarship aimed at explaining the late empire's strategies for survival. Continuity is no more natural than change, however, and we must explain how the Chinese achieved the reproduction of empire. Indeed, the future of the Chinese empire in the early thirteenth century was hardly any clearer than the possible futures confronting much of Eurasia, with Mongol armies invading China, Russia, the Middle East, and Europe. Western Europe was spared the Mongols through luck, not any virtue of their own.[4]

For the Chinese, Mongol rule represented a redefinition of relations among steppe and sedentary peoples. Steppe influences on China had been important in earlier centuries, but never had a group from the steppe been able to conquer the Chinese empire without also incorporating considerable elements drawn from Chinese political practices and sensibilities. The Song dynasty's failure to stop the Mongols came after desperate government efforts to increase taxation and build up military forces led to widespread popular resistance among people forced to supply the defensive effort (Chafee 1993:330–35). Mongol rule in China turned out to be but a century interlude. The Ming dynasty that followed in 1368 made aggressive efforts to obscure the influences of Mongol rule on their own practices, an effort modern historians have in large measure supported.[5] But even the articulation of principles and the implementation of policies with a historical pedigree from earlier centuries required effort. The mere fact that political practices resemble those of the past is no guarantee of success. Scholarship aimed at explaining the reproduction of empire as a political problem rather than simply assuming empire as a natural inertial condition for China is still limited.

Scholarship on the formation of European states, in contrast, is well developed, but the logic guiding analyses has often been framed within a backward projection from the nineteenth and twentieth centuries to examine the early modern origins of later success stories. This view treats a particular kind of European political change as the norm for development, while the apparent continuity of political practices in late imperial China mark it as stagnant.

Three difficulties hamper our ability to examine state making in China and Europe. First, European patterns of state formation are distorted by a focus on winners. Preoccupations with what made England and France in particular successful tend to slight not only the dynamics that produced later winners such as Italy or Germany, but the dynamics that made losers out of the many smaller polities like Wales or Venice and reduced the size of once-large countries like Poland and Sweden. Rather than look backward from the nineteenth or twentieth centuries at the process of state formation in Europe we need to look forward from 1100 to capture the possibilities for state formation within which certain winning strategies

---

[4]The late Joseph Fletcher, Jr. (1986:47) affirmed the internal political reasons for the failure of the Mongols to continue their assault into India, Europe, and the Middle East. "The classic pattern of the steppe empire, as I have suggested above, was one so closely tied to the ruler's person that when he died, it stood in real danger of collapse. If it were to be preserved, the preservation would have to be based on political maneuvering, struggle, and probably civil war. All of these followed the deaths of Ogodei and Mongke. The Mongols had little choice but to break off their campaigns." The Mongols' difficulties with political succession arrested their abilities to expand even further across Eurasia.

[5]In contrast, Joseph Fletcher, Jr., a great proponent of the impact of the Mongolian conquests on China and other sedentary civilizations, suggested (1979–80) that a Turco-Mongolian monarchic tradition developed in the Ottoman empire. He was unable to complete a similar analysis for Ming China before his untimely death.

came to dominate, a perspective for which Charles Tilly (1975, 1990) has argued persuasively.

Second, there is the much larger problem of our expectations of what a modern state should be. Some analyses of non-Western areas assume that a modern state will have characteristics like those of modern Western states—democratic political institutions, large-scale bureaucracies, and the like; we measure degrees of modernity according to the presence or absence of particular institutions. We are often more able to say how a system doesn't work than to explain how it does work; as in the case of economic history, the search for absences leads to poor explanations. Other analyses begin from the premise that non-Western political structures are very different from European ones but that the spread of the European state system creates the standards according to which all states must act. Much of the literature so regularly uses European experiences as a model that the Chinese state usually seems anomalous. For instance, Bertrand Badie and Pierre Birnbaum in their book *The Sociology of the State* (1983) give us two definitions of the state—one for "true" states that emerge in Europe and a second for the "states" that make up an international system of states. Within this double perspective, late imperial China lacks a true state and gets one only by the second definition when Europeans arrive to extend their international order. Badie and Birnbaum consider non-Western states in terms of their deviations from European conventions of "differentiating" politics, religion, and economics. By making the European state-making experience the norm, the long histories of rule in other countries tend to be distorted.[6]

Historians of China have not encouraged an appreciation of Chinese state formation and transformation by nonspecialists. Their efforts compose a third feature of the problematic situation for analyzing Eurasian state formation in recent times. Chinese historiography, applying two perspectives that at times contradict each other, has taken a generally dim view of the state. One prominent view of the late imperial Chinese state stresses the autocratic and despotic nature of rule. This vision of strong centralized control contrasts sharply with a second common view of the late imperial state as an inefficient, lumbering bureaucratic machine.[7] Both viewpoints assign the state a minor role in explaining modern Chinese history—progressive developments take place outside the state. A third view of the Chinese state stresses the role of local elites, especially the degree-holding gentry, in creating and recreating a social order on top of which they sit. Gentry manip-

---

[6]For his part, Bertrand Badie has in a more recent work (1987) undertaken a comparison of European and Islamic patterns of political modernization which recognizes not only different dynamics of change but the possibility of distinct end points for modern political systems.

[7]For a learned and distinctive view of Chinese despotism, set up in contrast to a construction of a Chinese "liberalism," see de Bary 1991:57–73; on how the ruler's relationships with high officials should temper and guide the despot's actions see de Bary 1993:52–81. The lumbering and incompetent state may be seen in Ray Huang's depiction of the late sixteenth and seventeenth centuries and in Kung-chuan Hsiao's monumental analysis of local control in the nineteenth century (Hsiao 1960; Huang 1981).

ulated and managed officials to serve their own purposes, including keeping out officials seen as competitive or meddling.[8] No matter which of these three vantage points we adopt, we lack much incentive to pinpoint more precisely how the Chinese state's transformation compares with European state-making experiences.

To escape this situation, we must consider the late imperial Chinese state's survival problematic but important and view the very different conditions in Europe from an analytical perspective that can capture similarities and differences. I examine four clusters of issues: challenges, capacities, claims, and commitments. Two of these, challenges and capacities, are structural. By "challenges," I mean the problems set out within specific historical settings that states attempt to solve. Problems include domestic ones posed by relations with elites and common people as well as foreign ones presented by other territorial powers with ambitions; goals are those concrete projects that states deem necessary or desirable to promote or secure their rule.

"Capacities" refers to the human and material resources the state can mobilize for its purposes and the effectiveness with which it can achieve its goals. I've already suggested that political power can be initially conceived in terms of the abilities to mobilize resources and exercise control; "capacities" refers to the ability to mobilize resources and to deploy them effectively. States need not share the same capacities to extract resources, nor need they use these resources for the same purposes or with the same success.

The two other themes, "claims" and "commitments," are strongly shaped by culturally specific categories for ordering political and social life. Claims take the forms of demands for state action or limitations on state actions placed by both elites and common people; definitions of what a state is expected to do and what it is not allowed to do both fall under the category of claims. For their part, states may also exercise claims on resources and people which elites and common people recognize as appropriate, acceptable, or necessary. States come into conflict with their subjects when they seek to expand their claims at the expense of elites and common people.

"Commitments" are ideologically expressed preferences for certain styles of rule. States make promises about the principles they will use; these commitments can be about processes of decision making or about maintaining or promoting particular social conditions.

These four categories of challenges, capacities, claims, and commitments highlight different dimensions of state formation and transformation. Connections among these dimensions deserve a brief mention. For instance, the goals that a state defines result both from the conditions set by the structural category of challenges and from the repertoire of political possibilities created by the more culturally shaped category of commitments. Similarly, the capacities that a state

---

[8]Japanese scholars saw the gentry as a tool for the state to use, while American scholars have stressed ways for gentry to stake out their own space (Mori 1975–76, 1980; Shigeta 1984, Wakeman and Grant 1975, Brook 1993).

constructs are shaped by the kinds of claims that elites and common people can mount. Social claims can limit state capacities to raise resources or exert control, as well as stimulate the development of state capacities to compete more effectively against them. I assign no logical priority to any of these categories and therefore take no position on the relative importance of material and structural features of state making and the cultural components of these processes. It is difficult enough to disentangle them and label them, let alone to develop persuasive arguments about their relative importance.

I use the four categories of challenges, capacities, claims, and commitments as a taxonomy to pinpoint similarities and differences among Chinese and European state-making processes. Though the focus is very much on processes, I do not claim to do even minimal justice to the narrative of changes that take place with respect to any of these categories. For purposes of this analysis it is not necessary to reconstruct in any detail the particular ways in which capacities changed or how commitments were refined. Nor is it necessary or appropriate at this point in the analysis to address a particular state's strengths or weaknesses. Variations among challenges, capacities, claims, and commitments do not reduce easily to a unidimensional notion of strength or weakness. Once we have developed a framework within which the basic processes according to which Chinese and European states were formed and transformed can be better understood, we can assess state strengths and weaknesses. In order to delineate the distinct trajectories of state making bringing China and Europe into the nineteenth and twentieth centuries, I start my review of challenges, capacities, claims, and commitments in the twelfth century.

The Formation of European States

Challenges

Control over the myriad political entities dotting the map of Europe in 1100 changed repeatedly in succeeding centuries. For nobles, clerics, and urban elites, the principal challenge during the next several centuries would become the preservation and, when possible, expansion of their powers. Complex networks of political relations among different noble lines, created through intermarriage, meant that lordship over a particular territory and its relationship to other territories could change over time. One royal house could control spatially separate territories. Instability of control over bishoprics was caused not by marriage, but by the buying and selling of rights to these ecclesiastical units. Urban elites joined nobles and clerics in becoming subject to the state-making aspirations of monarchs. All these elites made efforts to compete with would-be state makers, seeking to define through negotiation and conflict the dimensions of political control emerging above them. From the territorial state maker's point of view, the organized presence of three distinct groups—clergy, nobles, and burghers—challenged an aspiring ruler's goal to assert control and gain resources.

Important dramas unfolded for territorial rulers regarding their relations with each of these groups. One important story line centered on the long-term transformation of church–state relations. Initially antagonists competing to define their realms of authority in the 1100s, over the next several centuries clergy increasingly identified with their governments instead of with the papacy; by the nineteenth century churches had become subordinated to states and the papacy reduced to one of several church institutions. In between, the clergy became one important group organized to defend their claims.

Apart from the clergy, European rulers were challenged by nobles. In England, France, Sweden, and Spain, rulers generally succeeded in distinguishing themselves from nobles and created various strategies for asserting their superiority during the sixteenth and seventeenth centuries. The papacy and the Holy Roman Empire checked the development of monarchy in Italy and Germany. Moving further east, we find an example of an absent monarchy in Poland and the mounting of bureaucratic absolutism in Prussia.[9] The variable success of nobles vis-à-vis territorial rulers was in part conditioned by the strength of an independent burgher presence. In places such as France, where strong urban groups posed their own challenges to would-be monarchs, rulers could play nobles and burghers against each other.

The process of royal state formation in Europe was centuries in the making. For France, it was Philip Augustus (1180–1223) who put his own men in provincial offices, thereby beginning a process of royal centralization that proceeded in fits and starts for nearly six centuries (Strayer 1970:50–51). Successful state makers were those monarchies that managed to expand their powers over urban and rural elites. During the sixteenth and seventeenth centuries, the driving challenges behind monarchs' desires to gain control over elites were more international than domestic. Early modern European states were constructed through a process of mutual warfare, which propelled much of the expansion of major state capacities.

Capacities

The acceleration of state expansion in the sixteenth and seventeenth centuries followed the development of bureaucratic capacities to tax and make law in previous centuries. European governments relied on lawyers and clerics to staff their growing bureaucracies. Not all states were equally likely to engage in battle, but warfare, or at least the creation of the capacity for organized violence, became a main pursuit for most successful states. Organized and commanded according to new rules and lines of authority, armies became one of the innovative organizational structures of successful early modern states. To support these armies, states were compelled to extract new revenues. England was most successful at raising new revenues from commercial sources. In part, this can be attributed to the wealth

---

[9]Anderson 1974 compares the developments in strong Western European absolutist states—England, France, Spain, and Sweden—with Eastern European variants—Prussia, Austria, and Russia; both differ from cases of weak governments, like those in Italy and Poland.

created by economic changes which the English state could tap by creating new fiscal strategies. But economic change alone hardly guaranteed political success, since the displacement of the Dutch Republic by England as Europe's most dynamic country can be viewed in part as a Dutch political failure to capitalize on economic changes. France was somewhat less successful than England in meeting its revenue needs, but it also vastly expanded the mobilization of revenues by the central state in the seventeenth and eighteenth centuries. All across Europe, successful states were those able to mobilize resources (Ardant 1975). Expanded fiscal capacities required expanded bureaucratic organization to create and channel the flows of resources gained by European states.

Charles Tilly (1990) has analyzed the spatial variations among European paths of state making. He contrasts as extremes states that rely principally upon mobilizing coercive resources and those that largely depend upon amassing capital resources. At the coercive-intensive end lay a state like Russia, while at the capital-intensive end lay a state like the Dutch Republic. In between the extremes lay the more familiar success stories of England, France, Spain, and Prussia which, for all their differences, combined coercive and capital concentration in their state-making processes.

Thomas Brady (1991) makes similar spatial distinctions. Countries like England, Spain, Portugal, the Netherlands, and France embarked upon absolutist state making as monarchs centralized power at the expense of aristocratic, urban, and clerical elites. In another group were areas like the Italian- and German-speaking regions, where Catholic institutions remained important and governments were fragmented.

The variations among European states that Tilly and Brady have identified all took place within a common matrix of sixteenth- and seventeenth-century challenges and capacities: European states aimed to develop their resource bases in order to compete with other territorial states; this process forced them to seek revisions in their relationships to urban, aristocratic, and ecclesiastical elites. Constructing new bureaucratic capacities to mobilize resources and to field armies is perhaps the most salient component of European state formation after 1500. These new capacities of successful territorial state markers met the challenge of competition with other states. Collectively, these states formed a system. To succeed in inventing new sources of revenue and in creating new armies, territorial rulers had to displace or evade the claims on resources already made by nobles, urban elites, and clergy. In return for their acquiescence to new taxation, these elites made their own claims on territorial states.

Claims

Would-be centralizers were surrounded by other power holders with their own bases of power and authority, be these strong municipalities, nobles, or the Catholic Church. Fourteenth-century European kings dealt with their elites not as powerful individuals, but as members of corporate assemblies or "estates" (Brady 1991:134). The entry of towns into politics destabilized the balance of power between territorial rulers and princes, forcing monarchs to deal with elites organized as corporate estates (Poggi 1978:42–46). In this political structure, the "law" meant specific clusters of rights claimed by estates and by rulers. Different estates had their own legal entitlements to be defended by their corporate powers (Poggi 1978:72). Before the sixteenth century, no crown west of the Elbe River in Germany could tax on its own authority; all levies had to be accepted by assemblies of elites known as Parliament (England), *parlements* (France), or *cortes* (Spain). In many countries, clergy and nobles were able to defend their tax exemptions or at least sustain preferential treatment. As state makers expanded their fiscal and war-making capacities in the sixteenth and seventeenth centuries, they had to recognize claims made by various elites. Building on medieval traditions of municipal government and noble authority, some European elites, including those in England and France, made claims to a political voice. In many situations, like the English, issues of taxation were enmeshed with issues of political representation. By 1300, the king of England was able to impose taxes on the property of all men across the country. He consulted Parliament, an assembly composed of nobles and representatives of the boroughs, on these matters. Certainly the powers of Parliament constrained the ability of the English king to act, but as Joseph Strayer (1970:45) has argued, Parliament's assent to issues presented by the king had meaning only because the king was recognized to have sovereign power. In the 1688 Revolution the English Crown acquired greater authority over taxation.

In France, a contest over judicial and legal authority between the *parlements* and the Crown was repeatedly acted out, culminating in the mid-seventeenth-century Fronde, in which the Crown's authority to raise new taxes was challenged by princes and *parlements,* as well as by common people opposed to the central government's move to extract additional revenue (C. Tilly 1986:91–101, 140–45). Further east, in Prussia, the move toward absolutism included the shift of tax collection away from the estates as the ruler acquired direct control over an urban excise tax on consumption goods; this move allowed the ruler to fund his army without depending on the estates (Poggi 1978:53).

In different ways, the English, French, and Prussian rulers succeeded in establishing powers that made elites subordinate to them. Brian Downing (1992) explains why elite claims for representation proved less successful in some countries than in others. Many medieval European states had institutions to represent elite interests. In countries where monarchies relied on the domestic extraction of resources to build armies in the sixteenth and seventeenth centuries, medieval constitutionalism was usually dismantled and a military bureaucratic absolutism displaced the previous balance between monarch and elites. The failure of a European sovereign to achieve a measure of autonomy in exchange for recognition of certain claims could spell disaster. Thus the weakness of the Polish state was reflected in the veto power that nobles individually could exercise over the selection and subsequent actions of the Polish king. Separate from the claims exercised by elites, other claims were forwarded by common people. Lacking formal political representation before the nineteenth century, common people exercised claims on government through protests that highlighted government failures to meet popular claims or government decisions to transgress popularly perceived limits to government powers.[10]

Constructing state power in Europe often meant acknowledging an increasingly well-defined boundary between what the central state could do and what lay beyond its powers. Where that boundary was drawn was by no means stable over time or the same in different countries. Those states able to expand their capacities to extract resources and to field armies developed a measure of autonomy from the elites and common people they governed. Where elite and popular claims constrained state action, monarchs and their royal administrations lacked much autonomy.

The formation of this boundary between the centralizing state administrations and society at large is basic to European ideas about "civil society." The creation of the modern European state and civil society were parts of a common process defining a particular construction of state–society relations in which sharp lines could be drawn between state and society. The state grew, but with boundaries drawn more precisely over time. The state–society divide became a principal axis as the central state displaced urban authorities and estates as the agent granting privileges and setting rules, a role that had previously been enacted locally or regionally. The state created a public social realm subject to its taxation, law, and administration (Poggi 1978:79–83).

Commitments

European states made three major commitments to society in order to achieve increasingly effective rule. One was the commitment to provide legal systems that affirmed the rights of individuals and estates. With these systems, rulers administered justice, for which they were responsible according to medieval church theories of sovereignty.[11] Church theory also promoted a second kind of commitment that European governments made. Religion assigned to the Christian faithful the duty of charity. By the 1530s, charity was in some places provided by governments inspired by Christian doctrine (Bossy 1985:144–46). In succeeding centuries, secular rulers worked to acquire the Church's moral functions in society, taking on commitments previously conceived as religious in nature, including, by the nineteenth century, such responsibilities as education. During the early modern period, however, European governments did not articulate many commitments to their subjects, and these commitments served state interests at least as much as private ones. But while "justice" served the interests of order more

---

[10]Common people exercised their claims on the government through small-scale forms of popular protest like conflicts over food supplies and tax resistance, a subject discussed in Part III.

[11]Strayer 1970:23. Harold Berman has argued that "the basic institutions, concepts, and values of Western legal systems have their sources in religious rituals, liturgies, and doctrines of the eleventh and twelfth centuries, reflecting new attitudes toward death, sin, punishment, forgiveness and salvation" (1983:165).

perhaps than the rights of individuals, courts also provided a context in which disagreements and disputes among people and with rulers could be pursued. The third commitment governments made, often grudgingly, was to political principles of representation that defined the manner in which elites were to negotiate with rulers.

Affirming most commitments was not a major concern for European rulers despite the paternalistic cast of rule. Negotiating competing claims was a far more important process, one through which governments dealt with people and from which commitment to political procedures was established. European rulers confronted nobles, urban elites, and clerics whose various powers and authority they aimed to displace, compromise, or complement. The processes of negotiation between territorial rulers and these elites produced institutions to limit the powers of rulers. We can therefore view territorial state formation as a mixed process of negotiations and impositions from above, the blend varying among cases. Since European rulers did not invest much effort into affirming commitments, it was difficult for people to develop expectations of proper actions by officials from meeting their commitments. Rather, expected behavior from officials came through negotiating claims or bargains. In China, a different balance of claims and commitments characterized politics. Nor were the challenges and capacities of government the same in China as they were in Europe.

The Reproduction and Elaboration of the Chinese State

Challenges

The primary challenge to Chinese rulers in the second millennium of imperial rule was not the creation of any radically new state in competition with other political actors, but rather the reproduction and transformation of an agrarian state, a state that governed an ever-larger population settled across greater stretches of territory. The Chinese state was not one of many roughly similar political units which had to expand to compete in the manner of a European state. Domestic order in China spanned an area equal to the territory of many European states. This order hinged upon effective social control, an understanding of which marked classical political texts as well as the political practices of preceding dynasties.

The scale of challenge posed by domestic order in China did not mean that foreign challenges were absent. The major ones in both the first and second millennia of imperial rule came from the steppe to the north, where mobilization of massive military power by seminomadic peoples threatened Chinese rulers, even when the empire was united during the Han (206 B.C.E.–220 C.E., Tang (618–906) and Song (960–1279) dynasties. The threat from the steppe included dismembering China, though some steppe incursions, such as the Xianbei formation of the Toba Wei, did not divide China, but in fact were instrumental to the formation of unified rule culminating with the sixth-century founding of the Sui dynasty. In later centuries, conquest was achieved by the Mongols in the thirteenth century and by the Manchus in the seventeenth century. Successful conquerors, with the notable exception of the Mongols, adopted many Chinese principles and structures of rule. The Chinese state domesticated its conquerors even as steppe peoples added new features of rule. For the Manchus, whose Qing dynasty became China's last imperial government, adopting Chinese ideology and institutions of rule were the means to gain acceptance and establish effective control. Beyond China proper, the Qing expanded the empire into Inner Asia and strengthened the span of its world order according to visions and policies of rule attuned to the sensibilities of peoples inhabiting the steppe.

Capacities

In military terms, the Chinese empire was often weak compared to various groups along China's inner Asian frontier, including the eighth-century Tibetans; twelfth-century Jurchens, Khitans, and Mongols; and the seventeenth-century Manchus, to name just some of the more powerful groups. So weak was the Chinese state between the tenth and fourteenth centuries that some scholars consider the Middle Kingdom to be part of a multistate system in this period (Rossabi 1983). The Song dynasty's military vulnerability to a collection of northern peoples was in part a conscious choice following the An Lushan rebellion (755–763), when the Tang government reduced radically the capacities of military commanders to achieve independent bases of power at the cost of increased military vulnerability to peoples on the steppe. Song military weaknesses accounted first for the loss of northern China to the Khitans and Jurchens and then the Mongol conquest of the entire country. The Mongols, of course, proved themselves a formidable military force not only in China but across much of Eurasia in the thirteenth and fourteenth centuries.

The challenge of Chinese military weakness persisted beyond the Mongol collapse. But despite these weaknesses, or perhaps in part as a response to them, the Chinese state succeeded in creating a framework for its international relations that placed other countries in a tributary status, a ritual position confirmed by the presentation of tribute, the presentation of gifts by the Chinese to the emissaries, and various agreements on a set schedule of visits every several years. In certain instances it is clear that the maintenance of the tribute order was considered expensive by the Chinese state so that the frequency of tribute missions was limited. It is equally clear that the Chinese government often sought to buy the good will of potential military threats through exchanges on favorable terms (Hevia 1995). From a Chinese point of view, the tribute system met the challenge of ordering the Chinese world with the Chinese state at the center. The increasingly formal states that emerged along China's peripheries, such as Korea, Vietnam, and Japan, adapted Chinese ideology and institutions to their local situations. China's diplomatic relations with these states and with others not influenced by Chinese cultural practices generally asserted China's centrality and superiority. Foreign governments generally allowed the Chinese to promote this view without necessarily accepting it themselves.

When the Manchus established the Qing dynasty, they based their governmental structure in large measure upon the previous Ming dynasty's bureaucratic system. Thus the common observation that China could be conquered but its
system remained intact is important for us in a comparative context, since China
was not threatened with the frequent possibilities of dismemberment or absorption faced by smaller European political units or even larger ones like Poland.
When the Chinese state failed to avoid military defeat, a ruling house or dynasty
fell sometimes with a subsequent period of disunion, but after the establishment
of the Ming dynasty in 1368 there was only one more dynastic transition in the
next five and a half centuries. Concern for military threats was concentrated on
the borders, especially across the northern frontier. More troublesome was the
challenge of maintaining domestic order. The possibility of rebellion spurred the
Chinese state to devote considerable effort and attention to monitoring and controlling the domestic population.

China's civilian administration, like civilian administrations in general, was
geared toward collecting taxes and maintaining domestic order. In functional
terms, all governments must raise revenues and must do so at least partially
through levies upon some of their subjects. All successful governments also find
ways to exert control and keep order, but the means developed to achieve this
goal vary considerably. In Europe, the centralizing states of the early modern period collected taxes, established courts, and in certain specific areas, notably capital cities, organized charity and famine relief. In China, political aspirations to
affect the moral and material order of society were far grander.

For most of imperial history, the state's principal source of revenue was land
taxes. Unlike in Europe, no institutionalized sets of interests explicitly constrained
Chinese state authorities in setting tax rates. Instead, government taxation rates
were set by officials who believed that light taxation allowed the people to prosper, and since a prosperous people was held to be crucial for the maintenance of
a powerful state, tax rates were low. Some officials, at least, no doubt realized that
attempting to raise tax rates would have the unhappy consequences of promoting resistance and even rebellion. Thus, while the Chinese state did not explicitly compete to establish its claims to land taxes with other organized interests that
could exercise independent claims, as the Catholic Church and aristocracies did
in Europe, the late imperial Chinese state extracted resources at a relatively light
rate.

Collection methods varied over time, but tax collection was always recognized
as an important official task. In the Ming and Qing dynasties, local officials cate-
gorized land according to its productivity and collected taxes, first in kind, but after the sixteenth century increasingly in monetary form. For most of the nearly
five and a half centuries in which these two dynasties ruled, agricultural revenues
met routine expenditures; extraordinary demands were met through a combination of land surtaxes, commercial taxes, and "contributions." The same local officials who collected taxes also promoted agricultural production and stored grain

for distribution to poor people in the lean spring season.[12] In addition to their responsibility for material welfare, officials in the Ming and Qing dynasties were expected to organize the delivery of didactic lectures to illustrate virtuous behavior and persuade common people to live in accord with Confucian precepts.[13] Special bureaucratic capacities were created to maintain the Yellow River, administer the Grand Canal connecting the fertile Yangzi region to the capital area, and to collect and ship a special grain tax known in English as the grain tribute (*caoliang*).[14] In the eighteenth century, when many of these capacities were particularly well developed and with reliance principally upon agricultural taxation at a deliberately low rate, the state even managed to build up a revenue surplus.

From a purely Chinese perspective, central state capacities appear in many ways to have diminished after the tenth century. As the area and population of the empire expanded, neither the numbers of officials nor the level of fiscal extraction kept pace with the empire's growth.[15] Between the Tang and Song dynasties, the state gave up attempting to control land distribution and market affairs directly. After the Song dynasty, the state simplified its management of the economy, becoming increasingly willing to forgo direct control in favor of strategies to influence indirectly an economy increasingly controlled by private interests. But such a decline in capacities cannot be interpreted simply as a sign of growing weakness, as is sometimes done in Chinese studies. Were this judgment generally reasonable, we would consider all decisions to diminish the level of state control or involvement in economic matters to be signs of weakness. This would contradict our general sense of early modern European state making, in which national states increasingly allowed merchants the freedom to create national markets unencumbered by state regulations. One basic component to the story of nineteenth-century capitalism's triumph is its wresting from government control certain key economic activities. Regarding China, the picture of a secular decline in government strength is also qualified by excellent research on eighteenth-century archival sources to document the growth of central government capacities under the Manchu emperors (Bartlett 1991). What matters more generally to our assessment of state strengths and weaknesses is gauging the capacities the state created and how these capacities were used. To make this effort, we can first look at the Chinese state's claims and commitments.

---

[12]Taxation and political economy more generally are examined further in chapter 6.

[13]The strategies employed by Chinese officials to create local order are examined in chapter 5.

[14]On the Yellow River, see Shuili bu 1984:298–347; for the Grand Canal, see Hoshi 1971:161–262; on the state's role in frontier developments, see Peng 1990, Wang Xilong 1990, and Wang Yuchuan et al. 1991 for land clearance specifically; Ma and Ma 1990 and Yuan 1991 for more general analyses. On the granary system, see Will and Wong 1991.

[15]G. William Skinner made this observation years ago (1977:19–20). The idea of a "secular decline in governmental effectiveness" pegged simply to the declining number of officials per capital offers a useful first approximation. Other factors beside per capita size of the government intervene to make the government bureaucracy more or less effective at different historical moments.

Claims

The late imperial Chinese state faced no powerful elites that could place claims on the state in ways that legally limited the state's boundaries of action. The destruction of the aristocratic elite by the mid-tenth century meant that there were no challenges to the emperor by elites with independent bases of authority; the only nobility that remained in the Ming and Qing dynasties were people related to the emperors. Nor were there any municipal elites with claims to urban autonomy. China's late imperial elite was composed in large part of people who had succeeded in passing the civil service examinations, a portion of whom then went on to government service. Those who did not serve in government shared with the officials a Confucian ideology cultivated during their preparation for the civil service examinations. Degree holders, both those serving as officials and those often called "gentry" who were not part of the government, were joined by wealthy landlords and rich merchants to form an elite that shared a broadly based perspective on social order and the state. Whatever differences of opinion existed, they did not crystallize into institutionally separate social classes or estates, because China's social structure lacked such distinct social groups. The Chinese state could therefore actively enlist elites to help officials to govern, an activity less conceivable in Europe because the power and autonomy of nobles, burghers, and clerics would make the central government less confident about the intentions and activities of its elites.

Chinese elites after 1000 did not face an aggressively expansionist state developing new central institutions and strategies to strengthen state power with an aim to extract ever-larger sums of revenue, the situation of most European elites after 1500. Thus Chinese elites had less incentive to demarcate clear boundaries limiting state authority and power. State authority was in effect bounded by organizational and resource limitations—officials were simply too few to pose a clear and constant threat to elites and their abilities to pursue their own agendas. In terms of visions of local social and political order, these agendas overlapped significantly with the vision promoted by the state from the eleventh century onward. Elites and officials certainly disagreed at times about taxes; relations between local elites and officials were by no means always amicable. But tensions never became the focus of claims that elites made upon the government for formal limitation of state activities. Instead, officials and elites came to share a set of Confucian commitments to culturally specific strategies to create social and political order.

Commitments

The Chinese state's ideological commitments developed from a political philosophy that assigned a high priority to maintaining popular welfare and that associated ruling with instructing the people. The state's authority rested upon a mandate conferred by Heaven and revokable upon strong evidence of misrule— floods, famines, and the like. To avoid such phenomena, officials were motivated to intervene in ecological and economic matters. The basic idea of legitimacy was premised upon supporting the people and regulating their livelihoods. Popular support was crucial to maintaining the Mandate of Heaven. This position, associated with the philosopher Mencius (372–289 B.C.E.) was not consistently stressed, but even when material welfare was not prominently promoted, the alternative formulations stressing moral control or coercive control recognized the people as a persistent potential threat to the Chinese state. The ideology of rule was moral, and this necessarily carried commitments to shape the peasant's mental world and sustain his material well-being.

The very familiarity of Chinese maxims for rule leads specialists to discount their significance. Given the limited capacities of the late imperial state to affect popular welfare, at least by modern standards, we have even more reason to pass quickly over the ideological vision of Chinese rule expressed in its priorities and commitments. But these commitments take on clearer importance when we realize they differ in substance and intent from the kinds of ideological commitments developed by early modern European states.

To appreciate the differences in state-making processes in late imperial China and early modern Europe, we need to compare the two directly. But it is difficult to compare two very different historical experiences without taking one as the standard against which to consider the other. To avoid the commonly recognized problem of measuring a non-Western situation according to European standards, I propose comparing Chinese and European state-formation experiences in two ways, one common but problematic, one strange but revealing. First, let us evaluate Chinese state making from a European perspective—not, however, a European perspective of some abstract sort, but a historical type as empirical as the Chinese case with which it is compared. Then let us invert customary practice and evaluate Europe according to Chinese experiences. By reversing subject and object in the comparisons, we may create new perspectives on state making.

Chinese State Making in European Perspective

The formation of national states in Western Europe has a number of basic features. Reinhard Bendix (1964, 1978) stresses the transformation of authority relations when citizenship expanded and large-scale bureaucracies were created. For Charles Tilly (1975, 1990) the formation of national states was driven by warfare and revenue extraction. Neither set of processes—the spread of citizenship and the formation of bureaucracies or warfare and revenue extraction—seems immediately relevant to the late imperial Chinese empire, where authority relations were not transformed, citizenship was a culturally foreign concept, large-scale bureaucracies had already existed for more than one thousand years, and the Chinese state was never simply one of several similar states competing with each other. The Chinese state's fiscal health varied over time; surpluses in the eighteenth century were preceded and followed by periods of intense need, but responses to fiscal scarcities did not spawn much in the way of new bureaucratic powers. Does this mean we have nothing worth comparing? Not at all. Bendix and Tilly both raise problems worth considering in a Chinese context. Borrowing from Bendix, we might ask how authority and power relations determined the separation of state and society in China. What kinds of claims and commitments shaped the division between state and society? Borrowing from Tilly, we can ask, among other things: What are the basic threats to the state's security? How is the reproduction of an agrarian empire different from forging national states amidst interstate competition? Do different challenges and capacities develop because the situations of an agrarian empire and interstate competition are so different?

European state-making experiences defined a range of relationships between state and society likely in different European countries. As Bendix and others have made clear, the shifting bases upon which authority was predicated increasingly made certain social groups the key actors in defining acceptable and unacceptable political authority. The same process that defined the state's capacities also defined its commitments to certain political principles promoted by social elites who made claims to procedures whereby their voices were not merely heard but counted in specific ways. The dynamics of Chinese state formation and reproduction do not create such sharp distinctions between state and society. Indeed, the separation of state and society in practical terms even diminished from the twelfth century forward as officials increasingly relied on local elites to help them implement a common agenda for promoting domestic order, an agenda that included social persuasion, surveillance, and welfare. For their parts, European states had mixed success imposing their will on local elites and on patterns of local rule and control, with the particular balances between central and local power varying among European countries. In the Chinese case, an uncertain and shifting line between state and society responded to different dynamics of change through late imperial and postimperial times. We will explore those dynamics more closely in the next chapter.

If we shift to the subject of European warfare and fiscal extraction as the processes that drove state expansion, we discover that China did not experience these two intertwined processes in anything like a European fashion. The Chinese had a revenue base that did not grow continuously, but fluctuated according to needs; these needs were kept in check after the mid–twelfth century, in part by a delegation, sometimes implicit and at other times explicit, of political and social responsibilities to elites. The post-1500 Chinese state faced periodic fiscal crises, often stemming from military campaigns, but this problem did not bring forth new fiscal systems as it did in post-1500 Europe. The fiscal problems were broadly similar in the sense that state capacities to extract resources fell short of what was needed in both China and Europe. But in early modern Europe, the gap was chronic and always threatening to grow; it was exacerbated by competing claimants whose rights to resources had to be sidestepped or dismantled. In late imperial China, the gap between revenue and expectations was episodically critical, but the central state generally asserted its claims on resources without obstruction by others. The state's principal claim was on the land; the Chinese had created a relatively effective organizational infrastructure to collect agricultural taxes for several hundred years before sixteenth-century reforms gradually converted collection in kind to money payments. At times individual households were expected to turn over payments directly to local bureaucrats or their aides; at other times local groups were organized and assigned collective responsibility for tax payments. In either case taxation was usually flawed by inefficiencies and difficulties, but extraction did take place and often met expenditure requirements.

European states did not all have well-established bureaucratic structures to collect taxes from the land. They often scrambled to tap new sources of revenues on which there were no previous claims. Their frequent reliance on commercial taxes and a public debt were not important in late imperial China before the late nineteenth century.[16] Pre-nineteenth-century Chinese officials often considered reducing expenditures rather than raising revenues. When these officials considered fiscal reform, they frequently grappled with issues centered on the incidence and equity of the tax burden rather than efforts to raise additional revenues by new means.[17] Chinese officials often felt obliged to defend the imposition of taxes. European states, in contrast, aimed to extract as much as they could.[18]

In both China and Europe, states aimed to raise resources, control their subjects, and manage relations with groups beyond the ruler's territory. But these basic functions in different historical situations created distinct configurations of political challenges and capacities, different mixes of claims and commitments. Chinese politics did not develop the representative institutions of European politics nor the basic system of interstate competition. Those features of Western state making intimately attached to these particular institutional and ideological aspects of European history should therefore not be expected in China. The reproduction of agrarian empire was a process driven by a different political logic than the formation of European national states. If we take the European cases as the norm, much of late imperial Chinese history becomes irrelevant because it does not relate to issues of political representation, warfare, and fiscal expansion. What happens when we look at European developments from a Chinese perspective?

A Chinese Perspective on European State Making

During the centuries that European state making was largely propelled by warfare, the Ming dynasty fell and the Manchus invaded from the north to found the Qing dynasty. Military campaigns along China's northern and southwestern frontiers took place in both Ming and Qing times. The anxieties of a militarily weak

---

[16]The Song state, however, did rely on commercial revenues which at times exceeded half their total income.

[17]On Chinese fiscal institutions generally, see Zhou Bodi 1981. For an example of the reform aspect of Chinese fiscal problems, see Dennerline 1975. Fiscal reform and tax remittance issues were closely related in China; tax resistance is addressed in chapter 10. For European fiscal practices, see Ardant 1975; Webber and Wildavsky 1986.

[18]As Bernard Guenée puts it, "Without worrying about the theoretical justification, it [the state] imposed taxes on vital goods whenever possible" (1985:150).

Ming state were replaced by an aggressive and expansionary Qing state, which in the late seventeenth and early eighteenth centuries extended imperial rule over portions of Inner Asia and Tibet. Qing armies succeeded in establishing the borders of China that would become the basis of postimperial Chinese claims to territory.

Apart from their military successes, which allowed them to incorporate new territories and secure peaceful borders, Qing rulers elaborated earlier Chinese strategies of rule focused on techniques for domestic social control. The ideal social order was a settled agrarian society, but social order spanned both cities and the countryside. Chinese rulers aimed to make both urban and rural areas safe; people on the margins of settled society, in both urban and rural areas, were considered dangerous. Officials shared with elites a common Confucian understanding of the importance of moral indoctrination and material welfare to successful rule. Coercive forms of control were of limited utility because state capacities to mobilize the resources necessary for widespread reliance on police power were not available. The threat of potential intervention, however limited in actual practice, was one of the means by which social order was sustained.

Taking moral instruction as a basic aspect of rule, the Chinese state aimed to shape the education of both elites and common people. For would-be officials, study of the classics, commentaries, and histories formed the core of a curriculum taught in schools sponsored by both officials and elites. As preparation for a series of examinations, the content of which was defined by officials, elite education created a world view that linked state and elite. Elites, of course, had ideas and interests that lay outside the examination system and preparation for it; elites could pursue their interests in poetry or Buddhism, for instance, without necessarily challenging state expectations for elite belief. For the population at large, the state made efforts to order key religious practices; central to these efforts was the definition of a pantheon of gods and spirits to whom imperially recognized sacrifices would be made. The state often aimed to coopt gods with active popular followings into the officially sanctioned hierarchy. Many deities, however, remained local in their followings. The state did not actively proscribe all deities it did not recognize as official. Rather it only singled out those it feared to be potential mobilizers of popular protest.[19] To shape popular beliefs and reduce the appeal of heterodox thought, the state promoted public lectures by local educated people who explained the virtues of proper Confucian behavior. Emperors promulgated edicts rich with advice for the common people about working the land, respecting social hierarchy, and paying their taxes (Mair 1985).

---

[19]For the Chinese state's relationship to religion in late imperial times, see Watson 1985 for a statement about the state's concern for proper ritual and performance (orthopraxy) more than proper belief (orthodoxy). Duara 1988b, Pomeranz 1991, and Pomeranz forthcoming offer alternative views on the coopting of popular cults by the state. Wolf 1974 presents a clear view of the correspondence between the categories used in religion and by the bureaucratic state. Zito 1987 argues for a close relationship between family-based rituals and city god cults.

As a set of related strategies to define the intellectual's education and the preferred beliefs of the common people, Chinese state efforts find little parallel in European settings. In the medieval period, the Church played the major role in
education at both elite and popular levels. Interpreting education in the broad
Chinese sense to include moral indoctrination, the Church controlled the production of saints and their positions within the Church hierarchy much as the Chinese state aimed to regulate the pantheon of Chinese gods. In issues of education
and moral indoctrination, the Catholic Church took on the roles associated with
the state in China. Late medieval and early modern European states were less directly responsible for education than was the late imperial Chinese state and therefore reached people in fewer ways. The Chinese effort to reach the minds and
hearts of peasants contrasts strongly with European states, which left such matters to religious authorities.

We think it a "modern" trait for states to push education and to attempt more
generally to shape the beliefs of the people. European states began these efforts
in the nineteenth century as they moved, on the model of France, to mobilize
their populations around sentiments of national identity. Though Chinese efforts
at education and moral training between the twelfth and nineteenth centuries did
not lead to a nineteenth-century European-style "nationalism," they do represent
efforts by a state to influence belief and behavior patterns of the general population well before such activities were imagined, let alone pursued, in Europe. What
we conventionally think of as a "modern" trait is such only if we limit our view to
European examples and insist that the purpose of activities like state-sponsored
education and moral training need be undertaken for specifically nineteenth-century European purposes. There is no early modern European government equivalent to the late imperial Chinese state's efforts at dictating moral and intellectual
orthodoxy, nor were such efforts particularly important to Europe's state-making
agenda, as they were in China. Early modern European states did not share the
Chinese state's view that shaping society's moral sensibilities was basic to the logic of rule.[20] From a Chinese perspective, the lack of concern for education and
moral indoctrination in Europe constitutes a basic limitation on European
rule, no less important than the absence of representative political institutions in
China.

When we turn to issues of material welfare, we find a tradition of intervention
in subsistence issues in China that dwarfs European government efforts to address
the insecurities of agrarian economies. In the Han dynasty, creating a class of self-
sufficient peasants to whom land was allotted by the state meant creating a group
of people who could pay taxes to support the state. By 1100 direct state land

---

[20]Of course, the Catholic Church took a great interest in people's moral and spiritual lives, as the Inquisition makes abundantly clear. Catholic states certainly cared about the Inquisition, but without the
Church the movement cannot even be imagined. In China, the state takes a direct and primary role in
defining orthodoxy. There is no European-like institutionalized division of labor between a religious
organization guiding moral and spiritual lives and a government controlling their material and physical
lives.

grants to peasants no longer played the same role they had played in earlier times, but officials continued to ponder the advantages of land distribution schemes and to recognize that broadly based landownership was the foundation of a stable agrarian social order. To this end, the late imperial state promoted the settlement of new lands and the expansion of China's frontiers, especially in the eighteenth century. More generally, state concerns for material welfare shifted from production-oriented activities to consumption. The search for social order led to state policies designed to stabilize the supply of various goods, especially food. In earlier centuries when officials took over the storage, transport and distribution of goods, be these salt, grain, cloth, or minerals, they often conceived of these operations as money makers. By the eighteenth century, the state recognized salt as a money maker, but managed food supplies for welfare reasons. During the Qing dynasty, a sophisticated system of food-supply management was created in which the central government gathered information on grain prices, weather, and rainfall from local officials in order to predict when and where in the empire serious food shortages might occur and to react to difficulties when they did appear. The centerpiece of state efforts at intervening in food-supply conditions in both routine and extraordinary ways was a granary system which stored several million tons of grain. Located mainly in county seats and small market towns, granaries represented official commitments to material welfare beyond anything imaginable, let alone achieved, in Europe (Will and Wong 1991:507–26).

Amidst considerable policy variations the Chinese state generally followed a basic philosophy of expanding and stabilizing production and distribution in order to create a steady source of revenues and a stable social order.[21] A socially secure and fiscally sound state depended on a healthy and happy people. Not that the state was some sort of noble, disinterested party. Far from it. The Chinese state pursued policies designed to reproduce and enhance its capacity for stable and secure rule. The general purpose is not surprising or unusual. What matters is the set of choices made to pursue this general goal. These differed from the specific goals and strategies conceived within European traditions.

In Europe, food-supply management had largely been in the hands of local political authorities until the centralization drives of early modern state formation

---

[21]Modern scholars have tended to discount the state's impact for at least three sets of reasons. First, sinologists confront administrative texts that say more about how officials expected things to be done than how they necessarily were done, as well as public and private writings that complain about how things went wrong—the combination creates a belief in the irrelevance of ideals to actual bureaucratic practice. Now that we are gaining greater access to archival materials, we are becoming better equipped to evaluate realistically the mundane matters of administration. Second, social scientists have minimized the state's impact because the impact does not neatly fit any of the categories of effort that characterize modern state activities; obviously, the late imperial Chinese state did not attempt to foster economic development in terms identifiable to a development economist of the last quarter-century, but this does not necessarily mean the state had no vision or capacity to implement meaningful economic policies. Third, historians have minimized the state's role because the issues the Chinese state took seriously are not always ones that loom large in the historical literature for other parts of the world, e.g., Chinese concerns about land distribution and food-supply management.

propelled central governments into the business of adjudicating the competing claims of local consumers, long-distance markets, and urban consumers. Such intervention as states began to make after the 1520s was inspired by religious doctrines and practices. But even with Christian motivations, European governments never created even modest networks of granaries to cushion bad harvest years and the machinations of the market. Principally anxious about urban public order, especially in capital cities, European states did little to coordinate food-supply conditions across broad stretches of territory.

Especially lacking in any kind of assistance were peasants. European states did not consider peasants a target for material control. European states varied in their policies toward the land and the different classes of people in agrarian society. During the seventeenth and eighteenth centuries, Eastern European states were supported by landed elites who benefited from their control over serf labor, while both land and labor were more mobile in Western Europe. France had many areas with large peasant populations, while England experienced land consolidation through a series of enclosures, but amidst all these variations the range does not extend to include government policies directly aimed to promote peasant welfare beyond some minimal efforts to keep peasants from losing their land. E. L. Jones has argued that early modern European states became more interventionist, supplying increased services and public goods (1987:139–49). Yet a comparison of the ways in which Chinese and European states affected people's most immediate and basic needs, their subsistence, suggests that despite the increased efforts of early modern European states, in important ways their efforts remained more limited than those of the Chinese in the same era. This European lack speaks to the limitations of European state concerns and their agendas for rule. Material means of control mattered in China long before they became elements of the modern Western welfare state. To think of state concerns for popular welfare as a very recent political practice makes sense only if we again limit ourselves to Western examples.[22]

Social order in China also meant political coercion. The threat of coercion lay behind the Chinese state's efforts to register the population and encourage people to report the suspicious behavior of their neighbors. The state was uneasy about all associations that had a potentially oppositional character, whether they involved groups of intellectuals, boatmen, or peasants. Officials feared heterodox beliefs because sentiments were generally considered closely tied to actions and the "wrong" ideas could lead easily to threatening actions. Any one who was not firmly settled on the land was also a potential danger, whether a merchant, a soldier, a monk, or a beggar. For the Chinese state, most of the great threats to social order came from the countryside, not the cities. The Chinese worried about keeping people close to the land and controlling their geographical movements. They confronted a dilemma between allowing, and even encouraging, people to

---

[22]The logics of Chinese and European political economy are addressed directly in chapter 6. For more on food-supply issues, also see chapter 9, where conflicts over food supplies are analyzed.

move to less densely settled areas and forcing them to remain peacefully in their native areas. In periods of state strength, such as the eighteenth century, the state often encouraged migration and worried less about enforcing local social order through coercive mechanisms. Conversely, when state power was weaker, as it was in the nineteenth century, the state turned to more coercive means to sustain local order, became more suspicious of geographical mobility, and grew more sensitive to its weaknesses in frontier areas.[23]

To keep track of the population the Chinese registered households in two ways. Households were registered for land taxation purposes; after 1100 they were also registered periodically in order to create groups of households mutually responsible for each others' behavior (*baojia*). Gentry were explicitly excluded from playing leadership roles since officials feared they could manipulate these positions. A crime committed by a member of one household could implicate other households in the group unless they reported it. Thus Chinese coercive control envisioned a settled agrarian society in which people's behavior was the responsibility not simply of the individual or even his family, but of his neighbors more generally, people who in many places were also kinsmen. Chinese law recognized the social context of crime in several ways—the seriousness of the crime was determined by the social relations of the criminal and the injured party. This relationship was then set within the context of kin and neighbors.

Kin relations played an even larger role in coercive control. The extended kinship group tracing its ancestry to a common male ancestor formed a lineage. As a corporate group the lineage maintained rules for membership that allowed it to expel individuals for improper behavior. To be cut off from the lineage was to experience social ostracism and could force the wayward individual to migrate. Lineages also played a modest role in material welfare since elites within a lineage would be expected to support poorer lineage members; some lineages formed charitable estates for the purpose of supporting widows, orphans, and the indigent. Lineages also formed trusts to support education. Thus moral, material, and coercive means of control were adapted to some degree by lineages to complement state strategies.

European society lacked extended kinship networks organized in a highly corporate fashion. The range of strategies kin groups in China could pursue to reproduce social order were therefore lacking. As regards coercive control itself, European states differed in which level of government could exercise jurisdiction over which kinds of crime, and these standards were always focused on the individual. National state making included the centralization of many coercive forms of control exercised over individuals. European states, therefore, like the Chinese central government, eventually developed greater control over the punishment of crime, but they achieved this without the institutions basic to late imperial rule.

---

[23]The most comprehensive English-language single-volume survey of late imperial state efforts at social control remains Hsiao 1960; the book offers rich documentation concerning Chinese views on social control during the Qing dynasty; also see Tsurumi 1984 and Wakeman and Grant 1975.

At the heart of Chinese coercive social control lay the assumption that the government should have the capacity to learn any source of potential ill or wrongdoing, even if it was not able to realize this goal. This assumption recognized no qualifications of individual rights or estate privileges. Again, European governments lack institutions and strategies adopted by the Chinese state to create and reproduce social order across an agrarian empire. The Chinese goal of surveillance seems disturbingly similar to modern political efforts at control. Here too, we cannot easily fit the Chinese practices within our expectations of pre-twentieth-century states when our norms for state behavior are derived exclusively from Western practices. What become a modern Western concern for pervasive social control was in certain areas already an aspiration and even an expectation in late imperial China.

European states could not coopt elites as easily as the Chinese state could. Aristocratic elites enjoyed competing bases of power and authority. Their strength, variable across Europe, to be sure, defined the crucial problems for state makers that the Chinese had long since solved. The range of strategies that European states could consider for coercive control was more limited, just as were those for material and moral intervention. Flanked by aristocracies and the Church, European state makers were constrained by claims placed on them by other actors and limited by their own organizational capacities.

Looking at early modern European state making from a Chinese perspective, we can find little evidence of several features basic to the Chinese case. Those features absent in European cases—deep concern with elite and popular education and morality, active promotion of material welfare especially of the poor and of peasants, invasive curiosity about and anxiety over potentially subversive behavior — did not emerge for several centuries after they first appear in China. The assumptions and assertions of power by Western states have grown in modern times, taking on features that resemble some of those in an older tradition of Chinese political practices. Ideas and institutions that are specifically "modern" in the West are simply not "modern" in China. Looking at the earlier absences in European state making from a Chinese perspective highlights how recently some of the traits we label generally "modern" actually appeared in Europe.

Trajectories of Political Change

The Chinese trajectory of state making is not dominated by the simple secular changes found in Europe, where a clear sequence from empire through parcelized sovereignty to the formation of larger states defines the basic outlines of political change. None of the key dynamics for European modern state formation—warfare coupled with fiscal centralization and expansion or shifting authority relations from royal rule to popular sovereignty—matter to China's late imperial state dynamics. It should therefore not surprise us to find that European narratives of state formation have very little to say about the Chinese empire and its dynamics of reproduction and transformation.

European agendas of rule differed dramatically from those in China. In Europe, centralizing territorial rulers competed with institutionally distinct and powerful aristocracies, clerics, and urban elites. Central state concentration of power was accelerated by sixteenth- and seventeenth-century warfare among European rulers anxious to expand their power. In China, the emperor worked to develop and sustain a bureaucracy able to meet routine tasks of administration and respond to crises swiftly and effectively. After 1100 there were no elites with strongly institutionalized corporate positions of power and authority independent of the state. The state's relationships to its elites therefore fell into a set of patterns unlike those found in Europe.

When we look at bureaucratic capacities we find early modern European states focusing on the construction of a cadre of central government officials to achieve territorial administration of their countries and extract ever-larger amounts of revenue to fuel growing armies. In China, bureaucratic capacities were not driven by the combination of voracious revenue needs and military buildup. Instead, bureaucratic capacities addressed two principal kinds of control—the maintenance and reproduction of a social order spanning urban and rural China and the maintenance of special administrative capacities to maintain the Yellow River, the Grand Canal, and the salt monopoly.

In contrasting the bureaucratic capacities of early modern European and late imperial Chinese states, a brief assessment of the information and competence required to fulfill government duties suggests a core of common kinds of activities flanked by forms of knowledge and expertise found in one case and not the other. In both Europe and China, the maintenance of military organization mattered. But the techniques used were not always the same: Chinese armies often grew at least part of their own food supplies and posed a less pressing resource problem.

As regards taxation, we can contrast European efforts to raise taxes, which were constrained by the claims exercised by elites, with the Chinese elite's absence of any capacity to place formal claims on the taxation process. In the Chinese case, however, the government expressed a commitment to light taxation, a commitment it generally honored. Perhaps a more striking set of differences is the absence in Europe of a Chinese agenda for domestic rule including moral, material, and coercive strategies of control that relied upon elites to share official priorities and policies for achieving local order, a subject to be pursued in the next chapter.

Another way in which the Chinese and European cases clearly differ lies in the contrast between "domestic" and "foreign." These categories derive from modern state-making distinctions and apply only partially to earlier periods. But asking how these terms fit Chinese and European situations can still be revealing. For the European states, the long arc of domestic state making from the twelfth to the nineteenth centuries defined an increasingly large and coherent "domestic" realm that gradually encompasses and integrates previously disparate populations. "Domestic" has a limited meaning when the disputes and marriages of royal houses can redefine the relationships among sometimes geographically separated populations. Such populations may become subjects of the same state as state-making imperatives of fiscal extraction and warfare tie their political fates together. European warfare defined the international arena more sharply in terms of competition than it did the meaning of "domestic."

China's international order was, in contrast, an extension of its domestic order along a continuum that recognized zones more than borders and considered these to be culturally constructed as much as geopolitically defined. China was at the center of the world order; the government took on a civilising project to bring as many people as possible under its political and cultural hegemony. The same general principles of moral, material, and coercive strategies of domestic rule which we will look at more closely in the next chapter were applied to the international sphere as well (Yang 1968). China was not one of several ambitious and competitive states seeking to order domestic space and expand its international presence at the expense of similar competitors. In important ways, the dynamics of Chinese state formation and transformation fail to obey European dynamics of historical change. The Chinese state made greater efforts at both coercive and material control than European states—on the one hand, aiming to keep accurate registers of the population and to maintain a regular flow of tax revenues and, on the other, investing far more in social welfare efforts. Even more striking is the Chinese state's inclusion of ideological control cast in moral and educational terms. The ambit of Chinese imperial authority and power stretched far beyond those of European states in spatial scale and substantive variety. When we look at European state making from a Chinese perspective, we can find several significant instances of European state limitations, such as inability and unwillingness to manage subsistence conditions in rural as well as urban areas and unimagined responsibilities for defining the moral education of both elites and commoners. These limitations of European states suggest that certain types of historical change are consequently unlikely to occur. Early modern European states were not likely to become activist paternalistic states with a strong sense of ruling a social order in which people's moral behavior and beliefs mattered to state legitimacy and success.

Thinking of absences and unlikely possibilities in European trajectories of change creates a sense of a larger universe of historical change within which European patterns become simply one family of possibilities. This sense improves our understanding of historical changes. When we jump to a more general level to stress the differences between premodern state and modern ones, the distinctions we draw are generally based empirically on Western cases exclusively. We implicitly deny the possibility of finding important traits in premodern states that are not exemplified by Western cases.

The problem is not simply privileging Western traits to define what is modern throughout the world, thus ignoring other traits, such as those important in late imperial China. The less obvious but equally serious problem is assuming that certain state strategies and behaviors do not exist historically until modern Western states adopt them, which leads us to ignore evidence of practices that fail to fit our expectations. This is not the increasingly well-recognized problem of universalizing the Western experience to the exclusion of features absent in the West. Rather, it is the parochializing of the world to fit the particular trajectory of state formation found in Europe. The late imperial Chinese rulers were engaged in moral, material, and coercive strategies of state making that were undertaken by Western states only in later centuries.

It is hardly news to claim that most of our ideas about political change privilege European traditions. Conventionally, we look back at European history to discern patterns of development. The limitations of this retrospective focus on those activities that created winners are well known. How to transcend the limitations associated with these basic views is far less obvious. A refusal to universalize Western practices is only one step. We must furthermore take alternative trajectories of historical change seriously. Analyzing the formation of domestic social order in China and Europe will allow us to pursue these comparisons in the next chapter.

5

CONSTRUCTING DOMESTIC ORDER

European states in the sixteenth and seventeenth centuries had to make choices about how to relate to aristocratic, commercial, and clerical elites as well as to peasants and townspeople. Their options were shaped by the particular social structures and ideologies that defined proper roles and expectations for rulers and subjects. Would-be territorial states shared similar challenges and faced similar claims; the successful ones created similar capacities. The Chinese empire faced a different constellation of challenges. No elite or popular claims limited state authority. Rather than centralize power through compromise and conflict with other power holders, the Chinese state aimed to create institutions of social order at the same time as it avoided meddling in ways likely to stimulate hostile responses. Not surprisingly, the political ideology elaborated under these conditions differed dramatically from the political ideologies developed in European countries.

Social and Political Order in Europe and China

Looking across Europe in 1100 and viewing the large number of very small political units dotting the landscape, three types of elites can be easily distinguished—nobles, clergy, and urban commercial elites. Each had a distinct social role—to fight, to pray, and to make and move goods. Each was organized in a distinct fashion: nobles enmeshed in feudal relations, clergy organized by the Church, and commercial elites organized to pursue profit and power. Before territorial states were formed, the late medieval political order was largely a local or regional phenomenon with one of these elites at the center of overlapping jurisdictions: clergy in bishoprics, merchants in municipal governments, and aristocrats in feudal relations. The formation of territorial states created the challenges of defining local political order within a new larger state construct and of defining political roles for nobles, clergy, and merchants. Though no group was homogeneous and variations in composition and outlook gave rise to intra-European differences, the general social and political distinctness of these groups stood in stark contrast to Chinese social structure, in which such groups did not have corporate identities; there were consequently no struggles among them or with the state. The specific accommodations reached among these three elites and European political rulers, however much they varied among themselves, all addressed a particular problem in European state formation—how a centralizing state would establish territorial authority in concert or competition with elites that played changing political roles.

From the European state's point of view, its three kinds of elite each performed a distinct and useful function. Nobles, or at least a large percentage of them in medieval times, derived their raison d'être from supplying military service to the Crown. Merchants were useful because their activities were a source of tax revenue and loans for needy rulers. Clergy took on the duty of establishing moral order throughout the realm. Coercive, material, and normative components of constructing social order were associated closely with three institutionally distinct elites. The centralizing territorial state called on the three to play roles it deemed desirable, but the elites did not always agree with state preferences. These disagreements led to different kinds of accommodation and conflict between European states and their elites. In some cases, including a band in the north from England through Scandinavia and further south from Spain, east through Burgundy, the Swiss Confederation, and Italian city-states, parliaments representing elite interests achieved control over taxation and warfare in the late medieval period, though they were not always able to hold onto these powers in the sixteenth and seventeenth centuries (Downing 1992:10). Where absolutist states greatly increased central power, elites lost political power. But the contest continued as royal sovereignty was increasingly compromised and even replaced by various kinds of popular sovereignty after the French Revolution.

In late medieval times, European social order was imagined on two radically different spatial scales. At local levels, social order was created first in rural community settings, cities, and manors, and then in small territorial units of bishoprics, duchies, principalities, and the like. At a far grander level could be found the Church's mandate to order the world. European states emerged at an intermediate spatial scale to take on some functions encouraged by the Church, like providing justice, law, and sometimes charity. Elites of society, assembled into estates, negotiated with would-be territorial rulers (Poggi 1978, Dyson 1980). Within studies of European history, the distinction between estates and classes and the analysis of the shift from a social order based upon estates to one based on classes has long been a focus for research and debate.[1] But if we take a broader per-

---

[1] The medieval materials that gave rise to an image of old regime society organized into orders has been studied by Duby 1980. Roland Mousnier has produced a detailed study of sixteenth- and seventeenth-century France centered on the concept of "orders" (Mousnier 1979). His principal intellectual

spective that includes the Chinese case, we see that estates and classes are intimately linked and in many ways the dynamics of change are historically particular to European cases.

Late imperial China had no estates, and notions of class did not matter to the construction of political order as they did in Europe. In China, the same ideological vision perceived local and central order to be of one piece. The units of social order were not estates but families, lineages, and villages. Elite families spanned different economic and social functions, but the vision of social order did not privilege those functional differences. While Chinese thought recognized functional differentiation into scholars, peasants, merchants, and tradesmen, these did not become the primary units for organizing social order. They were never accorded institutionally distinct corporate status. Elite families were those that managed to diversify the pursuits of their sons into government service, management of family lands, and commerce. At any point in time the basis of elite status for a particular family could be possession of a civil service degree and official post, wealth made from trade, or major landholdings. Some families were more likely to reproduce their success in one kind of elite activity than another. In general, there was a continuum of possibilities without any sharp distinctions among elite members that were reproduced over time. In Europe as well there was social mobility among aristocrats and men of commercial wealth, but these European elites possessed institutionalized voices which Chinese elites lacked. European elites also possessed military forces of their own; towns lost their own forces before aristocrats, who fielded independent armies in France as late as the Fronde rebellion of the mid-seventeenth century. Chinese elites lacked both military force to organize revolts and civilian voice to express their interests against those of the state. While European elites had institutionalized voices that circumscribed the limits of the ruler's authority, Chinese elites participated in extending the reach of state power and authority by sharing a common Confucian agenda for promoting social order. Where Chinese elites disagreed with the government, they depended in most cases upon the limitations of state capacities to avoid open confrontation. They did not set out to demarcate in sharp and explicit ways a space of their own. They did, however, set out to advocate a kind of localism in which elites and local officials could act more independently of the central government.

The emperor, for his part, worried about the danger of horizontal cliques compromising the vertical bureaucratic ties of the central government. Knowing that the fall of the Ming dynasty had been attributed to fighting among officials, eighteenth-century emperors may have opposed localism as a way to protect the dy-

---

antagonist has been the Russian scholar Boris Porchnev, who analyzed the old regime in terms of "classes" and class conflict. A convenient introduction to both perspectives as well as the work of other scholars is Woloch 1970. But not only Marxists have applied the concept of "class" to the ancien régime. The pioneering historian Marc Bloch devoted several chapters to "social classes" in the old regime in his classic work *Feudal Society* (1961, 2:283–358). Despite Bloch's use of "class," however, many later scholars have chosen to stress the differences between a society of "orders" under the ancien régime and a modern "class" society; see, for example, Blum 1978:418–41.

nasty. The differences between state–elite relations in China and Europe alert us to structurally distinct situations that provide frameworks within which domestic order was created.

In the early modern period, European states competed for power with aristocratic elites and watched, at times anxiously, for popular rural protests. But urbanization created an even more pressing source of concern for many governments: the domestic social order they aimed to create was largely an urban social order governed by the state's bureaucracy.

The problem of domestic order for the Chinese empire, in contrast, involved both urban and rural areas. Of the two, rural social order was much more important to Chinese rulers. They feared peasants, not as individuals, but as people drawn or even duped into rebellious roles by unscrupulous leaders who were always the prime targets for punishment. This perspective followed from Chinese principles that defined people by their social roles and relationships, not in terms of either corporate identity or abstract individuality. If the late imperial state did not face the difficult European problems of breaking the powers of aristocracies and free cities, it did nevertheless face its own serious problems. Unlike European rulers, Chinese rulers were not seeking in late imperial times to create new centers of power and authority, to subjugate groups that had previously been relatively independent elites. The Chinese challenge was to reproduce social order as an equilibrium condition within the limited technologies of rule available.

The constraints were several. The bureaucracy, a very large and complex organization, was nevertheless limited in size. Official presence was limited to the county seat, beneath which were several towns and hundreds of villages and populations ranging from several tens of thousands to hundreds of thousands. But the state could not just increase the numbers of local officials and expect greater success; additional officials would not only have cost more financially, but have raised the organizational costs of vertical bureaucratic integration and control over personnel. Coordinating the roughly 1,300 county magistrates at the bottom of the hierarchy was difficult enough. The central state was limited in the amounts of information it could secure from counties across the empire. Rule making and policy implementation were repeatedly qualified by particular social and ecological conditions, making the task of creating domestic order far more complex than any simple application of the same principles and policies to all areas. The root of the empire's difficulties lay in the inadequate number of local officials to rule across an agrarian empire in the manner desired by the state. A solution to the problem of creating effective local rule was central to the states' success in securing the empire during late imperial times.

Domestic Order in Europe and China

During the Middle Ages, European government was largely local in scale. At one extreme was fragmented Italy with its many city-states. At the other extreme was England, where the king was crucial; there was no landownership without a lord;

there were no lords without royal recognition. In general, medieval continental Europe had no overarching authority to which lords or city burghers were subject. The early modern state-making experience changed this by creating absolutist states across Western Europe.

The experiences of local communities varied. In England, local authorities sustained a tradition of independence stretching back to Roman times despite the importance of the king. The imposition of local rule by central government meant the incorporation of power holders into a larger system. Justices of the peace were appointed by the Crown, but served without salary. Leadership was in the hands of gentlemen. The Prussian *Landrat,* like the English justice of the peace, was appointed by the central government, but unlike his English counterpart the *Landrat* was paid for his work, which centered on mobilizing and managing men and horses for the military, a function quite unlike the English focus on local peace and welfare issues (Bendix 1978:199–200, 329). Local government in France, in contrast, had been more formally organized under *parlements,* the members of which possessed wealth and/or noble birth. By the seventeenth century, the French Crown had succeeded in taking over many fiscal, military, judicial functions from the *parlements* in most of the provinces, if not without conflict, as the Fronde rebellions remind us.[2] Local administration in outlying areas like Brittany and Languedoc remained independent.

Political community in feudal Europe was rooted firmly in local settings. In all state-making efforts, centralizing governments faced local elites with independent claims to local power and authority. Some combination of cooption or displacement was pursued by centralizing states as elites generally aimed to protect their autonomy. Just as the English experience promoted the separation of the economy from the state, the English experience also promoted the separation of society from the state. A strong civil society could largely govern itself. Many affairs not in secular hands could be managed by religious organizations both in England and on the continent. The complement to a state that meddled little with the economy was a state that played a minimal role in matters of local welfare. In both France and German areas, the local autonomy of many cities continued through much of the absolutist period. Matters of local administration remained distant from the centralizing government. Despite important variations in state-making processes among European countries, certain themes are found to some degree in all cases.

The state-making process centralized the extraction and control over larger amounts of resources but did not create new kinds of political community. Resistance to centralizing efforts appealed to traditions of political autonomy that would later promote the expansion of political representation and democracy. Representation allowed elites to resist state demands.

Administratively speaking, local governments retained varying degrees of autonomy through the eighteenth century. In most of Europe, rulers established lo-

---

[2]The Fronde and other forms of tax resistance are addressed in chapter 10.

cal officials paid by the state. The French crown maintained authority over local officials even though those officials were not always responsive to the ruler's desires. In England, local government was more a creature of local society, staffed by unpaid local elites (Guenée 1985:117). European rulers formed territorial states by subordinating urban and rural populations near the capital and in peripheral areas, with varying degrees of local autonomy. The extreme case of local autonomy occurred as an offshoot of European political traditions.

The greatest local government autonomy was not in Europe but in the American colonies, as Tocqueville explained in his sharp and clearly idealized contrast between European, especially French, forms of local government and what he saw in Jacksonian America. Whereas in Europe, local government had been incorporated into centralized structures to serve national states, in America, government began with local townships, then built to the state level; the federal government came last, its powers limited by the authority already assigned to lower levels. The Anglo-American tradition of local self-government is consciously conceived as a participatory democracy quite separate from the state as a centralized bureaucratic machine. The degree to which representative democratic institutions developed in the nineteenth century was correlated with the strength of local government institutions able to define and defend spheres of authority separate from the central state. In the U.S. case, the discrete authority of local government became embodied in the tradition of local governments having their own taxes, usually property taxes, to support services and functions deemed local in nature (Wallis 1984).

Institutional differentiation among levels of government, each of which had distinct duties, may have become most fully developed in the United States, but differentiation existed throughout the West to some degree. Common to all Western cases was the creation of institutionally distinct political interests and power in society that became the basis for local levels of government and social order. Centralizing territorial states faced the challenge of establishing their authority over these units through some combination of persuasion, negotiation, and force (Blockmans 1994).

Not surprisingly, this European context for domestic political order does not prepare us adequately for considering the creation and reproduction of order in the Chinese case. The central Chinese state's concern for social order embraced rural society far more systematically than did that of European states. The degree of vertical integration necessary in the Chinese case to achieve central control over social order was far greater than in any European case, given the vast differences in the spatial scale of Chinese and European societies. China did not have an institutionally autonomous and ideologically articulated notion of local government founded on notions of democratic participation and opposition to the central government. Again not surprisingly, Europeans have not always been impressed with imperial Chinese approaches to social order.

Tocqueville was rather skeptical of the virtues that centralized administration had brought to China. European travelers often spoke approvingly of China's social order and harmony, but Tocqueville suspected they were achieved at great cost:

> China appears to me to present the most perfect instance of that species of well-being which a highly centralized administration may furnish to its subjects. Travelers assure us that the Chinese have tranquility without happiness, industry without improvement, stability without strength, and public order without public morality. The condition of society there is always tolerable, never excellent. I imagine that when China is opened to European observation, it will be found to contain the most perfect model of a centralized administration that exists in the universe. (Tocqueville 1960, 1:94)

Tocqueville believed reports of Chinese central administrative control. But he suspected that having such centralized power reduced local initiative and popular enthusiasm. Tocqueville's vision of a Chinese emperor and central bureaucracy achieving a tranquil social order resembled the one that the ruler and officials themselves no doubt held, although they recognized it to be a goal, not a reality. The more common complaint of both Chinese officials and modern scholars has been the central government's various difficulties and limitations in trying to rule agrarian society in imperial times. The challenges faced by central state and county officials in late imperial China have alerted scholars to the fragile and, certainly by twentieth-century standards, limited capacities with which Chinese bureaucrats faced their mission of ordering society. Yet conventional wisdom fails to take the measure of the Chinese problem with social order: no other state in world history has confronted the challenge of creating instruments of domestic rule over two millennia. The very length of the empire's existence indicates that it succeeded to some degree.

The equilibrium political position for China was agrarian empire. Nor was this equilibrium stagnant. Territory, and especially population, expanded in late imperial times, in particular during the eighteenth century. We cannot hope to understand Chinese dynamics of state formation and transformation without considering this distinctive set of conditions.

During the second millennium of imperial rule, the settlement of growing numbers of people across ever-larger areas demanded innovative strategies for local government. While many techniques certainly elaborated upon older institutions and policies, at their core lay what we might call a Neo-Confucian agenda for social order which suggested to local elites new ways to promote social tranquillity and popular welfare. Zhu Xi and his contemporaries championed the role of elites in buttressing social stability through good deeds, perhaps as alternatives to undesirable government activities.[3] More generally, however, elite efforts were seen not as substitutions for but as complements to official efforts to maintain lo-

---

[3]For example, the replacement of Wang Anshi's green sprout loans (*gingmiaofa*) by Zhu Xi's community granaries (*shecang*) was conceived as a shift from government-sponsored monetary loans to grain loans by elites.

cal social order. In Qing times, this mix of official and elite efforts assumed particular configurations and reveal how political norms were translated into social practice across an agrarian empire.

Much scholarship on local social order in late imperial China has stressed the roles of nongovernmental actors. The state has often seemed inconsequential to analysts. The vast scale of the empire guaranteed that labor-intensive strategies of official rule and control were impossible. But while Neo-Confucian principles of social and political order created complementary roles for officials and elites, many interpretations look largely at elites. The importance of gentry households and other local elites to the maintenance of local social order has long been noted by scholars. Fei Xiaotong (1953) made the gentry the basic intermediary between officials and peasants well into the twentieth century. More recently G. William Skinner's (1977:19–20) observation that the size of the state, relative to its population, contracted over time has often been the point of departure for scholars who expected elites to play a greater role in local affairs than did local officials during the Ming and Qing dynasties. The Japanese have examined more directly the interests and motivations of the gentry themselves; Shigeta Atsushi (1984) outlined a theory of gentry control over local society that others have elaborated since his death. The Japanese literature, highlighting the lower Yangzi experience, tends to stress the gentry's assertion of control over tax and welfare in local society. In certain ways this control came at the expense of the state in the late Ming as well as in the Qing dynasties, but in others gentry control represented state power in the countryside. While possible antagonists, gentry and officials shared enough common ground to make them jointly define the political elite (Mori 1975–1976).

The American literature has focused on nineteenth-century changes in state–society relations in which local elites assumed ever-larger responsibilities. William Rowe's two books (1984, 1989) on the central Chinese riverport of Hankow during the nineteenth century present the emergence of a new kind of city in which the management of urban social order rests crucially upon the efforts made by merchants and other elites to organize the city. Mary Rankin's work (1986) on parts of lower Yangzi China in the decades following the mid-century Taiping Rebellion (1850–64) tracks the activities of local elites who assert expanded roles for themselves as they re-establish social order after the largest civil war in world history, a conflict that crippled government control over the empire's wealthiest regions and caused several million fatalities. Rowe and Rankin have related their analyses of social change in nineteenth-century China to the concept of a "public sphere" in which elites gradually expand their activities (Rowe 1990; Rankin 1990). Using this concept, comparisons can be made with European social changes in the early modern and modern periods.

The distinguished German philosopher and social theorist Jürgen Habermas analyzed the term "public sphere" (*Offenlichkeit*) in his effort to clarify a realm of public opinion and political activity that emerged in postfeudal European societies. Habermas (1989) offers an explanation for the appearance and demise of the public sphere. The public sphere was the arena in which reason could be heard and rationality could advance. The collapse of the public sphere has meant that ir-rationalities of increasingly powerful governments and consumer cultures have re-duced social capacities to reason collectively and thus live democratically.[4]

Those who espouse a Chinese variant of the public sphere sometimes relate the nineteenth-century phenomena studied by Rankin and Rowe to the roles of the gentry in late Ming and early Qing society. The spatial dimensions of the argu-ments that move from the late Ming forward are generally confined to regions along the Yangzi River, especially to places in the lower Yangzi. A second key lo-cus of evidence comes from new urban centers in the nineteenth century. Often omitted are less urban and less economically developed regions. Nor is a recog-nition of the eighteenth century as a period of state activism different from both the seventeenth and nineteenth centuries salient in discussions of a Chinese pub-lic sphere.[5]

Institutional Bases for Social Order

The variations in eighteenth-century China's granary system suggest that the pub-lic sphere some scholars have found in China needs clarification. The eighteenth-century civilian granary system suggests that officials depended on a public sphere where they could and substituted for it elsewhere. The awkwardness of speaking of officials "depending" upon a public sphere suggests that the concept may fit Chi-nese politics and society poorly. The Confucian agenda for local order in eighteenth-century China did not privilege either elites or officials as the guardians of local order. It recognized that either group could be important in particular situations.

The eighteenth-century state's system for subsistence management included monthly price reports for grains in every prefecture of the empire as well as weath-er and harvest reports. On the basis of information from these documents, offi-cials made decisions on how best to use granary reserves and influence commercial shipments to equilibrate demand and supply within small locales and across great expanses. The collapse of this system in the nineteenth century created a range of scenarios similar to the conditions of the late sixteenth century. The decline of the granary system was occasioned by factors both within and without the system. From within, the granary system was undermined by difficulties officials faced in repeatedly mounting the organizational efforts needed to keep the system run-ning. The Jiaqing emperor took an important step in 1799 when he freed local community granaries from having to report their activities to local officials, who in turn no longer reported on these granaries to provincial officials. From with-out, military demands for grain increased; the additional funding required for

---

[4]Habermas 1989. I offer an extended evaluation of the "public sphere" concept's application to Chi-nese history in R. B. Wong 1993.

[5]Keith Schoppa (1982:7–8), the first scholar to use the term "public sphere" in the China field, was in fact attentive to spatial variations, but others after him have not always shown the same sensitivity to spatial issues.

restocking rarely arrived. Gone was the eighteenth-century system of official monitoring and coordination of granary activities within provinces and between them (Will and Wong 1991:75–92). But this does not mean that officials and elites stopped building granaries.

Officials and elites in several provinces continued their efforts to fund and manage granaries during the nineteenth century. Compared to eighteenth-century practices, granaries in some places did become more of an elite responsibility, since officials by themselves became increasingly unable or unwilling to sustain granaries by themselves. But more salient on an empirewide level was the overall decline in reserves and the absence of a centrally monitored and coordinated system. Reliance on local elites to sustain rural granaries was hardly new in the nineteenth century. During the late Ming and even under the Yongzheng and Qianlong emperors, community granaries in Jiangsu and Zhejiang were not subject to the kind of monitoring that became common for much of the empire. What the nineteenth-century granary situation suggests, however, is that a kind of Jiangnan model of elite activism may have become more common, along with less official leadership and certainly a collapse of systematic official oversight. Thus, if we want to imagine a Chinese public sphere, it emerges from the reduction of official activism rather than as a product of elite efforts to stake out a set of claims against the state, as happened in parts of Europe.

The history of local schools in the Qing suggests that variations in strategies of moral control resembled those of material control. The Chinese, more than any other state in the early modern world, made the principle of instruction (*jiao*) basic to its conception of political rule. During the Zhengtong (1436–1449) reign of the Ming dynasty, community schools (*shexue*) were established in many counties as an official undertaking (Igarashi 1979:296); by early Qing times only a few remained, at least in name if not always in practice. The most common form of local school in Qing China was called the "charity school" (*yixue*), established by the government in border regions to civilize local populations; in interior parts of the empire local elites responded to official exhortations to build charity schools (Ogawa 1958; Igarashi 1979). Angela Leung's work (1994) on charity schools during Ming and Qing times demonstrates the central role played by the leaders of local communities rather than by officials in the creation and maintenance of these institutions. Though her research is focused primarily on lower Yangzi examples, she includes evidence from some other places as well that suggests a major role for local elites in local education outside the lower Yangzi as well.[6] But how common was this lower Yangzi pattern?

---

[6]Certainly for the lower Yangzi, Leung (1994) has demonstrated that the nomenclature of community schools was more commonly employed in the Ming and charity schools in the Qing. She also finds for the lower Yangzi cases a clear shift in the relative importance of official and elite funding and management from Ming reliance on officials to Qing reliance on elites. But for other parts of the empire, such as Guangdong, the community school nomenclature is retained in the Qing dynasty (Guangdong TZ 1822:144.1–9).

In frontier provinces, the state clearly played a larger role in charity school formation. In the *Precedents and regulations of the Qing dynasty (Da Qing Huidian shili)* one finds frequent mention of official efforts to promote charity schools in Guizhou, Yunnan, and the more peripheral parts of other provinces like Sichuan, Hunan, and Guangdong (*Huidian shili* 396:1a–9b). Charity schools were especially associated with the education of minority peoples. The best-documented case of successful government promotion of charity schools is by the famous eighteenth-century official Chen Hongmou, who in Yunnan spearheaded the founding of 650 charity schools. As William Rowe's research (1994) has shown. Chen made his subordinate officials responsible for developing charity schools. Through repeated questioning, he made them increasingly uneasy about their failures to establish these educational institutions. He suggested that they turn to a variety of sources to fund the schools—local budget surpluses, customary fees, rents from estates attached to their bureaucratic posts, revenue from newly opened but previously concealed land, and contributions from local elites. Whenever possible, Chen sought land endowments for charity schools to give them a secure source of funding. Elites played a role in establishing charity schools through financial contributions as well as gifts of land, but their efforts were not the driving force behind the expansion of charity schools. In sharp contrast to the dynamics in the lower Yangzi, officials in Yunnan clearly played the leading role. The contrasting roles of elites and officials in charity school formation in the lower Yangzi and Yunnan parallel in their broad outlines the different roles that elites and officials played in community granary formation in economic cores and imperial peripheries during the eighteenth century. Between these two poles, charity school formation involved a mix of official and elite benefactors, just as community granaries did.

Schools and granaries complemented each other ideologically. The promotion of education and economic welfare were twin commitments of the local magistrate; thus the term *jiaoyang,* "to instruct and nourish," was considered a basic feature of government.[7] Moreover, the variable roles of officials and elites across the empire were also similar in both systems. But the organizational formats developed in the eighteenth century to coordinate these activities were separate vertically structured institutions rather than a single horizontally integrated local system. The eighteenth-century state achieved greater oversight over education and more control over grain reserves than had been accomplished by earlier dynasties. Local community granaries fit within a larger granary system that was itself simply one major component of a broad repertoire of state options to

---

[7]In the explanation of contents (*fanli*) in his magistrate's handbook of 1694, *A Complete Book Concerning Happiness and Benevolence,* Huang Liuhong (1984:61–62) shares with the reader his effort to gather materials on education and economic welfare for the topic of "instruction and nourishment" (*jiaoyang*); granaries are actually discussed in the next section of famine relief (*huangzheng*), as food-supply management for crises was a large enough subject to be distinguished from other policies for economic welfare.

influence food-supply conditions; local granaries had the straightforward function of feeding peasants during a particularly lean year and occasionally providing seed grain for the next year's planting. Local schools, however, had multiple functions. State-sponsored schools, especially in the empire's frontiers, were aimed at "civilizing" minority groups with indoctrination in Confucian moral and social order. In contrast, local schools in the interior were often conceived as the first step of study for boys with scholarly promise; some of those who did well in local schools could expect to continue their studies and pursue the greater goal of passing the civil service examinations. Because the state already controlled education through the civil service examination system, school administration itself needed less central control than the granary system.

Local efforts at creating and sustaining charity schools, like those aimed at mobilizing grain, involved both officials and elites. The fuzzy distinction between official and unofficial roles in education is visible in the county-level "studies official" (*xueguan*), whose position, in Alexander Woodside's words was "incompletely bureaucratized" (1990:182). Such vaguely defined roles confuse the distinction between official and unofficial.

Similar ambiguities may be seen in many societies. The parallel to the Qing studies official is the U.S. school board composed of elected representatives who are not clearly official or unofficial. In Western cases, the ambiguity between official and nonofficial is often tied to issues of representation, to the ways in which certain strata of society gain access to political participation. The ideological and institutional articulation of the continuum between official and unofficial was very different in China, where the concepts of representation and the separation of powers among levels or branches of government did not exist. The public sphere as an arena within which politically active populations can contest and influence state action was lacking in late imperial China. Instead, officials and elites jointly participated in the creation of institutions for social order. The particular inputs from each varied in different social, economic, and political situations.[8] The significant difference between eighteenth- and nineteenth-century practices was not between official and elite, but between practices monitored and even guided by the central government and those depending more completely on local initiatives from either officials or elites and usually from both together. What distinguishes nineteenth-century from eighteenth-century practices are the more explicit *local* limitations.

The Legacy of the Search for Material and Moral Control

Scholars have long noted the manpower and organizational limitations of the late imperial Chinese state that precluded its effective penetration of village society.

---

[8]My stress on a continuum between official and unofficial in China does not mean that the roles of officials and elites could not on occasion be contested; from Woodside's (1994) research on education, for instance, the role of "studies official" was subject to some disagreement. But such disagreements did not lead to the fundamental distinctions between state and society drawn in many parts of Europe.

This observation has often led us to expect, implicitly if not explicitly, that the state could succeed at few efforts to order local society and that, if the government did make such efforts, it would have to delegate responsibility to local elites. When joined to arguments that local elites had their own priorities and desires, this train of thought easily leads to the conclusion that the state was of at most limited relevance to local order.

The evidence for separate and even competing agendas is clearest on taxation issues.[9] On other issues, scholars often assume that private funding means that the interests served must be separate from the state. This chapter argues that in the realms of material welfare and moral indoctrination the state and local elites shared an agenda which during the eighteenth century was implemented throughout the agrarian empire through a mix of official and elite efforts coordinated, if not fully controlled, by the central state through vertically integrated reporting procedures. Officials defined the dimensions of their involvement in these concerns according to their assessments of local social structures and economies. What distinguishes in general eighteenth- and nineteenth-century government efforts at sustaining social order is the degree to which and manner in which higher-level officials sought to monitor local society. The eighteenth-century granary system, for instance, demonstrates the state's capacity to construct a massive and sophisticated structure to influence material welfare across diverse locales. While certainly a fragile achievement in fiscal and organizational terms, it was nevertheless sustained for many decades as a complex system of grain mobilization, storage, transfer, and distribution. Not surprisingly, a government capable of this kind of success also attempted to impose vertical control in other areas as well.

In the realm of moral indoctrination, the Qing emperors paid considerable attention to implementing the village lecture system (*xiangyue*). The term *xiangyue* in Song and Ming times had referred to a local community organization within which social harmony was to be promoted through proper instruction and material aid. In the Southern Song, the *xiangyue* which can be translated as "village compact," was conceived as a unit within which people could organize to fight fires, repel bandits, and care for the sick and poor (Wada 1939:51–52). During Ming times, the Hongwu emperor called for establishing the *xiangyue* as a local education institution in 1388. Famous figures like Wang Yangming and Lu Kun also championed the *xiangyue* as a local institution that twentieth-century scholars have seen as an instrument of self-government or local elite control (Matsumoto 1977:131–38; Wada 1939:119–26; Shimizu 1951:338–60; Handlin 1983:47–51, 198–99). But as Maurice Freedman noted many years ago, the early and mid-Qing rulers gave the term new meaning as a kind of public lecture system subject to official oversight (1966:87). In his "Sacred Edict" the Kangxi emperor offered sixteen maxims which counseled people to work diligently, spend carefully, treat kin and neighbors with propriety, promote correct learning, remit taxes promptly, and organize into groups to prevent thefts. Through the village

---

[9]For instance, James Polachek's (1975) essay on the gentry in Suzhou during the Tongzhi restoration.

lecture system, people were to listen to lower-degree holders (*shengyuan*) who elaborated upon these themes (Hsiao 1960). Not satisfied with his father's maxims offered in terse classical Chinese, the Yongzheng emperor issued his own amplified instructions, later augmented by many popularizations (Mair 1985).

The lecture system depended on elites without formal bureaucratic positions who recognized their Confucian responsibilities to preach correct behavior. The state made efforts to organize and monitor the lectures as an activity distinct from other local operations. In certain cases, the magistrates themselves were expected to give the lectures.

Already in the eighteenth century there were complaints about the limited efficiency of the village lecture system. In part, the problem was the lack of an analogue to the granary accounts that tracked the mobilization and disbursals of grain. But even if the village lecture system could not claim the organizational sophistication and success of the granaries, the political intent remains clear—eighteenth-century rulers intended the village lecture system to be a vertically integrated system that specialized in moral indoctrination. Officials were expected to keep track of these lectures.

Apart from these material and moral systems, the eighteenth-century state mounted a considerable effort to implement the *baojia* system to provide for mutual surveillance and security. Registering households created an institutional nexus between family and state to regulate the people's virtue (Dutton 1992). This virtue, promoted through moral and material methods of control, was the conceptual center of a stable social order. For all three categories of local control—material, moral, and coercive—the eighteenth-century state aimed to create distinct vertically integrated and functionally specific institutions through which a centralized state could organize local social order. These systems created explicit roles for elites, whose levels and dimensions of participation varied across the empire.[10]

European state strategies to create domestic order did not reach the level of Chinese food-supply management policies. Nor did European states make the efforts at moral instruction typical of late imperial Chinese officials and elites. Churches were the institutionalized guardians of moral order; ministers and priests engaged in moral lecturing. Li Xinchuan's critique of religious moral instruction in 1234 would not occur in Europe for several hundred years: "The country establishes schools in the prefectures and counties in order to clarify human relationships; this is the proper business of Confucians. In establishing schools, is there any reason not to oppose the flourishing of monks?" (Chafee 1994:316). Less obviously, European churches also kept track of populations more closely than governments did. Church registers of population more closely

---

[10]Another indicator of political concern for official control over local institutions comes from Chen Hongmou's efforts in Jiangxi Province to utilize lineages more formally in local administration. Chen (1763, 14:35a) argued that a leadership position should be created in every lineage and filled by an individual whose responsibility it would be to report to local officials on local order.

resembled Chinese government *baojia* records than any European government practice.[11] European states in their period of major formation between the sixteenth and eighteenth centuries did not imagine, let alone attempt, to implement the range of institutions of social order typical of China.

The success of high Qing Confucian strategies to promote local order clearly depended on official ability to convince elites to play roles defined for them by the state in accord with Confucian moral sensibilities. We might expect that the major weakness of these systems was the antipathy elites felt toward official efforts to bend their will to a state-defined social agenda; late twentieth-century social sensibilities resist political cooptation. Moreover, for the late imperial elite we know best, the gentry elite of Jiangnan, there is a record of resistance to official interference in local affairs that begins in the late Ming and certainly carries forward into the early Qing; gentry elites were able and willing to manage their own locales without state interference.[12] But the state may have perceived the situation differently. For if elites succeeded in sustaining the local social order without official participation, this merely simplified the tasks of ruling the agrarian empire and allowed official energies to be expended on other types of problems. The absence of official oversight would be least anxiety-provoking in those areas where elites were both able and willing to adopt Confucian social and moral outlooks. More generally speaking, the limits on eighteenth-century practices of sustaining local order were imposed less by antagonism between officials and elites than by constraints on bureaucratic capacities and shifting ideological commitments.

To return to food-supply management: the bureaucratic costs of surveillance over local operations could be substantial. In the case of granaries, gathering the accounts of many separate rural granaries, checking to see that the figures balanced each year, then aggregating them into reports was an operation that demanded skill and patience from local officials. As granaries became more common, the difficulties of performing these operations grew accordingly. If mistakes were made, it often became difficult to uncover them in future audits, so accurate monitoring became increasingly less likely.

The difficulties of monitoring local activities such as managing rural granaries were not merely an issue of organizational capacities. Higher levels of government might worry about the misappropriation of money or grain by local officials. Fears of potential meddling limited the role the Yongzheng emperor assigned to local officials in rural granary management. Worries again surfaced when the Jiaqing emperor decided in 1799 to end state monitoring of local rural granaries because he felt it was impossible to sustain official oversight without also suffering corruption in some county governments (*Renzong shilu* 50.24b–26a). The central government had to decide whom it trusted more—local elites who, guided by the

---

[11]European parish registers included more complete population data than Chinese *baojia* registers, which assists demographic analysis. In terms of population control, however, the Chinese system generated far more information than any Western government of its time.

[12]For examples using famine relief, see Mori 1969.

positive force of moral suasion channeling elite self-interest, would take care of local affairs on their own, or overburdened local officials who counted surveillance among their many duties.[13]

The relative importance of material and moral means to achieve local order, not surprisingly, varied over time. As China entered the mid-nineteenth century, state commitments to ideological and material order were overshadowed by threats of rebellion and the consequent challenges of mobilizing men into militia and extracting revenues to meet military expenses. The shift in fiscal priorities was accompanied by an increased reliance on local officials and local elites, who were expected to coordinate the many activities necessary to first defend and then sustain local order. This meant greater local coordination of material, moral, and coercive means of control and less vertical integration of functionally specific activities. These changes certainly diminished the central state's abilities to manage local affairs, though many provincial and local officials continued to confront problems of irrigation, river conservancy, and famine relief.[14] Indeed, flanking the purely military crisis of rebellion were social problems that continued to demand state intervention. Because official actions in the more peripheral provinces were driven by military considerations, we conventionally consider these areas separately from the economically more central regions. We focus largely on what might be considered a Jiangnan model of local rule, in which elites play prominent roles in providing the services that create social order.

I use Jiangnan as a model because there elites had played a salient role in local affairs since the late Ming. The empirewide context that gave Jiangnan elite practices their social significance however, changed between the late Ming and the late Qing. In the eighteenth century the government subordinated elite efforts to official oversight: in areas without strong elites, officials played more active roles. The empire's political integration of vast territories at the local level was predicated on central government recognition of varying roles for elites and officials. The central government's success, however, required a degree of coordination, oversight, and control that proved impossible to sustain amidst changing social and political circumstances. Jiangnan elites were least affected by the bureaucratic changes of the eighteenth century, because they were already primarily responsible for maintaining local order. When the eighteenth-century system fell apart, the Jiangnan model of local order emerged as a clear alternative.

---

[13]Some nineteenth-century local officials, however, continued to promote local granaries; see Hoshi 1985:297–98.

[14]Lest the diminished coordination and monitoring of local government activities be taken as a more general indicator of state weakness, consider two features of state activity. First, the central government was able to expand fiscal extraction dramatically in the late nineteenth century. Revenues expanded from a range of 30–40 million taels in the eighteenth century to an average of 83.5 million in 1885–94 (Wei Guangqi 1986:287; Hamashita 1989:79). Second, the government continued to mobilize armies to put down uprisings. Following military victories, officials like Zeng Guofan and Zhang Zhidong mounted efforts to reestablish social order and extend political control in the northwest and the southwest.

As late nineteenth-century elites were drawn more firmly into local government, the Jiangnan model became ambiguous: Is this the strengthening of the state or the growth of elite power? Both? Neither? Again, there is a continuum between what is formally in official hands and what is in elite hands; distinctions can be drawn, but the sharp institutional differentiation typical of European cases is not found in China.

The structural interchangeability of officials and elites doesn't mean, of course, that the policies the groups pursue are always the same. Moreover, elites do not necessarily identify more closely with the local populations than officials do. The institutional changes in government organization and practice between the eighteenth and nineteenth centuries included the central government's abandonment of such activities as granaries. What masks this institutional decline is the rhetoric of the Confucian agenda for local order which did not explicitly require any central government role. Zhu Xi's local institutions enlisted local elite participation in creating social order under local magistrates. The central state played an active role in promoting these efforts for much of the eighteenth century but played much less of a role in the nineteenth century. As a result, the Confucian agenda for domestic order could be articulated at different levels with no change in the basic rhetoric of presentation. In this sense, it possesses a "fractal" quality—at any level in late imperial China we may find expressions of a Confucian agenda for social order.[15]

This fractal quality admits no easy dividing line between state and society. The fractal quality of Chinese ideology allowed the principles of social order to be articulated by different levels of government. The institutions developed to implement local order could also be replicated on small or large scales. The elites and officials who created social order were linked in networks that also possessed a fractal quality. Local elites had connections within an area smaller than those of national elites, whose concerns for social order replicated local concerns on a grander spatial scale. There were, of course, disagreements over how best to achieve local order, many of which were articulated with respect to "feudal" (*fengjian*) and prefectural (*junxian*) ideals. But these alternatives were expressed within a common ideological terrain that included the same local institutions even if people differed as to how officials and elites would manage them.

The fractal nature of Chinese state–society relations meant that officials at all levels accepted the same agenda for social order. To be sure, preferences among material, coercive, and moral institutions of control varied over time and differed across regions. In general, the state's reliance on elites enhanced its capacity to rule, but relations with elites also highlight the chronic fluctuations in that ca-

---

[15]The term "fractal" was invented by the mathematician Benoît Mandelbrot to refer to the replication of certain irregular geometric patterns on different spatial scales in which the degree of irregularity remains constant. Thus fractals look the same whether so tiny as to be viewed under a microscope or so large as to be recognizable only from an airplane. See Gleick 1987.

pacity. At the base of these fluctuations was the instability of public institutions such as granaries and schools, which depended on periodic infusions of new resources and constant organizational energy to run effectively. Because elites and the state shared overlapping sets of interests, elites sometimes welcomed the delegation of state responsibilities to them. But elites were also oriented toward local society and could fend off the state either to defend the common people or more often to protect their own claims on resources and to control over local society. There were no clear divisions of responsibilities either between elites and officials or among different levels of the bureaucracy. Even where there was some functional differentiation and specificity, such as in the reporting procedures for granaries, there was no delegation of authority, resources and responsibilities for granaries. Instead routine surveillance and extraordinary investigations flowed from the central government when the state had the capacities and commitments to do so. When these capacities and commitments were less present, the reproduction of social institutions like granaries varied more dramatically across the empire, dependent upon the initiatives and efforts of local officials and elites. But since the logic of constructing social order based on these institutions was the same whether articulated locally or by the emperor, the fractal quality of government masked actual changes in the way China was ruled.

Terms like "public sphere" and "civil society" are hard pressed to embrace this multifaceted fractal quality, which is foreign to the early modern European experience and which obscures the axis of change in the implementation of political norms. The axis of integration between center and locale forged during the eighteenth century collapsed in the nineteenth century without affecting the basic social principles composing the agenda for local rule and order.

An Agrarian Empire's Decline into Modernity

From the point of view of social institutions, China's nineteenth- and twentieth-century history first appears to affirm notions of modern social change predicated on European patterns. The further decline of the granaries, which in the eighteenth century had been organized into a system of reserves spanning most of the agrarian empire, removed from view a kind of institution quite foreign to our European-based notions of modern social change and their stress on sharp divisions between the state on one side and a private economy and civil society on the other. The image of modern society based on these notions no longer describes very effectively late twentieth-century conditions, but the power of the concepts continues to shape our expectations of social change. Thus the disappearance of rural granaries in China fits comfortably with our notions of the decline of "traditional" empires and the rise of modern states. Even if our initial skepticism of granaries is overcome by evidence of their operations and we acknowledge their implications for material welfare, we can dismiss them as "traditional" since they do decline in importance in the twentieth century.

Changes in education also fit the conventional story line of a collapsed empire. The demise of Confucian education and its displacement by Western subjects meant that education was no longer primarily moral indoctrination. Postimperial governments made great efforts to promote a redefined curriculum of knowledge combining Western subjects with Chinese ones. As with the granary situation, the twentieth-century Chinese government's recognition of Western-based education affirms our expectations about social change.

If we move forward just a few decades, the Chinese parallels to European changes become less complete and persuasive. Rural subsistence management reemerged after 1949 as a basic political challenge. Though the specific institutional arrangements and the ideological presentation of these activities do not closely resemble Qing practices, the persistence of food-supply issues in local agrarian society is unmistakable. Central government officials have faced difficulties moving grain surpluses controlled by powerful provincial leaders, raising questions about flows of grain similar to those of earlier centuries. Complaints about peasants forsaking agriculture for trade echoed those made in late imperial times.[16] Politics and education have also become enmeshed again since 1949. The state's attitudes toward elementary education resonate strongly with late imperial perspectives as the state seeks to impose its own moral vision of society through the education of young children. Of course, elementary education now includes many kinds of instrumental knowledge first learned from Westerners. But the presence of these "Western" subjects doesn't speak unequivocally for a more general Westernization.

Nineteenth- and twentieth-century social and economic changes with roots in the West are obviously different from earlier historical parallels. Such changes have become models, opportunities, and constraints on China, especially since the second half of the nineteenth century. Though China had a long history of urbanism, nineteenth-century treaty ports clearly added new dimensions to the scene. By the second and third decades of the twentieth century, Chinese cities were the sites of new social groups, including industrialists, workers, and students; new forms of economic production and consumption; and new kinds of political expression such as mass demonstrations and boycotts. Urban centers became the most obvious places to expect a public sphere and a civil society. Certainly in Europe it is the cities that house these social formations. But where politics in Europe always had a strong urban component with classical roots, Chinese politics had long been agrarian and imperial. The Chinese institutions reviewed in this chapter were rural in orientation or intended to blend urban and rural. The new Chinese urban developments, including twentieth-century analogues to civil society, had to be linked in some manner to the rural society which China had been for so many centuries. The basic problem with many discussions of a public sphere and civil society is not, therefore, that they have misidentified similarities, but

---

[16]These issues are addressed more fully in R. B. Wong 1988.

rather that they fail to situate the similarities in their respective contexts and thus draw out their implications. The danger of working with a term like "public sphere" is that insufficient framing will elicit expectations for patterns of social or political change that are not in fact well founded.

Differences between China and Europe can be as striking as the similarities posited by discussions of public sphere and civil society. Consider, for example, the role of kinship in state formation. As Lawrence Stone puts it: "The modern state is a natural enemy to the values of the clan, of kinship, and of good lordship and clientage links among the upper classes, for at this social and political level they are a direct threat to the state's own claim to prior loyalty" (1979:99). The Chinese state continued to rely on kin groups as it became "modern." Social and political changes created ambiguous roles for lineages through the first half of the twentieth century. Feng Guifen, a famous late nineteenth-century thinker, for instance, saw the lineage as the basis for state efforts to nourish and educate the people. He established a tight conceptual connection between the lineage and the state by appeal to the *zongfa* system of ancient times; as a kinship-based political system, the *zongfa* system did not distinguish kin group from the state. By promoting a larger role for lineages in local government, Feng affirmed the continuum between state and society at the same time as he made the lineage serve the state's efforts at local government. As he envisioned the local scene, the state could implement surveillance, community granaries, and militia, with lineages as a base. The lineage thus provided the organizational focus for the increased interactions of officials and elites whose activities were increasingly considered components of the state's strategies of rule (Feng 55:5b–6b). Feng's approach would not be found in any nineteenth-century European government.

Feng Guifen's approach, however, also differed from the positions that eighteenth-century officials and the Qianlong emperor had taken. Where eighteenth-century officials and rulers emphasized vertical control over locales, Feng suggested a "feudal" (*fengjian*) system of government predicated on a much greater degree of horizontal mobilization. Feng's promotion of lineages in the lower Yangzi called for recognition of the lineage as a multipurpose, quasi-official organization. He saw this as a development that would strengthen, not weaken, local government. But successfully strengthening local government reduced the vertical integration of state decision making. It is ironic that the absence of vertical integration makes these elite activities appear to some Western scholars to be public and hence modern, in contrast to what had been official and bureaucratic and hence traditional. In fact, the change lies not so much in what elites began to do as in the reduction of what officials had been doing to promote and control elite activities.

The relationship among Chinese elites, local governments, and central state continued to be contentious and uncertain in the first half of the twentieth century. Philip Kuhn's now classic article on local government set out clearly some of the likely possibilities for local government development in the early twentieth century (Kuhn 1975). He argued for the constraints imposed on participatory and representative forms of local government by a national state committed to maintaining vertical control over local authorities. Other work appearing in English since Kuhn's piece has explored the interplay of Western political ideas and Chinese political concepts, as well as the institutional features of local government operations in the late Qing and Republican periods (Min Tu-ki 1989; Roger Thompson 1988, 1995; Duara 1988).

The same analytical tensions and choices between local participatory government versus subordination and integration under central government that Kuhn presents for Republican China confronted officials and elites during the French Revolution. In this European case, local representative government was affirmed. China's repertoire of ideological principles and institutional forms did not make the French outcome at all likely in the Republican period. The late empire had no set of representative institutions or a "public sphere" like those found in Europe. Both were key elements in the process of European state making, though they may not have been always complementary. Absolutist states seeking to bypass the *stande* encouraged a public sphere for expression of opinions (Poggi 1978:83). Yet, this same public sphere became an arena in which intellectuals pursued critiques of the state. Chinese social order lacked both representative local government and a public sphere. A Confucian agenda for social order committed officials and elites to the common construction of an ordered world. Chinese ideology and institutions of rule are sufficiently different from European ones to make analysis of Chinese state activities in late imperial times difficult, if not impossible, through exclusive appeal to Western categories of analysis. Yet these categories became increasingly relevant as postimperial state making problems and possibilities include Western inspired ones. The reproduction and expansion of empire depended upon a range of strategies in large measure foreign to European state making processes. For China the process of post-imperial state making combines issues on the agenda of agrarian empire and those created through contact with the West.

The presence of a Neo-Confucian agenda for local rule shared by both officials and elites does not mean that officials and elites always agreed upon their respective roles in local society. They could compete with each other as much as they might complement each other. Moreover, to stress the Confucian context of strategies for local order doesn't mean that Buddhist and Taoist elements are not present amidst the broader cultural sensibilities within which officials and elites acted. European cases display parallel features. Just as Chinese elite-official relations could range from antagonistic to complementary, so could relations between European elites and centralizing states vary between conflict and cooperation. The variations are important to explaining particularities within Europe and within China. But to compare China and Europe, the contrast between the politically institutionalized positions of European elites and the fractal quality of Chinese social order is more important. Within their respective ranges of variations, European elites were more likely to have antagonistic relations with their state makers than Chinese elites were to be in serious conflict with their state.

Europe's public sphere was an arena in which politically engaged populations could express their claims against states. Processes of formal and informal bargaining took place to create government policies and political practices that social groups found acceptable. Within the social space of the public sphere, groups with shared interests could establish an identity and pursue their claims against the government. A public sphere makes sense only where such claims are a salient feature of state–society relations. In late imperial China, claims were far less important than commitments. Officials and elites were connected not by competing claims but by common commitments to the principles and strategies formulated to construct social order. Western forms of local government developed a set of resources and responsibilities differentiated from other levels of government. These forms of differentiation complemented the separation of state and society by making the state a group of bureaucratically distinct authorities.

No comparable division of authority took place in late imperial China. The fractal nature of political rule in China means that the state was less clearly differentiated internally and that the lines between state and society were not drawn as sharply. When we consider how the creation of social order is tied to state formation and transformation in China and Europe, we discover important differences in the dynamics of state–society relations. Other important differences in state formation, reproduction, and transformation emerge when we turn to state relations with the economy.

6

POLITICAL ECONOMIES
IN EUROPE AND CHINA

Our explorations thus far suggest a contrast that once stated may seem obvious but is all too often ignored. In economics, the possibilities at both ends of Eurasia were broadly similar until the fundamental discontinuities of the nineteenth century, discontinuities that gave Europe not only a different set of material possibilities but a set that in most ways seems preferable. In politics, however, what Chinese and Europeans could envision and implement, and what they sought to avoid, diverged much earlier and along lines that allow for no obvious ranking. Having presented an assessment of the economic similarities and the political differences, we can now explore the reciprocal effects of politics and economics. Given the differing political agendas at each end of Eurasia, were shared economic constraints more of a problem for state makers in one place than in another? Conversely, were the political problems in China or Europe more easily solved within their shared economic world in one place than in the other? Did the different goals and strategies pursued by state makers in one place do more to push economic development to the limits of Smithian and Malthusian growth than in the other? Or did one set of tensions between economic and political possibilities make it more likely that the limits of growth in the classical economist's world would be transcended? To address these questions we must abandon the useful but artificial distinction between politics and economics that we have used up to now. It is time to compare the political economies of Chinese empire and European states.

Scholars of European history who disagree strongly on how European states effected economic possibilities nevertheless agree that the results were positive. Some speak of European states creating institutional infrastructures to support and even stimulate private entrepreneurial activity, while others show European governments supporting the monopoly activities of the wealthiest

127

merchants.[1] In contrast, scholars of Chinese history either claim that the state had a negative influence on economic possibilities or at best was irrelevant. The late imperial Chinese state is generally viewed as an inefficient bureaucratic machine headed by arbitrary despots; both bureaucrats and emperor could interfere with the well-being of merchants and thereby block more positive developments. This view is shared by both scholars working within Marxist traditions and those who do not. Moreover, scholars who see positive developments in the commercial economy, whether Marxist or not, emphasize the private sector rather than the state.[2]

Thus, as in the study of European history, a generally similar view of the Chinese state's economic role can be identified among scholars whose analytical frameworks are in many respects incompatible. Together, the positive assessments of European states and negative assessments of the Chinese state display a surprising consistency that spans all manner of intellectual disagreement.

How can we account for this situation? The most obvious explanation would be to agree with the general view. However different our explanations, we might all agree that at least some European states promoted economic change. No matter how greatly explanations of Chinese historical change diverge, we might all accept that the Chinese state failed to promote the development of industrial capitalism. But this easy solution asserts a series of connections between government policies and economic change that merit further reflection. With the advantage of hindsight, we, of course, know that dramatic economic differences separating China and Europe became starkly visible by the second half of the nineteenth and the early twentieth centuries. We can find important differences of political economy even in earlier centuries.

A simple attribution of significance to government policies based on later economic developments is easy to make but may not be accurate. Scholars also often take a second step and infer motives, assigning to state policies the purpose of developing (or hindering) economic change. Both steps lead to problems. The first asserts a causality running from politics and government policy to economic performance, often spanning considerable temporal distances. But analysts have yet to agree on whether, and how, politics and economics intersect. Some scholars emphasize mercantilist strategies, others government lawmaking and regulation of private economic activity. If we cannot agree on which government policies positively affect economic change, how can we determine which policies were significant and why?

The second step, which attributes motivations or purposes to those responsible for policies, is equally problematic, since it assumes that the economic results

[1]The Nobel Prize recipient Douglass North (1981, 1990) is a leading exponent of the position that states fostered economic growth by providing secure property rights. Other scholars, such as Immanuel Wallerstein (1980), tie economic success more closely to government policies and political power.

[2]Hong 1983 exemplifies critiques of the despotic state; Ray Huang 1974 gives a detailed portrayal of the bureaucratic limitations of the sixteenth-century fiscal system. Many of the essays in Nanjing daxue 1981, 1983 demonstrate the Chinese Marxist view of private-sector developments. Elvin 1973 is a non-Marxist view of private-sector developments and limitations.

of policies were intended when in fact they may not have been. Hindsight allows us to create from apparent consequences a set of intentions that may or may not accord with what officials themselves thought they were doing. When we look more closely at the policies and political philosophies of states in China and Europe, we can discover if our conventional contrasts between early modern Europe and late imperial China adequately account for how different types of political economy fit within distinct patterns of state making and, by the nineteenth century, increasingly divergent patterns of economic change.

In both China and Europe, many government policies toward the economy were not conceived in terms of developing or stabilizing the economy but were the product of state goals and needs. Particular needs, such as raising revenues, were shared by states throughout the world but were approached differently. The actual impact of revenue strategies on the economy might, subsequently, differ from the intended purposes of taxation policies.

Raising Revenues: Common Challenges, Different Capacities

Chinese and European states, like all governments, faced the challenge of mobilizing resources. Rulers needed to pay their bureaucrats, support ritual displays of the court, and pay for military operations. Rulers in diverse settings relied on similar sources of revenue, including rents from their own estate lands, agricultural taxes, poll taxes, and commercial taxes. But, as we've already observed, there were important differences between Chinese and European fiscal strategies—would-be state makers in Europe competed with other power holders (nobles, clerics, and merchants) to redefine and expand their claims on resources. In China, a division of claims on resources in which the state was assured its modest percentage held generally steady over many centuries.

European rulers anxious to become territorial powers in the early modern period were at once chronically resource hungry and lacking in adequate, routine methods for revenue raising; officials therefore had great incentives to innovate in order to tap resources previously beyond their grasp. Since land revenues were encumbered by claims from both local lords and the Church, West European rulers looked to expand their revenues through tapping commercial revenues. First, rulers imposed additional taxes on consumption and trade; to solve his fiscal insolvencies, Louis XIV, for instance, relied heavily on a proliferation of consumption and commercial transit taxes (Dessert 1984:17–20). In Spain as well, "the Crown's revenues were extracted overwhelmingly from the market sector of the economy" (I. A. A. Thompson 1994:151). European rulers, by the late fifteenth century, turned to rich merchants for loans before they began to develop their infrastructural capacities to tax their own subject populations.[3]

---

[3]For example, Jakob Fugger, founder of the famous Fugger merchant dynasty, made a loan to the duke of Tyrol secured by a share of the output from the duke's silver mines (Jeannin 1972:3).

The poverty of rulers continued to drive them to invent new ways to borrow money. Loans were sometimes secured against receipts of future tax revenues. In other cases, rulers sold the rights to taxation in return for advance payments; tax farming was thus a form of short-term credit that depended on wealthy merchants believing that rulers would make it worth their while to lend money to the state. When states defaulted on loans, at times deliberately, merchants and other wealthy people were, in effect, taxed. But rulers had growing incentives to repay their loans in order to secure steady sources of credit. Rulers who participated actively in the formation of credit markets worked to transform their short-term debts, brought on usually by war-making needs, into long-term debts that were easier to manage.

Apart from loans, which at some point required state revenues to fund their repayment, were new taxes. The new demands that rulers made lacked any claim to "customary" acceptance. Taxation was not embedded in any long-standing tradition defining appropriate state action. Explanations and reasons for taxation were invented and struggled over as European rulers expanded their claims on resources. The Church, urban interests, and nobilities posed constraints on the capacities of would-be territorial rulers to raise revenues. After 1650 the Church paid taxes in most countries, as did aristocratic and commercial elites. The expansion of central states' claims on resources came through negotiations and agreements that recognized elite privileges and rights. Negotiating over taxation was at the base of the process creating representative governmental institutions. The political logic of constitutional government was intimately tied to the efforts of state makers to solve their fiscal problems (Hoffman and Norberg 1994).

For some European state makers, expansion overseas became a source of revenues, though resource mobilization was hardly the only or even the main reason for maritime movements. Spain and Portugal began to move into the New World at the end of the fifteenth century, setting up local administrations as part of a Catholic mission to create social order. Spain's political reasoning in the Philippines broadly resembled that taken in the New World, but Portugal adopted quite a different approach in other parts of Asia, where their goal was to dominate trading networks dealing in various commodities, especially spices. Portuguese power in Asia was displaced beginning in the late sixteenth century by the Dutch, whose success in trade was also based on their leading role in the spice trade centered in Southeast Asia. The Dutch in turn declined in importance as the spice trade became less lucrative in the seventeenth century and the English, who focused on South Asia and textiles, became an ever-larger commercial and, after the mid-eighteenth century, political presence. European governments gained revenues by granting monopoly rights to their trading companies in Asia.[4] Although territorial states hoped to, and did, gain revenues from maritime expansion into Asia, overseas adventures could be expensive. The Spanish in the Philippines, for

---

[4]For an overview of European expansion, see Parry 1966. Furber 1976 gives country-specific comparisons of European maritime operations. Several excellent studies of maritime empires are included in Tracy 1990 and Tracy 1991.

instance, relied on the galleon trade bringing New World silver into Asia; so great was this traffic that the Madrid government imposed limits on the volumes of silver going to the Philippines in order to keep more of it in Europe (Steinberg 1987:54–55). The Dutch and English governments minimized their commitments by avoiding direct political rule of overseas territories and by delegating state-like powers, including military power, to chartered companies. Thus they maximized the revenues gained from maritime expansion while limiting the costs of colonial administration. European rulers suffered the uncertainties attending overseas expansion as part of their competition with each other in Europe.

Revenue raising in Europe had both domestic and foreign dimensions for many successful state makers. In domestic terms raising revenues committed rulers to negotiate with the elites they aimed to subordinate; deals were struck that involved competition and compromise over resources. When governments struck deals that granted monopoly rights or other kinds of production and trade restrictions, they hampered the development of their economies through open and free competition. When French and Spanish kings traded property rights for tax revenues, they solved state needs for revenues, but the formation of various local monopolies discouraged competition, innovation, and the efficient use of resources.

In contrast, the Dutch Republic and England solved their revenue needs without granting many monopolies, at least domestically. They secured revenues through agreements with elites on taxation policies. Their economies also proved to be the most dynamic of the early modern period. European rulers recognized that their international conflicts included fights for control of resources and revenues associated with maritime expansion. Mercantilist competition over limited—if not, as they believed, fixed—levels of wealth guided European state efforts to amass resources at the expense of fellow state makers.

Little about the political context within which Chinese rulers raised revenues resembled those of European territorial rulers in the 1500s. Chinese governments between the tenth and twelfth centuries increasingly relied on commercial revenues as the economy began its commercial expansion, and agricultural revenues declined. In the thirteenth century Mongol rulers levied commercial taxes at low rates and developed new institutions to tap revenues in agriculturally rich regions. Reliance on agricultural revenues became basic to Chinese state administration after the fourteenth century, when the Ming dynasty's founder, Ming Taizu, promoted an agrarian social order with little place for commerce. The methods by which land taxes were assessed and collected changed as commerce began to expand once again in the sixteenth century, but the intimate connection between the art of ruling and taxing the people who worked the land remained. People protested taxes when they thought they were unfairly levied; they did not challenge the state's claim on tax revenues in principle.

One of local officials' basic tasks was collecting and shipping tax revenues. The Chinese bureaucracy was organized to mobilize tax payments from millions of peasants and to transfer them according to central government directives. Most tax payments in the fourteenth and fifteenth centuries were paid in kind or as labor service; by the mid-sixteenth century, commutation to payment in silver was initiated, a process that was completed during the next century (Huang 1974). The increased commercialization of the economy in this period made it possible for the state to contemplate tax collection in silver. This change increased the government's ability to move resources among different parts of the empire; between 1500 and 1800 the central administration elaborated numerous institutional procedures to move funds across provincial borders as routine transfers and as responses to crisis concerns.

The Chinese state developed an infrastructural capacity to mobilize and disburse revenues quite beyond the imagination, let alone the abilities, of European state makers in this period. Taking Europe as a whole, separate flows of resources made their ways to capital cities and sites of major projects, such as building the Spanish Road. Beyond the flows created by territorial rulers within their respective countries, additional resources flowed in from the New World and Asia. Silver and spices created additional revenues for rulers in competition for wealth on an expanding spatial scale. But considerable portions of European revenues remained in their provinces of origin owing to a division of authority over these resources among central and provincial officials; in Languedoc, for instance, roughly a third of total revenues stayed within the province in 1677 with the balance being sent to the central French government (Beik 1985:260). There were fewer institutionalized political barriers to hinder Chinese fiscal flows, to the center as well as the peripheries, as decided upon by the central government and coordinated by lower-level officials. In general, Chinese rulers could manage fiscal flows over far greater spaces than European rulers could. European overseas activities yielded uncertain returns, the benefits accruing to only a few states. Moving resources through greater spaces gave the Chinese state certain opportunities that European states lacked. When faced with an acute need for resources in one area, the Chinese government could sometimes move resources from another area rather than having to raise additional revenues.[5] This means it had fewer incentives or pressures to develop new mechanisms to tap new revenue sources. The greater area over which it could raise and then move revenues meant that increasing extraction within any smaller area was less necessary than it proved to be in European countries.

When the Chinese state did face a financial crisis of insufficient revenues, it often relied upon "contributions" (*juan*) of various kinds. The most important kind of contribution during the Qing dynasty were "contributions" for lower-level degrees (*juanna*), which entitled a person to sit for higher exams and possibly receive an official position. Other "contributions" were simply surtaxes on the land tax. Still others were made by rich merchants, especially those who enjoyed government favor in the salt monopoly (Xu 1950; Will and Wong 1991:27–30,

---

[5]This was especially true for subsistence issues. On the movement of resources for subsistence issues from the mid-seventeenth to the mid-nineteenth century, see Will and Wong 1991.

49–53). None of these three types involved the kinds of negotiations and decision making that raising new taxes did in Europe. The very term "contributions" stressed the giving of resources over the demanding of them. This view of revenue raising no doubt distorts the particular features of different types of *juan*. It obscures, in particular, the coercive component of land surtaxes, the social status and political opportunity that accompanied buying a degree, and the process whereby merchants agreed to make a "contribution." In this latter case, the norms defining appropriate amounts are uncertain. The impression given by the term *juan* is that merchants met an expectation to help the government as opposed to a responsibility to pay taxes. What is certain is the absence of the kinds of negotiations that delimited merchant payments in Europe through a process of recognizing claims and bargaining. Also missing from China's pre-1850 scene was much reliance on *borrowing* from merchants. The government had no tradition of mortgaging future revenues to meet current needs. Indeed, to the contrary, the government often put its surplus revenues in merchant pawnshops to earn interest. The Chinese state had no reason to develop the kinds of credit institutions that European states promoted in order to secure loans. Late imperial state involvement with credit markets was principally regulatory—the state set legal ceilings on the rates of interest that pawnshops could charge borrowers (Pan 1994). The Chinese state and merchants did not develop the kinds of financial institutions—banks, joint-stock companies, chartered companies—created by European states and merchant elites. These European institutions served the state by developing the concept and reality of a public debt and helped merchants and aristocrats to construct new institutions of European commercial capitalism. As regards fiscal resources, credit, and capital, the late imperial Chinese state did not promote the institutions of capitalism that developed in early modern Europe. European governments stimulated the development of institutions beneficial to capitalism, not so much as a goal in its own right, but as a solution to their own fiscal needs.

Commercial revenues did not bulk as large for Chinese leaders as they did for successful territorial rulers in Europe. Domestic transit taxes were levied in China, but in the mid-eighteenth century they accounted for only a small percentage of total revenues. In 1766, for example, they accounted for some 11 percent of total revenues; adding the revenues from the salt monopoly and other miscellaneous commercial taxes raised the figure to only a quarter of total receipts.[6] The central government aimed to monitor and in a few cases to control commerce, but trade was never as exhaustively exploited by Chinese rulers as it was by European ones. In part, this was because the Chinese tapped agricultural revenues so much more effectively than European rulers could. But it was also a result of gov-

---

[6]See Zhou Bodi 1981:421–43. The importance of commercial revenues changed dramatically after the mid-nineteenth century. Wei Guangqi (1986:227) estimates that agrarian revenues accounted for 77 percent and commercial revenues for 23 percent of total revenues in 1849; the figures were 40 percent and 51 percent, respectively, in 1885 (the balance came from other sources), and 16 and 69 percent in 1911.

ernment decisions to tax relatively lightly in order to allow the people to prosper; since a prosperous people were expected to be a contented and peaceful people, light taxes had their own self-serving political logic for officials. A burdensome government that levied heavy taxes was more likely to provoke rebellion, possibly raising a serious challenge to social order. The threat of social disorder then required additional resources for military preparations, thereby exacerbating popular dissatisfaction and unrest. Thus Chinese officials reasoned that they should keep taxes light.

The eighteenth-century central government's concerns over collection and use of commercial revenues specifically led it to avoid growing reliance on them. In contrast to the clear procedures in place to collect and move agricultural taxes, certain commercial taxes, like license fees, were not routinely collected and forwarded. Rather than have local officials collect funds that the central government could not monitor, let alone control, the state preferred to avoid taxing commerce as heavily as it could have.[7] In contrast to the Chinese state's success with agricultural revenues, many European states could not extract much revenue from the land. At the same time, the central government in China was wary of allowing lower levels of government to raise commercial revenues because unreported increases of resources in local hands could make these officials more independent from oversight and control.

The Chinese government developed routine, light, and legitimate taxation of agricultural revenues mobilized by the state's bureaucratic infrastructure. European state makers, in contrast, relied on extraordinary taxes, often commercial in origin, and seldom argued over their intrinsic legitimacy; instead, rulers often secured agreement for new taxes through negotiations. Tax farmers collected the taxes as a business, contracting to provide the ruler with a certain amount of money and then making their profits through collection of surpluses. European taxation was enmeshed in claims and in negotiations between states and elites. In China, resource mobilization was more about reciprocal commitments, to keep taxes light while raising enough funds to provide certain goods and services. The Chinese state relied on a mix of official and private initiatives to mobilize resources for local institutions, including such projects as the granaries and schools discussed in chapter 5. This flexibility explains in part how the government could meet its commitments in diverse local situations. In Europe, resource claims were more sharply divided among different groups that competed for resources.

The economic impacts of revenue-raising policies differed in China and Europe. European states' efforts to amass wealth in a mercantilist competition with other states promoted some economic expansion, but often at the expense of others. Early modern European merchants and governments enjoyed complex relations of mutual need and support qualified by potentially competing interests, the

---

[7]See Mann 1987. Zelin (1984:51–52) speaks of local government in the eighteenth century holding back commercial revenues rather than forwarding them to the central government, exactly the sort of practice that sometimes concerned high officials.

merchants to secure larger and more dependable sources of profit and governments to extract more resources. Whatever promotion of economic expansion resulted from European revenue policies, this was rarely a deliberate, let alone primary, purpose. Chinese revenue policies directed primarily at agrarian production between the mid-fourteenth and mid-nineteenth centuries neither promoted economic expansion through competition nor facilitated institutional changes. Tax holidays facilitated land clearance, and generally light rates meant that productivity increases accrued mainly to cultivators. Relations with merchants were more limited both economically and politically than they were in Europe.

Raising revenues was a common challenge to states across Eurasia. Between the sixteenth and eighteenth centuries, Chinese and European rulers developed distinctly different capacities to meet their needs for resources. For European rulers, raising revenues involved them in repeated negotiations with elites with whom they competed to make claims on resources. In contrast, Chinese rulers engaged in no formal bargaining process and confronted no institutionalized opposition to their access to revenues. Chinese revenue raising was constrained by the bureaucracy's capacities to mobilize agricultural revenues across an empire and by the commitment to keeping taxes from becoming a heavy burden. With such contrasting fiscal philosophies and strategies, it should come as little surprise that the larger political economies within which these policies were embedded also differed dramatically in China and Europe.

Chinese Political Economy in the Late Imperial Period

The Chinese state maintained an active interest in the agrarian economy, promoting its expansion over larger stretches of territory and its stability through uneven harvest seasons. This agenda had its origins in the centuries preceding imperial unification. The canonical texts taught rulers benevolent ways of rule. We may well wonder how much of an impact these lessons had on rulers of the Warring States period (480 B.C.E.–221 B.C.E.), each of whom was attempting to increase his military and financial resources to expand and defend his territories against antagonists each poised to do the same.

In imperial times, these ideas about benevolence took on deeper meaning. Land distribution schemes in the Han, Sui, and Tang dynasties were modeled on classical precedents to stabilize the people's livelihoods—if people all worked their own holdings, then society would be relatively egalitarian and stable. These social welfare efforts were intimately linked to the logic of resource extraction. The goal of land distribution was the continued recreation of a society of small landowners, each of whom paid taxes to the state. The state was therefore creating its tax base when it allocated land.[8] Moreover, the imperial state during its first millennium of rule repeatedly attempted to establish its autonomy from the magnate families whose independent bases of power were a major threat to state security.

---

[8]The link between land distribution and taxation is reviewed dynasty by dynasty in Zhou 1981.

In short, resource extraction, social welfare, and state autonomy were all goals of state land distribution schemes. By 1100 the magnate families had all been destroyed; a new kind of local elite emerged, the kind that would adopt the Neo-Confucian agenda of social order described earlier. Commercial expansion with cash cropping, improvements in transportation, credit, and marketing institutions also increasingly made land a private commodity to be bought, sold, and passed on to one's sons and less a resource that the state could aspire to distribute. The Song state's expectations of a social order based on Neo-Confucian principles were not immediately pursued by the first Ming emperor. Distrustful of elites and desiring an agrarian world of simplicity and self-sufficiency, Ming Taizu's image of an ideal society faded under succeeding emperors as Ming society again became subject to dynamics of commercial expansion and elites schooled in Neo-Confucian virtues.

By 1500 the late imperial state possessed a complex tradition of policy options to shape economic activity, both to raise revenues and to achieve a stable social order. Official choices fluctuated between two general approaches. First, the state could choose activist and interventionist policies to control or direct economic activities; such efforts included the regulation of mining and the exchange of salt vouchers for grain shipments to troops in the northwest.[9] Second, the state could satisfy itself with monitoring private-sector efforts and even informally delegate responsibility or depend on others to help to achieve its goals; examples include market surveillance and reliance on elites for famine relief (Mann 1987, Will 1990). In between the extremes of direct state control and indirect monitoring lay all sorts of efforts to redirect, channel, or limit private-sector economic practices.

Despite considerable variation in techniques, there was basic agreement through the eighteenth century about the type of economy officials sought to stabilize and expand. They supported an agrarian economy in which commerce had an important role. Disagreements over long-distance versus local commerce, over planting grain versus cash crops, were animated by subsistence anxieties.[10] But in the eighteenth century these differences did not open a large gap between competing visions of how to organize the material world. Commercial activity had come to enjoy a recognized and accepted place in the agrarian economy.

Two centuries earlier the outcome had not been so clear. The expanding commercialism of the sixteenth century provoked anxieties among many educated people. Their criticisms often included nostalgia for simpler times when the pursuit of profit was not so widespread. The continued economic expansion powered by Smithian dynamics rendered the imagining of a simpler world impossible. Chinese officials and thinkers came up with ways to tame commerce and create for it

---

[9]Debates on mining policies during the Qing dynasty are detailed in the archival source materials collected by Qing specialists at People's University; see Zhongguo renmin daxue ed. 1983:1–72. The same collection includes many documents on state capitalization of major mining operations. On salt vouchers and grain shipments to the northwest during the Ming, see Terada 1972:80–119.

[10]The tensions between long-distance and local commerce and between cash crops and grain will be addressed in chapter 9 where grain seizures in China and Europe are compared.

socially acceptable functions. Not all merchant activities were equally acceptable, but the stereotypical notion of a government opposed to merchants and commerce is poorly supported empirically.

Officials understood the basic ideas of market supply and demand, consistent with Adam Smith's notions of how markets promote specialization and exchange. But at the same time they opposed the monopoly behavior of merchants who held grain off local markets to push prices upward. Government policies toward the food supply included, in the eighteenth century, the maintenance of more than one million tons of grain for sale and loans in the lean spring season and in years of especially poor harvest (Will and Wong 1991). Subsistence issues made grain commerce of particular interest to the state. Where markets failed to provision people adequately, officials were likely to take an active role. Government efforts at stabilizing grain distribution complemented elite efforts at making grain available at local levels. The efforts of both officials and elites to influence grain circulation complemented official attempts to promote expanded production through clearance of new lands and improved productivity of existing fields through better seed selection and water control. Grain was a special case because of its fundamental importance to survival. More generally, the late imperial government allowed trade to be carried on without much government oversight and with modest taxation. Most cash crops and handicrafts—fruits, vegetables, medicinal herbs, paper, leather goods, textiles, etc.—circulated across the country through a well-developed marketing system.

In certain situations, however, officials abandoned their support for multiple buyers and sellers in favor of regulated exchange through a small number of merchants. First, the salt monopoly was a revenue maker for the state; licensing the distribution of salt made the state money and made a small number of merchants extremely wealthy. Second, foreign trade was often regulated. Some of this trade belonged within the tribute system, which offered a political as well as economic rationale for exchanges between foreign governments and merchants. Other foreign trade was controlled because the goods involved were of strategic importance. Hence the tea and horse trade with the northwest, for instance, was regulated because of the crucial importance of horses to the military and because revenue could be made on the tea sales. But when trade was neither foreign nor intended primarily as a revenue maker for the government, it was generally given free rein by the state, as long as officials believed that no small number of merchants were able to manipulate supplies and hence prices to the detriment of the consuming public at large.[11] Officials thereby supported commercial exchange without promoting concentrations of merchant wealth.[12]

---

[11]On salt, see Xu Hong 1972 and Chen Feng 1988; overseas foreign trade in the late imperial period is reviewed in detail by Li Jinming 1990 and Lin Renchuan 1987. For the horse and tea trade and northwestern trade more generally, see Lin Yong and Wang Xi 1991.

[12]The eleventh-century official Wang Anshi, a reformer responsible for promoting an activist set of government policies to raise revenues and order society, went so far as to help small-scale merchants with government credit to make them more competitive with large merchants.

While they believed markets to be socially useful, late imperial officials worried about people leaving the land to take to the road in search of profit. Their concerns included worries that people in perpetual or periodic movement were potentially dangerous to social order, which was defined in terms of a sedentary agrarian society in which men worked the fields and women wove cloth and tended the home. Late Ming literature often counseled its readers against the dangers of men taking to the road for months or even years at a time.[13] Another worry more directly connected to the economy concerned a growing taste for luxury and extravagance acquired by people who pursued profits from trade. The superior man was not swayed by the pursuit of advantage or profit; instead he was guided by his quest for Confucian virtues of benevolence and righteousness. The merchant pursuing profit (and not virtue) needed some external constraints on his behavior so that lust for luxury did not overcome Confucian sensibilities of restraint and moderation.[14] Confucian anxieties over the unbridled pursuit of profit qualified Chinese understandings of the market's social usefulness. Chinese officials recognized the virtues of market principles of supply and demand yet abhorred the aggressive pursuit of wealth and prominent displays of extravagance. Within the late imperial Chinese political economy, officials could comfortably promote market exchange and understand how an expanding commercial economy afforded peasants additional opportunities to make a living. But official support for a market economy in which benefits reached the many peasants who bought and sold goods did not mean that the government therefore favored concentrations of wealth gained through market manipulation. Chinese official support for commerce did not mean promotion of commercial capitalism as it developed in Europe.

The ideal Chinese political economy was an agrarian commercial economy in which expansion came from opening new lands and improving productivity on already cultivated fields. Rural industry was clearly conceived as complementary to cash crops; giving women more work to supplement income from the fields was one way to maintain the household economy amidst population expansion. Market exchange helped to balance supply and demand. The Chinese political economy tied production to distribution through its commitment to reducing or ameliorating relative inequalities and guaranteeing absolute minimal standards for survival.

---

[13]One famous example of this sort of literature is "the Pearl-Sewn Shirt" in which the opportunities for amorous misadventures depend on the husband's absence from home on commercial ventures. See Birch 1958:37–96.

[14]Chinese Confucianism may well have afforded resources for merchants to construct a positive view of their activities similar to the example of the Osaka merchants studied by Tetsuo Najita (1987) who promoted a self-justification of their activities in Confucian terms. But differences in social structure between the two countries, specifically the contrast between Japanese merchants who formed a social class distinct from warrior and noble elites and those in China who remained more closely tied to large landowners and officials appears to have limited Chinese possibilities for a distinctly merchant vision of their properly Confucian social role to gain an independent basis from which to compete with the ideals expressed by agrarian and official elites.

In general, the Chinese state promoted agricultural production—opening new land, repairing and expanding water control in order to expand and stabilize production of both grains and cash crops. It also influenced and occasionally regulated commercial distribution of some goods, most importantly grain, in order to achieve equity within local economies and balance across regions; and, when convinced no serious social problems between immigrants and natives would occur, it encouraged migration to form new settlements so that populations and resource bases remained in relative balance. State efforts in these general areas supported a range of economic situations at the end points of which were two distinct types of agrarian economy: a series of small-scale, self-sufficient economies reproduced across an expanding empire; and a complex, large-scale interdependent economy to be monitored and if necessary managed by the state. Increased production and regulated distribution could occur in either type of economy, while migration could create new small-scale economies or frontier communities later integrated into the larger society. The state promoted economic prosperity through both kinds of economies. Officials believed that such actions helped them to gain the support of the people and thereby affirmed the government's mandate to rule.

Images of social stability could be based on the multiplication of healthy cells or on effective ties among diverse elements composing a complex compound. The former, which did not explicitly require a central or even local government's efforts, was present throughout the late imperial period; it was linked to the fractal vision of social order analyzed in Chapter 5. The latter, typical of the eighteenth century, required far more of the state. Through its land reclamation policies, creation of a granary system, and movement of resources into frontier regions, the state actively tried to develop those parts of the empire that private-sector activities alone were not likely to change. In economic cores, the state worried more about inequalities among rich and poor but expected elites to help poorer people to survive and the state to keep local order. This vision of economic prosperity was far more difficult to sustain for long periods of time. As the state enlarged its territory, officials promoted economic expansion to improve material conditions, believing them to be the basis for social order and political stability. When the state became weaker in the nineteenth century, the former idea of creating economic health on more limited, local bases reemerged. In general, officials advocated the development and spread of best practices in agriculture and handicrafts, the basic sources of production in the economy. They supported the principles of market exchange and sought to protect buyers from monopoly power. To the extent that the state succeeded in realizing its aspirations, it increased efficiency and promoted maximum production within the constraints of available technologies.

European Political Economies: From "Just" Prices to Just Prices

Political economy in medieval Europe was generally conceived on a scale reflecting the small size of most political units. Political and religious leaders focused on the importance of markets providing goods without the extreme price variations associated with the manipulations of wealthy merchants. The political context for constructing domestic markets was the displacement of municipal administrations and regional aristocratic assemblies as the primary bodies in charge of economic matters by centralizing territorial states that focused on amassing revenues. As small political units were increasingly challenged by rulers with territorial ambitions, wider commercial networks developed. Territorial states developed as larger market hierarchies penetrated the countryside and integrated many rural people and town dwellers into commercial exchanges with large cities. This development was different from the earlier exchange among major metropolises, which included luxuries brought in from Byzantium, Russia, and the Middle East, as well as goods traded along the Silk Road. In the early modern era, an expansion of maritime international trade was powered by merchants who forged close relations with rulers in the political economy of mercantilism.

Mercantilism, the dominant philosophy of political economy in Europe between the late sixteenth and the early eighteenth century, posed a close relationship between power and wealth. For a state to become powerful, society had to become wealthier. This was achieved by expanding economic production in rich core areas and by extending trade across the country and especially beyond it. Merchants and rulers shared an interest in promoting national production and economic unification in order to keep wages and interest rates low and the land fully exploited. Internationally, a key goal was to build up a positive balance of trade which would increase the domestic money supply, money being essential for prosecuting wars. Analysts treated states like individuals or firms; success was measured by spending (importing) less than one's income (exports). Rulers believed that one nation's commercial gain was achieved at another's loss. Thus competition for wealth on a global scale became a component of European state making. European states promoted the production and commerce of their private entrepreneurs, whose successes contributed to the consolidation and prosperity of competing states.

Foreign trade became a crucial battlefield for states, but early modern maritime trade was often a risky business. A combination of natural misfortunes and man-made dangers threatened commercial voyages. Bad weather and poor winds could delay or destroy a vessel; pirates could do the same. While little could be done about the weather, the arming of ships to defend merchants against pirates was a key component of economic success. The Mediterranean hegemony of the Venetians was based on their ability to protect merchants from predators. But the military skills that protected could also be turned against other merchants. European rulers were anxious to safeguard their own merchants yet eager to plunder ships of other countries. What made maritime trade especially lucrative was monopoly control over some greatly desired good, like tea or pepper. Merchants who enjoyed monopoly privileges backed by armed force to keep out competitors could make great fortunes. The neoclassical economic norm of competition among multiple buyers and sellers was in reality bounded by the two extremes of piracy and monopoly.

When Europeans went to Asia in the late fifteenth century, they arrived first as pirates and interlopers seeking to establish themselves forcibly in the Asian trading network. They achieved their greatest successes in places where they could establish monopolies. In ports where they did not enjoy military supremacy, they became simply new players in the game of Asian trade. Some analysts argue for important differences among the strategies of various European states to gain advantage in Asia; certainly there was a general shift from purely predatory actions to efforts at exacting tribute and establishing monopolies. But the underlying role of military force and coercion was a constant throughout; military power was as important to the European "discovery" of the world as it was to state-making competition within Europe (Parker 1988).

While centralizing governments aimed at concentrating coercive powers domestically, they often allowed these powers to be held by chartered companies in Asia. The close connection between wealth and power in mercantilist logic appears in the variable division between public and private powers within Europe and overseas, in Asia. In the political economy of mercantilist empire, states and merchants initially played complementary roles—states wanted a part of merchant profits and merchants wanted state support to secure greater profits. Mercantilists, however, felt no particular concern about the legitimacy of political power wielded by Europeans over Asian populations. Still, this was not immediately a serious problem for Europeans. What undermined the mercantilist logic were private traders seeking to take advantage of the general framework set up by the chartered companies. English private trader efforts, for instance, undermined the monopoly power of the East India Company in the late eighteenth century.

Adam Smith's critique of mercantilism posed the "free market" economy as the desirable alternative. Domestically, the proponents of free markets had been waging a battle to dismantle various medieval restrictions on trade during the seventeenth and eighteenth centuries. The subsequent changes have been viewed in different ways. One approach to these changes stresses a shift from an active localist political paternalism in the marketplace anxious to defend "just" prices to a laissez-faire strategy by a central government determined to expand the scale and volume of trade (E. P. Thompson 1971). Another approach highlights the state's role in setting the ground rules and affirming the individual property rights that gave people the security and incentives to pursue their self-interest knowing that the fruits of their efforts would be protected (North 1981).[15]

From whatever vantage point one approaches the changing political economy of early modern Europe, in particular that of England and France, one can find new political principles at work. The national state made alliances with certain economic actors as individuals in order to undercut the claims on resources and market control enacted by local political authorities anxious to defend the interests of

---

[15]Not all analysts, however, have stressed the positive features of markets. The uncertain political implications of free-market ideology are traced in different ways in MacPherson 1962, Pocock 1985, and Appleby 1992.

local groups. Local people favored open markets with multiple buyers and sellers. They opposed rich merchants who aimed to establish control over local markets and create connections with distant ones.[16]

As arguments in favor of freer domestic commerce were being aired against the local protectionism that E. P. Thompson called "moral economy," arguments against monopoly control in overseas trade were also being made. Reflecting distinct political and economic situations, the arguments against local protectionism and overseas monopoly came to share the intellectually powerful common denominator of free trade. After Adam Smith trumpeted the virtues of the market and the evils of mercantilism most persuasively, David Ricardo offered the further insight that "comparative advantage" guaranteed that all parties to trade could gain from free market exchange even if one of the parties was uniformly less efficient and productive. Once it could be argued that everyone benefits from trade, irrespective of their initial endowments and skills, free trade made moral sense. The English government could disengage itself from overt manipulation of economic affairs. As the government championed international free trade, English colonial administration grew.

Flanked by growing colonial power, the free-trade logic of England's industrializing economy proved inadequate to establish economic connections between China and Britain. After failing to sell enough cotton textiles or any other English goods to balance their imports of tea, the government agreed to a strategy of growing opium in India for sale in China. England's nineteenth-century economic successes were not, therefore, achieved simply because of its Industrial Revolution or its superior position in a world of free trade, but resulted in part from the English government's continued capacity to set terms of exchange politically and economically, a relic of mercantilism.

The European transformation of political economy began with two rather independent sets of changes, both enacted by the centralizing state. First was the formation of national markets, especially in England, France, and Holland. Second came the intrusion of European traders into Asian trading networks and the movement of European traders and settlers across the Atlantic to the New World. The Industrial Revolution took place in this context of national markets and international trade. The dynamic of industrial changes linked to expanding domestic and foreign commerce was distinctly European. Other parts of the world occupied positions with their own greater or lesser possibilities for economic development.

Comparing Chinese and European Political Economies

When scholars have compared Chinese and European government policies toward the economy, they have often asserted that the Chinese government failed to adopt policies to promote economic development (Hall 1985:53; Jones

---

[16]See Tessie Liu 1994:69–71 for a French example. Additional French and English examples are introduced in chapter 9.

1988:141). They have suggested that European policies led to particular economic changes and that governments deliberately pursued these changes. To make more balanced and revealing contrasts we should remember that state policies did not always produce the intended effects or anticipate the actual results. More important, the evaluation of Chinese policies according to European standards is an incomplete exercise in comparison. Since the motivations behind the Chinese and European political economies were different, I will again evaluate each in terms of the other. Let's begin with attitudes toward production, then move on to evaluation of policies toward markets, merchants, and trade, including brief thoughts on policies toward consumption.

European policies toward production emerging from the medieval period principally concerned urban craft production. Guild regulations on quality, price, and production volume were dismantled as textile production moved to the countryside. While centralizing states did not assert control over rural industries comparable to that of medieval urban authorities over urban industries, they sometimes aspired to control trade of rural textiles.[17] European policies toward production did not extend into the countryside. Not only did they exempt rural industries from the kinds of control typical of medieval urban industries, but they also placed agricultural production largely beyond the political economy of centralizing states. Physiocrats could argue that agriculture was the sole source of wealth, and Adam Smith could stress the importance of agricultural production, but officials did little to expand or improve that production. From a Chinese point of view, these are striking limitations.

Promoting land clearance and irrigation, Chinese officials considered the expansion of agricultural production to be an important goal. Qing emperors ordered the production of agricultural manuals, the information in which was to be disseminated by officials and elites. For example, the Kangxi emperor ordered the compilation of a work on flora in 1708, while the Jiaqing emperor ordered a high government official to compile a work on textile production in 1708 (Deng Gang 1993:127). Most impressive was the imperially ordered compilation of the *Shoushi tongkao* (Compendium of works and days), a five-year project undertaken by fifteen court scholars. The Qianlong emperor personally wrote the preface to this massive tome, stating in part:

> The foundation of society is agriculture. . . . [I] gave my edict to the court scholars to search widely to collect information regarding the significance of phenology, the different soil types in the North and South, the timing of tillage, methods of storage and the management of sericulture and animal husbandry. . . . This compilation contains all works written on agriculture and [states that] the peasantry will receive respect, and that people will work hard; and that the whole society, the ruling and the ruled, will exert themselves unremittingly. (Deng Gang 1993:35)

---

[17]For an example of an inspector of manufacturers exasperated over his inability to subject rural textiles to the policing of trade that was an urban monopoly, see Vardi 1993:147.

Chinese agrarian political economy served a broader political strategy for promoting social stability. This same outlook framed official approaches to rural industry.

Unlike rural textile weaving in Europe, which was often the work of male weavers who no longer tilled the fields, Chinese textiles were woven by women. Chinese state promotion of production envisioned a household division of labor in which men ploughed the fields and women wove textiles at home. Household handicraft production for the market helped to anchor people in their communities and kept them from becoming mobile labor in search of jobs in cities or other regions. Officials wished to promote economic production in a manner that allowed them to champion a social order in which women stayed at home even as their work became increasingly destined for markets (Mann 1992).

The cultural context for the development of rural industry in China was thus created, at least in part, by explicit official desires to perpetuate an ideal agrarian social order amidst a growing commercial economy. The state's concern over both economic and social issues is clear. The overall coherence of a political economy in which the reproduction of particular statuses was conceived by the state as part of a larger program for social order confirms how Chinese views of political economy were part of a larger world vision.

European states did not pursue such grand visions of ordering the agrarian economy. Agrarian social organization varied dramatically across Europe. In some areas of Central and Eastern Europe, nobles wielded a heavy hand over peasant lives, but in most of Western Europe, peasants pursued their interests and desires without any political force, moral or coercive, shaping their decisions directly. The widespread custom of sending young women into domestic service formed a common phase in the life cycle; this customary mobility made the transition to urban employment, including factory employment, a relatively straightforward move, at least far easier than in China where a political and social ideology constantly celebrated women's roles within the household (Hohenberg and Lees 1885:145–46, 190, 210–13; Mann 1992). When such twentieth-century opportunities were created by foreign forces in the hinterlands of major cities, especially that of Shanghai, many women streamed into the cities to fill the textile mills. There was consequently a rupture in the Confucian political economy of women's work. The point is not that it was impossible to move Chinese women into urban factories, but rather that such a move seemed neither reasonable nor desirable as long as a Confucian political economy dominated, and that a Confucian political economy thus could not easily accommodate industrial change. Regardless of ideological preferences, if the material advantages of one option outweigh those of another, some people will take the former despite the resistance of others.[18]

---

[18]Jack Goldstone (1996) suggests that the Confucian family system hampered Chinese industrialization before 1911. He cites South China lineage rules to account for the movement of silk spinners in this region into factories relatively early (pp. 16–17). But if removal of the Confucian family system leads to industrialization, factories should have sprung up far earlier, for the lineage system he cites was

Shifting from production to commerce, Chinese and European government attitudes toward markets and merchants had some traits in common. Both Chinese and European officials understood the principles of supply and demand. Both believed that markets and merchants could serve useful social purposes. For Europeans, markets became a tool to calm the passions of warlike people; commerce was a more acceptable outlet for man's aggressive tendencies because it could succeed in taming these passions (Hirschman 1977). Chinese thinkers also pondered men's passions and their desire for profit. But they had no notion of the merchant as warrior substitute. Instead, they faced the Neo-Confucian problem of how superior men could govern a world in which smaller people acted in pursuit of profit. Neo-Confucian political and moral leaders could never bring themselves to promote the virtues of the market as a tool of social control (as Europeans might), but this inability to valorize profit making politically doesn't mean that they opposed the principles of market economy. Chinese leaders still valued merchants and their markets for the social good their activities brought.

But while Chinese officials appreciated the merchant's role, they remained anxious about the pursuit of luxury that trade engendered. Officials reasoned that extravagant weddings and funerals as well as the consumption of finer objects wasted precious resources. They proceeded from the assumption that social wealth was limited; therefore elites should not squander these resources on unnecessary indulgences. A theme of frugality surfaced in the eighteenth century after consumption of marketed goods expanded. We currently lack much research on patterns of Chinese consumption to parallel the rich literature on this topic in European studies. Craig Clunas (1991), who pioneered the study of late imperial consumption, cautions us against assuming that the development of European consumption patterns was unique. But since the role of consumption in Europe is not yet clear, comparisons are difficult to make.[19] After the burst of commercial change in the Ming dynasty, eighteenth-century officials discouraged ostentatious consumption of luxury items. Conspicuous displays of wealth were frowned upon. Reservations about conspicuous consumption did not prevent merchants from going about their business but may have limited the demand for certain goods.

The creation of long-distance market networks in Europe was in the hands of capitalists whose profit-driven behavior was tied in some commercializing locales

---

operating long before the 1870s. More important, I suspect it was industrialization that influenced the family system rather than the reverse. Once the transformative possibilities of technological change became known in China, they created new institutions, such as factories, and modified other institutions, including family systems. When industrial methods achieved clear productive superiority, the Confucian family system did not stop new technologies from being adopted. Now Confucian principles no longer made sense, and they were abandoned.

[19]Some historians have argued that England began to form a consumer society in the eighteenth century. De Vries's "industrious revolution" pushes the increase in market consumption back to the mid–seventeenth century. More research on Chinese patterns of consumption is needed, as is an analysis of how consumption patterns may have affected economic change.

to class differentiation. In China there were changes in tenancy rates, sometimes associated with commercialization, but none of the sharp redefinition of rural social structures entailed by enclosures. Different political arguments about the role of commerce did not clearly promote or constrain the economic role of markets at either end of Eurasia. But state policies did affect official relations with wealthy merchants, which in turn created different institutions of political economy. European merchants provided far greater resources to the states than Chinese traders did, while European states were motivated to meet their own fiscal needs, not by any abstract desire to develop the economy itself.

Much European commercial wealth was tapped by needy governments anxious to expand their revenue bases to meet the ever-escalating expenses of war. From the fourteenth through the eighteenth century, the Chinese government, in contrast, taxed trade lightly, except on rare occasions. Amidst the mercantilist competition among European merchants and their governments for wealth and power, maritime expansion played a role of particular importance. Both European merchants and their governments benefited from their complex relationship, the former gaining fabulous profits, the latter securing much-needed revenues.

The late imperial Chinese state did not develop the same kind of mutual dependence on rich merchants. Lacking the scale of fiscal difficulties encountered in Europe between the sixteenth and eighteenth centuries, Chinese officials had less reason to imagine new forms of finance, huge merchant loans, and the concept of public as well as private debt. Not only did they depend little on mercantile wealth to support the state, they also feared the potentially disruptive consequences of both concentrated wealth and the *pursuit* of such wealth. This opposition to what might have become a kind of commercial capitalism, had the government needed the merchants more and thus been supportive of them, does not mean that officials opposed markets and commerce more generally.

I argue for a crucial political component to my distinction between market economy and commercial capitalism, based on Fernand Braudel's discussion of economic behavior, actors, and institutions.[20] Market exchange among many buyers and sellers at prices determined by supply and demand conditions is economically and socially very different from the transactions masterminded by a small number of very rich merchants who can set the terms of exchange with producers and consumers to make large profits, often minimizing competition through monopoly and force. European governments created the conditions for commercial capitalism both within Europe and across the globe. The Chinese

---

[20] Braudel's monumental three-volume work *Civilization and Capitalism, 15th–18th Century* (1981–84) develops a basic distinction between market economy and capitalism. Braudel, especially in vol. 2, argues for the widespread presence of market exchange in Eurasia in the early modern period. He suggests that capitalism, however, is more of a distinctly European phenomenon. While not all scholars agree with Braudel's arguments about the uniquely European character of commercial capitalism or his ideas of how capitalism builds on a market economy, the basic distinction between market economy and capitalism is an important one. A more concise presentation of Braudel's idea of the differences between market economy and capitalism can be found in Braudel 1977:39–78.

state, in contrast, had no incentive to promote any sort of capitalism. This statement is different from the common complaint that the Chinese state somehow blocked market activities and commerce.[21] The Chinese state, I argue, supported a market economy in an agrarian society but did not promote much commercial capitalism, excepting those merchants engaged in monopolies for salt and foreign trade. Chinese officials created conditions for the formation of considerable merchant wealth either when they needed to tap merchant wealth for resources, as with the salt monopoly or when they were controlling foreign access to China. In general, Chinese rulers had no reason to imagine, let alone promote, the mercantilist policies invented by European rulers.[22]

It is hard to imagine intense striving for foreign trade in a Confucian political economy. Chinese officials did not see overseas exploration as money making for the state; nor did they imagine for very long that overseas explorations could be politically empowering. Chinese officials had little use for foreign trade revenues. They knew from Zheng He's early fifteenth-century voyages that large expeditions were exceedingly expensive operations. As for Chinese traders who pursued trade with Northeast and Southeast Asia in growing numbers between the sixteenth and eighteenth centuries, the government adopted different policies according to whether they viewed this trade as a threat to domestic security or a source of social stability. With an agrarian ideal of sedentary life, all people in motion were potential sources of anxiety, be they monks, merchants, or pilgrims. Those whose sphere of movement brought them into contact with foreigners were even more suspicious because these were people most likely to be exposed to heterodox beliefs. Worst of all, maritime trade was growing more bellicose in the sixteenth and seventeenth centuries as Europeans brought armed force into what had been peaceful Asian trading networks. The line between trade and piracy was becoming obscure. Ironically, however, Chinese state efforts to prohibit foreign trade in order to improve social order only increased piracy because they made all trade by definition illegal. Government hostility to trade vacillated in the seventeenth century with concerns for the livelihoods of those who depended on the sea to survive. The awareness that some people in coastal areas depended on trade for their livelihoods inspired proponents of trade to urge the government to allow foreign trade (Shen 1985; Li Jinming 1990; Lin Renchuan 1987).

---

[21] See Balasz 1964; Hall 1985; Hong 1983; Jones 1981, 1988.

[22] There are scholars who have characterized some Chinese policies as mercantilist. Paul Smith's (1991) study of the Song dynasty Tea and Horse Agency characterizes Wang Anshi's policies as "mercantilist." Helen Dunstan (1997) has identified one general concern of eighteenth- and early nineteenth-century officials with wealth as mercantilist. Kenneth Pomeranz (1993) also used the term to highlight late nineteenth-century concerns for strengthening the state at national, provincial and local levels. These scholars all have good reasons for employing the term "mercantilist," but the policies they review do not always parallel European ones. Thus, when explicitly comparing European and Chinese policies as I am here, it seems prudent to limit the use of the term "mercantilist" to European cases. Even though there are certain ways in which the term applies to some Chinese policies, for most of the period I am covering, the differences between Chinese and European policies are, in my opinion, even more striking.

Because European mercantilist states of the early modern period conceived themselves to be engaged in a competition for wealth and power, they stressed foreign trade and in particular the importance of massing silver at the expense of other governments and merchants. In contrast to European states, the Chinese government saw merchants as but one of many sources of fiscal security and political power and legitimacy. As a result, Chinese merchants, especially the many of modest scale, had a socially useful function but no political importance as a group. European merchants, however, as part of the urban elite, played an important political role as well as an economically crucial one.

Whether we consider institutions or ideologies, European and Chinese systems of political economy exhibit basic differences. European mercantilism gave competing European states a common interest in expanding the spatial dimensions of their economies. Early modern colonialism was one project to build the wealth and power of European countries. One country's successes came from displacing another from some colonial site or by beating others to new unclaimed spaces. The fates of the societies into which Europeans inserted themselves was not part of the mercantilist calculus. European states were especially interested in competition with their rivals for resources, products, and money. Strong economies competed with each other to amass money and exploit gains to be made from colonies.

This logic of political economy stressing competition with foreign states had little in common with China's stress on domestic exchange expected to benefit all parties. The Chinese state supported the expansion of production and trade but could not imagine, let alone approve, of a scheme in which a competitive zero-sum game pitted provinces against one another. Chinese officials expected commerce to be generally fair and effective in distributing goods according to supply and demand. Where commerce was poorly developed, the state invested money to promote production and exchange. Rather than extract resources from peripheries, the Chinese state was more likely to invest in them. Political expansion to incorporate new frontiers committed the government to a shift of resources to the peripheries, not extraction from them. Late imperial Chinese political economy obeyed a set of principles very much at odds with those of mercantilism.

China expanded its empire through a combination of moral, material, and coercive means with a principal goal of achieving security and stability. As a territorial empire, the government recognized spheres of influence. While not borders in the modern geographical sense, the Chinese state nevertheless imagined spatially defined zones contiguous to each other. European empires of the early modern period were, of course, fundamentally different. The mercantilist goal was to amass as great a portion of the more or less fixed wealth in the world as possible.

European dynamics of imperial expansion embraced commercial, political, and military factors; the benefits of naval power were not merely military since mastery of the seas meant the capacity to reap material rewards by controlling long-distance trade. The Chinese did not perceive foreign trade to be so lucrative. Though they had a considerable navy in the early fifteenth century, certainly the most powerful in Asia, they did not envision using it to establish militarily an economic position of dominance. Unable to see any point—moral, material, or military—to plundering others, the late imperial Chinese state moved between the sixteenth and eighteenth centuries to regulate its contacts with foreign merchants whom it considered dangerous. As Europeans became bellicose in Asia, the Chinese moved to protect their empire from these potentially disruptive influences. They allowed Chinese merchants to pursue their trading activities in Southeast and Northwest Asia without incorporating them centrally into their political economy, a move obvious to European thinkers.

Chinese political economy was intended to capture the benefits of expanded production and exchange through policies that increased production and stabilized trade. Officials promoted the spread of best practices with the goal of closing the gap between what was economically possible and what current practices permitted. Within the limits of its capacities, the government succeeded in its aim of achieving a kind of static efficiency. But aiming for and achieving short-term static efficiencies does not exceed the basic limitations of an organic economy. In fact, early modern European political economy could not break the bounds of an organic economy either. The crucial distinction between the Chinese and European political economies was the greater adaptability of the latter to industrial possibilities. As I suggested earlier, commercial capitalism was logically independent of the changes that E. A. Wrigley labeled the shift from an organic to an inorganic economy. But European institutions of commercial capitalism were able to take advantage of industrial possibilities swiftly. The Chinese political economy, although it had some well-developed market institutions, lacked the range of financial markets, business organizations, and resource bases created by commercial capitalism supported by European states bent upon making themselves stronger and wealthier than their competitors.

Industrialization in Capitalist and Agrarian Economies

The great economic transformation of industrial capitalism was to integrate and expand economic production and distribution on spatial scales undreamed of before. One way to gain a sense of this transformation is to consider once again the connections among Braudel's three levels of economic activity—material life, market economy, and capitalism—after the Industrial Revolution. Industrialization accelerates the integration of material life, market economy, and capitalism to levels not possible in preindustrial times. Nineteenth-century Europe became more commercially integrated at the same time as industrial capitalism took a commanding position in the economy. Indeed, the integration achieved through roads, railroads, and canals was itself constructed through a combination of state and private mechanisms to amass capital and with technologies developed during industrialization. Integration of a different sort took place across the globe as increasing portions of the world were brought into a Western-dominated economy. But some analysts exaggerate, in my opinion, the nature and significance of these connections forged by Western political economies with the rest of the world.

Certainly commercial capitalism and industrial capitalism forged a network of political and economic linkages that began to take shape in the sixteenth century. But it has proven all too easy for scholars to read backward from a mid-twentieth-century perspective to the nature of economic and political relationships in the past. The sixteenth-century "world system" linked a few seaports and their hinterlands across a great maritime space, but created few economic linkages within the societies at any distance from these ports. Varying degrees of exchange and integration within different social and cultural universes took place more or less independently of this maritime network. Thus Chinese domestic trade developed on a European scale but had little connection to overseas trade. In other places, however, a stronger integration into maritime networks could prove fatal to major economic activities, like that experienced in South Asia where Asia's greatest textile producers were destroyed by British cottons (Perlin 1983). While the production of cotton textiles was decimated in India, it continued in China with both positive and negative effects from international trade.

One way to see immediately that the Europeans did not create a world economy defining all the roles even in the nineteenth and twentieth centuries is to recognize that industrialization fits into distinctive political economies in various ways. Industrialization need not blend with a market economy to form advanced industrial capitalism as it has in Western Europe and North America. The key elements of the European experiences are as follows: a connection between Smithian market expansion and industrialization, and the link between capitalism and the market economy described by Braudel. Braudel's capitalism is the amassing of superprofits by rich merchants who avoid the control of market forces; capitalists are those actors who can invoke monopoly power and grasp large amounts of resources with impunity. Industrialization begins to connect the market economy and Braudel's capitalism in the nineteenth century.

Industrialization did not develop swiftly within a Chinese political economy of agrarian empire for several reasons. One was a lack of institutional flexibility, an inability to create new economic institutions easily. In part this occurred because the commercial institutions the Chinese had already established worked well. Industry's initial lack of superiority in consumer products, in particular textiles, meant there was little incentive to develop an alternative institutional framework.

Another issue was that, in areas where new industry did not overlap with earlier forms of production, as in new armaments and shipping, its conceived purpose was to strengthen the state. Since Europe never had an elaborate agrarian political economy, it had nothing to displace that matched the Chinese system's scale and importance. Through the eighteenth century, Chinese political economy attended to its main concerns—mobilizing sufficient resources and promoting social stability—by consciously limiting its fiscal extraction and spending bureaucratic energy and financial resources on projects to prop up the empire's economic and social infrastructure.

In the nineteenth century, Western challenges created a new preoccupation with wealth and power, similar to earlier European mercantilist anxieties. The Chinese now faced the challenge of strengthening the state through policies that helped it amass both wealth and power. Industrialization could be, and was, pursued to strengthen the state. But industrialization was not seen as benefiting society generally. In a political economy suited to agrarian empire in which improvements were achieved by affording people opportunities to gain what others already enjoyed, where equalizing conditions for production was seen as a means to promote expansion, industrialization was potentially disruptive and subversive because it could create regional disparities and promote class differences.

European political economy did not create industrialization, nor was the European political economy deliberately designed to promote industrialization. Instead, European political economy created a set of institutions able to promote industrialization once it appeared. The European political economy was not burdened with issues of regional or class equity, so Europeans could ignore the economic problems of areas not favored by industrialization and the problems of class differentiation that concerned Confucian thinkers. The ideology of free trade argued that everyone benefited from trade, but nineteenth-century European governments and capitalists continued to see themselves as competing, no longer just to accrue wealth and power but to advance their societies and make "progress." Despite these differences, industrialization did take place in twentieth-century China, but this China was no longer an agrarian empire.

7

THE CHINESE STATE
AFTER 1850

The international system of states created by European expansion imposes real constraints on and sets specific expectations for proper behavior among states. Separate from interstate behavior are the dynamics of domestic changes in state–society relations. While some analysts privilege the interstate axis, most also recognize the domestic axis of state–society relations. The major challenge for our analyses of state formation in the nineteenth and twentieth centuries is to show how the interstate and domestic axes together define the space within which groups reproduce and transform their states. The relative importance of the two axes may well vary from country to country as a function of size and length of organized political history preceding contact with the West. According to both criteria, the domestic axis of Chinese state making in the nineteenth and twentieth centuries commands our attention.

The domestic axis of state making in nineteenth- and twentieth-century China was not, of course, free from Western influences. Western states provided models to be imitated (or consciously rejected) by others. Leaders deliberately adopted strategies for achieving political goals (imported from beyond the society) that represented specific kinds of political change. But new expectations for change based on what others have achieved in very different environments do not guarantee success. Unintended consequences are often the product of a rather poor fit between blueprints for change and current realities. Provincial assemblies in late Qing China, for instance, were unable to achieve a stable and secure role in either a constitutional monarchy or a republican form of government. They helped to topple the imperial system but did not come out of the 1911 Revolution with clear and effective functions (Fincher 1981, Nathan 1985). Just as state making in China and Europe had very different dynamics before the nineteenth and twentieth centuries, they continued to differ even as Western models became available and as China became more fully part of a world system based on Western concepts and experiences.

State Making in Nineteenth-Century China

Conventional wisdom tells us that the nineteenth-century Chinese state was unable to cope with the challenges of domestic rebellion and foreign pressures (Fairbank 1978). In part, this assessment rests upon the ultimate failure of the dynasty in 1911 and the tracking of its "inevitable" demise back to its troubled relations with foreigners and rebels. A retrospective view easily ignores how the state perceived its problems and what it actually could and did do to address its difficulties.

From a modern nationalist point of view, the Europeans imposed a series of unequal treaties that compromised Chinese sovereignty. The failure of China to gain acceptance in the international system created by the Europeans contrasts with early twentieth-century Japanese success in gaining equal diplomatic status. True enough, but how did China fail? Was China so weak that the state was simply unable to prevent a series of humiliating treaties being imposed on it? Perhaps not. China's tradition of dealing with foreigners, largely the steppe peoples to the north, formed the frame of reference within which China first approached Europeans (Fletcher 1978:375–85). Allowing Westerners to reside in specific places in China and making them responsible for their own affairs (extraterritoriality) made good sense to the Qing state based on Chinese experience with steppe peoples. Regulating foreign trade with the use of foreigners as Chinese customs officials meant that the Chinese relied on intermediaries to deal with the foreigners; since customs revenue later became much more important than originally anticipated, the Qing government's initial desire to use foreigners and to agree to a low tariff could not have seemed as unreasonable to Qing officials as it does to us. Moreover, before the Sino-Japanese War of 1894–95 and the Boxer Uprising of 1899–1900, when foreign powers imposed massive indemnities, at least some Chinese could feel reasonably confident that they were handling the new challenges of foreigners. Ultimately, they would discover that dealing with Western foreigners using strategies developed for Inner Asian peoples did not work. But we invoke a kind of tragic fatalism if we argue that Chinese approaches to Western foreign relations were necessarily doomed to failure. Domestic challenges to the state seemed far more threatening in the nineteenth century.

From 1850 to 1873 the Chinese state faced major rebellions across much of its territory. The Taiping Rebellion (1850–64) began in the mountains of Guangxi and moved through central China and then along the Yangzi River to proclaim its capital at Nanjing; establishing a regime that effectively precluded Qing control over part of China's richest region, the suppression of the Taiping demanded major mobilizations of resources and new strategies for forming armies. To the north raged the Nian Rebellion (1851–68); Nian armies roamed the Huai River region and, because they were deemed less of a threat than the Taiping, were not suppressed until after the Taiping was defeated. Separate from both of these were the multiple uprisings by Muslims in the northwest and southwest, the last of which was not suppressed until 1873.

Mobilizing men and resources to defeat this diverse spectrum of rebels demanded both fiscal and organizational innovations. In addition to implementing internal transit taxes (*likin*) to raise funds to support the armies fighting the various rebels, foreign loans secured against future customs revenues were used to put down the Muslim revolts. Some provincial officials became increasingly powerful through their control over new regional armies that defeated the rebels. But most of the regional armies were demobilized in the 1870s, and the central state could celebrate its success at meeting the mid-century challenges of rebellion. Indeed, the conquest of Xinjiang and formation of routine civilian administration in this northwest frontier region in the 1870s reflects impressive military strength, at least in the arena of competition and concern that had been the Chinese state's principal focus before Westerners became a serious threat. While the imperial state did not enjoy the degree of central initiative and control common in the eighteenth century, the empire remained an integrated political unit with policy making coordinated across its provinces. This state proved militarily powerful enough to consolidate its borders far inside Central Asia, a sharp contrast to our expectations of military weakness based on interactions with Westerners.

Internationally the Chinese lost influence in Vietnam to the French, but until the Sino-Japanese War of 1895 the central government could reasonably feel secure in its foreign affairs. Slow modifications in its view of the world and foreign relations to accommodate European approaches were taking place. The Zongli yamen under the grand Council was established in 1861 to deal with foreign relations in Peking. In addition, there were two commissioners to deal with foreign affairs in Nanjing and Tianjin who reported directly to the emperor. Officials began to establish steamship lines and railways, and to move from heavy industries with military applications to light industries like textiles. The state proved able to mobilize vast new sums of money, first to put down the rebellions and then to expand the range of activities it supported in the late nineteenth century.

In 1849 the government raised some 42.5 million taels of revenue, 77 percent of which came from agriculture and the balance from commerce; thirty-six years later revenues had climbed to more than 77 million taels, the increase being largely the result of a quadrupling of commercial revenues. The capacity to increase revenues in this manner is hardly the sign of a weak state; one sign of centralizing power among early modern European states, after all, was their growing capacity to extract revenues. The development of Chinese central government control over customs revenues is a clear indication of the state's ability to create new infrastructural capacities. Expenditure levels remained in the range of 30–40 million taels annually between the 1720s and the early 1840s; they then doubled to 70–80 million taels annually between the 1860s and early 1890s (Hamashita 1989:66).

Much of the increased revenue was raised through the Maritime Customs collections; in addition to being used as security on foreign loans and paying for suppressing the 1867 Muslim rebellion in northwest China, customs revenues were used in the 1880s to build railroads (Hamashita 1989:68, 72). When the late nineteenth-century central government is not judged by its failure to survive beyond 1911 but is instead compared with the eighteenth-century central government, its fiscal capacities were clearly augmented, in part because it adapted certain foreign methods of raising funds.[1] But these increases were nothing compared to the nearly 302 million taels of revenue gathered in 1911, the final year of the dynasty—agricultural taxes had grown from roughly 30 to roughly 50 million taels, with another 45 million from miscellaneous sources. More than 207 million came from commercial taxes—whatever the late Qing state's weaknesses, raising money was not among them (Wei Guangqi 1986:227). Unfortunately, the Japanese indemnity equaled a full year's receipts and the Boxer indemnity was one and a half times that. These are the charges that made China's fiscal situation so precarious and ultimately untenable. Such a catastrophe was not by any means predestined. A less onerous burden would have left the Qing state in far better fiscal health.

And yet China's weak financial condition, however undesirable, was not the immediate cause for the dynasty's fall. Instead, what proved decisive was the central government's inability to control its newly formed army units, staffed by officers trained in Western military skills, and the provincial assemblies, composed of elites pressing for a formal voice in policy making. Had the state proven more successful in managing these challenges, it is conceivable that even the extraordinary fiscal strains put upon the state by foreign powers could have been surmounted. In any event, it was not old problems that brought the dynasty down, but new forces and difficulties intimately associated with foreign relations. Buffeted by uncertainty on many fronts, the Qing state lost its ability to articulate and implement an agenda for rule.

Focusing exclusively on the forces that brought the dynasty down, however, causes us to miss the relevance of the late imperial agenda of rule for the postimperial period. We fall prey to the easy assumption that the late Qing state's failure to meet the "modern" threats of the foreigners accounts for all the challenges faced by postimperial states. This approach implicitly dismisses as irrelevant what the late imperial state did to achieve and reproduce social order domestically. In particular, we downplay the significance of state control over local social order, an order that continued after 1911 to be largely agrarian and to cover tremendous stretches of territory.

Considering China's nineteenth-century state in terms of challenges, capacities, claims, and commitments offers a perspective on nineteenth-century changes

---

[1]Hamashita 1989 and Peng Zeyi 1983 both discuss the expansion of state revenues and expenditures after the 1860s. Like Wei 1986, they generally see a weakening of central government control over finances. Li Sanmou, however, reminds us that, even if provinces did develop considerable autonomy in the collection of new taxes, they used them in the 1860s and 1870s to fulfill central government financial needs (Li Sanmou 1990:334). By the closing decades of the nineteenth century, the central government asserted more control over revenue mobilization and disbursal.

based on earlier dynamics rather than the future collapse of the dynasty. Within such a framework, the conventional view of a weak state does have some foundation. In particular, the central government of 1850 had diminished capacities to mount and sustain the kinds of bureaucratic management typical of the mid-eighteenth century that would have promoted economic infrastructure and met social welfare concerns. This decline was in part the result of a shift from providing services to promoting defenses against rebellion. In military terms the state showed great flexibility and success, both in raising needed revenues and in mobilizing the men needed to put down the rebels.

The return to peace also found officials renewing their commitments to agrarian social order and prosperity. Officials, sometimes in concert with gentry elites, sponsored land reclamation and development projects, as well as social welfare institutions in the years following the rebellions. When a massive famine struck northern and northwestern China between 1876 and 1879, the central government, elites, and foreign-inspired relief efforts intervened in a major and dramatic fashion. The government's limited bureaucratic and fiscal resources alone were no match for a famine of this magnitude. A new form of nonstate initiative for famine relief, relying on the energies and resources of Jiangnan elites, played a key role in overall relief efforts (Rankin 1986:142–47). As the government proved inadequate to the task of moving resources, Jiangnan elites developed new abilities and desires to address domestic crises well beyond their home area. In their own areas, the Confucian view of local order underwent some changes. In the postrebellion years Jiangnan model of local order incorporated gentry into officially supervised bureaus, strengthening the formal quality of elite participation in sustaining local order. But the vertically integrated political infrastructure that made these efforts a state-coordinated empirewide program was less in evidence than before.

The diminished capacities of the central state in post-1850 China can be explained, in part, by the new challenges imposed by imperialism. Kenneth Pomeranz (1993) has argued persuasively that this was the reason for the shift in state commitments in inland North China. The central government chose to abandon areas it had previously maintained along the Grand Canal in order to concentrate resources in coastal areas where the threat of imperialism was more immediate and dangerous, and shifted its priorities to mobilizing new revenues and meeting foreign challenges.

A second form of foreign challenge with greater implications for the domestic axis of state making came with the blueprints for local reforms, including police forces and schools, as well as plans at the national level for building new armies. The new organizational structures proposed in the last decade of Qing rule would have displaced earlier forms of central government organization and expanded the functions of local government. But the institutional changes necessary to realize these reforms could not be completed before the dynasty was toppled by the revolt of New Army troops no longer loyal to the emperor and by provincial assemblies of elites who no longer believed in the central government's ability to secure China's future in the dramatically changing world of the early twentieth century.

Chinese Trajectories of State Making in the Twentieth Century

Assessments of "modern" political change in China, not surprisingly, often appropriately, and perhaps even unavoidably focus on ideas and institutions of Western origin. While there may be good reason to defend Western political values and to make normative judgments about regimes we like and do not like around the globe, our analytical capacity to discern political dynamics should not be restricted to the possibilities defined by those values. Identifying foreign with modern and domestic with traditional is typical of political figures as well as later analysts; such an exercise reveals how political possibilities are imagined. But such exercises often neglect the historical contexts within which political institutions are created, sustained, transformed, and destroyed.

The European epic of modern state formation embraces two narratives—the cheerful story of parliamentary institutions and democratic ideology and the drama of aggressive centralization of power by growing national bureaucracies that increased their claims on social resources through fiscal extraction and engaged in war. Indeed, the two processes proceeded in uneasy tension as much as they complemented each other. The late imperial Chinese state's labors to implement a Confucian agenda for domestic order as part of its efforts to promote the continued reproduction of the agrarian empire created a dynamic unlike Europe's. How the ideological and institutional dynamics of Chinese state transformation changed after the collapse of the last dynasty remains poorly understood.

We can distinguish two related components of China's postimperial state-making dynamics. The first concerns the familiar problem of ruling rural China: officials made renewed efforts to penetrate village society in order to mobilize additional resources and organize more activities. Here the issue is how local government integration into higher levels of state activity—either provincial or regional, as during the warlord years, or national, which was the goal of the Nationalist Party during the Nanjing Decade (1927–36)—differed from late imperial experiences. How were normative, material, and coercive methods of control over the countryside reconfigured in the twentieth century? Since the agenda of political rule could not escape the constant presence of Chinese peasants, what opportunities for redefining state rule existed?

The second issue is the concentration of political resources and power in the urban centers of core regions, paralleling the concentration of economic resources, labor, and capital in the same areas. Central government increasingly became urban government in the first half of the twentieth century. Officials faced new kinds of challenges, such as forming a banking system; they also gained new capacities, such as the bureaucratic ability to consolidate control over various commercial taxes. People in cities did not expect the same commitments as peasants did, but they did make new claims on the government. These developments were certainly influenced by Western ideas and practices, but were they leading to patterns of thought and behavior common in the industrial and urban West?

Finally, postimperial urban developments suggest a larger problem regarding the relationship between urban and rural: how could urban polities constructed increasingly by elites separated from the countryside create capacities and commitments to rule rural China? The dynamics of postimperial state transformation in rural China and in urban China were not clearly tied together either ideologically or institutionally.

Ruling Rural China in Postimperial Times

The transformation of local social order in the unsettled years of warlord rule and the Nationalist decade involved competing and complex processes. On the one hand, elites took more explicit and formal roles in village governance; ties between landlords and officials grew closer as rent and tax payments were increasingly enmeshed in richer areas like Jiangnan (Bernhardt 1992:161–88). On the other hand, villages in some areas tended to become increasingly corporate and to close themselves off from forces of violence and extraction, be these bandits, civilian officials, or warlords. Governments in the first half of the twentieth century aspired to various goals: all worked to mobilize more revenues, while some aimed to supply new services like schools (whether desired or not), and the Nationalists in particular made normative Confucian appeals through their "New Culture" movement. Effective government penetration into rural areas varied dramatically in the twentieth century, with more pronounced extremes than in late imperial times. Where government succeeded it became more intrusive, but where it failed it was increasingly irrelevant in a militarized and dangerous environment. What then might have happened differently in the Chinese countryside during this period? What could have twentieth-century state builders in China have done? How would those alternatives have compared and contrasted with Western developments?

Philip Huang gives one answer to these questions in his 1985 study of North China. In the context of his interest in agrarian economy, Huang presents an analysis of village–state relations in modern China. He begins with the Qing dynasty when, he suggests, the state had little impact on peasant lives. He sees government attempting to make its presence felt principally through tax collection, a process he finds bedeviled by corruption and inefficiencies. North China villages, largely free of state administration, lacked gentry elites or lineages that would have created networks beyond the village. For Huang, the North China village was a collectivity largely isolated from the state (and the market). He sees two distinct processes affecting villages in the twentieth century: (1) closure against intrusion from outside; and (2) collapse of community amidst proletarianization. He contrasts these processes with a counterfactual about "local political change" as "modern bureaucratization." Huang suggests "Had the Republican government developed a truly modern administrative apparatus, had the Guomindang actually possessed the machinery with which to implement its ideal of a modern party, then the story of local political change would have been simply one of modern bureaucratization. Agents of the state would have penetrated deeply into local society and village communities, in the fashion of the People's Republic" (Huang 1985:289).

This argument posits the phenomenon of modern bureaucratization which depends on a "truly modern administrative apparatus." The concept of bureaucratization was initially developed in the study of Western political changes. One defining characteristic of a modern Western state is its bureaucratic infrastructure, giving it the capacities to mobilize revenues and make decisions on a rule-bound and routine basis. What modern Western bureaucracies end up choosing to do seems obvious; political life has many apparently necessary features—laws, armies, schools, social services, and a framework for economic activity. But the Chinese case reminds us that end points of bureaucratization can include as central features phenomena that are not salient in Western cases.

Huang's counterfactual assessment of political change during Republican times assumes an arc of deeper state penetration of local society "in the fashion of the People's Republic" which is not at all the pattern of bureaucratization and use of administrative apparatus found in the West. Such changes are not characteristic of modern states; local political change in China is not simply a story of modern bureaucratization. It is as much a story of popular mobilization and social control, a narrative in which new local leaders and outside cadres both played the roles of heroes in the search for villains and enemies. The driving concern to order agrarian society in postimperial times makes sense only in the context of how Chinese politics in late imperial and postimperial times imagined the possibilities for ruling and the resources with which they could construct institutions of rule.

In the late imperial period, the state pursued material strategies to affect peasants' lives as well as coercive ones. The state's success at these efforts, not surprisingly, varied across space and time. To posit, as Huang does, a Qing baseline that is empirically based on post-1850 North China conditions ignores the far greater successes the state achieved in affecting village society in the previous century.[2]

Also missing from Huang's picture of the state's relationship to agrarian China is an assessment of the efforts made to shape the country's moral universe. The role of education and moral exhortation in the Neo-Confucian agenda of promoting local order has already been presented. Both officials and elites participated in this endeavor, in generally complementary ways. The government well understood that it possessed material and coercive powers far too limited to rule

---

[2]To take a north China example, the plan to establish 1,005 charity granaries to serve 39,687 villages of Zhili in the late 1740s suggests a vision of activity well beyond what Huang assumes to be the Qing situation. Actual construction fell short of this target, but nevertheless raised more than 20,000 tons of grain reserves for peasant use; every village did not need such a granary for the project to affect villagers' lives (Will and Wong 1991:70–72).

the empire without simultaneous appeal to ideological control. The notion of ruling as educating became a central component of the political tradition. Official concern for popular religion manifests this focus clearly. Late imperial officials allowed much popular religious activity to go unchallenged but aimed to coopt particularly efficacious deities into the official pantheon and to proscribe those deities deemed dangerous to the Confucian order. The result, as we've seen in chapter 4, was several kinds of political and social activities foreign to Western states and social elites before the nineteenth century.

Prasenjit Duara's work on Republican China foregrounds the importance of cultural issues in his explanation of state making in this period. He argues that the nineteenth-century state ruled North China largely through reliance on culturally determined norms shared by imperial state and rural society alike; the religious arena was a central location for elites and the state to exert leadership. Duara uses cultural logic as the baseline from which postimperial state making takes place. In brief, he argues that twentieth-century efforts to extract additional revenues undermined the logic of legitimacy and authority at work in the nineteenth century. State making became "involutionary," because the state received a smaller proportion of a larger absolute take; tax farmers were amassing larger sums and in the process evoking social opposition to the state's new efforts.[3] Where Huang focuses on coercive to the exclusion of normative means of control during the Qing, Duara stresses a shift from moral or normative methods of control to coercive ones. Thus he highlights a change toward expanded resource mobilization in the twentieth century. Duara's dynamic of change stresses the growth of fiscal extraction and the decline of culturally shared norms between officials and local communities. These shifts in normative and coercive means of control were accompanied, I believe, by a continued decline in material means of control. Social and economic infrastructures, including water control and credit markets, as well as welfare measures in the form of food-supply management and famine relief, failed to reach the levels of the nineteenth century, not to mention the eighteenth. The similarity between twentieth-century Chinese state making and early modern European state making, that is, the combination of warfare and fiscal extraction, is made sharper by the decline of normative and material means of control far more common in late imperial China than in early modern Europe.

Duara's twentieth-century story of "culture, state and power" in North China is framed by an opening statement of twentieth-century Chinese similarities to early modern European state making and a concluding contrast between the two. One way in which Duara sets up his story of twentieth-century North China is by using state making in Western Europe as the norm. "The similarities include the

---

[3]Kenneth Pomeranz's work (1993:188–93) suggests several revisions of Duara's involutionary thesis. Most important for present purposes are Pomeranz's suggestions that: (1) the success of new state extraction in providing services varies with political priority assigned to areas of economic wealth and centrality; and (2) local social structures affected the likelihood of success that state agents would have in raising revenues or providing services.

impulse toward bureaucratization and rationalization, the drive to increase revenues for both military and civilian purposes, the often violent resistance of local communities to this process of intrusion and extraction, and the efforts by the state to form alliances with new elites to consolidate its power" (1988:2). He concludes the work by searching for what separates his Chinese case of involution from European state making. Basing himself on Immanuel Wallerstein's reading of the great French medievalist Georges Duby, Duara suggests that modernizing states go through a phase in which entrepreneurial brokers are crucial to extract revenues from the population; successful modern states are those that manage to create formal state structures to displace both feudal elites and entrepreneurial brokers. Having depicted this European model of modern state making as a general process, he suggests that the Chinese case is part of a larger family of twentieth-century cases in which vastly increased roles for the state spawn brokerage structures that are difficult for the state to replace with bureaucratic practices. Non-Western failures generally contrast with European state-making success which "was more organically linked to other social, political, and economic processes" (1988:257).

Duara's China–Europe comparison ends by contrasting the distinctive historical arc of change in Europe with the particular context within which new twentieth-century states, including postimperial China, find themselves. Duara's conclusion about successful state making, like Huang's discussion of modern bureaucratization, posits a general process common to all successful modern state-making dynamics. For Duara, failure to follow this general pattern of change signals the absence of key phenomena "organically linked" to state making in European history. This kind of taxonomy encourages us to remember what China did not become, a condition it shared with many other countries. But to explain what did in fact happen, consideration of linkages between late imperial and postimperial transformations of the Chinese state should prove helpful. When we put Duara's postimperial state-making story into the temporal perspective of late imperial Chinese history, however, we confront the problem of knowing what the "state" is.

When Duara writes about the state, he has in mind either county-level administrations or provincial governments, not the central government. Hence Duara's analysis contrasts provincial and county governments with centralizing European states. The Chinese central government, as well as its relationships to local and provincial levels of government, are left out of the equation. This leaves unanswered the question: How did the central government become the core of a "modern" state? Provinces and regions under warlords and gentry elite rule were in large measure independent of the Beiyang regime that ruled in Peking (1916–27), and even after 1927, when the Nationalists established their government in Nanking with putative authority over the entire country, the government's control over taxation and personnel decisions never exceeded a handful of provinces near the capital. After Yuan Shikai's presidency there was a chronic devolution of power from the center to provinces and locales for both personnel and fiscal issues. Local order and social control became increasingly defined in terms of coercion with fewer normative or material instruments of control available for use. Normative strategies of order basic to Confucian views of ruling depended on a set of assumptions shared by elites and masses and expressed in lectures on the Sacred Edict and in school curricula, but in postimperial China the shift in content and increase in costs for a new educational system prompted widespread resistance. Neither the substance nor the scales of postimperial rule over rural China were clearly marked. Just what kind of state would emerge to rule postimperial rural China was not clear at all. Both Huang and Duara appeal in part to European norms of state making to establish counterfactual scenarios of how China's postimperial state could have developed. If the arguments I have made about the distinctive dynamics of state formation and transformation in China and Europe have merit, we can expect framing the possibilities for ruling twentieth-century agrarian China in terms of European state-making dynamics to be inadequate. But before we consider the implications of an alternative perspective on state rule over agrarian China, let us consider the ambiguities of state transformation in urban politics.

Urban Politics and the Postimperial Public Sphere

Cities figure prominently as bastions of bourgeois strength in European state-making dynamics. Centralizing state makers in early modern Europe labored to subordinate these powerful elites as they simultaneously faced aristocratic and clerical elites, each with its own claims on symbolic and material resources. In postimperial China, cities also housed powerful elites who had begun in the late Qing to organize themselves politically and socially through a variety of political assemblies and social associations. In the twentieth century, elite organizations such as chambers of commerce, education associations, and industrial associations were joined in urban politics by associations of workers organized according to occupation, including the most menial such as night-soil carriers and even beggars. Urban associations of various kinds had begun to play larger roles in municipal governance in the nineteenth century as William Rowe's important work on Hankow established (1984, 1989).

Officials viewed many of these merchant elite activities positively. Efforts at moral and material promotion of social order fit conceptually within the same continuum of official and elite activism directed toward broader territorial administration in earlier centuries. As long as elite roles in cities were limited to local urban issues, the nineteenth-century state could pursue its larger vision of creating order across the agrarian empire.

By postimperial times, urban elites had begun to make claims on the political process and to represent not only local but national concerns. The central government's challenge became how to subordinate elite and popular groups to state will, to utilize their strengths to create a stable urban order without granting them a larger political role that might compromise or constrain government power. This challenge was quite different from the one facing the late imperial state and its

Confucian elite who shared a Neo-Confucian agenda for sustaining local social order. Twentieth-century urban elites created formal organizations for a variety of economic, social, and political purposes. They claimed a formal political voice that was institutionally more explicit than the ones late imperial Confucian elites had sought in building on the reform movement of the last years of the Qing dynasty to produce possibilities and expectations for political voice.

Nationalist government leaders had little desire to promote parliamentary rule. They attempted to define elite roles principally in social and economic terms without sanctioning any formal and separate political presence according to models and ideals imported from the West. The Nationalist government depended on urban China for most of its resources. It subordinated other would-be rulers through the force of its military. But it didn't survive international competition—the Japanese took Manchuria in 1931 and invaded China proper in 1937, ending Nationalist rule over the entire country. Nationalist state-making dynamics of administrative centralization proceeded without the representative political institutions that developed in parts of early modern Europe and expanded throughout the nineteenth century, inspired by the French Revolution. But Chinese cities did have an arena that resembled in some ways the public sphere of early modern Europe.

A number of scholars have employed Jürgen Habermas's concept of "public sphere" to analyze late imperial and postimperial state–society relations in China. I have already expressed my reservations about applying the concept of "public sphere" to the domestic order of late imperial China. But in the closing years of the Qing and especially in the postimperial period, the emergence of elite opposition to government at local, provincial, and national levels makes a Chinese public sphere more probable than before. In the late nineteenth century, nationalist sentiment was promoted in a new and expanding Chinese press that was read by elites, many of whom soon turned against the dynasty. Provincial assemblies, chambers of commerce, and political as well as educational societies mobilized resources to oppose government actions. These developments resonate with European changes and create new conditions under which to consider the possible meaning of "public sphere" and "civil society" in China. The late imperial Confucian state, its strategies for domestic social order, its agrarian political economy, and its world order had little to offer this new urban scene.

David Strand addresses the new conditions in urban China using the concepts of public sphere and civil society. He shows how twentieth-century Chinese cities became sites for groups of people to organize a range of economic and social activities separate from the government and also to mobilize political opinion in opposition to the government. This fits his definition of "civil society"—an arena composed of social groups pursuing activities separate from the government. Strand (1991:11) suggests that the alumni associations, newspaper associations, native-place associations (*tongxianghui*), student associations, guilds, and chambers of commerce occupy the social ground between state and family described in Tocqueville's depiction of 1830s Jacksonian America. The public sphere, for Strand, is the place where such groups organize to express support for or opposition to government policies; it is an explicitly political arena in which "traditional" bases of corporate mobilization and self-regulation combine with "modern" ideas of citizenship for the expression of new demands on government. Strand links the political activities of these groups to their past behavior by suggesting that it is their previous roles as providers of necessary social services that gives them their claim on government attention. This tradition is the Chinese equivalent to the juridical basis of the public sphere in the West. Strand's interpretation suggests structural parallels, the result of distinctive historical trajectories but all leading to a public sphere and a civil society. This argument doesn't mean, of course, that all societies have the same kind of public sphere or civil society, but rather that all modern societies can be understood by appeal to a common terminology.

In Strand's analysis, public sphere and civil society are principally urban phenomena. The organizational bases and mobilization techniques found in cities are different from those found in rural settings. Intra- and intervillage organization were based on family, lineage, and on occasion other units such as village compacts, militias, and granaries. Only in urban areas were there native-place associations and merchant guilds in late imperial times. The traditional bases that Strand argues mattered to the early twentieth-century public sphere and civil society were largely urban as well as traditional. Some of the organizational forms were new in the late nineteenth and early twentieth century. While they relied to some extent on earlier resource strategies, they could not have been imagined without the Western models on which they were based.

Strand certainly recognized the foreign component to the early twentieth-century scene. But both he and others, like Mary Rankin and William Rowe, appear to believe that the long-term Chinese historical trajectory is more important.[4] This view is also suggested by Rankin and Esherick, who argue toward the end of their edited volume on local elites, "We have just reviewed a series of initiatives, dating back to the late sixteenth century, through which local elites gradually established a public sphere for their activities in philanthropy, education, local defense, water control, public works, fiscal affairs, and, in the twentieth century, in professional associations, journalism, political organization, economic development and local self-government" (Esherick and Rankin 1990:340). Taken for granted in this statement are the changing scenarios within which elite initiatives take place. "They were developing new strategies and new institutions to protect their positions and to guide political developments in accord with their interests and ideals" (Esherick and Rankin 1990:340–41).

This perspective, which stresses long-term Chinese historical changes, implicitly and effortlessly domesticates foreign possibilities and problems to fit into an

---

[4]Rankin (1990, 1993) relates the organization of social activities by elites in the late nineteenth century to elites' involvement in famine relief, water control, and education in the sixteenth century. Rowe's reconstruction of China's historical trajectory (1990, 1993) highlights those elements he finds similar to features of European history, including commercial firms, financial institutions, merchant networks, regional urbanization, and a printing industry.

already present trajectory. Moving from the understandable desire to debunk nineteenth-century notions of Chinese stagnation, this late twentieth-century alternative creates a Chinese trajectory of change modeled on parallels to an idealized European one. Even as Chinese historical changes are separated from European developments, they are reunited as functional equivalents to European changes. As a result, historical change continues to be defined by European experiences. We still implicitly, if not explicitly, expect a simple, general, and unilinear process of social and political change. In fact, the social practices of the seventeenth and eighteenth centuries were only contingently related to late nineteenth-century political challenges. The ways in which newly constructed urban spaces did and did not build on nineteenth-century patterns particular to China need to be analyzed more closely.

A larger challenge yet remains of assessing the linkages between urban and rural dynamics of state making and social change. Just as economic linkages between city and countryside were compromised by new dynamics of development, so too political linkages were less effective than they had been before the emergence of new patterns of urban change. How, then, did the central government retain its power? Why didn't competition among warlords create new provincial states engaged in war and competition? Why was the natural result of postimperial state making not a group of Chinese states, similar to the European states created in previous centuries?

State (Re)building and Nationalism in Twentieth-Century China

There were three spatially distinct scales on which state building took place in early twentieth-century China. Within many counties, local government capacities were expanded. At provincial levels the development of new institutions of civilian rule competed with the growth of new forms of military power. Finally, at the central government level, new bureaucracies were formed and older ones reformed. The postimperial possibilities of Chinese state making were defined by the dynamics taking place at each of these levels and the linkages among them.

Local governments' penetration of society in the Republican period was an extension of complex processes at work in the late nineteenth century. Elites became more formally involved in local affairs, blurring the distinction between official and elite. Elites staffed the various bureaus established during the late Qing New Policies. The push to create modern schools and modern police forces, combined with the need to pay off the Boxer indemnity and to fund a modern military, led to increased taxes on local society. The dynamics of local government expansion varied across China, in part reflecting different roles of officials and elites in late imperial times. In Jiangnan, for example, elites took on more formal roles through their own initiatives. Continuing the trend of acquiring material, coercive, and normative means of social control that began no later than the sixteenth century, consultative gentry assemblies were established in the late nineteenth century. In early twentieth-century Shanghai, a city council was formed, with separate executive and legislative branches to carry out a range of tasks entrusted to the gentry by imperial government officials, including selling cheap rice, suppressing opium dens, dredging waterways, building and repairing roads and bridges, removing garbage, and lighting streets (Elvin 1969). The scale and sophistication of local government developed by Shanghai gentry may have exceeded practices implemented elsewhere, but the gentry's active role in forming local governments was hardly unique to Shanghai elites.

In less wealthy areas officials played a larger role in expanding local government and in the process asserted the importance of administrative hierarchy, seeking to integrate local government into a system of state control reaching down from the center to the province, the prefecture, and finally the county. The North China governors of Shanxi and Zhili were ordered by the central government to experiment with local self-government in the early 1900s, just as they and other North China governors were ordered a little more than a century and a half earlier to experiment with charity granary reserves (Will and Wong 1991:69–72). Governor Zhao Erxun in Shanxi followed an authoritarian model, while Yuan Shikai developed a set of less authoritarian institutions more similar to Japanese practices (R. Thompson 1995). The elaboration of local government under strong official control continued in the postimperial period as well; Yan Xishan, for instance, created a village system which replicated late imperial practices of tax collection (*lijia*) and mutual surveillance. A program for stronger local government in Guangxi also resulted from provincial-level official initiatives, in this case to serve military mobilization (Kuhn 1986:340–43).

Because state-building initiatives at the local level often meant extracting revenue and men for increased levels of conflict, people in many local settings mobilized to protect themselves against what was experienced as a kind of government predation. Increased efforts at state penetration were met with increased efforts to avoid the state's hunger for resources. Since villages were increasingly taxed as a unit, this gave local communities a shared interest in resisting taxation. Villages also aimed to resist bandits, whose numbers were augmented by demobilized and unemployed soldiers. Efforts to expand the capacities of local government took place at the same time as local government's ability to insure stability and peace became less certain.

Not surprisingly, no postimperial state could mount systematic welfare or economic policies designed to stabilize and expand the agrarian economy. Nevertheless, such efforts were made on more modest scales. The impetus behind such efforts could range from a Confucian commitment to ordering the world, a motivation that animated Liang Shuming's efforts in Shandong, to Western-influenced projects such as those by Jimmy Yen in Hebei and Tao Xingzhi outside Nanjing (Kuhn 1986:353–59). These efforts cut against the isolation and withdrawal that some parts of agrarian China experienced. The impetus behind them was a belief that agrarian society and its economic base had to be improved. The responsibility for achieving these improvements fell, as they had in late imperial times, on a combination of elites and local officials. But neither Confucian nor Western-influenced rural reconstruction proved viable. Only the various experiments that the Communists conducted in their base areas continued after the Japanese invasion of 1937 to represent a kind of local government activism stimulating production and expanding taxation.

At provincial levels two new dynamics beginning in the last decade of the Qing continued into postimperial times. First, the formation of assemblies seeking a role in a constitutional form of government held out the possibility of new institutions for civilian rule. Second, the mobilization of armies increased the importance of military interventions in political decision making. This mobilization began with the collapse of the Qing dynasty as the New Army revolted in Wuhan and continued through the formation of regional armies that ushered in a period of warlord strife. The relative importance of civilian and military expansion varied among provinces. At one extreme Yunnan in southwestern China was basically under military rule (Sutton 1980). At the other extreme, government in the lower Yangzi region around Shanghai featured far more participation by civilian elites. In between fell the cases of Hubei and Hunan in central China (McCord 1993). It is important, as McCord has argued, to note the evidence of growing civilian government in some provinces during the warlord era. Earlier research tended to stress the military dimension to state power in the years following Yuan Shikai's death in 1916 (Pye 1971, Chen 1979). At the same time, it is important to note the crucial but ambiguous roles that military power played in state-building dynamics of the postimperial period.

For almost a millennium, military competition *within* China had not been a basic feature of politics. When military issues were important, they generally arose along China's northern frontiers. Domestic rebellions created threats, but these were only partially military and more broadly issues of social order. Now a process with certain striking parallels to some aspects of early modern European state building emerged. Growing armies stimulated the development of new abilities to extract increasing amounts of revenue from the population. These armies competed, some growing and others shrinking as alliances shifted to create new balances of power every several years. These military alliances, however, did not coalesce into new states as happened in Europe. At the same time, the formation of Chinese provincial assemblies paralleled the creation of representative parliaments in European countries, but again, the Chinese institutions did not secure the same place in government that European legislatures held.

The partial parallels between Republican political changes and early modern state making are set within contexts that differed in important ways. Although militarization in postimperial China stimulated increased resource extraction, it did not produce new bureaucratic organizations to mobilize and manage revenues. For their part, provincial assemblies were unable to create for themselves a necessary role in government; they could not make and sustain an effective claim to decision-making power. Civilian bureaucratic administration remained the core of government. The formation of provincial military units and assemblies undermined the central state's capacity to rule, but not enough to eliminate it as a site for state building in the postimperial period.

The manner in which the Qing dynasty fell in 1911 was unprecedented—provincial governments declared their independence from the central government. Yuan Shikai, president of the Republic from 1912 to 1916, succeeded in reasserting central control over the provinces, though opposition to his policies resulted in two more declarations of provincial independence in 1913 and 1916. Yuan succeeded in reasserting some central government control over revenues and a role in personnel decisions in the provinces. But the fragility of central government control emerged clearly after his death. By the early 1920s, the Beijing government was a central government primarily in the sense that foreign governments recognized it as such, thus allowing it to receive customs revenues and arrange foreign loans. This government recognized that its reach beyond a part of North China was limited.

Meanwhile, most of the country was under others' control. Most specialists argue that the Northern Expedition of the Nationalist Party in 1926 reunited the country, making the succeeding decade from 1927 to 1937 the only period between 1911 and 1949 that the country was united. Arthur Waldron (1995) has argued, to the contrary, that the Peking government in 1921 was no less a ruling government than that created by the Nationalists. Moreover, the Nationalists would never have had the opportunity to make their move had the government leaders not been dislodged in a surprising set of military maneuvers. Waldron argues for continuities between Beiyang and Nationalist regimes that other analysts have not seen. Such continuities suggest that the Beiyang regime was a stronger central government than we have tended to assume, while the Nationalist regime was weaker than often believed.

Where the Nationalist government excelled was at the central government level of state building, where officials established new specialized bureaucracies and reformed older ones. The central government succeeded in improving its capacities in key areas, especially fiscal matters, banking, and international relations. Many of the central government's state-building successes enhanced its control over urban society, facilitated economic development, or improved performance in international diplomacy. But next to these positive signs are signs that the central government no longer controlled the governments that ruled beneath it. The state was no longer unitary.

The late imperial Chinese state had been unitary: its power was not divided among different types of government authorities; there were no aristocracies, estates, provincial parliaments, or independent cities with separate bases of governmental authority. The late imperial state's vertical integration rested on central government control of finances and personnel decisions; no other political authority independently laid claims to resources or selected officials without the central government's approval. The collapse of the dynasty brought a halt to central control over finances and personnel decisions. Control over the mobilization and flow of resources had become increasingly complex in the second half of the nineteenth century as transit taxes initially collected by provincial officials were brought under central control and taxes on international trade were collected by a special bureaucracy staffed by Chinese and foreign officials. The civil service system had already undergone dramatic changes in the final years of the Qing dynasty, changes that made postimperial officialdom less coherent than it had been in earlier centuries. The prospects for creating a unitary state in postimperial times looked less promising than they had in the agrarian empire. Why then didn't the kinds of disintegration common to other empires, like the Ottoman or Austro-Hungarian, take place in China? In part, because the Chinese state had traditionally constructed Chinese identity culturally by promoting common moral and material practices that served simultaneously to construct social order and promote political stability, it had a broader social base to support political integration than other empires.

Under Manchu rule, the construction of Chinese identity became more difficult, because the Manchus also strove to maintain their own identity and those of other northern peoples. They envisioned the Qing empire as a political system composed of different peoples; within this system they generally applied principles of cultural sinification to peoples south of the Great Wall. Across the larger empire, the Qing emperor presented himself variously as a Buddhist king, a Central Asian khan, and a patron of the Dalai Lama. But within China proper he acted as a Confucian emperor. While recognizing the empire's great diversity, the state aimed to create order by defining the acceptable boundaries of cultural and religious difference. This Confucian-inspired project of creating a set of cultural practices deemed to be the foundation of proper personal behavior and social order united a society within which popular beliefs ranged far beyond the dimensions of a Confucian template.

Whatever its limitations, the state's drive to control Chinese cultural practices contributed to the definition of a Chinese identity. A late imperial fusion of culture and politics was part of the basic construction of state–society relations. The state played an explicit role in promoting this identity, especially in periods of official activism (both local and central) and in southern frontier areas where Han Chinese sometimes came into contact with people whose customs differed dramatically from their own.

The cultural construction of Chinese identity in Qing times has particular relevance for understanding twentieth-century Chinese nationalism, a relevance obscured by some influential assertions about modern state making and nationalism. Ernest Gellner, in his *Nations and Nationalisms* for example, presents a picture of what he calls "agro-literate polities" that seems virtually antithetical to China, the world's largest such polity. For Gellner, the fusion of culture and polity is the essence of modern nationalism and occurs only when industrialization begins to transform agrarian societies. In agro-literate societies, he says, "almost everything militates against the definition of political units in terms of cultural boundaries" (Gellner 1983:11).

Gellner forcefully argues the common belief that so-called premodern states were unable to exercise much cultural influence over their subject populations. In many historical cases this is no doubt true. There are, as Gellner notes, cases of sophisticated agrarian societies that seek to differentiate people into separate groups or castes, such as South Asia. There culture is divided horizontally and vertically, preventing it from becoming an integrative force. In Gellner's view, politics and culture remain separate in agrarian societies. As John A. Hall remarked, in delineating nationalism: "There have always, of course, been distinctive cultures, and particular upper classes have had some sense of shared ethnic solidarity. But the power of the nationalist idea—that people should share a culture and be ruled only by someone co-cultural with themselves—seems historically novel" (J. A. Hall 1993:3).

Historically specific, yes, but limited to the modern world and first taking place in Europe, no. The legitimacy of Manchu rule within China proper depended on Manchu emperors and officials pursuing a Confucian agenda of rule. Were we to grant the premise that the mix of politics and culture is a unique feature of modern nationalism, we would have to treat imperial Chinese state-making strategies as "modern." The Chinese state and elite shared a common Neo-Confucian agenda for creating public order both before and after the Manchu conquest. Peasants too were members of the Neo-Confucian cultural order, even if this Confucian structure did not embrace and domesticate all popular beliefs.[5] The cultural sense of "Chinese" that was constructed in late imperial times and the intimate relationship between this construction and political action forms an important part of the immediate context of the Qing empire's collapse. Amidst the uncertainties regarding state building in the postimperial period, two plausible scenarios did not in fact develop.

Given the far weaker lines of control between central and provincial levels of government than had existed in the late imperial period, one possibility was a federal structure, with each province handling its internal affairs and a central government charged with foreign relations. Certainly provincial governments had acted independently to some degree since 1912. They made de facto claims of autonomy with respect to finances and personnel. But in fact little effort went toward the formation of a federal structure of government. To form a federal system of government would have required an agreement to divide powers and responsibilities among levels of government. This would have represented a fundamental bureaucratic change, since the late imperial Chinese state had been a unitary state in which the central government assigned responsibilities to bureaucrats at different levels of administration without compromising its own authority. In the late imperial state, most officials in the counties, provinces, and capital were responsible for the same basic functions; the result was a fractal political order. There was a hierarchy of authority but no division of powers. While no central state en-

---

[5]My argument is not that elites and common people agreed on all cultural matters. Indeed, the gap between them began to open in the eighteenth century as stricter Confucian control over popular practices was attempted. What matters for the present argument is that officials, elites, and common people shared a cultural universe in which expectations of proper and desirable behavior spanned all groups.

joyed the ability to act as a unitary state throughout the country between 1912 and 1927, the logic of bureaucratic administration remained that of a unitary state spanning as much of the former empire as feasible. Federal systems usually emerge as a way to coordinate the authority of previously more autonomous and institutionally powerful bodies. The postimperial Chinese situation was not one in which provincial-level power holders held institutionalized authority with which the center could then negotiate and bargain.

A second plausible scenario was for the military competition among warlords to lead to the formation of a system of competing states within China. Alternatively, the civilian leaders struggling to form new institutions of civilian rule could have aimed to forge "independent" provinces. Provinces did in fact declare their independence three times between 1911 and 1916, but in each case they were declaring independence from a particular central government in protest against its actions, not as a prelude to the creation of institutionally autonomous positions. Perhaps the major reason fully autonomous provinces did not develop lies in the difficulty of integrating new armies and assemblies with older state institutions in a way that would give them larger roles. In addition, however, it mattered that no smaller groups could create a notion of "nation" to displace China. No provincial-level process of state building could introduce a process of political engagement to persuade people that they were an identifiable group with a particular history and consequent right to their own political system. The late imperial state's construction of a Chinese identity was so successful that the formation of alternative identities on which to mobilize people in opposition to other Chinese was difficult to imagine. Neither independence nor a federal system would make sense in a political situation in which people did not forge politically significant identities able to displace the notion of Chinese identity created and reproduced in late imperial times.

A third scenario for state building did develop in which postimperial Chinese nationalism and the Qing empire's construction of unity clearly differed. Areas beyond China proper in which the eighteenth- and nineteenth-century governments had not promoted sinification increasingly separated from the Chinese state and nation, despite the state's plans to rule all the territories of the Qing empire. With its establishment in 1912, the Republic of China promptly declared its authority over the "five peoples" of the former Manchu state—Manchus, Hans, Mongols, Muslims, and Tibetans. The first president of the Republic, Yuan Shikai, proclaimed that Mongolia, Xinjiang, and Tibet would be treated administratively as provinces.

Given the central government's uneven control over provinces, one might view Republican control over these three areas as simply the end point of that government's limited territorial integration. The Mongolians and Tibetans went further, however. Because they had national identities distinct from the Chinese, the Mongolians were able to achieve political independence in Outer Mongolia and have it recognized by the Republic of China, while the Tibetans established de facto political independence in the central and western parts of the area populated by

Tibetan people. Inner Asian nationalisms were largely shaped by and at times sub-ordinated to international power politics involving the Russians, the Japanese, and the Chinese.[6] The net result has been the separation of regions such as Outer Mongolia from China and persistent uncertainties about the integration of oth-ers, notably Tibet, into China today.[7]

Within China proper, the shared cultural identity promoted by the late imperial government was one important factor in the development of twentieth-century Chinese nationalism. This cultural identity provided a persuasive but weak basis on which people could recognize shared features. It helps to explain why competing nationalisms formulated at the provincial level did not displace a larger Chinese na-tion. China's new political context of competition and conflict with foreign powers helps to explain why twentieth-century constructions of nation and nationalism in China would form an uneasy relationship with earlier notions of cultural identity.

The nationalist view that developed in the late nineteenth and early twentieth centuries in reaction to confrontations with Western powers was at least as much "racial" as cultural and put together as much from Western as from Chinese ma-terials. In a world of social Darwinism, in which the Chinese nation was strug-gling to avoid extinction, only a strong and fit China would survive the threats of Western and Japanese power. This type of nationalism was distinct from the cul-tural construction of a Chinese identity in its focus on the Chinese state's rela-tions with foreign governments. In the 1910s and 1920s, for example, urban Chinese criticized the Chinese government's agreement to loans from Japan and China's treatment by Western powers following World War I; opinions voiced in the press provided the sentiments around which elites and urban common peo-ple mobilized to form mass boycotts and demonstrations. This kind of national-ism was certainly a twentieth-century phenomenon and generally fits with the idea of nationalism as a recent historical phenomenon. Elites perceived their situation in national terms because of the system of states in which China now had to act. The demands and anxieties caused by China's situation spurred both elites and common people to demonstrate against a government they feared would not rep-resent the nation's interests effectively.

---

[6]The fates of these areas is enmeshed in complex international politics. The constructions of ethnic na-tionalisms begins for some of these groups during this period, e.g., the Turkic Muslims become Uighurs in the early 1920s. For a succinct account of the fortunes of the peoples in these areas in the postim-perial period, see Fletcher 1979:41–51.

[7]Evelyn Rawski (1996) discusses the relevance of the Qing conquests to the problems of ethnic na-tionalism in China today. By focusing on China's inner Asian peripheries, where non-Han peoples cre-ated identities quite distinct from the vast majority of the Qing empire's population, she calls into question the validity of the Sinicization thesis. She overlooks the complexity of the Qing enterprise. In the more densely settled parts of China, where well over 90 percent of the population lived, the Manchu rulers had aggressively promoted a Chinese cultural identity among most people. Had the Qing not ex-panded Ming China's borders, the problems of ethnic nationalism on China's frontiers might not have arisen. But had the Qing rulers not set out to create an agrarian social order through ideological, ma-terial, and coercive mechanisms, there might not have been a twentieth-century China to worry about those frontiers.

The Gellner-Hall theory of nationalism doesn't describe, let alone explain, the late imperial Chinese case or the changes in the postimperial period. Whereas the late imperial Chinese state, which should not, according to Gellner and Hall, have developed a national identity, did promote one, the twentieth-century Chinese state did not, as Gellner and Hall would have predicted, create a nationalism that served both elite and commoner. Instead, a gap opened, then widened, between the Western-influenced culture of the increasingly urban elite and the popular culture of the still largely rural masses.

The state proved unable to play much role in constructing the nation for several decades. China's peasant masses in the 1910s and 1920s did not share the elites' view that the country was in crisis. The new nationalism that developed in Chinese cities was part of the growing cultural gap between cities and countryside, epitomized by the May 4th cultural iconoclasm, which rejected much of late imperial China's culture, the very Confucian precepts that had given rise to China's politically constructed cultural identity.[8] Thus the new nationalism directly challenged earlier forms of Chinese identity. Clearly a product of recent contacts with Westerners, it was not indigenous to Chinese society. The nationalism of the May 4th era pit largely urban Chinese against the dangers and challenges of Westerners and the Japanese. Issues of wealth and power became fused. The relevant state was the state facing these foreign threats, the relevant society the urban society that recognized them.

Other forms of state power, those facing the challenge of ruling rural China, worried about raising revenues and suppressing social disorder. While peasants protested against foreign missionaries and sometimes gained from economic ties to international markets, rural China's problems and possibilities remained largely rooted in domestic soil. Some issues, such as opium cultivation and consumption, were the result of foreign contacts, but many others were structurally and cognitively the same as those of a century or two earlier: anxieties about subsistence and family—hopes for more land or a good marriage for a son or daughter—were at the heart of the very Confucian ideal that urban China rejected.

If there were two kinds of nationalism in China during the 1920s and 1930s, how could they be reconciled? The conflict was serious. Neither partisans of urban nationalism nor rural farmers had much tolerance for the other's anxieties and desires. The issue was further complicated because the new sense of Chinese identity was not limited to Chinese living in Chinese cities but extended to those who had emigrated as merchants, miners, coolies, and farmers. Sun Yat-sen targeted these people in his appeals for funds in the late Qing to foment political change in the migrants' homeland. What kind of synthesis could be built from the two basic types of nationalism, one culturally based and spanning rural China, the oth-

---

[8]Myron Cohen (1991) has stressed the degree to which the twentieth-century creation of nationhood in China entailed a rejection of earlier cultural constructions of national identity. This rejection notwithstanding, intellectuals and officials have labored to create a nationalism that incorporates both May 4th iconoclasm and earlier definitions of Chineseness.

er politically motivated by contacts with foreign powers and including Chinese living in cities and abroad? Political elites envisioned uniting the country in order to save it from foreign dangers. In *The Principle of Nationalism* Sun Yat-sen wrote:

> An easy and successful way to bring about the unity of a large group is to build upon the foundation of small united groups, and the small units we can build upon in China are the clan groups and also the family groups. The "native place" sentiment of the Chinese is very deep-rooted too; it is especially easy to unite those who are from the same province, prefecture or village.
>
> As I can see it, if we take these two fine sentiments as a foundation, it will be easy to bring together the people of the whole country. (Sun Yat-sen n.d.:43)

Sun Yat-sen's logic for building Chinese nationalism posits building blocks of identity. He starts with the smallest block, family groups, on which he places larger lineage groups; on this group he then balances ever-larger blocks based on territorial identity, village, prefecture, and province. The crowning piece is the nation. But this inverted pyramid seems very unstable. Can nationalism really be built out of kin and smaller territorial sentiments? Not easily. The shared sensibilities that the late imperial state did so much to promote are not adequate to mobilize large numbers of rural people to oppose an outside threat; their similarities did not create commitments to sacrifice for each other unless the outside threat became visibly a local problem. Late imperial efforts had already created what Benedict Anderson (1991) refers to as "anonymous solidarity" among people of different provinces, making it both less likely and less necessary to create a similar kind of identification among people of the same province. Sun's image of mobilizing people based on local loyalties had an empirical base in his travels outside China. But he was perhaps misguided in anticipating the power of these institutions and sentiments to create a sense of nation within China. The "nation" he observed overseas was formed in distinction from and even in opposition to the larger host society. The national consciousness he found in small groups of Chinese residents abroad would be more difficult to develop within China, where small groups of Chinese did not immediately confront others who were not Chinese. Building nationalism out of native-place sentiments in rural China therefore seems an unlikely project.

The urban situation, however, was different, as Bryna Goodman's study of native-place ties in Shanghai between the 1850s and 1937 has shown. These were not simple, timeless, or traditional native-place sentiments. Rather, Goodman shows a new kind of native-place organization developing in 1930s Shanghai to link people in Shanghai with people from their home districts to promote the community-transcending goal of a nation. The rhetoric stressed the nation's formation out of progressively larger groups. As Shanghai educational reformer Huang Yuanpei wrote in 1933:

> How should we save China? Many people have ideas, all of which require one thing: People must abandon their selfish individualism and begin to form

small groups. Then they should knit together small groups into large groups and unite large groups into one great national group. When the entire country becomes one group, the mass foundation for the nation will be established, the nation will be strong and long-lived.[9]

When Huang and others built their national project from groups with urban social bases, they appear to have succeeded. Whether protests against the accidental killing of a Ningbo native by a Russian sailor or the organizing of the anti-American boycott in 1905, native-place organizations were the units responsible for the protests in Shanghai. Issues of nation were represented by local urban groups with bases of mobilization that linked Shanghai to areas beyond the immediate community (Goodman 1995).

The "nation" was an abstraction to be concretized on different spatial scales. National salvation was to be achieved through efforts of officials and people working in particular parts of China. Lacking an institutionalized structure spanning the entire country, elites and officials motivated to save the nation worked at more modest levels. State-building efforts at provincial levels were thus not easily seen as contributing ultimately to the goal of independent provinces. Instead, provincial state building served a national purpose. The image of nation became a focus for state-building efforts that incorporated local, provincial, and central governments without actually connecting them institutionally. The concept of nation provided a new fractal focus for Chinese politics.

Before 1937 the project of saving the nation was very much an urban project led by a mix of political, social, and economic elites whose efforts were articulated by intellectuals, most of whom accepted a May 4th distinction between a backward, rural China mired in Confucian traditions and a progressive, Western-influenced urban China leading the country in its battle for survival. The Anti-Japanese War (1937–45) changed the spatial dimensions of Chinese nationalism by making resistance to the Japanese an issue of immediate moment to people in both cities and the countryside. Questioned and qualified in many ways since its publication in 1962, Chalmers Johnson's thesis of the Communist Party mobilizing peasants around a core of national resistance to Japanese aggression is relevant because it alerts us to the Communists' success in representing the nation. Not all peasants may have conceived their struggle as a national effort, but at a minimum we can recognize that peasants were mobilized successfully by Communists who for their part claimed to represent the interests of the peasants as the Chinese nation. Moreover, the nation the Communists represented was principally the backward and isolated rural China, not the economically more advanced urban China. Their Chinese "nation" later expanded to embrace urban China as well, as the Communists moved from participating in victory over the Japanese to defeat of the Nationalists and the establishment of the People's Republic in 1949.

---

[9]Huang Yanpei, *Shanghai Pudong tongxianghui mujin goudi jianzhu xuanyan* (Manifesto for Shanghai Pudong Tongxianghui land purchase and building construction fund-raising), pamphlet, Pudong Tongxianghui archives, Shanghai, cited in Goodman 1995:300–301.

The enemy faced by rural Chinese was in fact the same enemy faced by city dwellers. Sharing a target brought rural and urban forms of Chinese nationalism closer together but did not resolve their basic differences. How a rural-based and culturally conservative, antiforeign nationalism would engage a Western-inspired, urban-centered nationalism after the mid-century was uncertain.

8

CHINA AFTER 1949

The division of labor in Chinese studies has made the links between imperial and postimperial state making hard even to see, let alone understand. Until recently the 1911–49 period has been set off from the late imperial period and from post-1949 China. Few people have worked on issues of state making across the 1911 divide in a systematic fashion; fewer have done so across the 1949 divide. As a result, many contemporary specialists work within frameworks that stress China's similarities to other socialist and former socialist countries, the more general problems of developing democratic systems, or the state's role in China within a larger international context. Political continuities are usually not obvious, whereas the differences between China's twentieth-century state-making experience and that of earlier centuries are easy to spot.

The absence of analyses that span a long time frame is reasonable. Between 1911 and 1949 the state-making challenges were unification of the country and defense against foreign aggressors. The revolution that culminated with the establishment of the People's Republic defined a new set of relationships among state, society, and economy. There have been solid grounds, therefore, to consider the twentieth-century state-making experience of China in comparative terms, to look at the problems and possibilities that China shares with other non-Western countries.

The general literature on twentieth-century states reinforces our perception of disjunction between twentieth-century China and its past. Many treatments of twentieth-century states in general include at least one, sometimes two, and occasionally all three of the following themes. First, the state is portrayed principally in terms of its role in the economy—how state actions support capital accumulation, economic growth, and the dominance of the bourgeoisie in capitalist economies. Second, the state is defined in terms of its political institutions and ideology of rule—how the state formulates policies consistent with democratic ideals. Third, the state is defined in terms of a rational bureaucracy that facilitates modern management (Alford and Friedland 1985).

Each of these general perspectives is represented in Western works on China. On the state–capitalism relationship, studies of China emphasize the failure of the late imperial state to promote modern economic growth, while economic development in Republican China has been seen as a quintessentially private-sector phenomenon. These evaluations contrast with analyses of state-sponsored efforts after 1949, even when scholars stress links between economic performance before and after this date.[1] The state-ideology theme has enjoyed attention among scholars who have looked at experiments in democracy beginning with the late nineteenth-century representative assemblies.[2] Finally, issues of bureaucracy have been at the center of efforts to analyze the PRC party and state.[3] Though important work has been produced within each perspective, these themes alone form an inadequate set of theoretical options for analyzing Chinese state making. Together they do form a framework for looking at European state making because capitalism, democracy, and bureaucracy generally developed together there, but since bureaucratic capacities developed in China without the ideologies and institutions of either a capitalist economy or a political democracy, China clearly has had a different historical trajectory. Therefore, examining its components solely according to themes deriving from Western history is unlikely to capture all the relevant features of political change and increases the likelihood that we will downplay or even ignore important issues within Chinese traditions of state making.

A second perspective on the contemporary Chinese state that at first glance appears very different from the social science literature highlighting issues of economy, ideology, and bureaucracy views contemporary problems as rooted in a history filled with failures. Much of this literature sees nothing to build on within the Chinese past and present. In the 1920s the educated Chinese rejection of their past was a basic theme to much May 4th–period thinking. Today, there is a double rejection of Confucian and Communist ideologies. By denying the importance of dynamics of change in China's past to understanding the present and possibilities for the future, this perspective in effect argues that the past is irrelevant to China's current challenges. Fundamentally, it too focuses on China's similarities with other twentieth-century countries because both perceive the possibilities for advancement in terms of Western categories, not Chinese history. The widely viewed and strongly debated *River Elegy* television miniseries, for example, views China's indigenous culture as the product of an inward-looking and isolated civilization ruled by an authoritarian state unable to create the kinds of

---

[1]See Feuerwerker 1984 for the late imperial period, Rawski 1989 for the Republican period (1911–49), and Perkins 1975 for the post-1949 economy in historical perspective.

[2]See Fincher 1981 and Nathan 1985 for analyses of the issue of democracy in historical and contemporary times. Fincher argues strongly for considering the Chinese experiments between 1905 and 1914 with constitutional reform, self-government, and provincial assemblies as examples of political experimentation undertaken in Asia as well as Europe. Nathan neatly locates contemporary debates about democracy within Chinese efforts of the last century to grapple with this Western concept.

[3]The classic statement is Schurmann 1968; Lieberthal and Oksenberg 1988 is a more recent effort to attack the problems of bureaucratic organization.

changes that transformed the Western world. The solution to this tragic situation is for China to open outward and engage more fully with foreign experiences.[4]

Important continuities certainly connect imperial and postimperial times, but the failure to recognize and explain which features are reproduced and which are not means that we cannot explain the continuities as the product of historical dynamics. To perceive the past as a dead weight that crushes the present and to imagine the only escape into the future as lying beyond the dimensions of the domestic past limits the search to models derived from foreign historical experiences. Neither ignoring the domestic past nor selective memory of features deemed negative adequately explains how the Chinese state has in fact acted since 1949. The purpose of examining post-1949 state-building dynamics from a historical perspective is neither to praise nor to blame state policies and preferences but rather to show how institutions and ideologies promoted since 1949 can be better understood. The contemporary Chinese state is a very different state from that which ruled in late imperial times. Still, it has connections with the country's imperial past, and not only negative ones. To understand more fully the Chinese state's present possibilities, we may reconsider the three topic areas of economy, bureaucracy, and ideology within the historical trajectories leading from the late imperial period forward.

State–Economy Relations

The economy the Chinese Communists inherited in 1949 was one that already had a modest industrial base concentrated in the Shanghai region and the Northeast. A few other urban centers had more meager industrial bases. Postimperial industrialization was concentrated in a few areas and, before the Japanese invasion, was largely a private-sector phenomenon. Industrialization began in China in the absence of a strong and vertically integrated state. The establishment of the People's Republic in 1949 fundamentally changed the political context for industrialization. The new government had several immediate traditions of political economy to draw upon in principle and in practice. All the governments active in wartime China—the Japanese, the Nationalists, and the Communists—had control over at least some production, and in both Nationalist- and Communist-controlled areas they also regulated distribution. In principle, however, none of these experiences was most important to the Communists after 1949. Instead, the Chinese created a five-year economic plan modeled on Soviet experiences of industrialization that emphasized developing a heavy industrial base. In fact, the logic of state-run heavy industries resonated strongly with the approach of the previous Nationalist government. Japanese efforts to control heavy industrial production in their areas provided a second example of how governments controlled the economy. When these experiences are added to the Communists' own at-

---

[4]The Chinese television miniseries *River Elegy* is discussed in Barmé and Jaivin 1992:138–64. For further discussion and translations of the scripts see Su Xiaokang and Wang Luxiang 1991.

tempts to manage poor and backward agrarian economies, an alternative to a major state effort to control the economy is difficult to imagine. The new government began to expand the heavy industrial base it inherited from the Nationalists
and to stabilize the light industrial base, then in private hands but gradually so-
cialized over the first seven years of Communist rule.

One of the important decisions taken by the government in the 1950s was to
broaden the geographical basis of the industrial sector. In 1949, 80 percent of all
industrial production was located in the six coastal provinces and the Northeast,
an area that comprised 18 percent of China's land and 42 percent of its population. In contrast, northwestern China (about 33 percent of the country) had but
2 percent of its industry (Zhu Cishou 1990:7). Efforts were made to develop met-
allurgy, machine-building, resource, and chemical industries as well as light industries in each of China's major regions, and particularly in those regions with
relatively little industry: the North, Northwest, and Southwest. In the Northeast,
where heavy industries were well developed, the government aimed to develop
light industries; conversely, in eastern China, which had a light industrial base,
heavy industries were promoted (Zhu Cishou 1990:55–57). Though the Chinese
government did not admit it, its commitment to giving China a broad industrial
base built on Nationalist government efforts to establish an industrial sector in
the Southwest during the war. The Nationalist effort, of course, was driven by
wartime losses of territory, while the Communist plan was intended to cover the
entire country.

Communist policies also represented the unacknowledged application of a policy of widespread economic development developed by the Qing government for
the agrarian economy two centuries earlier. Both the techniques and significance
of socialist industrial development differed from the Qing political economy of
agrarian empire, but the logic of creating comparable economic activities across the
entire country was a common theme. Much as the Qing dynasty's political economy stimulated agrarian prosperity across a vast empire, the Communist political
economy promoted industrialization across an equally large agrarian country.

For the overwhelming majority of China's population, who continued to live
in the countryside, the new industrial developments of the 1950s mainly meant
taxation of agriculture to provide capital for industrial expansion. Peasants saw little material benefit from the creation of a heavy industrial base. The industrial policy of the 1950s government differed little from that of the Nationalists, or for
that matter, the late nineteenth-century Qing government: all three spearheaded
the development of heavy industry with military purposes in mind. None of the
governments conceived of industrial policy primarily as a tool for developing the
economy generally. But, unlike the late Qing period when provincial officials usually took the lead in promoting new industries, in the 1950s central planners made
the decisions about industrial projects. These decisions included locating projects
in the interior as part of a conscious strategy to expand the country's industrial
base. Chinese industrialization in the 1950s and 1960s, therefore, was seen largely as a process that would strengthen the country as a whole.

Before 1957 decisions on industrial investment and production were made by centralized ministries. There followed a period of decentralization that recognized that the information flows necessary to create a centrally run economy were harder to achieve as the economy grew more complex. Further decentralization to provincial levels took place in the 1960s. These changes along the continuum of a vertically integrated bureaucracy affected which level of the bureaucracy was most engaged in guiding industries, but did not revise the state's basic leadership in industrialization. As long as the Chinese state bureaucracy was once again vertically integrated, as it had become after 1949, shifts in the locus of responsibility for different activities didn't significantly change the state's capacities to direct economic development.

The political economy of agrarian China after 1949 was in many basic ways separate from the policies of industrialization. Chinese leaders explicitly pursued a kind of dual economy in which planners aimed to control both industrialization and the agrarian economy. Agriculture, like industry, was subject to central planning, with production and distribution decisions largely determined by the central government. The government influenced agricultural output through production assignments, quotas, and price policies. As industrial decisions were decentralized to provincial and lower levels of government after 1957, the goal of grain self-sufficiency was promoted within provinces. Fears of subsistence crises and the limited abilities of officials to move grain swiftly to relieve famines prompted an effort to create a margin of security within provinces. This kind of decentralization did not threaten the power of the central state. Making lower levels of government responsible for their own subsistence reduced pressures on higher levels of government to manage production and distribution. The dismantling of commercial grain circulation in the 1950s and 1960s made the decision to encourage more grain production a sensible alternative. To reduce rural income inequalities, inspire increased output, and achieve greater control over the rural economy, the government collectivized peasant production. This fundamental change away from household-level farming that had characterized the rural economy for centuries has been duly stressed in the literature. Government policy makers determined the amounts of different crops to be planted across the country and held peasants accountable for what they produced. But the contrast between Communist policies and earlier government policies is less stark than conventionally assumed.

Political efforts to regulate the agrarian economy were also made in earlier periods, but the government then had less capacity to impose its preferences. While some warlords forced peasants to plant opium, coercion was not, in general, a government option before 1949. The Qing government aimed to increase production and regulate distribution, especially of grain supplies, but officials did not demand that peasants plant particular crops. Officials in areas with expanding cash cropping sometimes worried that the reduction of area devoted to grain cultivation might lead to inadequate local supplies of grain. They felt anxious about depending heavily on commercial imports to feed the people living in their jurisdictions. For example, the Liangjiang Governor-General Gaojin chastised officials and people alike for failing to recognize the importance of grain production in the lower Yangzi region during the 1770s. To Gaojin, the shift from grain to cotton planting exacerbated reliance on commercial grain imports and created potential supply problems that the government's granary system could not meet. He noted that cotton required less labor than rice but commanded higher prices and thus he did not expect market conditions to lead peasants to shift from cotton to rice production. He therefore advocated administrative restraints on additional land being shifted to cotton cultivation and for official encouragement of rice production (Gaojin 1775). The governor-general's concerns seem to have had little impact on peasant decision making.

Other officials were less worried than Gaojin; many of them positively encouraged the expansion of handicraft production and cash cropping as sources of higher peasant incomes. But Gaojin's stress on promoting local grain supplies foreshadows the better-known efforts of the post-1949 Chinese government to foster local grain self-sufficiency. With more limited capacities to determine agricultural production, late imperial officials contented themselves in large measure with regulating food-supply distribution. They supported private market exchange when they thought these transactions would move grain from surplus to deficit areas, but where markets failed to insure subsistence security, officials took it upon themselves to build up grain reserves or arrange shipments into needy areas.

The post-1949 state reduced the role of markets in rural areas as it increased its direct mobilization of agricultural resources. The government's concern for local self-sufficiency in grain echoed one kind of eighteenth-century concern, but it drew more immediately on experiences in wartime, when reliance on imports was impossible and grain production was promoted as a means of national defense. I am not suggesting, therefore, that Communist officials consciously decided to replicate late imperial policies. I am proposing rather that the actual gap between the policy choices of the mideighteenth and midtwentieth centuries was not so large as we conventionally assume it to be.

Within the agrarian economy, small-scale rural industries developed, first as part of the late 1950s Great Leap Forward, and then as elements of a continued strategy of expanding the supply of materials and goods available to agriculture. While the building of so-called "backyard steel furnaces" was a well-known fiasco, the development of chemical fertilizer plants was far more practical, if less widely publicized. The formation of township and village enterprises (TVEs), small-scale industries owned collectively, can be considered a development based on rural industries that in late imperial times operated at the household level. Whereas Qing dynasty handicraft production was limited to a small range of goods, mainly textiles, TVEs engage in a broader variety of activities. Though the links between small-scale collective industry and late imperial rural handicrafts are not simple causal ones, the similarities merit attention. These modern rural industries, at least before 1978, were firmly integrated into an agrarian economy and institutionally distinct from the political economy of urban industrial China, just as late imperial handicrafts were a component of agrarian political economy. In late imperial times officials feared urban growth because cities were more difficult to govern; Chinese policies were geared to an agrarian social order. To reproduce the viability of the household economy, the government promoted activities, such as craftwork, that kept women at home and productive. Communist bureaucrats, too, feared urban growth, because they recognized the peril in population concentrations that weighed too heavily on public infrastructures, with some people enjoying secure jobs in state-run enterprises and bureaucracies while others scrambled at the margins of society. In both situations, rural industries took on social as well as economic importance. The place and importance of TVEs changed dramatically after 1978.

The striking changes in China's economy since 1978 have been the object of countless studies. Scholars don't agree on the causes, the degrees of success, or the likelihood of continued success. Some have stressed the increased role of markets and the increased specificity of property rights to explain China's recent economic growth. Others have noted the dramatic increase in foreign trade and investment. Some argue that further growth will be difficult without continued progress toward market institutions, while others insist that the success of reforms is attributable to the government's refusal to condone a "big bang" adjustment in prices. Some argue that economic reforms favoring market capitalism will drive the Chinese political system into liberalizing its policies and accepting democratic practices. Others suggest, to the contrary, that China's economic successes are akin to other authoritarian government initiatives in East Asia and that economic achievements were possible because they were not disrupted by political uncertainty. Amidst these disagreements, let me sketch how Chinese political economy has changed, but in ways that make a particular kind of sense in light of earlier practices.

From the earliest efforts at self-strengthening in the 1860s, China's political economy has conventionally distinguished agriculture from industrialization. Even in the quarter-century before the Japanese invasion, when most of China's industrialization was a private-sector development, links to the agrarian economy varied in strength and span. The creation of rural small-scale industries as collective enterprises in the two decades after the Great Leap Forward (1957–59) affirmed the continued separation of the agrarian economy and associated industries from large-scale industry. The economic reforms have fundamentally changed the institutional separation between agriculture and industry through the promotion of small-scale industries, the vast majority of which are collectively owned by villages, townships, or county governments, not by the central government or individuals. The growth of these industries has stimulated the development of small towns and brought the higher wages of industry to a new generation of factory workers, many of whom continue to live in villages or return to their rural homes frequently. A social and economic continuum between industry and agriculture now exists where previously there was rigid institutional separation.

The development of TVEs has been crucial to the success of agriculture in this period. While many have proclaimed the virtues of a return to household production and the ability of peasants to decide for themselves what crops to plant and sell, the success of these changes would have been far less dramatic without the movement of agricultural labor into local industries. New local industries absorbed previously underemployed surplus agricultural labor. The increased absorption of agricultural labor into off-farm employment has been a key factor in reducing labor surpluses and thereby raising labor productivity in agriculture. The creation of local factories—often with far less technological sophistication, capital investment, and organizational complexity than are found in larger private or joint venture enterprises—is a key component of recent economic changes in China. Without these new industries tapping agricultural labor power, a return to household farming could have meant more of a return to production conditions of the 1930s when surplus agricultural labor was a basic feature of many rural situations.[5] In terms of markets, the economic reforms have meant in part a return to pre-1949 patterns of commercial exchange. The reestablishment of China's rural marketing system and its further expansion along the lines begun centuries ago echo some structures and patterns of late imperial political economy.

Perhaps the most important contrast between the reform-era agrarian political economy and the late imperial political economy is the dominant role of government agencies as buyers at contemporary crop markets. The willingness of government policy makers to use market mechanisms to procure grain and other crops makes any equation of market with private and plan with government simply false. Expectations that increased production by firms for market exchange would mean the growth of a vigorous private sector at the government's expense are further confounded by the *collective* nature of the new township and village industries. These are not privately held firms; the entrepreneurial leadership often comes from local Communist Party secretaries. Though the property rights specifications vary among cases, these firms are generally subject to county government oversight and control. Some analysts have even likened county governments to complex firms that make decisions on how to invest resources in different lines of production (Walder 1995; Oi 1995).

The example of local industry that most contradicts our assumption about economic reform comes from a village called Nanjie in the north-central province of Henan. Here the Party secretary has spearheaded the efforts of the village's 3,100 inhabitants to develop local industry. So successful have these efforts been that the twenty-six village-owned enterprises, including a brewery, a printing plant,

---

[5]Despite the importance of the TVEs, their capacity to absorb surplus labor is not unlimited. A 1994 estimate put the number of workers absorbed by TVEs at some 100 million; nearly 200 million peasants remained as surplus agricultural labor. As the capital intensity and technological sophistication of TVEs has risen, increases in output are not translated into growth in employment. Between 1978 and 1984, an increase of 1 percent in the gross value of TVE output was tied to an increase of 0.57 percent in employment; by 1992 the same increase in output value meant an increase of only 0.15 percent in employment (Solinger forthcoming: chap. 3).

and plants for processing instant noodles and snack foods, employ some 9,600 migrants. The first surprise comes when we discover that these migrant workers earn more salary and welfare benefits than village residents—in 1994 migrants made 2,160 RMB in salary annually and an additional 1,440 RMB in welfare benefits; the figures for residents were 2,300 RMB salary and 900 RMB welfare benefits. But it turns out that salary and welfare benefits aren't a complete measure of well-being, since all residents are entitled to furnished three-bedroom apartments, each with a living room, kitchen, flush toilet, and shower. They earn "star ratings" for socialist virtues such as public spirit, work enthusiasm, political participation, personal hygiene, and the studiousness of their children. On a one-to-ten scale, most households have eight or nine stars, which entitles them to free benefits: gas and electricity, medical care, kindergarten through college education, life insurance, and weekly supplies of food; those with fewer stars get fewer benefits and are forced to purchase needed goods on the market. With a white marble statue of Mao Zedong built in 1993 for some 260,000 RMB (roughly $30,000 U.S.) standing guard over the village and workers reading Mao's essays on serving the people and combating liberalism, this village's economic successes are firmly rooted in a socialist vision of collective effort largely discredited elsewhere in China.[6] If a village can invoke Mao Zedong and distribute services freely to those of its residents who have proper political attitudes, then the flexibility and openness of the economic reform process is indeed startling.

Economic reforms in China have in general exhibited two related components: (1) decentralizing bureaucratic power over industries to lower levels of government, and (2) market institutions. Each poses an analytically distinct challenge to a unitary state. Decentralizing decision making over enterprises has not made enterprises necessarily freer of state regulation and control. But in fact industry has expanded greatly in the reform period as an increasing portion of its output is produced by local industries. Local governments depend on revenues generated by these industries and therefore promote them. At the provincial level, competition to develop industry has led some analysts to conclude that economic reform is best carried out at this level. Both these changes represent challenges to the unitary state: local levels of government are developing their own resource bases, while provincial levels are developing their own policy packages to promote growth, policies that are not seen as national, but as particular to a province.

Many analysts have commented on the devolution of power from the center to lower levels of government. Certainly the development of local industries fits within this broad set of changes. But more particularly the emergence of county governments that are economic competitors signals the end to a unitary state in which higher levels of government could expect lower levels to share a common agenda for promoting production and exchange. While the role of local governments in China's new political economy is growing, the central government con-

---

[6]Kaye 1994. I am grateful to Dong Zhenghua of Beijing University for bringing this case to my attention.

tinues to make large investments despite serious reductions in its resources. The center continues to set many of the rules and to negotiate with provinces and large cities over tax revenues and regulations governing industrial development. Some scholars have argued that the center has succeeded at reform by creating policies that benefit lower levels of government. But as Dorothy Solinger (1996) has noted, not all large municipalities or provinces have succeeded under the reforms because, as she explains in her account of the central Chinese city of Wuhan's experiences, the center has not approved the same kinds of favorable conditions there as they have for various coastal provinces. Wuhan's relative lack of success reminds us that China's economic reforms have not had equal impact across the country.

Some analysts have argued that the province is the appropriate unit to take charge of reform initiatives. Provinces, according to this view, should be given increasing freedom and flexibility to set laws and regulations to promote growth. The most successful provinces will in turn serve as models for others. But if provinces are set loose, won't those with historically favorable endowments simply do better? The critiques of what inland provinces perceive as the center's favorable treatment of coastal regions—special economic zones, favorable tax packages, and greater freedom in contracting with foreign enterprises—suggest that the center's role has yet to be determined. The March 1996 National People's Congress included complaints from provincial leaders whom the center has labeled "warlords". The central government offered no guarantees that it would meet the inland provinces' demands for central government funds.[7] Just how far China's future political economy can stray from one in which the central government plays a strong role in shaping the flows of resources among provinces remains to be seen.

Market reforms pose a different challenge to the unitary state. Markets have become increasingly important for both producer and consumer goods, for capital as well as labor. Officials appear to have transcended the vacillation and ambivalence about markets evidenced between 1949 and 1980 (Solinger 1984). Peasants have far more freedom about crop choices and more ways to dispose of their products. Fewer industrial inputs and outputs are strictly controlled by a central plan; that some still are, however, means that political corruption can affect access to certain resources and products. Creating market institutions has been a considerable challenge. Financial markets, for example, are complex operations once they begin to mobilize and move large sums of money among many people. Copyright issues recognized in principle become difficult to enforce in law. Adjudicating contract disputes stimulates new forms of negotiation and resolution. For all these activities the basic formal structures are developed from Chinese interpretations of foreign practices. But these new institutions do not exhaust the meaning of the "market" in recent years.

---

[7] *Foreign Broadcast Information Service,* 19 April 1996, p. 44. I'm grateful to Dorothy Solinger for bringing this information to my attention.

Local political leaders have an interest in local economic development exempt from any central planning. The market is a crucial instrument, but its spatial dimensions deserve careful analysis. Large-scale integration does not result from these rural industrial developments (Oi 1992:124). Simple contrasts of centralized and market economies fail to capture either the analytical or the spatial dimensions of the recent changes. These rural industries vary considerably in their ownership and management structures—some are owned by private people, others by collectives, yet others by local governments. They all work, at least in the short run. Each is an improvement over what previously existed locally. But regional competition, while offering a solution to local fiscal needs, also promotes protectionism and therefore inhibits national market integration. The prominence of rural industries in China's contemporary political economy is related to the character of commercial exchange and rural industries in earlier decades as well as to the challenges of establishing a secure fiscal base for local governments.

The Chinese state can adopt specific economic policies already tested in other settings, but these policies will affect China in unique ways because of its demographic and territorial size. Thinking about "markets" or "industry" abstractly without attention to the institutional frameworks, both political and economic, within which these terms acquire social meaning, may lead to interpretations that fail to capture the real possibilities present at a particular point in time. The Chinese state's priorities for economic change may also differ over time and from those of other states at earlier points of history. I earlier argued that rural industry is a form of industrialization that seems particularly suited to China economically, irrespective of the particular institutional frameworks imposed politically. In relation to political challenges, rural industrialization also provides a source of funds to solve local fiscal problems.

Chinese industrialization is now more closely tied to the agricultural economy. The connections overcome separations between industry and agriculture present in late Qing and Republican times. Rural markets not only play the roles they did in late imperial times, but have expanded their importance. The range of goods and types of firms active in the economy dwarf those of two hundred years ago. If the central government gives up its role as the decision maker shaping the flow of resources across the country, then there really will be a revolution as the Chinese political economy breaks with the aspirations and achievements of earlier generations of policy makers.

We have seen the Chinese state downsize its commitments and capacities in the reform period. We have seen household decision making expand at the expense of both local community control and state directive, and we have witnessed an explosion of marketing activity, both within previously common circuits of exchange and across longer distances within China and beyond. These changes are taking place in the broader context of a global capitalism eager and able to take swift advantage of cheaper Chinese labor for production of a range of goods from light industrial consumer items to heavy industrial ones. Some of these goods have entered international markets, while others are consumed within the country. It is tempting to see these economic changes as necessary and natural results of "freeing" the Chinese economy from the shackles of government control, but in fact the recent changes are neither natural nor logically necessary. They are, however, key to economic growth possibilities. It isn't just global markets in general that matter. China has been integrated into global markets before. Especially important have been the systematic transfers of technology and organizational formats that have powered economic change within China.

The economic changes in post-1978 China have depended both on dramatic institutional changes within the country and on global capitalism having reached a point at which expansion into China could have that kind of transformative impact. It may seem obvious to point out the importance of China's developing a legal infrastructure and new kinds of factor markets that make possible the combination of capital, labor, and technology that motors a good part of the economic change taking place. Less obvious, perhaps, is the fact that international trade in the 1930s did not have the same effect. A major and positive rupture has certainly taken place. The material benefits of a modern industrialized economy are beginning to reach larger numbers of Chinese. How well Chinese leaders will plan future economic infrastructure, manage a wide range of ecological problems exacerbated by industrial development, and adjust to the loss of their current complement of comparative advantages is unknown.

The political economy of industrial development today differs from late imperial agrarian political economy in part simply because more possibilities exist today. The late imperial political economy stressed the replication of best practices adapted to local conditions. Few forms of economic competition among regions or provinces were imaginable in an organic economy. When such competition did occur, the government preferred to ameliorate and obscure the conflicts by finding solutions that minimized the importance of competing interests. The central government moved grain, money, and people across the empire with an aim of promoting a dynamic balance of population and resources. China's political economy from 1949 to the late 1970s expressed a similar outlook. Industrialization was a new process to be spread throughout the country by central government decision making. But the wealth produced by industrialization far outstripped the dimensions of the late imperial economy. Despite state efforts to spread industrialization, interregional gaps in economic development widened.

Now lower levels of government pursue economic development with a conscious sense of competing with each other. Can a unitary state in which central government decision making is implemented through a vertically integrated bureaucracy be sustained? If not, then what happens to the state's massive bureaucracy?

State–Bureaucracy Relations

The post-1949 bureaucracy is certainly larger and more complex than the late imperial bureaucracy. Nonetheless, efforts to distinguish modern bureaucracies from premodern ones can mislead us. The contemporary bureaucracy faces certain problems that would have been familiar to the late imperial state. For example, should the government form primary relationships with households or collectives? In late imperial times, the question was asked principally concerning taxation;[8] in the post-1949 period it has applied to both production and extraction.

Another issue is cadres. We look at the local cadre and see one symbol of the contemporary state's penetration of local society. But the local cadre, paid out of local funds and recruited out of local society, has little hope of moving out of the area. The local cadre occupies a socially and politically ambiguous role, as did the gentry in late imperial society, of being both part of local society and representative of the larger political order, even though the organization of politics and local society have changed. What remains a structural constant is the tension between horizontal and vertical ties that the local political elite experiences, which defines the possibilities and limitations of central state influence and control in local agrarian settings.

Research on local government issues often tends to highlight one of the two basic dimensions of the local scene. Some work stresses the vertical patron–client axis, while other work argues for the density of horizontal ties that outweigh vertical ties in significance. No doubt both axes are significant, however much scholars disagree over their relative importance. Both types of analysis accept as a given the degree to which China's modern state has made large-scale and systematic efforts to govern rural society. The challenge of ruling large agrarian populations is hardly unique to China, but the Chinese state's capacities to do so are certainly unusual. The range of efforts undertaken by the Chinese is no recent historical development. The political preoccupation with rural society flows out of a state-making tradition with an intense focus upon agrarian society.

Urban society, of course, is quite separate from rural China. Until the 1980s, the post-1949 state maintained a strict administrative separation between the two. Now new social problems and challenges come from the increasing numbers of people in the "floating population." Links between urban and rural China notwithstanding, cities remain organizationally different from the countryside. Urban China is the site for the continued formation and elaboration of groups asserting some measure of autonomy or independence from the state. The state bureaucracy in the city has declined in ways that open up spaces in which Chinese now seek social freedoms akin to those imagined and struggled for in Western countries. The public sphere and civil society so lacking in late imperial China have developed in fits and starts during the twentieth century. But Western ideas about state and civil society, for instance, have hardly been a natural modern development. The continued association between *wuguanfang* (unofficial) with *buzhengtong* (unorthodox) affirms the absence of an autonomous sphere for the expression

---

[8]The basic distinction was between a system in which households were selected to forward the payments of others in the village and one in which peasants were expected to go individually to the county seat to pay.

of group interests.[9] Similarly, a Chinese historian's quip to Perry Link about "government-organized nongovernmental organizations" replicates a structural ambiguity present in late imperial China (1994:35). The issue of the bureaucracy's scale and penetration of society, in both imperial and postimperial times, is related to the scale and complexity of nonstate organizations. The ability of the state's bureaucracy to penetrate has been a function of its capacity to create new organizations and at least influence, if not control, those that are nongovernmental.

Economic organizations have been in the vanguard of institutions establishing corporate identities apart from the state. As other social and cultural groups prove able to achieve this separation from the state, a public culture, public sphere, and civil society all become more likely. But the Chinese state aims to achieve a control over non-governmental organizations that rivals the aspirations of the late imperial state. The capacity of these organizations to define their own spheres of activity varies according to state policies, although their potential for autonomous activity exceeds that of groups in rural society.[10]

For the party-state, rural rule involves issues of local order and vertical integration of state bureaucracy not unlike those of late imperial times. Within the same ambiguous spaces in the continuum between state and local communities, institutions like village compacts (*xiangyue*) have a plastic and uncertain identity, much as they did in late imperial times. Whether officials know how current practices relate to earlier ones is unclear. They are at pains to distinguish their government from a "feudal" past, yet they are equally eager to affirm its embrace of Chinese culture. Moreover, village compacts and household registration today do not merely replicate earlier practices; they are adapted to today's social order (Anagnost forthcoming; Dutton 1992).

Nevertheless, contemporary practices do resonate with the past. Addressing reform-period efforts at policing, Michael Dutton notes conscious appeals to Maoist ideals of community policing, but he sees links with late imperial practices as well. "It is this collective cultural memory that is unconsciously 'recalled' when mass line mechanisms are operationalized in contemporary China. Hence, while the Party may politically recall such mechanisms and institutions as socialist, their real strength derives from their ability to tap into a much deeper historico-cultural memory. Thus, while the socialist and dynastic period are radically different, the

---

[9]The association between *wuguanfang* and *buzhengtong* is pointed out in Link, Madsen, and Pickowicz 1989:2.

[10]Consider briefly a Japanese contrast. With a repertoire of Confucian concepts of rule similar to the Chinese augmented by native Japanese notions, the Japanese were far better able to adapt some Western principles of rule. A key part of their capacity to do so results, I believe, from the spatial scale of coercive control and resource availability in Japan, whose geopolitical and economic dimensions resembled those of a European country far more than China's did. Japan's domestic challenges were more similar to those of a European country, its leaders saw its foreign challenges as more like China's. In both cases the forging of strategies to deal with the Western threat involved the emergence of new national identities. In the Japanese case, Meiji state makers succeeded in constructing a nationalism that served expansionary aims.

cultural referents they address and the ways they constitute the social subject share common ground" (Dutton 1995:427–28).

The state in post-1949 China has aspired to be a unitary state with effective rule over the entire country. A unitary state was achieved in late imperial times as the central government controlled appointments, procedures, and revenues. The eighteenth-century state not only cultivated a corps of officials who shared basic interests and agendas for rule with senior bureaucrats in the capital, but also incorporated local elites into its strategies. The nineteenth-century state developed new extraction capacities in the form of transit taxes, which were at first under provincial control but were gradually in the late nineteenth century brought back under central control. In the first half of the twentieth century there was competition among different levels of government and among would-be national governments for control over the customs revenue. Twentieth-century Chinese central governments lost control over the revenues previously collected by the late imperial state. The People's Republic quickly reasserted central control over revenues and disbursements; use of revenues remained local, as in the eighteenth century, but the center once again decided how to use them. This too reflects the logic of a unitary state that generally refuses to recognize the legitimacy of sectional interests. It represents a basic structural bureaucratic continuity between late imperial and post-1949 state aspirations and capacities. The decentralization of power to provinces need not logically undermine a unitary state if different interests are reined in or controlled by a combination of ideology and coercion. In recent years, however, neither shared goals nor pressures have worked effectively, in part because the possibilities for revenue collection have expanded greatly with the development of the economy itself.

Eighteenth-century central government uncertainties about letting county governments expand their collection of guild licensing fees expressed the state's awareness that local officials might develop their own power bases if they were allowed to mobilize revenues. The nineteenth-century central government succeeded in asserting control over transit taxes and began to oversee the collection of maritime customs duties. Postimperial central governments lost control over agrarian revenues, a situation the PRC reversed in its early years. But the success of the central government's control over tax collection and use depended on the reproduction of a unitary state.

In principle, the fiscal system is still unitary, even in the reform period. Analysts have noted that the Chinese fiscal system is unusual in having local governments collect revenues for the central government. But since local governments are intended to be part of a vertically integrated bureaucracy that forms the backbone of the unitary state, the distinction between local and central is less significant institutionally than it is in a federal system or in any other political system that delegates power to subnational levels of government. Revenues in China continue to be designated as central, local, and shared. This format is a clear descendant of late imperial fiscal organization. But what was a functional system earlier acquired dysfunctional features after 1978. This fiscal structure, already problem-

atic in the three decades preceding economic reform, has more recently proved unable to take much advantage of economic expansion; and perhaps even more serious, it has promoted economically irrational behavior as local governments seek to
expand their fiscal power (C. Wong 1991). In the 1980s, with the rapid succession
of industries subject to county taxation, the central government found itself unable
to establish its claims or to define how tax money should be spent. Considerable
amounts of revenue raising and control have developed to provincial and county
levels of government. The central government reasserted its authority with the rev-
enue-forwarding agreements of 1994, but the fiscal powers of a Guangdong or a
Shanghai continue to exceed those of any eighteenth-century province.

The ideal of a unitary state seems less likely to be realized than ever before.
Pressures mount to create new fiscal principles and policies that can tap economic growth more effectively and allocate resources in ways agreed upon by central,
provincial, and local officials. The central and subnational governments will continue to remake their relationships, but whatever alternative to a unitary state they
are able to create will have to solve basic fiscal issues if it is to succeed. With a measure of institutionalized separation at each level of government comes a clearer
sense of the different interests and concerns of China's many parts. Sharper distinctions between social groups and the state are also being drawn. The kind of
Chinese state that replaces the previous unitary state will reveal much about what
will happen to China more generally. To become persuasive, this new state must
elaborate a successor ideology to both the Confucian and Communist ideologies
that have supported a unitary state.

State and Ideology

Sharp contrasts between Confucian and Communist ideology are conventionally
drawn—Confucian harmony versus Communist conflict; Confucian hierarchy versus Communist equality; Confucian conservatism versus Communist radicalism.
Differences matter, but the contrasts can be blinding. When compared to Western
traditions, similarities between Confucian and Communist ideals emerge clearly.
Confucian statecraft repeatedly expressed a commitment to leveling inequalities—
land distribution schemes and calls for limits on private landholdings, for instance,
were made in every major dynasty. Communist land reform in Confucian perspective represents the greatest triumph of land redistribution in Chinese history.

Confucian goals for regulating people's livelihoods and nurturing their minds
are goals comparable to the Communists' goals since 1949. The substance and
symbolism of the goals has changed, but the state's basic commitment to the people, to molding their personalities and creating social and economic security, is
part of a long Chinese tradition.[11] In both imperial and contemporary times, peo-

---

[11]The reasoning I develop here partially resembles Lucian Pye's argument (1985:196), but what he in-
terprets as "profound cravings of dependency on the part of the Chinese masses" I see as positive expectations of claims to be placed on the authorities.

ple have expected the state to intervene on their behalf. These expectations can be considered parts of paternalistic or dependent relationships, but we should also remember that pressures on the state to fulfill its role form a kind of "contract"; should the state fail to meet its obligations, peasants have a Mencian "right" to rebel. This connection between state and subjects is distinct from Western traditions of political rights and formal institutional mechanisms to express opinions and influence decisions. Confucian and Communist visions of rule are both hierarchical and authoritarian. They both construct an ordered society across different levels of political space and see authority relations between unequal people as basic to the construction of society.

The new Communist state faced two distinct domestic challenges in 1949: creating a set of institutions and an ideology (1) to span both urban and rural China and (2) to rule all China. The profound differences between urban China and rural China in the late 1940s and early 1950s made it difficult to conceive of policies and institutions that could bridge the two. The new Chinese state opted in 1949 to create organizationally distinct political and economic structures for urban and rural China. The state closely controlled the few institutional linkages it created in the 1950s. For some of China's largest cities—such as Peking, Shanghai, and Tianjin—separate municipal administrations were created outside the vertically integrated system from center to province to prefecture and county.

The solution to establishing Communist rule throughout the entire society relied upon possibilities that existed specifically in a Chinese context. The Chinese Communists aimed to reduce social and economic inequalities both within regions and across them. The Communists expanded the state's role in creating a new status hierarchy to displace the older Confucian hierarchy of literati and officials. Being a Party member became the principal way to achieve status and power in China after 1949. Just as in late imperial China, the most important social status depended on government sanction.

Again as in late imperial times, the elite was expected to serve the government. The Communists expressed a desire to reduce social and economic inequalities that Confucians shared. In political terms, they created a new kind of elite without an independent and institutionalized basis of power and authority. The absence of a tradition in which elites have institutionalized bases of power has made it difficult for people to imagine principles that would let them claim autonomy. China's conceptual resources have been augmented by foreign ideas and principles, but the persuasiveness of those ideas depends in part on their receiving institutional expression.

The narrative of Communist victory became a postimperial alternative to Confucian imperial discourse for uniting and ruling the country. Despite the parallels, Communist ideology actively distanced itself from traditional political thought. As a result, many studies assume there is little relationship between Chinese Communist ideology and earlier forms of political belief. But some scholars have discerned continuities. The intellectual historian Yūzō Mizoguchi, for instance, has argued that the late imperial notion of public (*gong*) was carried into postimperial times, culminating with Chinese socialists taking *gong* to its logical conclusions (1980, 1991:63–81). Mizoguchi argues for a kind of continuity that is revolutionary, suturing what we conventionally assume to be a radical rupture. Communist ideology deliberately obscures the similarities and resonances between Communist sensibilities and those of late imperial times.

The Confucian and Communist visions differ in the degree of their totalizing aspirations. The Confucian agenda sought to order the world, but in late imperial times generally tolerated Buddhist and Daoist doctrines as long as they were not seen as fomenting social disorder. The Communist agenda has had to battle on two distinct fronts, with "feudal superstition" and "bourgeois" thought. The Communist visions forged from the 1920s through the 1960s offered a spectrum of views about politics, economics, and society that combined foreign ideas with native ones. Facing its own past and the world at large, Communist ideology has repeatedly criticized the persistence of old cultural forms and the adoption of Western ones as well. Securing orthodoxy has been more problematic for Communists, in part because the affirmation of their revolutionary identity has rested as much on an opposition to their own "feudal" past and the "bourgeois" West as it has on any positive set of goals and values.

Confucianism and Communism are effective ideologies for unitary states because they are both fractal ideologies, espousing a similar vision of proper order on any spatial level. The divisions of labor that can occur politically and socially depend on the interchangeable roles of people in institutionally distinct positions. All are expected to agree upon priorities and to implement the decisions made by higher levels of authority. Goals are national in scope; cadres at each level are expected to share the agenda for social order articulated by the center. Fractal agendas for rule share key assumptions about what ruling entails. Many analysts have noted the authoritarian nature of both late imperial ideology and Communist ideology, but, more than its authoritarian nature, it is the fractal character of the unitary state that is important.

The general collapse of Marxism-Leninism has made it difficult for Chinese leaders to articulate an ideological vision still tied to a set of universals that can then be replicated and applied all the way down the line. Instead, to the extent that leaders make normative appeals, they have become insular and parochial, a defense of the Chinese nation. The state has staked its legitimacy on its success at fending off foreigners and reestablishing security and integrity. But the project of forging a national identity on such bases fails to create much meaning for Chinese nationalism. The problematic legacy of May 4th iconoclasm, of which Marxism is a part, features an ambivalent, if not openly antagonistic, attitude toward China's Confucian past. The state is thus in a difficult position, because it has tried to represent two kinds of nationalism. It makes itself vulnerable to political critiques of being part of an agrarian bureaucratic past, unable to lead the nation through the twenty-first century. This argument was an implicit component of the widely celebrated and criticized *River Elegy* television series of 1988. The six programs aired twice, in June and in August 1988. They proclaimed the death of traditional Chinese civilization, part of which they suggested was an authoritarian state. The symbol of China's traditional culture is the yellow soil of the agrarian past; the symbol of China's future is the blue ocean connecting China to a vast world beyond its borders. One key consequence of the assertion that traditional culture was moribund was China's lack of a national tradition or cultural identity appropriate for its future.

If *River Elegy* is correct, the nation based on the countryside can no longer play the role of history's subject. Such expressions of unease over China's future give voice to the problematic meaning of nation and its uncertain relationship to the state. To displace a nation rooted in the soil with a subject floating on the seas is to create a precarious situation, open to several possibilities, including the invention of a different nation to serve as subject for Chinese history.

In recent years some intellectuals have argued that the nation's dynamism and future lie not with the bureaucratic and landlocked North leading an anti-imperialist struggle but with the innovative maritime South long in favor of contacts with foreign countries. This southern nationalism speaks of China's tradition of overseas contact, of a commercial dynamism and social openness distinct from the bureaucratic and imperial North absorbed in the politics of a land empire (Friedman 1994). Significantly, this critique does not clearly promote a separate southern identity. It does not challenge China as a nation but the state's ability to represent the nation; rejecting Peking's nationalism leads to a shift of nationalism to the south. While a challenge to state constructed notions of nationalism, the southern variant still affirms China as an integral unit. Such a recentering of the Chinese nation can be seen as a response to the *River Elegy* critique of the Chinese cultural past, a critique that includes precisely those elements composing the common cultural construction of Chinese identity. By diverting the center of national tradition to the maritime South, some critics are inventing an alternative lineage for the Chinese nation, as well as a future to be mapped out across the deep blue seas. Hence criticism of the bureaucratic state tradition and its role in defining Chinese cultural identity need not forsake all notions of a Chinese nation. Instead, it can attempt to free the concept of nation from the state's control. In other cases, however, there are indicators of stronger efforts to establish identities separate from a national identity. Prasenjit Duara (1995) has argued for a Cantonese "provincial narrative of nationalism." Diana Lary (1996) has shown how archaeological study of the Nanyue kingdom, centered on present-day Guangzhou, has been shaped into a source of cultural identity distinct from that of the northern Han conquerors. Whether this identity becomes the basis for larger claims of autonomy, a possibility related to claims of separateness made in the 1920s and 1930s, is for now, at least, difficult to predict.

Even a brief review of Chinese examples of common themes in the literature on modern states reveals that they lie along a temporal trajectory unlike that taken by Western states. There are parallels, to be sure, but a limited search for similar phenomena will only tell us in what ways the Chinese state has become like us. It easily normalizes the differences as Chinese failures. To stress a Chinese trajectory of state making does not deny the clear presence of changes to the Chinese state. The post-1949 state certainly exceeds earlier twentieth-century bureaucracies in terms of its moral, material, and coercive resources. Its deployment of these resources and its methods of control have created a society in many ways strikingly unlike the world of the late imperial period. But one may say the same of Europe. Indeed, in many ways the European changes seem far greater than those in China. Europe moved from a myriad of little independent political units to national states—much more dramatic and dynamic than the reproduction of an agrarian empire and its transformation in the twentieth century. Why has the Chinese state existed for so long?

The Persistence of the Chinese State

In perhaps the only case since the Enlightenment in which an analysis of European state making gained perspective from studies of China, Charles Tilly (1990:127–30) generates insights about European state making based upon G. William Skinner's analyses of urban hierarchies in late imperial China. Skinner (1977:275–301) distinguishes two kinds of urban hierarchies, one an administrative hierarchy and the other a commercial hierarchy. Political control flows down the first hierarchy, while goods and services are channeled into larger concentrations as one moves up the second. The two hierarchies intersect and even overlap, but they remain analytically distinct because they are created by separate processes.

The administrative hierarchy is a set of county, prefectural, and provincial capitals with the national capital in Beijing. The commercial hierarchy is composed of networks of market towns ranging from local periodic markets through the centers of large regions that Skinner calls macroregions. Tilly explains in European cases how states mobilized resources and established administrative control via these two hierarchies. At the same time as Tilly sheds new light on comparable processes in China and Europe, his juxtaposition implicitly poses anew the question of how and why European national states were formed out of materials so similar to those that in China were shaped into an agrarian empire. What accounts for the different spatial scales on which social control and material resources are secured in China and Europe? Why didn't China develop a stable system of political states? Why didn't some European state achieve control over a far larger area?

In medieval Europe, locally organized powerful elites had institutionalized bases of power in the countryside or cities. Successful territorial state making meant coopting elites through a combination of persuasion, force, and material benefit. The dispersion of wealth and of the political capacities to mobilize men and resources made it difficult for any one state maker to gain control over multiple nodes of capital. Territorial state makers, wrestling with elites near at hand and other state makers farther away had no opportunity to conquer all other entities in their particular state system.

China, by contrast, had no corporate groups, no elites with their own bases of power and authority, either in the cities or in the countryside. Controlling the status system, the government created and reproduced important segments of the elite. Elites could negotiate with officials or find themselves in conflict over issues such as taxation. But the negotiation of different interests in China did not create the same range of rents and privileges traded in for tax revenues that could be found in several European countries. Moreover, negotiations did not affirm and even reinforce juridically defined privileges and rights of elites vis à vis the government. Thus it is difficult to imagine in Chinese history, especially after the Song dynasty, the emergence of institutionalized opposition to state rule that could have kept the Chinese state from extending its rule over an agrarian empire. The limits that emerged were more often geophysical than political—mountains, steppe, and oceans determined much of the empire's borders.

More threatening to imperial unity were military challenges. Between the tenth and fourteenth centuries, challenges from the north variously cut up the empire, and in the seventeenth-century transition from the Ming to the Qing dynasties, military opposition to the Qing took place on the southeast coast and throughout the southern reaches of the empire. But military challenges could not establish durable alternatives to imperial rule.

Tilly's use of Skinner's two urban hierarchies alerts us to the common spatial structures of political and economic resources across much of Eurasia. If we think of economic hierarchies as systems of material resources to be tapped politically, the question becomes how states build their capacities to tap these hierarchies and in the process what kinds of political hierarchies they create. It is very clear that China developed capacities to extract revenues on a routine basis early in its imperial history. After the tenth century, these capacities could be defined and defended, because there were no competing claims on these resources from elites able to challenge the state for political control. There was an economic division between rents and taxes that allocated resources to both landed elites and the state, with landed elites unevenly distributed across the empire and the state able to tax everywhere. Late imperial state making promoted social order by encouraging elites to serve alongside officials. The state's commitment to social order was shared by elites. This kind of state making did not encounter many of the challenges faced by Europe.

The imperial Chinese state was hardly a static or monolithic structure during the two millennia it provided China's basic structures of rule, but it was consistently guided by a vision of a unified empire. Certainly there were extended periods of disunion, especially in the first millennium of imperial rule, but no new ideologies of rule emerged in these periods, no new leaders seeking to establish their autonomy on the basis of new logic of rule. The norms persistently favored unified empire. Early Chinese successes in creating the infrastructure to support this vision meant that ideological and organizational resources were always available to re-create and reshape an imperial system in later centuries. Indeed, the capacity of the Chinese state to rule a vast territorial empire depended on general ideological acceptance of the state. Were the state required to defend itself militarily throughout the empire, the strain on coercive resources and instruments of control would have undermined the survival of the state's imperial rule. Military power was never dispersed throughout Chinese society. Multiple pockets of coercive power rarely developed to challenge central power. Particular rulers succumbed, but periods of disunion did not create many competitive military power holders.

China's survival as an agrarian empire makes sense before the nineteenth century. But why was a unitary state re-created in the twentieth century? In a well-known work on state making in twentieth-century non-European settings, Joel Migdal (1988) asks why strong states emerge in some countries but weak states more commonly in others. In Europe, he suggests, state-making imperatives during the past five hundred years have issued from the competition among political units in a state system. This competition drove states to increase their domestic social control. But in non-Western areas the forces of capitalism and colonialism undermined the social institutions of peasant society. Acute challenges confronted successful states: a major war, revolution, or massive migration. The states that succeeded under these conditions had strong bureaucracies and were blessed with skillful leadership.

The Chinese case qualifies Migdal's scheme in three ways. First, the capacities of the late imperial Chinese state developed without a state system dynamics. Second, widespread Chinese commercialization before the arrival of Western capitalism meant that the disruptive influences of economic change were less severe; Chinese political and social institutions were not destroyed by the international economy. Thus the ability of the Chinese state to assert itself may well be as much a reflection of its past achievements and expectations as a response to new conditions. Third and finally, the central state reasserted its control over politics because its right to do so was not challenged by institutional and ideological alternatives.

The imperial state's ability to reproduce and transform itself created a force for unity, even after the system collapsed. Nonetheless, Chinese political order has traditionally always been close to anarchy. Order has been fragile because it has not been institutionally constructed out of checks and balances; rather it has been imposed through moral suasion, provision of material benefits, and coercion. None of the instruments to achieve order has proven organizationally stable. Institutions for moral suasion (the village compacts), for welfare (granaries), and for coercion (mutual responsibility groups) were difficult to sustain because they had no specific and permanent basis for reproduction. Constructed along many points of a continuum between state and society, they had no socially and politically secure position. Often created in response to imperial exhortation, they took a kind of energy and commitment that resembles the enthusiasm brought out in post-1949 political campaigns. But because the vision of social order was fractal, even when political integration by the state could not be assured, no strong forces aimed to replace the empire with smaller competing units. Hence disunion did not ultimately carry much threat.

The unitary state in Chinese political practice depends upon the strength of bureaucracy in both institutional and ideological terms; its possibilities for success are enhanced by the absence of a strong state–society split (no corporate groups, no parliamentary roles) and the lack of competing visions for organizing politics or for opting out of politics (and society). In late imperial times, the unitary state could promote its own reproduction through its political economy, welfare policies, and visions of social order. Even when the state was institutionally weak, its fractal ideology kept the ideal of the unitary state alive.

The conditions that sustain a unitary state no longer exist in China. The government no longer represents the principal source of status and power in society. Alternative ideas for organizing government and society threaten to remake both. The contemporary Chinese state lacks some of the capacities typical of the late imperial state in times of great strength. The ability of the eighteenth-century state to combine vertical integration of its bureaucracy with a fractal vision of social order mobilizing elite participation created stable political rule. The contemporary state has serious problems defining relations among different levels of government. The contemporary state also faces the nineteenth- and twentieth-century challenges of urban and industrial society. To confront these twin challenges, it seems only sensible that some combination of Chinese and Western strategies will be necessary. Western state making has little guidance to offer on producing political security and social stability in a rural society of millions of peasants. Chinese traditions of state making only began to cope with cities and industrialization in the 1870s in response to foreign contacts. For more than a century it has been unclear how to create a new kind of state that can span the divide between urban and rural in a country the size of China. China's past political practices are often viewed as traditional, feudal, backward, and obstructionist, while Western practices are modern, advanced, and ideal. Such valorizations obscure China's long arc of state making and consequently limit clear visions of alternative futures. Not only have current leaders failed to embrace democratic principles and to recognize claims placed on the state, but they have dismantled the set of commitments that they affirmed in the first quarter-century of their rule. Much attention has been focused on China's failure to create a new political system, but it is by no means clear that success at such an endeavor would necessarily solve the challenges inherited from the agrarian empire.

Like all countries set upon by Western powers in modern times, the Chinese have faced the challenges of adopting and adapting foreign categories and constructs to their native situations. Before 1980 Chinese particularities were generally described as objective conditions, while the utility or positive meaning of Chinese cultural categories were denied. One alternative to this denial of a role for Chinese culture and tradition is a new Confucianism, an idea that appeals to both native and foreign thinkers. The affirmation of Confucian values and visions is an argument for the present relevance of Chinese traditions. But this affirmation is defined by a Western discourse on Chinese culture. So—less obviously, perhaps—are the criteria for assigning value to Confucian traits. This makes it difficult to discern how the Confucian order itself was conceptualized in different historical periods and difficult to appreciate how a Confucian order specifically or a Chinese order more generally can be constructed in a non-Western manner. The new Confucianism looks for certain cultural values and their instrumental roles in shaping a contemporary definition of social order.[12] A functionalism defined at least partially by external criteria, this Confucianism is intended to replace the discredited logic of socialism, which itself once erased the Confucian categories of understanding. Since the new Confucianism is envisioned as compatible with a range of political regimes, from a "people's republic" to a Singapore or a Taiwan, it doesn't argue for a return to a unitary state with a Confucian ideology. The state-building logic that persisted in some basic ways from imperial times through the watersheds of late Qing reforms, the 1911 Revolution and the Communist Revolution, is now perhaps finally exhausted.

History and Theory

We have placed late imperial and modern Chinese state making in comparative perspective in order to point out similarities and differences that often escape scrutiny and analysis. For the postimperial period, many scholars have implicitly or explicitly compared the Chinese state to Western state making while labeling the West modern and the East, insofar as it is not Western, as traditional. Eurocentric models apply poorly to the Chinese case if we view them as guides to paths of development. If, however, we think of the functions that modern European states take on, we can compare these states' agendas with those developed in China during late imperial and postimperial times. All states must perform certain functions, such as raising revenues, guarding against threats from neighbors, and assuring domestic social stability. But the relative importance of these functions, their concrete and substantive definition, and the organization of the society with which the state deals can all be different.

There are far fewer independent political units in the world today than there were in 1200. The world has witnessed much state formation. As time went on, the traits of a successful state became more uniform. But important differences remain among states in respect to what they must face (challenges), what is demanded of them (claims), what they can do (capacities), and what they want to do (commitments).

The modern world is filled with states, but the ones we have today still bear the marks of the different paths they have traveled. There is no single state-making process. Before 1800 similar problems occurred at both ends of Eurasia, but they were formulated and dealt with as parts of larger agendas that remained distinct. Managing subsistence, raising taxes, and exerting social control were all elements of state making, but they did not fit together in the same way. Ideologies mattered. Different issues took on special importance in different settings. Thus

---

[12]Efforts to locate a relevance for Confucian thought have steered clear of formal politics and represented the ideology more as a culturally specific social or individual philosophy (Fudan daxue 1991).

European states could provision urban populations without the grand and elaborate ideology of paternalistic responsibility that motivated Chinese efforts, while the idea of no taxation without representation would have struck an eighteenth-century Chinese as a strange idea. Some challenges faced by early modern European states resembled those confronted in China. These similarities remind us that Europe's problems were not unique any more than Europe's expansion made its state-making logic universal.

Since 1800 non-Western parts of the world have increasingly been integrated into larger political and economic networks created by European expansion. It has been easy, therefore, to think about states in other parts of the world either in terms of this system or in terms of the traits that Western national states developed. But that China should exhibit links to the past is no more peculiar than that Europe should do so. Of course, not all parts of the world have state-making traditions as strong as the Chinese. They did, however, have histories unrelated to Europe's pattern of political development before their fateful encounters with the West. Unless we look for the historical dimensions to their state-making experiences, it is difficult to see how we will identify the general and the particular in different state-making processes.

Searching for multiple paths of modern state formation alerts us to a broader range of factors than scholars generally consider when looking at twentieth-century politics. We usually select some set of traits initially developed in the West and then expect them to be adopted by other countries as they become more "modern." Twentieth-century Chinese state making includes challenges inherited from the late imperial past. Bureaucratic capacities are no doubt far greater in many ways than they were two hundred years ago, but they remain inadequate to achieve the degree of centralized administrative control over the countryside that so many officials in both imperial and postimperial times have considered ideal. Postimperial commitments cannot be expressed in openly Confucian categories, but Communist ideology has created some clear parallels. How these capacities and commitments will change in the future is difficult to anticipate. But predictions completely divorced from an awareness of the trajectory from late imperial to postimperial state making are unlikely to be valid.

An earlier generation of Western scholars more confident in the march of the West's universal values sometimes ridiculed Chinese efforts to combine a Chinese "essence" with Western techniques, but the recent sensitivity to wide-ranging critiques of Western ideas has weakened the conceptual link between modernization and "Westernization." At the same time, however, many Chinese thinkers have engaged in a wholesale rejection of Chinese tradition; today, some thinkers reject both Confucianism and Communism as part of the same tradition. The disavowal of tradition comes from a judgment of its failures. The measuring stick for China's failure is the West's successes. But the consequent rejection of Chinese tradition and embrace of things Western limit the critical capacity to evaluate and discriminate among features of Chinese belief and Western values.

Two flawed assumptions are particularly problematic. First, it is generally assumed that all traits of Western economic and political systems are in some important way linked; this assumption makes unnecessary analysis of how these systems change over time; it also allows those who criticize Western systems to argue that any negative traits are necessarily embedded features. Second, there is an implicit assumption that Western and Chinese values must be in conflict, so that acceptance of one set requires the rejection of the other. The principal critique of this has been to assert the independent presence in China of Western values, an effort often ridiculed for its forced nature (Levenson 1968). The assumption of contradiction presumes displacement as the only basis for ideological change and fails to recognize the hybrid formation that emerges from a blend of complementary ideas. Such failure can lead to an inability to build on the past, thus limiting the hybrid's chances of success.

A position stressing hybrid evolution is at odds with recent writing about capitalism and democracy being the ideal, final state toward which all societies aspire (Fukuyama 1992; P. Anderson 1992:279–375). There are several problems with this latter view. Among other issues, the liberal conjunction of politics and economics is based on a contentious view of Western history; it assumes clear and fixed goals in a complicated and shifting situation; and it is blatantly Eurocentric. If capitalism and democracy in their Western forms are not inevitable, what can be achieved and how will vary from one path-dependent scenario to the next. Economic institutions can have considerable variations, and political ones even more.

In conventional Western assessments of the modern market economy and capitalism, markets are a basic component of capitalism. Communist assessments in both the former Soviet Union and China have generally accepted this identification. But where Western analyses promote the virtues of markets and capitalism, Russian and Chinese economic policies generally avoided what they considered dangerous vices until the 1980s. Late imperial Chinese thinkers, however, could distinguish between the beneficial impacts of markets allocating products and services according to supply and demand and the manipulative power of rich merchants who made huge profits by controlling prices, one basic component of capitalism. Confucian ideology supported markets and decried scheming merchants. Though post-1949 Chinese leaders have not consciously called upon this Confucian distinction, they have proven more able to promote market exchange than their Russian Communist counterparts.

Chinese policy makers and theorists have repeatedly asserted a basic distinction between a commodity or market economy and capitalism, a distinction most Western analysts find forced and hollow.[13] Yet Fernand Braudel has made just this

---

[13]Chinese works have considered the nature of China's socialist commodity economy since the founding of the People's Republic in 1949; see Zhang, Zhang, and Wu 1979 for a collection of essays and bibliography on commodity production and pricing under socialism written in the 1950s, 1960s, and 1970s. A major subject in the early years of the reform era was commodity circulation; see the collection of views on the issue Zhongguo shehui kexueyuan 1980. More recent works have

distinction in discussing an earlier period of European history. Can we be sure it doesn't apply in China today? Consider the similarities of Confucian and Communist views on political economy. Late imperial ideology accepted markets and understood how they could promote economic welfare. The same ideology also aimed to control degrees of inequality and guarantee minimal subsistence to all. But late imperial Chinese ideology never completely accepted the profit motive; virtue always lay beyond pursuit of material advantage. Communist ideology has also had difficulties accepting the pursuit of profit. Like Confucians, Communists aimed to reduce inequality and provide for the material security of everyone in society. With these similarities, perhaps it isn't so surprising that both argue for the virtues of markets and yet do not support capitalism. But even if this distinction between market economy and capitalism can be made, the recent double rejection of at least some Confucian and Communist sensibilities leads to the question of what will guide future Chinese understandings of economic change.

Many Western analysts assert that free-market economics will not only bring Chinese understandings of the economy more into line with our own, but will lead to political transformation. They argue that the free-market transformation of China sets in motion processes of political change toward pluralism and democracy. Certainly China has introduced new laws to address property rights and facilitate and protect the movements of capital and labor in people's pursuit of profit. There are also clearly more kinds of organized activities taking place outside direct state control than was true in the first three decades of Communist rule. But the chain from economic to political change may be less strong than some of us would like to believe. Political change depends on both ideology and institutions, neither of which has yet become completely divorced from the past.

For all the differences in the arcs of political change in China and Europe, the two areas find themselves at the end of the twentieth century in somewhat parallel situations. In China, the tremendous economic boom of the 1980s and 1990s has increased the amounts of resources and products within the country's several regions. Since the 1980s, different levels of government have negotiated about how to divide the new sources of tax revenue thus formed. Decentralizing power and reducing the government's role in economic management means that the central state's role is subject to continued redefinition and often reduction. In Europe, the movement toward a European Union involves the delegation of certain national government powers to a supranational body. These moves are qualified by the more limited geopolitical integration of Europe in military and strategic terms; NATO, whose member states retain veto power, displays less authority at a supranational level. Just how far these moves toward political integration will go remains to be seen. Not all countries of Europe even participate in these larger political groups. But enough has occurred to admit that the European national

---

addressed China's commercial geography (Zhang, Tao, Dai, and Ke 1988), and in a series entitled "Marxism and Contemporary Realities" Wang Ruisheng (1987) has considered the relationship between the commercial economy and spiritual culture.

state is by no means the stable and everlasting political form scholars assumed it to be twenty or thirty years ago. As European states agree to delegate certain powers to supranational bodies while the central Chinese state finds its powers and responsibilities reduced, a new kind of parallel between Chinese and European state making is emerging: both China and Europe must redefine relationships among different levels of political power.

Putting the contemporary Chinese state in historical and comparative perspective reveals specific traits of state making in China and Europe and alerts us to what they have in common. While Europe may never be more than a loose union of largely autonomous states and China never less than a country with a highly visible central government, in neither case are state-building processes closed.

PART III

POLITICS, PROTEST, AND SOCIAL CHANGE

The basic template of modern European history was determined by the entwined processes of state making and capitalist development. No analysis of another part of the world can comfortably make the same claim. First, no other area's modern history has been powered as exclusively by its own internal engine. Second, and from some analytical perspectives less obvious, no area's modern history can be viewed simply as the product of its contacts with expanding Western power. To understand how Chinese patterns of economic and political change have been affected by connection with Western powers since the mid-nineteenth century, I have argued for the necessity of reconstructing the dynamics of economic expansion and state transformation that preceded these important contacts.

In Part III, analyses of social protest provide a focus for looking more closely at some of the economic and political similarities and differences in the long-term patterns of Chinese and European historical change. Small-scale conflicts offer a well-defined unit of analysis that display clear similarities in the cases of grain seizures and tax resistance. The points of conflict are the same; participants exhibit similar interests; and officials have broadly similar options for dealing with the problems. When we place grain seizures and tax resistance within the broader frameworks of Chinese and European political economies, however, we observe differences that complement and qualify the similarities. State-building dynamics in China and Europe form alternative ideological and institutional contexts. Analyzing these contexts clarifies some of the similarities and differences in Chinese and European economic and political dynamics that we examined in Parts I and II.

Large-scale collective actions, like revolutions, are much harder to compare for several reasons. First, the events themselves are complex processes composed of multiple components. Second, there are very few cases to examine. Third, the search for what sets revolutions apart from situations in which revolutions do not

207

occur generally removes them from the long-term dynamics of political change. As a result, revolutions are often reduced to a few common elements and viewed only in the immediate, short-term contexts of political and social crisis. I explore the effectiveness of setting the Chinese and French revolutions in long-term perspective and applying to them categories and strategies of comparison developed in Part II for analysis of state formation and transformation. This approach is intended to complement and to offer an alternative to other efforts to reconsider the Chinese and French revolutions in ways that diminish their general significance, particularly their positive attributes.

The study of large-scale and small-scale conflicts is no longer as prominent in historical studies as it was in the 1960s and 1970s. Working within very different historiographical contexts, scholars in both China and the West once found good reason to study social protests. In China, a mechanistic Marxist theory claimed that class struggle was the force driving historical development. As this theory has lost its persuasive power, historians in China have become commensurately less interested in examining social protest. In studies of European history, social protest analyses were a key component of the "new social history." Social history's displacement by cultural history has pushed analysts to explore how people and texts create meanings that can be reconfigured in multiple ways over time. Within the latter context particular events with claims to meaning and significance established by larger patterns of historical change are simply not very relevant.

In both Chinese and Western historical studies, the decline of interest in social protests reflects a change in historiographic tastes, as well as skepticism about the nineteenth-century social theories that once predicted the patterns of change that would lead to the modern world. Scholars in many disciplines have rebelled against the teleology of social theory that promised a particular end point for historical changes, in part because reality has not confirmed the theories. As often happens, this rebellion has not produced a coherent alternative program for social theory. We find specialists in the social sciences and humanities introducing a far wider range of situations and problems than nineteenth-century social theories ever confronted. This increasingly global range of issues assaults us with a rich diversity of themes for which the categories of earlier social theory are inadequate. For all the welcome and positive stimuli these efforts introduce, there is also a danger. Because recent research trends threaten, implicitly if not always explicitly, to separate the analysis of historical change from the building of alternative social theories, the intellectual protest against teleologies may sever an important link in the process by which we construct social theories.

To date, the rejection of nineteenth-century social theory has been only a rebellion. Some may dream of a revolution in social theory, but few agree where it is to be found. In the conclusion, I suggest how comparative history can help us to build better social theory. This is no revolution, to be sure, but perhaps it is a reform that will salvage the enterprise connecting historical analysis and social theory as the histories we confront include more of the world.

9

GRAIN SEIZURES
AND POLITICAL ECONOMY

Between the late seventeenth and mid-nineteenth centuries, food was frequently a focus of popular protest in Western Europe. Scholars have vividly described these events and cogently analyzed their relationship to the political and economic realities of this period (Rudé 1964, 1974; E. P. Thompson 1971; L. Tilly 1971; C. Tilly 1975). Less well known are the strikingly similar types of conflict that took place in late imperial China. Chinese crowds gathered to demand lower prices, to block the shipment of grain beyond their local areas, and forcibly to seize grain that was hidden in storehouses (R. B. Wong 1982).

Not surprisingly, on both continents conflicts over food often occurred when poor harvests reduced the availability of food. Such was the case between 1771 and 1773 in many parts of France when harvest failures triggered popular demands for lower prices and a halt to the sale of local grain to distant markets. The more general economic crisis brought on by poor harvests was labeled by one official in Languedoc as "no work and no bread" (Kaplan 1976, 2:565). The same relationship between harvest failure and reduced employment was drawn in a Chinese account of conditions under which grain seizures or food riots took place in the northwestern part of the empire during the Qing period:

> When plentiful harvests reach the market, prices are low and there is work for hired laborers in all areas. Everyone can make a living. When flood or drought comes, prices rise and there is no work or wages for hired laborers. One or two crafty people take "eating the big households" as their slogan and people rise up in a swarm. There is fear everywhere. (Zhongguo renmin daxue 1979, 1:289)

That there exists a close connection between harvest quality and level of general economic activity finds support in both European and Chinese grain seizures which took place in bad harvest years. While poor harvests unmistakably increased the likelihood of grain seizures, the postulating of a simple causal relationship between poor harvests and conflicts over scarce supplies is an incomplete, and indeed misleading, characterization of grain seizures and their settings.

A straightforward association between poor harvests and grain seizures is contradicted by the evidence. There are any number of instances of poor harvests which were not followed by a large number of grain seizures, as was the case in France during 1709; in China, countless local gazetteers list years of bad harvests for which there is no evidence of grain seizures.[1] Thus poor harvests alone cannot explain the outbreak of grain seizures. Moreover, there is evidence of scarce supplies and grain seizures in years unmarked by especially poor harvests. Consider, for example, the plaintive statement by the *élus généraux* of Burgundy in December 1766: "The province of Burgundy experiences in a year in which the countryside has produced an abundant harvest all the hardship of dearth and is on the brink of feeling the horror of famine" (Kaplan 1976, 1:208). In France, the increasingly free flow of grain over longer distances, supported during the 1760s by central government policies of grain liberalization which upheld merchant rights to move grain beyond their places of origin, produced local scarcities and increased the likelihood of grain seizures. Likewise, the county and provincial officials who quelled the grain seizure disturbances that broke out in many parts of central China in the spring of 1743 considered the mobilization of grain for export to other areas and the consequent failure to make grain available locally to be the reasons for popular protests (R. B. Wong 1982:772–74, 780). It appears, therefore, that grain seizures in China and Western Europe were the outcome of competing claims on the food supply, claims that defined alternative and at times incompatible patterns of food circulation and distribution. The threat of poor harvests clearly created supply insecurities against which people had little insurance. Protecting their access to food when it was threatened by competing claims, however, was not primarily a struggle of men against nature, but a deliberate confrontation between men (and in Europe often women) lacking food and those controlling it. Poor harvests merely exacerbated an already contentious situation.

The resemblance between grain seizures in China and Western Europe includes both types of events and at least some features of the situations within which these conflicts occurred. The presence of competing claims on unstable food supplies formed a common scenario in both parts of the world. These similarities prompt a series of questions about the context of grain seizures, their causes, and their integration into larger social processes. Were the economic conditions for grain seizures the same in China and Western Europe? Did the state play a similar role in both cases? Are grain seizures an indicator of other common features in the historical experiences of East and West? Observations on grain seizures in China and

---

[1]Rudé 1974:23; Chinese local gazetteers often list the years of exceptionally good and bad harvests, but they do not include instances of food riots for each occurrence of substandard harvests.

Western Europe suggest answers to these questions. We begin by locating grain seizures within the patterns of food-supply circulation and the politics of food-supply management in China and Western Europe.

Chinese Grain Seizures

The circulation of grain in late imperial China embraced a set of transactions ranging from the buying and selling of small quantities on local markets to the accumulation, transport, and sale of large amounts across great distances. Peasants shouldered small amounts of grain to nearby markets or more distant towns and cities. Alternatively, they sold their grain to peddlers or the local wealthy. Both peasants and peddlers sold grain directly to consumers, to brokers who managed rice shops, and to rice merchants who bought large amounts of grain for shipment to other areas. For their part, the local wealthy both stored grain for future local sales and sold grain to brokers and merchants. None of these transactions represents an innovation of the seventeenth or eighteenth centuries; evidence for each type can be found as early as the eleventh century.[2] Many of the business practices established by rice merchants and brokers during the Song period endured well into the twentieth century, and customs governing local exchange retained supporters for the better part of a millennium.[3] The temptation to invoke an image of timeless continuity is strong. There is, after all, a temporal durability to some of the institutional forms that reinforces a general vision of a traditional, unchanging China. Yet a vision of stagnation that focused on selected institutional forms would be myopic; it would fail to acknowledge changes in commercial organization and in patterns of commercial food-supply circulation.

The expansion of commercial activity during the Ming and Qing dynasties was premised upon the specialized production of different cash crops and handicrafts (Li Wenzhi 1981). This process generated growing numbers of people who relied on grain purchases for their survival; in many cases grain traveled long distances. The most important developments took place along the Yangzi River. As cotton and silk textiles developed in eighteenth-century Jiangnan, increasing amounts of grain flowed into the region from upstream provinces. More generally, many areas were integrated into complex networks of grain circulation. These networks were based primarily on waterways, which provided the cheapest venue

---

[2]The basic study of eleventh-century grain trade appears in Shiba 1968:142–85 [English abstract 1970:50–80]. For the northwestern grain trade between the fifteenth and seventeenth centuries, see Terada 1972:120–79. The important eighteenth-century rice trade from Hunan to the lower Yangzi region has been analyzed by Shigeta 1975:1–65.

[3]For an analysis of grain marketing in the first half of the twentieth century see Amano 1953, 2:217–51. Reduced price sales and loans by local granaries and wealthy individuals were probably less common than in previous centuries, but the ideal of storing grain to provide poor peasants with food during seasonal shortages and years of bad harvest continued to enjoy support; the state's efforts between 1934 and 1936 to implement granary reserves is examined province by province in Neizhengbu tongjichu 1938.

for grain transport. Growing grain networks did not, however, guarantee geographically broader channels of circulation. Grain trade routes were not only susceptible to disruption by wars and rebellions, but might also contract when increased demand for grain closer to the sources of surpluses reduced the amounts of grain reaching more distant places. For instance, during the nineteenth century, the central province of Hubei attracted more grain from Sichuan and Hunan, its neighbors to the west and south, grain that had previously passed through Hubei on its way to the lower Yangzi region. By the early nineteenth century in south China, Guangxi grain production was increasingly consumed within the province, which left less grain for sale to its eastern neighbor, Guangdong. Finally, some counties which had previously sold grain to other parts of the province began to consume more of their production locally; Qiyang in southern Hunan is one example of a county that was producing surpluses for sale elsewhere in the early eighteenth century but later began to consume larger amounts of locally produced grain.[4] In these examples, commercial trade provided grain to consumers at varying distances from the sources of surplus. Reacting to changes in relative demand, grain circulation in each case contracted. This type of development ran counter to the general process of increasing economic integration of different areas through specialized production and trade. Areas of specialized production which relied on grain imports competed with areas of diversified production which retained locally produced grain for their own consumption. Production specialization among areas and production diversification within smaller areas prompted distinct, but loosely integrated, patterns of grain circulation. The expansion of cultivation to marginal hill lands and demographic growth over the eighteenth century brought declining returns to both land and labor in some areas and as a result deepened the tension among different types of grain circulation.

Within the shifting patterns of grain circulation, the volumes of grain that flowed in any particular direction during a specific year could fluctuate widely as a function of relative harvest conditions. Rice merchants sought out the areas where rich harvests brought cheap prices and reacted to severe shortages elsewhere by shipping additional supplies.[5] The flexibility of grain sources and destinations meant that the overall danger of shortages due to harvest failures was

---

[4]Han-sheng Chuan and Richard Kraus (1975:77–78) note the apparent contraction in the volumes of grain moving down the Yangzi River between the early eighteenth and early twentieth centuries. G. William Skinner suggests that increasing populations in Sichuan, Hubei, and Hunan explain the decline between the 1720s and 1840s in grain volumes from these areas reaching the lower Yangzi (1977:713, note 30). The decreasing ability of Guangxi grain production to supply Guangdong is brought out clearly in two memorials that the governor general of these provinces (Li Hongbin) and the governors of the two provinces (Su Cheng'e and Lu She) presented to the throne in 1830; these memorials are in the *caizheng: cangchu* category of *zhupi* memorials at the Number One Historical Archives, dated Daoguang 10/9/20 and 10/9/21. For the Qiyang example see *Yongzhou fuzhi* 1867:5.16b.

[5]The influence of relative harvest conditions on the grain trade is discussed in the opening part of Hunan governor Yang Xifu 1748.

reduced. During the eighteenth century people in many parts of China who usually consumed locally produced grain as well as those who depended on imports could expect additional grain imports in years of poor harvests. This security was not, however, without its drawbacks. The constant variation in the amounts of grain available and needed in different areas each year precluded perfectly stable grain flows and increased the possibility of contention over the proportions of grain supplied to one area versus another. A growing population and an expanding food supply were brought into approximate balance every year as harvest fluctuations determined the exact amounts flowing in particular directions as a function of areal specialization of production.

During the eighteenth and nineteenth centuries, grain seizures occurred in almost all Chinese provinces.[6] The demands for lower prices in importing areas were similar to those voiced in areas vulnerable to grain exports. The successful retention of grain by people in exporting areas simultaneously threatened the food supplies of people in importing areas. Good harvests yielded enough grain to fill both local markets and larger grain networks. In years of bad harvests, grain seizures occurred in locales where grain production both fed people near at hand and entered trade networks extending beyond the immediate area.

The places where grain seizures occurred were not necessarily themselves suffering particularly poor harvests; poor harvests elsewhere could increase demand on local production, simulating the demands produced by poor local harvests. Massive flooding or prolonged drought over several seasons might ruin all food crops, leaving little grain for anyone. A series of very poor harvests or a few complete harvest failures across a wide area threatened people beyond the boundaries of the actual grain seizure.[7] Grain seizures also took place during full-blown subsistence crises, but such crises were not necessary for grain seizures to occur.

Anyone involved in commercial grain circulation could become a target of popular protest in times of scarce supply. Rich households (*fuhu*) who could sell or lend grain locally also sold grain to merchants for transport to other areas. Withholding grain from local markets to sell elsewhere made rich households vulnerable to charges that they were hoarding (*tunji*) or forestalling (*juji*). When grain seizures took place, rich households were frequently assigned part of the blame for the disturbances. The description of the grain seizures of the winter and spring months of 1742 and 1743 given by Chen Hongmou, governor of Jiangxi Province, is typical: "The local rich first hear that rice is expensive in many provinces and that officials and merchants will come to buy rice. They believe rice prices will continue to rise. Hence they are unwilling to sell at current prices" (1763:15.20b–21a). A 1751 report on grain seizures in Wenzhou and Taizhou prefectures of Zhejiang Province echoes Chen's description: "many cases of grain seizure begin when the rich hoard their grain and refuse to sell" (Zhongguo ren-

---

[6]Two documentary collections conveniently provide accounts of food riots across most of China, Zhongguo renmin daxue 1979, 1:281–309 and 2:562–93; Li 1955, 1:973–84.

[7]For an excellent analysis of famine and state relief, see Will 1990; also see Wong and Perdue 1983.

min daxue 1979, 1:295). An essay on the grain seizures in southwestern Hunan during the 1830s condemned rich households even more strongly: "Those who are causing the trouble in the area are the rich who protect their grain. They resist till death lowering their prices" (Deng Xianhe 1851).

Undertaking external trade at the expense of the local market could prompt protests against merchants as well. Rice merchants who loaded boats for transport elsewhere and brokers who amassed large amounts of grain for sale reduced the availability of grain locally. Both were challenged by people who seized grain. Nor were retailers immune from attack; shopkeepers who raised prices and limited sales had their grain forcibly seized by crowds.[8]

The central government rarely tolerated people's blocking the commercial circulation of grain and thus interfering with merchants' activities. Demands for lower prices, however, did sometimes meet with state approval. When the Yongzheng emperor heard of rioters in Fujian being arrested for demanding a one-*fen* reduction in the price of rice in 1726, he criticized the official responsible for arresting them before seeing if the price had indeed been lowered.[9] Because the state supported the ideal of grain circulating locally at "level" (*ping*) prices, rich households and merchants who hoarded grain and drove up prices were criticized.

The people's expectation of low prices and state intervention to stabilize prices did not, however, legitimize their direct confrontation of rich households and merchants. Officials usually arrested troublemakers quickly. Forcible seizures of grain were often seen as the actions of "wicked people" (*jianmin* or *diaomin*). On other occasions, officials noted that harvest failures prompted people to riot; the people causing the trouble were not necessarily the consistent troublemakers suggested by terms such as "wicked people."[10] The range of official reactions to grain seizures reflects broader state food-supply policies.

The basic aim of the Qing state's efforts to manage food circulation was to insure access to grain for those strata of the population and those parts of the empire that were unable to depend solely on their own production and exchange. Long-distance trade, according to regional price differentials, created movements of grain from areas with surpluses to those needing grain imports. The eighteenth-century state recognized the importance of these circulation patterns and consequently endorsed the activities of traveling merchants whose profits came from linking distant sources of supply and demand. The state even encouraged traveling merchants to undertake specific transfers of grain in response to poor harvest

---

[8]For example, merchants leaving Guangzhou in the summer of 1741 were stopped by crowds who wanted grain to remain within Guangzhou. Similarly, long-distance trade from Guangxi to Guangdong was blocked at various points along the route in the spring of 1742 by people who expected to buy or borrow the grain being exported. The brokers who supplied the traveling merchants in Guangzhou during the summer of 1741 were also attacked, while five rice shops in Xiamen county of Fujian each had grain forcibly taken during 1751. See Zhongguo renmin daxue 1979, 1:307–8; 2:580, 587–88.
[9]*Yongzheng zhupi yuzhi* 1738:2.5.64.
[10]Examples of the labels used to categorize food rioters can be found in Zhongguo renmin daxue 1979, 1:281, 284, 285, 294, 299.

conditions by lifting transit taxes and permitting the use of coastal routes otherwise restricted (Will 1990:208–25).

The state also took a direct and active role in long-distance grain movements. Portions of the grain tribute, a tax collected in kind from the fertile provinces along the Yangzi River and those provinces near Beijing, were diverted from their original destination and sent to provinces suffering immediate shortages. Evernormal granaries (government granaries located in county seats), which bought and sold grain to stabilize seasonal supply fluctuations, also received rerouted grain tribute shipments. The state also transferred grain among ever-normal granaries within a province or in different provinces to meet immediate needs for grain distribution and to increase reserves in areas with inadequate amounts of grain. Finally, market purchases of grain by ever-normal granaries sometimes involved officials of one county or province going to another county or province to buy grain (Will and Wong 1991). These official movements of grain overlapped with commercial circulation, sometimes augmenting and sometimes crosscutting commercial flows of grain. Together, state procedures for grain transfers and policies toward long-distance commerce directed flows of grain from surplus to deficit areas.

Furthermore, the state facilitated access by poorer strata of the population to local grain supplies. Ever-normal granaries mitigated seasonal fluctuations in grain prices through spring sales or loans and autumn purchases or repayments. Distributing greater amounts in years of poor harvest kept prices from soaring above levels common in years of good harvest. The state also promoted community and charity granaries which were stocked by contributions from the wealthy and levies on the land. These granaries placed a claim on part of the local grain production and guaranteed circulation within a small local sphere. Rich households were expected to make contributions to these granaries as well as give loans and sell grain at reduced prices in years of poor harvest (R. B. Wong 1982:768–69). State efforts, especially the promotion of community and charity granaries, reinforced "customary" circulation; that is, the pattern of loans, aid, and reduced-price sales that the rich made to the poor outside a "free" market nexus.

In sum, the state opposed hoarding by the rich and maintained granaries as a safeguard against years of poor harvest. Officials made efforts to increase local circulation and stabilize prices in order to forestall grain seizures. The expectations of those seizing grain were therefore grounded in assumptions about grain circulation shared by the state. Indeed, the failure of granaries to provide grain prompted riots similar to those witnessed at markets or storehouses of the rich.[11] Nevertheless, the arrest of people who blocked shipments of grain leaving an area

---

[11]For instance, in Yanshi county of Henan seventy to eighty people gathered to borrow grain from the granary which had already lent out a large amount of grain in the spring of 1747. They were dispersed, but a crowd of 150–160 people then gathered and broke into the official residence to demand loans. When Xiangxiang officials in Hunan had decided that enough grain had been sold at reduced prices in the spring of 1752, some people demanded more grain. After another day of sales, those continuing to demand grain were arrested. See Zhongguo renmin daxue 1979, 2:567–69, 569–70.

supported the claims of parties engaged in long-distance trade. These official actions decreased the amount of grain available and raised prices on local markets. The official reaction to grain seizures therefore reflected the state's twin commitments to stable local prices and to transfers of grain from areas with low prices to those with higher prices. The reactions to grain seizures, which affected all three spheres of grain circulation (commercial, customary, and state), were determined by the state's efforts to maintain its own sphere of circulation and to support and qualify both commercial and customary circulation.[12] The state's attempts to keep local areas well stocked represent its broader commitment to promoting equilibrium despite short-term instabilities. By contributing to the viability of rural economies, the state also reduced the food supplies available for urban growth, a growth that was part of European economic expansion in the eighteenth century, the time when grain seizures became common there.

European Grain Seizures

Much of the preceding sketch of Chinese grain circulation will sound familiar to European specialists. In Europe, as in China, competing claims on food supplies tied to different types of grain circulation formed the immediate context for grain seizures. During the eighteenth century, crowds in England, France, Italy, and Spain gathered to block the movement of grain, to demand lower prices for bread, and often to force sales of bread and grain at lower prices. Charles Tilly (1975) has located these events within two long-term processes: (1) commercialization and the formation of national markets for grain; and (2) state building and changes in government policies toward the food supply. The expansion of grain marketing was in turn a component of the growth of rural industry, which made rural populations dependent on commercial grain and bread; the growth of standing armies recruited largely from rural populations and fed by state grain purchases; and the growth of urban centers that relied on commercially marketed grain for their bread. These new loci of demand required grain be diverted into new channels, developed in part by state policies geared to increase central power and to support an urban public order. Let us begin our analysis with an examination of changes in English and French marketing structures.

Institutionally separate structures emerged to serve distinct sources of demand. N. S. B. Gras's classic account of corn marketing in England distinguishes three types of commercial circulation. During the twelfth century, trade mainly involved manors. The subsequent growth of towns encouraged the development of local markets. In the seventeenth and eighteenth centuries a metropolitan market and an export market jointly replaced earlier local markets (Gras 1915:200). Alan Everitt has made a more detailed study of food marketing, distinguishing the "open markets" or public marketplace of Tudor times from "private markets," that is, corn chambers, warehouses, and inns located in provincial towns. Institu-

---

[12]These spheres of circulation are discussed in more detail in Wong 1982.

tionally distinct, open markets served territorial units while private marketing encompassed larger areas, moving goods among regions that had begun regional specialization in production. Long-distance trade developed on the basis of family and personal connections; the increasing scale of transactions was limited by problems of illiteracy and the personal conception of credit. These constraints notwithstanding, private trade grew, the bulk of it serving provincial consumption (Everitt 1967:516, 530, 531, 549, esp 566–67).

In addition, three special markets developed to supply London, exports, and the royal household and armed forces. London's growth required a greater increase in private marketing than was necessary in other parts of the country; Gras has demonstrated the distinctiveness of the London market's organization, stressing the importance of the broker in mobilizing the supplies necessary to feed London's growing population. As London came to house about 10 percent of the English population in the eighteenth century, its growth was the principal force behind the development of the English grain market. Finally, the export market was tied to the feeding of troops stationed on the Continent which was, in turn, related to the development of channels to supply the royal household (Gras 1915:157; Everitt 1967:507, 524).

Everitt offers a cogent explanation of these developments:

> The rapid rise in the population and its increasing concentration in urban or industrial centers like London, Norwich, Tyneside and the West Country clothing towns, upset the balance of communities hitherto largely self-supporting, and compelled them to depend upon market supplies. The same concentration, together with the expanding scale of market transactions, the declining area of cultivable 'waste', and the increase of regional specialization prevented their being met by local resources. At the same time, the price rise of the sixteenth century seems to have led to an increase in agricultural productivity, while the shortage of ready money in the seventeenth century, so often complained of at the time, stimulated credit dealings. In the upshot some years showed a large surplus of certain commodities in the more productive areas, which only the private trade could dispose of. (Everitt 1967:564)

Demographic growth in the sixteenth century fueled the production of industrial and urban goods on a basis of regional specialization supported by increasing scales of trade through new structures of circulation. These structures of circulation included new types of merchants whose urban-based wayfaring produced a distinct vision of society. Everitt cautions us not to equate simplistically open marketing with the countryside and private marketing with the towns, but he uses this contrast to portray "incompatible views of society and social duty" that emerged with the development of new channels of food circulation (1967:568).

A. P. Usher's study of the French grain trade analyzes the structure of commercial grain movements before the eighteenth century and its subsequent transformation. Before the eighteenth century, local trade and long-distance trade were institutionally distinct. Town markets could be linked across a small area in a variety of ways—the grain of one producing market might supply one consuming area, or one large consuming market might be fed by a number of smaller producing markets. Wholesale trade was managed in two forms. A kind of wholesale wheat merchant known as the *blatier* used his capital to buy grain on one market and transport it to another. The scale of his transactions was quite small, and he could be banned from the town markets by local authorities. Another form of wholesale trade developed in fertile areas along major rivers. The residents of river towns formed granaries which were visited by merchants coming from large towns. In some areas, the granaries were formed by rentiers, by bourgeois buying on the market, or by merchants coming from large towns to make purchases. The multiplicity of actors who could start these granaries points to the shared interest of the rentier, local bourgeois, and merchant from the large town in developing the wholesale grain trade (Usher 1913:37–38).

The institutional cleavage between the town market and wholesale trade was bridged in the late seventeenth and eighteenth centuries, prompted by the need of growing urban areas to increase their supplies beyond the levels mobilized by the granary trade. Begun in years of dearth, a system of country buying emerged, distinguished by direct purchases of grain from producers. Merchants offered producers a steady demand, which brought producers directly into a larger marketing network (Usher 1913:39–40). In the French case, the transformation of marketing entailed the destruction of barriers between the local and wholesale trades. In both England and France, basic changes in the structures of marketing occurred between the sixteenth and eighteenth centuries and created the setting for European grain seizures.

Grain seizures became more frequent in a period of agricultural depression and economic stagnation, if not contraction, and continued into a period of rising agricultural prices and increasing economic activity. Expanding grain circulation absorbed much of the abundance from a series of good harvests. After 1750, when the depression, marked by low prices and relatively high wages, was over and these new claims on the food supply were firmly introduced, more frequent grain seizures took place as prices rose and wages fell.[13]

The state played an active, if sometimes ambiguous, role in these changes. Alan Everitt has argued that the English state's failure to accommodate the sixteenth-century growth of a new system of long-distance commerce was among the reasons for the Stuart downfall (1967:586). The state did not, however, merely adapt to the new market realities in succeeding decades. The growth of marketing was

---

[13]On the mid-seventeenth century to mid-eighteenth century agricultural depression, see Abel 1980:158–93. George Rudé's assertion that English food riots began soon after Parliament passed the first Corn Law in 1660 (1974:24) may be wrong. Disturbances that took place between 1595 and 1598, as described by both R. B. Outhwaite and Andrew Appleby, appear to merit the label "food riot" though neither of these two scholars makes appeal to the work of Rudé or E. P. Thompson (1971). See Outhwaite 1978; A. Appleby 1978:142–43.

not a simple, smooth, natural process driven solely by the logic of individuals rationally pursuing their own self-interest. Certainly, this is part of the story. Grain seizures highlight the competition between workers in two areas making claims on common food supplies. But how grain will flow in response to these competing claims is not simply a natural result of supply and demand on markets. E. P. Thompson has argued forcefully that free trade policies in England required the dismantling of statute law, common law, and customs, all of which placed distinct limits on the circulation of grain. Laws against forestalling, regrating, and engrossing were challenged and slowly removed between 1660 and 1772. The laws that were struck down had previously regulated the flows of grain by prohibiting buying up grain for reselling at higher prices on nearby markets or those far away. For Thompson, "the breakthrough of the new political economy of the free market was also the breakdown of the old moral economy of provision" (1971:136). The economic interests of the commercial class engaged in long-distance trade found political voice and in the century following 1660 were able to win the legal contests dismantling laws governing local markets.

For France, Louise Tilly's (1971) analysis of French grain seizures shows that the French state played a leading role in creating new channels for grain circulation. Late seventeenth-century officials Boisguilbert and Vauban attributed the problems of French agriculture to the system of regulated commerce in grain. There followed eighteenth-century decrees ordering free grain circulation, qualified in practice by numerous duties and regulations. There was also a shift in the authority over grain supplies from *parlements*, which often forbade grain movements out of their areas, to royal officials who sometimes forced wheat onto the market. Jurisdictional disputes were won by the crown at the expense of the *parlements*. The state centralized power and grain slowly began to flow more freely.

The French state was not, however, as clear a partisan for one set of interests as was the English. The eighteenth century was a period of protracted political debate between a provisioning ethic protecting local consumers and a grain liberalism favoring long-distance trade. As Steven Kaplan has shown in his two-volume study of the French food supply during the reign of Louis XV, grain liberalism represented a radical departure in social theory, but it was supported precisely by members of the most traditional and conservative elements of French society, major landowners and nobles of the sword and robe. Such men supported grain liberalism because it meant higher prices and better returns; they were not interested in the intellectual links between grain liberalism and other new ideas. For others, grain liberalism was difficult to accept because of its connections with other radical social attitudes and because grain liberalism itself entailed the rejection of social claims that caused revolt among the police and the people (Kaplan 1976, 2:682–87). Experimentation with grain liberalism at different points in the eighteenth century was qualified by the threats of shortage, to which the centralizing state sometimes responded with efforts to protect local supplies. Having wrested political power over food supplies from provincial assemblies, the central state bureaucracy vacillated throughout the eighteenth century in taking actions to defend local consumers' claims to grain in periods of scarcity.

Free trade policies fit nicely with years of abundance, but pressures for state intervention were compelling in years of poor harvest. Policy vacillation was, in part, a reaction to the wide fluctuations in harvests. There is evidence that the French state faced greater food-supply problems than did the English state. According to Andrew Appleby (1969), expanded crop diversity in England between 1590 and 1740 effectively reduced weather-induced harvest fluctuations. More stable supplies would have meant a diminished imperative to protect local consumers against new claims. It must be stressed, however, that more stable supplies need not have meant fewer grain seizures. A shrinking need for government intervention to combat threats of inadequate food supplies could have accelerated the state's unwillingness to protect local claims to the point that grain seizures became even more common. While changing cropping patterns could shift overall supply conditions, political decisions mediated access to supply and consequently influenced the likelihood of grain seizures taking place.

Grain seizures, supply scarcities, and human starvation are intimately related but crucially distinct phenomena. If starvation caused grain seizures, France should have had more grain seizures during the sixteenth and seventeenth centuries than in the eighteenth century, when mortality from hunger declined. Instead, grain seizures became a significant phenomenon as the most destructive subsistence crises subsided and the transformations sketched above took place. Moreover, when the state successfully protected the supply requirements of imperiled populations in the eighteenth century, as during the 1740–41 crisis in France, there were few grain seizures. In England, the period of frequent grain seizures was not one of subsistence crises. As Thompson says, "No evidence has yet been published to show anything like a classic *crise des subsistences* in England during the eighteenth century" (1971:133). Conversely, Emmanuel Le Roy Ladurie's Languedoc peasants did not block the export of grain during their subsistence crisis of 1526–35. The reason was simple—the Estates of Languedoc had already prohibited exports (Le Roy Ladurie 1974:135–42).

For Thompson and the Tillys, grain seizures occurred when people could no longer depend on officials to guarantee them access to food supplies as new forms and scales of commerce penetrated the local scene. People made their own claims legitimated by traditional rights and customs.

> Grievances operated within a popular consensus as to what were legitimate and what were illegitimate practices in marketing, milling, baking, etc. This in its turn was grounded upon a consistent traditional view of social norms and obligations, of the proper economic functions of several parties within the community, which, taken together, can be said to constitute the moral economy of the poor. An outrage to these moral assumptions, quite as much as the actual deprivation, was the usual occasion for direct action. (Thompson 1971:78–79)

The focus, in many studies of European grain seizures, on the new claims over the food supply which violated popular expectations rejects forcefully any simple causal relations between starvation and grain seizures. The attenuation of life-threatening subsistence crises in them decades preceding frequent grain seizures directs our attention to the "demand" side of the food supply situation, demand not simply as a quantitative indicator expressed theoretically on abstract markets, but as institutionally defined and politically enforced access to food.[14] The "supply" side, however, still merits attention. While famines were not a concomitant of grain seizures, hunger and fear of hunger were important. Both real reductions in food availability and the fear of diminished access to food were important ingredients in the grain seizure situation. Georges Rudé reminds us of both: "Food riots generally occurred, as one might expect, in the wake of bad harvests and shortages which sent prices rocketing upwards, and they may be said to have been the direct outcome of a fear of famine and not famine itself" (1974:23–24). Famine did not set the stage, but fear of famine put the drama into motion.

Georges Lefebvre rules out famine from the French scene in 1789 as he recreates the psychology of the food rioters:

> When things were short, hunger too started riots and in their train came a new or greater fear. The people were never willing to admit that the forces of nature alone might be responsible for their poverty and distress. Why had they not stored away corn during the years of plenty? . . . In 1789 they [the poor] said again and again that they could not possibly die of hunger. If the government saw fit to let the price rise, then all they had to do was raise wages too—or else make the rich feed the poor. Otherwise they would help themselves and have their revenge. . . . There was not famine, but it was too late to check rising prices. (Lefebvre 1973:24)

In Lefebvre's depiction, the participants in revolutionary grain seizures had their fears, but they clearly saw options for the government and for themselves. Hungry, yes; starving, perhaps. But famines were innocent—they did not cause grain seizures.

To summarize, centralizing states in France and England helped to create grain markets free from official interference. Officials no longer consistently guaranteed local food supplies against outside demand; they could no longer be counted on to lower market prices to "just" levels. Grain seizures emerged at the cleavages created by the commercialization of grain, in towns and villages where a new type of market expansion penetrated and transformed older patterns of exchange and when poor harvests forced choices among competing claims. After the 1850s grain seizures disappeared from Europe. Improved transport carried an increasing volume of food to urban markets. The rural social systems of Europe were

---

[14]Amartya Sen (1981) has argued that food-supply issues in poor countries today are embedded in a system of social and political relations; poor people have entitlements to food. Sen's perspective resonates with those found in both China and Europe two and three centuries ago.

transformed, in different ways to be sure, but in each case they became subordinated to urban centers, centralized states, and capitalist economies.

Grain Seizures: A Comparison

What can grain seizures tell us about conditions in China and Western Europe in the eighteenth century? Judging from descriptions of their actions, participants appear drawn to protest for broadly similar reasons. Whether Chinese or Europeans, they expected local officials and merchants to protect their food supplies. They considered certain price rises to be the result not of general supply and demand conditions but of the specific actions of merchants who kept food off local markets or officials who failed to keep prices stable. Despite dramatic differences in cooking and diet, Chinese and Europeans defended their claims to food in such similar ways that their expectations and understanding of the situations also seem closely parallel. Similarly, different officials in China and Europe defended structurally parallel interests—local officials were interested in protecting local supplies while higher-level officials generally wanted to encourage a freer circulation of grain. The understanding of what was at stake in a grain seizure contains elements that cross cultures among officials as well as among the populations engaged in protest.

Given these similarities of the grain seizure event in China and Western Europe, one might be tempted to search for an interpretation of Chinese grain seizures in a European context. If we take the European experience as the model for the historical development of capitalism and view the grain seizure as a conflict produced during the transition to capitalism, grain seizures in China could be interpreted as indicators of capitalist penetration and the resistance of lower strata to the reshaping of the economy and their incorporation into larger economic networks. Indeed, some Chinese and Japanese scholars have viewed grain seizures as class conflicts attending the penetration of a feudal society by capitalist relations (Fu 1941; Shigeta 1975:45–48; Kojima 1978:88–153).

Certainly, grain seizures were similar events in China and Western Europe. The similarity may be asserted to the degree that competing claims on the food supply were manifested in contradictions involving different spatial scales of grain circulation. Supply scarcities or fears of such scarcities defined the objective conditions and informed the subjective perceptions of crowds who took action because officials failed to guarantee them access to food. But similar events do not necessarily entail the same sets of conditions. Can we explain the presence of grain seizures in both parts of the world without invoking a shared principle of development? Let us review first commercial food circulation.

In England and France, an expansion of commerce was caused by institutional changes in marketing structures. New sources of demand led to additional claims on the food supply. The English open market system was penetrated by private trading, thereby propelling grain circulation into wider spheres. French country buying linked local and long-distance trade in an integrated fashion that made possible larger volumes of grain circulation across greater areas. New claims on the food supply were exercised by merchants whose marketing roles became sharply distinct from those of previous traders.

In China, expanding demand for grain was channeled through commercial institutions largely inherited from previous centuries. There were fewer changes in the organizational structure of marketing than took place in England or France. Specialization and diversification within the Chinese agrarian economy called forth increased commercial circulation of grain at local levels and across longer distances. No Chinese city grew at the rate of London or Paris to stimulate the expansion of grain commerce. The possibility of subsistence crises continued throughout the late imperial period, but the threat posed by poor harvests was simultaneously dampened by the variable flows of commercial grain. Long-distance demand grew in the eighteenth and nineteenth centuries, but so did demand closer to the sources of supplies. The possibilities for conflicting demands on the grain supply increased over the late imperial period with the expansion of commercial circulation at multiple levels to meet both economic specialization and diversification, as well as persistent harvest fluctuations with their threat of subsistence crisis.

In Europe, the deadly subsistence crises subsided as new sources and structures of demand created the conditions for grain seizures. In China, the continued possibility of famine accompanied eighteenth- and nineteenth-century grain seizures. The relative importance of new demands and lasting supply instabilities to the creation of conditions for European and Chinese grain seizures differed. A second set of differences in food marketing can be seen in the types of social relations expressed in commerce. In both France and England, merchants could ally with rich farmers at the expense of nearby consumers because those controlling local food supplies were not bound closely to the lower classes by ties of association or dependence, and hence were less likely, compared to Chinese rich households, to sustain a pattern of rural social relations that sometimes required rejections of merchant claims to grain.

In China, local market grain supplies were often dominated by rich households. Their ability to hold off the market a sizable proportion of locally produced grain gave them considerable power over the food supply.[15] At the same time, the grain accumulated by rich households fed the grain trade circulating beyond their immediate locales. Rich households enjoyed the luxury of choosing between higher profits from sales to merchants and lower prices from local sales which earned them the gratitude of their poorer neighbors. Their interests were served by balancing the desire for greater wealth and the need to support the people beneath them, whose continued existence was the foundation of the social order they headed.

---

[15]Yang Xifu, governor of Hunan in 1748 put the matter this way: "When the rich take grain to the market, they must get a good price. They refuse to sell cheaply. They have the power to control grain prices" (Yang Xifu 1748).

Turning to the state, policies in England and France both changed over the eighteenth century to support class interests benefiting from new claims on the food supply. Recognition of economic changes, concern for urban public order, and the need to provision their armies led the English and French states to adopt new policies. In both countries, the shift in the locus of political control over food supplies was part of the state-building process. In the French case, political control over food circulation had been in the hands of provincial aristocracies who lost their authority to newly created central government offices. In England, the promulgation of new laws replaced statutes defending local needs and priorities.

In China, the eighteenth-century state made efforts to centralize its control over grain movements by reducing the powers of provincial and local authorities to restrict the commercial movement of grain. Unlike the French state, the Chinese state did not need to strip semi-autonomous provincial assemblies of their previous powers; Chinese officials were members of a centralized bureaucracy who lacked independent bases of authority. Unlike the English state, the Chinese state did not have to reject established customs in favor of new laws; the central state could appeal to long-standing principles to encourage the circulation of grain.[16] The Chinese state's commitment to long-distance commerce required no radical rupture with past policies and practices. Moreover, the Chinese state's involvement in long-distance grain movements went beyond the efforts of either the English or the French. Shipping large amounts of grain over long distances to qualify and complement commercial grain flows was one basic dimension of a state sphere of grain circulation lacking a European counterpart. Chinese food policies entailed no displacement of lower levels of previously autonomous authorities. The Chinese state's efforts to promote long-distance grain markets lacked some of the incentives that centralizing European governments had to wrest food-supply control from local officials. The central government assumed itself to be responsible for all parts of the empire, and thus its support for long-distance grain circulation was less complete than in either England or France. The Chinese state was simultaneously committed to protecting local grain supplies and to promoting long-distance trade. Both its granary policies and opposition to hoarding were designed to ensure the circulation of grain locally at low and stable prices. Indeed, the state's success in creating massive stores of grain to mitigate seasonal fluctuations in grain availability and to counteract scarcities in years of poor harvest, positively increased popular expectations that it could intervene to protect the subsistence requirements of the population. The Chinese state's efforts at grain storage far exceeded European efforts in both plan and accomplishment.[17]

---

[16]Rotating service among provinces (excluding the official's province of origin), limited the degree to which officials would defend entrenched local interests at the expense of central government priorities; on central government opposition to lower-level officials restraining grain circulation, see Lang 1937:171–73.

[17]Brief remarks on famine relief appear in Wong and Perdue 1983:321–25; I make a more extended comparison in Will and Wong 1991:507–25.

The Chinese state's food policies had distinct local and empirewide dimensions. The state consequently applied different criteria to local circulation and long-distance trade making the state's view of the relationship between the two ambiguous. The opposition to hoarding demonstrated a desire for stable local prices rooted in a vision of the proper circulation of grain among different population strata. Frequent rejection of efforts by lower-level officials to halt grain exports from their jurisdictions demonstrated support for merchants moving grain from areas with low prices to those with high prices and reflected an awareness of the economic integration of different areas. The state's opposition to both holding grain off local markets and the blocking of transport leaves unclear the relative priority of local exchange versus long-distance trade. The admission by the Huguang governor-general, Yang Zongren, in 1723 that he did not anticipate a relationship between hoarding and long-distance trade underlines the common official separation of local exchange and long-distance trade into putatively unrelated parts: "I previously forbade hoarding by rich households, not realizing that purchases by merchants would consequently become scarce."[18]

During the eighteenth century, the failure to perceive the relationship between local exchange and long-distance commerce and assign clear priority to one type of circulation was partially obscured by the state's ability to take an active hand in long-distance circulation while strongly supporting the provisioning of local communities. Over the course of the nineteenth century, there was a decline in central government abilities to coordinate long-distance circulation and to build up local reserves. Grain mobilization for military campaigns gradually displaced efforts to manage civilian food supplies. The restoration of order following the mid-century rebellions did not reproduce the eighteenth-century successes in food-supply management.[19] The devolution of intervention in food-supply conditions to provincial and county levels in the nineteenth century represented a political retreat from efforts to effect an empirewide coordination of food policies. With the usual locus of political intervention in the food supply shifted to the provincial level, the central state was increasingly confronted by provincial officials making food-supply decisions on their own.

State policies in England and France encouraged economic integration within each country. Political centralization created economies that competed through the mercantilist era, ending with new forms of specialization and complementarity among the parts of Europe. The new marketing institutions and their accompanying claims on the food supply were created during a period of economic adjustment when parts of both England and France increased the amounts of grain production destined for other parts of Europe (England) and other parts of the country (France) (Wallerstein 1980:81–85).

---

[18] *Yongzheng zhupi yuzhi* 1.3.36.

[19] Nineteenth-century problems with the grain tribute are discussed by Susan Mann Jones and Philip A. Kuhn 1978; Hinton 1956. Difficulties with the local granary system during the nineteenth century, including the effects of grain mobilization of the military are analyzed in Will and Wong 1991:75–92. The Changsha riot of 1910 is considered in Wong 1982:781–82.

Political decentralization in China gave nineteenth-century provincial governments greater autonomy in their policies toward the food supply. Provincial officials faced a variety of food-supply situations; one common feature to their efforts was promoting increased production in order to meet the food requirements of growing populations. Trade within the province from surplus to deficit areas was desired in all cases, but officials divided their opinions on interprovincial transfers according to the province's position as a net exporter or importer.[20] When the central state no longer coordinated food transfers across provinces and less effectively restricted the ability of provincial officials to block the movement of grain from one province to another, food-supply integration across borders became more difficult.

Competition for food supplies produced a weak agrarian protectionism. This protectionism, exercised at the provincial level and below, reversed, at least slightly, eighteenth-century trends of political coordination and economic integration across provincial boundaries. In short, the political and economic frameworks within which grain seizures occurred in China and Europe were very different.

The contradiction between local claims and long-distance claims on the food supply was represented clearly in European grain seizures by alternative ideologies defending producing locales' claims to grain and promoting the advantages of making profits through satisfying consumer demand far away. In China this contradiction became a muted tension. A commitment to "level" prices carried with it condemnation of hoarding and forestalling, but the necessity of holding grain off local markets to supply other markets was tacitly accepted because traveling merchants performed the useful function of moving grain from areas where it was cheap to those places where it was dear. Two principles for the commercial circulation of grain, one applying to circulation within a small area and the other to movements between areas, uneasily coexisted, but were not brought out clearly as incompatible. The call for level prices was a warning to people who controlled large amounts of grain to keep availability stable through the seasons and across years of good and poor harvests. Acceptance of grain shipments according to relative prices shows an awareness of the need to balance variable supply and demand conditions across regions. The commitment to protect local food supplies was tempered by the recognition that some areas needed imports more than others. The political demands of sustaining social order across an empire and within each small corner of it were articulated through beliefs in principles that collided during grain seizures. A single ideological framework embraced alternative principles, each of which was grounded in its own logic. The different claims on the food supply did not, as in Europe, offer alternative

---

[20]Officials governing provinces that produced considerable surpluses often became nervous when merchants or officials from other provinces came to buy grain; officials serving in provinces habitually depending on grain imports trumpeted the virtues of trade. Examples of the former are given in R. B. Wong 1982. For an example of attitudes of officials in grain-importing provinces, see Chen Zhaolun n.d.

visions of how grain should flow in mutually antagonistic terms that were connected to larger economic and political debates. The ideology of an emerging market economy rejected the categories of economic concern and political actions that European food rioters sought to defend. Competing claims to the food supply based on antagonistic rationales placed high stakes on the outcome of grain seizures. The winners did not look back; the losers had less to look forward to. In China, no new ideology championed the claims of an ascending economic order.

Louis XV and the Qianlong emperor might well have understood something of the concerns the other had about managing food-supply problems. Certainly, both men faced vexing choices over how to meet competing claims on the food supply. However, state building in commercially aggressive European countries bore little resemblance to the eighteenth-century strengthening of central state control over a prosperous agrarian empire and nineteenth-century weakening of both central control and agrarian prosperity. Nevertheless, grain seizures took place in both parts of the world.

Implications

The similarity of the grain seizure event in China and Europe suggests that we have identified the same piece in two different puzzles. We know how the piece fits in one puzzle and take this as our lead for sorting out the pieces in the second puzzle. But the puzzles show different pictures. The grain seizure event emerged in European history as commercial capitalism entrenched itself as the dominant political economy. The expansion of commercial grain circulation in late imperial China within small areas and across great distances was an aspect of economic diversification within areas and specialization among different areas. By the mid-nineteenth century, grain seizures ceased to be a common form of conflict in Western Europe. Grain seizures were rearguard blows against the centralization of state power, the subordination of rural to urban classes, and the advance of capitalism. In China, the nineteenth-century state, beset by rebellion and imperialism, was less able to intervene in food-supply problems than the eighteenth-century state. The combination of economic specialization and supply insecurity continued to define the structural context for Chinese grain seizures. Claims on grain held by the rich continued to be made, while high prices were repeatedly protested and opposition to the export of grain persistently voiced. In the early 1900s, a young man named Mao Zedong was deeply impressed by the blockage of his father's shipment of rice along a small river in Hunan. Shortly thereafter, grain seizures in Changsha were entwined in the political protests that toppled the Manchu regime.[21] Grain seizures attended the demise of the imperial system and posed one of the challenges to be faced by leaders of the Chinese revolution.

---

[21]R. B. Wong 1982:781–82; on Mao's reaction to the food riot blocking his father's grain shipment, see Snow 1968:136.

Knowing grain seizures only as a type of conflict attending the building of European states and the consolidation of capitalism creates a sense of false necessity, a belief that grain seizures, such as those in China, must be embedded in processes of transformation akin to those found in Europe. Through comparison of Chinese and European grain seizures, we see that similar events embedded in different structures across widely separated parts of the world raise questions about explanations framed solely in culturally specific terms and those confidently forwarded as parts of universal causal sequences.

In economic terms, the presence of competing claims between local and long-distance trade created the structural conditions for protest in both China and Europe. But whereas there was a clear shift in European cases from local claims to long-distance claims, in China the two continued to be in uneasy competition for a far longer period of time. European food-supply conditions were transformed in the eighteenth century by productivity growth and in the nineteenth century, especially after 1850, by market integration made possible by the development of railroads and shipping. China experienced no remotely similar set of economic changes until the 1980s. Even in the 1990s the government threatens severe punishment for those who hoard or speculate on grain (*Wall Street Journal* 29 June 1994, A14). The presence of grain seizures in China and Europe reflects the existence of market economies in both. Their disappearance in Europe affirms the solution to subsistence worries under industrial capitalism. No such transformation has been completed to make Chinese peasants completely immune from food-supply insecurities and manipulation by entrepreneurs holding large supplies of grain.

Political differences also indicate how struggles over food motivated by similar interests and anxieties can become parts of very different trajectories of political change. In Europe, grain seizures starkly pitted the community against outsiders; women played major roles in the protests to defend the family and community. Local governments sought to defend their municipal autonomy and privileges against outside interference when acting to protect their local food supplies. Independent local rule buttressed a strong sense of local community. Centralizing states undermined municipal autonomy and integrated people into a national state not on the basis of community identification but as individuals with loyalties transferred to the larger political unit.

Chinese cases lack both the municipal autonomy of local government and the strong community identity symbolized by women taking to the streets to protest high prices and exports. By the early twentieth century, according to Lucien Bianco's (1991) research, a devolution in the degree of collective mobilization to protest high prices and exports had occurred. The weakness of community bases for mobilization is complemented by diminished state capacity to intervene to stabilize food supplies. We might surmise that there was, consequently, less reason for people to organize to protest since they could not expect government intervention to support them. Since 1949 the central state has become powerful once again and in some periods has pushed policies that promote community solidarity. But central power was hardly adequate to ensure adequate shipments of grain in response to subsistence crises, as the devastating famines following the Great Leap Forward demonstrated. The vacillating strengths of different levels of government and the varying degrees of integration among them are reflected in the contexts and likelihood of grain seizure events.

Viewed within a comparative perspective on China and Europe, grain seizures exist in two distinct trajectories of economic development and two distinct trajectories of political change. While produced under similar conditions of material insecurity coupled with competing economic claims to be adjudicated by competing political actors, grain seizures in China and Europe become similar scenes in different dramas.

10

STATE MAKING,
FISCAL NEGOTIATIONS,
AND TAX RESISTANCE

Struggles to define acceptable levels and forms of taxation took place in China and Europe after 1500. At issue in both areas were conflicts between government desires for revenues and popular conceptions of equity and justice concerning tax levies. In European settings, tax resistance stopped being a collective form of protest in the nineteenth century, when connections among representation, citizenship, and taxation were affirmed. In China, however, tax resistance persisted as a common form of collective action, growing more common in the nineteenth century and continuing into postimperial times. European states expanded their extractive capacities despite tax resistance strong enough to change the ways in which rulers raised taxes. In contrast, the nature of Chinese tax resistance itself changed over time; while it has never enjoyed the successes that some tax resistance episodes did in European history, tax resistance has continued to challenge Chinese governments. After a brief discussion of European tax resistance, this chapter considers the changing features of Chinese tax resistance between the eighteenth and twentieth centuries. Patterns of tax resistance in China capture changing state–society relations in late imperial and postimperial history. When compared with tax resistance in Europe, these patterns highlight similarities and differences in state-making experiences at both ends of Eurasia.

Tax Resistance in Europe

Tax resistance in the seventeenth and eighteenth centuries was a basic component of European state making. Two crucial features of state making are highlighted by tax resistance incidents. First, and most obviously, tax resistance took place as a reactive form of protest against the expanding claims of centralizing states for additional revenues required for warfare. Second, the effort to extract new revenues mobilized opposition against the central government on the basis of claims of local autonomy and in terms of corporate identity and privilege.

Throughout Europe, medieval parliaments and estates possessed the political power to levy taxes. In extreme cases, such as England, parliamentary bodies in large measure sustained their powers to initiate taxation in the early modern period. These situations were less likely to evoke resistance, because basic agreement to taxes was generally secured; major exceptions in England took place during the Civil War of the 1640s, when Parliament and the king competed to pass excise levies and billet troops, provoking considerable popular resistance (Underdown 1987:148–50). At the other extreme, tax resistance repeatedly punctuated the narrative of French state making, contributing to the revolutionary crisis of the 1780s and persisting as a less common form of collective action into the Second Republic. In a different kind of case, tax resistance was not common in Prussia, where state makers and nobles shared a common interest in warfare and taxed the towns and peasantry, neither of which was able to protect its interests very effectively.

Tax resistance occurred only when parties to the process could not agree on the levies set forth by the government and had some capacity to protest. Disputes over the levies were more likely to occur when government demands were great, economic conditions (harvests in particular) poor, and burdens perceived as inequitably distributed. Government need was especially great when prosecuting wars. Protests against taxes could lead to a failure to raise taxes, which in turn could force an end to the fighting. Public resistance to taxation, for instance, contributed to French defeats in 1697 and 1713 (Webber and Wildavsky 1986:242). Tax resistance was often associated with other forms of protest during difficult economic times: poor harvests and high prices could prompt people to protest food costs and availability as well as challenge tax levies and seigneurial dues. Equally important, people protested when they judged the allocation of the tax burden to be inequitable. This leads us to the second crucial feature of state making revealed by tax resistance: the construction of local order, corporate identity, and privilege.

European countries included nobilities and towns, each of which usually enjoyed privileges with respect to taxation either as individuals or groups. Towns were difficult to tax for several reasons. First, direct taxation was problematic because it was hard to establish assets and hence tax liability. Indirect levies were easier to calculate, but not always to impose, because kings had to strike bargains with town councils over taxation. Indeed, towns agreed to taxation in exchange for freedom to trade or for recognition of autonomous local government. To secure payments, late medieval kings would lower tax rates, restore debased currencies to promote trade, and grant exemptions from military service (Webber and Wildavsky 1986:184). The definition of local government in the period of state centralization depended on affirming independent spheres of political activity. Limits to central state power were set at the very time that their powers were expanding. Towns as corporate units had traditions of autonomy from the central government. In some cases, municipal officials were responsible for apportioning taxes among surrounding communities, leading to protests over whether or not the distribution of the burden was equitable or not (Bercé 1990:200).

While towns were difficult to tax and consequently often yielded a minor portion of state revenues, the nobility frequently enjoyed preferential rates, if not complete exemption. The *taille,* a poll tax levied by the French king after the late fourteenth century and the major source of crown revenues into the early modern period, was not applied to nobles; exemption from the *taille* was a key marker of noble status. Throughout Europe, efforts to reduce, revise, or remove noble privileges provoked opposition. The 1748 decision to tax previously exempt noble lands in Austria and Bohemia was part of a larger plan to reduce the power of the noble estates; opposition was vocal, but the crown in this case succeeded in reducing noble powers (Doyle 1992:305). Popular tax resistance did not usually flow from disputes between nobles and the crown, however. When peasant discontent joined opposition of urban leaders, including lawyers, notaries, and physicians, major revolts became possible.

French history gives the most ample evidence of sustained tax revolts. Between 1637 and 1648 major protests were launched against a new tax system in which provincial intendants sent out by the central government asserted taxation powers without the agreement of the estates. Another key set of changes promoted by the central government was expanded tax farming, the selling of taxation rights to merchants, thus creating collateral for bond issues which allowed the state to borrow funds at lower interest rates. To people who increasingly faced multiple indirect taxes, tax farmers seemed like illicit businessmen challenging local abilities to buy and sell goods freely. Most hated may have been the excise taxes on salt and wine. The notion of central government agents meddling in local affairs in this new manner prompted opposition not only among the people, but also by local town officials who were much more part of their communities than they were tied to the central government. Though local officials could not openly promote tax resistance, they often seemed, in the eyes of tax farmers at least, to be very slow in responding to popular disorder.

Tax resistance captures the difficulties encountered by rulers seeking to form centralized territorial states. Success depended upon dismantling previously existing rights, privileges, and expectations of towns, nobles, and peasants. Tax resistance was embedded in practices of negotiation and deliberation between central government officials and local elites. Peasants who became involved in these activities followed the lead of their local elites. Not all states faced the same fiscal pressures. Since fiscal extraction was largely driven by warmaking, smaller states without international aspirations faced fewer demands for revenues. Among the larger states, revenue demands changed over time as some became more active and others less so in military adventures—Spain avoided much involvement in wars after the mid-eighteenth century, while both France and England were increasingly enmeshed in military competition. But in no case did a central state become strong that could not wrest tax-levying powers from local and regional corporate bodies. In what became Italy and Germany, these local and regional bodies, sometimes towns and sometimes nobles, continued to be the major pro-state forces of their regions. Where kings shared fiscal authority with parliaments, as in the English case, the definition of government embraced elite representatives as part of the state apparatus; the English state was not an absolutist regime like France. But both England and France became stronger during the early modern period, and part of their growing strength came from creating new methods and procedures to raise revenues. Protests against the centralizing states' imposition of new taxes seemed to the state makers to be signs of social disorder, but for elites and common people alike, resistance was a defense of local and regional rights and resources.

Taxing the people was only one strategy for mobilizing much-needed funds. In addition, early modern governments relied on the formation of banking institutions, which made possible an array of credit techniques and a public debt. Where governments excelled at the use of these tools, as in England and Holland, the pressures on state bureaucracies to extract tax revenues were correspondingly diminished. The French Revolution reminds us that where states failed to meet revenue needs, major political crises could follow. At the heart of the revolutionary crisis was the state's inability to raise revenues sufficient to meet its war-driven expenditures. Tax resistance was no longer noble opposition to the loss of exemptions, nor was it an issue of towns or regions defending their local rights against an intrusive state. Nobles had agreed to taxation by 1695, and local and regional forms of institutionalized power had been increasingly limited during the eighteenth century. For their part, central government ministers even recognized, in the wake of the American Revolution, that taxation should not be levied without representation. But the central government lacked the credibility to propose successfully an acceptable institutional basis for representation. The state's inability to raise new taxes was a fundamental component of the revolutionary crisis that culminated in the overthrow of the French monarchy.

In both the American and French revolutions, issues of taxation were basic to the building of new states. The definition of legitimate principles of taxation was central to the construction of state-making authority. From an early modern concern with developing the capacities to extract resources, states redefined these capacities on the basis of affirming the role of representative decision making. Nineteenth-century states developed their bureaucratic capacities for raising revenues more efficiently. Concerns for fairness and equity were shifted from corporate or territorial units to individual citizens. Democratic sentiments affirmed earlier beliefs that representative governments should determine taxes. Tax resistance in Europe reveals state-making processes, the growth of bureaucratic capacities, and the development of ideologies and institutions of political legitimacy. In China too, tax resistance proves to be a diagnostic for uncovering state-making dynamics in late imperial and postimperial times.

Tax Resistance in China

In the 1890s, William Martin described a Chinese tax revolt in progress:

> Shops were shut and perfect stillness reigned, as, twenty thousand strong, they wended their way through the streets with banners flying, each at the head of a company and each inscribed with the name of a temple where that company held its meetings. "What is the meaning of this demonstration" I inquired. "We are going to reduce the taxes" was the laconic answer. Petitions had been tried in vain, and now, driven to desparation, they were staking everything on a last appeal, with its alternative—revenge. . . . The conflict was with the mandarins only; the rioters were under strict discipline, and still professed loyalty to the supreme government. . . . Their grievance was not taxation, but excessive charges made by local officers to cover the costs of collection." (Martin, quoted by Hsiao 1960:434–35)

This abbreviated account captures a kind of event, very large in this case, enacted numerous times across much of China during the late imperial period. Collective opposition to the payment of taxes was a modest drama of several acts. A common sequence began with a group of people, sometimes numbering less than a hundred, presenting petitions that protested collection practices to officials. The failure of officials to respond adequately according to people's expectations set the stage for violent actions—attacks on the bureaucrats' offices and homes. The arrests of troublemakers called forth larger crowds to protest the proceedings. Tax resistance was usually terminated through negotiated settlements, repression by military force, or some combination of the two. If not resolved, such actions could become pieces of a larger drama that directly challenged official rule.

Tax resistance events always had leaders and sometimes a considerable degree of formal organization. The kinds of leaders varied. The mobilization of participants could be informally managed through neighborhood, friendship, and kinship ties (the kinds of links that are difficult to document in sources) or, beginning in the nineteenth century, formally sponsored by a pre-existing organization—a secret society or militia. Some qualities of the tax resistance drama varied according to the kinds of actors brought on stage. Who protested, how they were organized, and what message they were sending the state changed over time.

The persistence of tax resistance through the Qing period and into the Republican era permits us to isolate elements of continuity amidst a complex compound of political change. A flash point for observing tensions between state demands and social expectations, eighteenth-century tax resistance was simply a minor incident that succeeded in renegotiating the terms of state revenue collection. But in the nineteenth century it became one feature of a larger challenge to state authority when protesters denied officials any access to local resources.

The kind of tax resistance and its location in a larger political context identifies the shifting character of state–society relations. The eighteenth-century resolutions of tax resistance issues affirmed two features of government maintenance of social order: some cases showed the state's coercive capacity, while others revealed the social sensitivity of the officials who adjudicated the disputes and restored a sense of equity and order on the basis of shared expectations of acceptable behavior. In the nineteenth century, when officials became unable to collect taxes, resistance revealed the limited and fragile grip of state control over local societies.

People protested tax payments when they believed officials had violated proper collection procedures and would reform their practices upon hearing popular complaints. Appeal to principles of equity and fairness were commonly made in three ways. First, people protested when they felt the tax burden was unfairly apportioned among households. Second, they opposed tax payments that failed to reflect harvest conditions. Third, they criticized official use of oversize measures, biased conversion ratios from grain to silver, and commutation rates that required more copper for a given amount of silver.

The apportionment of the tax burden among households was a difficult task because the size and quality of individual plots varied considerably, even within a single county, not to mention a province. Collection rates themselves varied dramatically in late imperial times across the empire, in very rough relationship to the productivity of the land in different provinces (Y. C. Wang 1973:84–109). Since little could be done to equalize the burdens across the empire as a whole, efforts were concentrated at local levels. But achieving equity among neighboring households was frustrated by two problems. First, as new lands were brought under cultivation in the early Qing dynasty, it was difficult to assure accurate registration. Thus the disparity of tax burdens, not their heaviness, was the source of tax resistance in western Hunan in 1698 (Zhongguo renmin daxue 1979, 1:330, quoting a *zhupi zouzhe* of 1698). Second, since households were not in fact equal, the definition of equity was not self-evident. Officials often expected more from the rich, as is shown by their calls upon the rich to demonstrate their virtue through contributions.[1] But the rich were often able to protect themselves and pay lower taxes in proportional terms than their poorer neighbors. The distinction between "large" and "small" households drawn for payment of the grain tribute in the lower Yangzi region played an important role in the mid-nineteenth-century protests that unfolded amidst the larger threats of a Taiping invasion.[2]

The fact of tax burdens being unequal is perhaps less surprising than the belief that taxes should be allocated equally in proportional terms at the local level. From a European perspective, certainly, the expectation that different social orders and corporate groups would have different exemptions and privileges was long a basic feature of old regime state–society relations. The Chinese belief in equity, shared by officials and ruled alike, helped make tax resistance likely when disagreements over equity arose.

---

[1]For contributions to fund granaries, see Will and Wong 1991:28–30, 49–53. On contributions for degrees and their more general uses, see Xu Dalin 1950.

[2]These examples are discussed below in the section on tax resistance in Jiangnan.

A second general cause for tax resistance was disagreement over the rates of collection appropriate to harvest results. To offer peasants relief from poor harvests, officials reduced tax liabilities and postponed collections (Will 1990:241–46). In years of poor harvest, peasants anxiously awaited official deliberations on tax liabilities. Sometimes officials reported that people pressed for exemptions without even allowing the magistrate to conduct an investigation. For instance, some thirty-four people from twelve villages in Xingtai, a county in southwestern Zhili, requested in 1731 a cancellation of taxes because a lack of spring rain had withered the crops. When the magistrate agreed to investigate crop conditions, some two hundred to three hundred people blocked his movements and demanded more forcefully a cancellation of the taxes. The immediate official response was to arrest the protest leaders. Whether the taxes were ultimately collected or not isn't clear (Zhongguo renmin daxue 1979, 1:310–11, quoting a *zhupi zouzhe* of 1731). In other instances we find evidence of disagreement over the implementation of principles that all parties accepted. Such was the case in the fall of 1768, when more than 120 people in the western district of Jiangyin, a wealthy county in the lower Yangzi delta, were arrested for insisting on additional tax remissions after officials had already made selective cancellations (Zhongguo renmin daxue 1979, 1:322–23, quoting a *junji lufu zouzhe* of 1768). Failure by officials to adjust adequately collections according to harvest conditions was a recurring theme in Qing dynasty tax resistance.[3]

A third source of opposition to tax payments was popular belief that oversize measures or crooked commutation rates were being used to extract additional revenue. This suspicion was reinforced in many mid-nineteenth-century cases in which different commutation rates were charged for wealthy and common households.[4] Popular suspicions of official malfeasance were mirrored by official worries that tax payers might use adulterated and inferior grains or silver of insufficient purity. These mutual suspicions highlight the uncertainties permeating tax collection.

Each form of opposition recounted above was motivated by a belief that officials had not followed appropriate procedures and principles. Opposition itself, then, seems rational. It served a specific and limited purpose and rested on beliefs that officials themselves understood and even shared. While officials usually could not tolerate disruptions without penalties, they did accept the rationales of those who protested. These kinds of tax resistance often succeeded in an eighteenth-century environment in which the state had few pressing fiscal problems. The situation changed in the following century when officials became less willing and able to honor the protesters' logic.

Tax resistance became more common as fiscal demands increased in the nineteenth century. Gone from the central government storehouses were the eigh-

---

[3]In addition to the 1731 Zhili case and 1768 Jiangyin case mentioned above, see an 1815 case from Songjiang (Zhongguo renmin daxue 1979, 1:323–24).

[4]Disparities in the conversion rates between copper and silver were an issue in the nineteenth-century tax disturbances in the Middle and Lower Yangzi regions discussed below.

teenth-century surpluses spent principally to suppress the White Lotus Rebellion, a movement that foreshadowed the broader and deeper challenges posed by the mid-nineteenth-century rebellions.[5] To meet urgent fiscal needs brought on by the nineteenth-century military challenges, officials turned to new commercial taxes and expanded sales of offices.[6] In this context, officials were, not surprisingly, less likely to respond to requests to reallocate existing tax burdens for equity reasons, to indulge requests for tax remissions and exemptions because of harvest conditions, or to avoid surreptitious methods for increasing collections. Already under pressure to respond to a growing crisis, the need to sustain a social order under siege diminished the power of positive paternalism and its associated flexibility toward tax collection. Promoted instead were the importance of raising revenues by any and all means and the necessity of imposing social order, militarily more often than not. Tax resistance actions became for officials a symptom of more serious disorders and were met with force.

The impact of the state's expanded fiscal needs was exacerbated by the silver deflation associated by contemporaries as well as modern scholars with the import of opium and export of silver.[7] Silver deflation meant that households had to sell more crops or goods to pay their commuted land tax payments, since they needed to earn more copper to meet their tax liability, levied in silver. Sluggish markets reduced demand and made the economic burden of taxes even greater. Yet the fiscal crisis of the first half of the nineteenth century was usually seen by contemporaries as a failure of individuals to act morally. Many believed that official corruption was the root of the state's fiscal difficulties (Suzuki 1958). This perception masked the state's basic problems—how to raise additional revenues without causing new instances of tax resistance that would exacerbate the already considerable disorder occasioned by the rebellions.

The large-scale nineteenth-century challenges to effective state rule tend to limit our awareness of those difficulties, like tax resistance, that earlier generations of officials had routinely faced and solved. The political transition from eighteenth- to nineteenth-century realities is in part captured by the changing character and context of tax resistance events in the two periods.

Tax Resistance in the Mid–Nineteenth Century

Middle Yangzi

The 1840s and 1850s were unsettled years in the Middle Yangzi region. Before the Taiping rebel armies had left Guangxi for their march through Hunan, tax re-

[5]See Suzuki 1952 on the White Lotus Rebellion and Jones and Kuhn 1978 for a presentation of the early nineteenth-century crisis.

[6]Mann 1987 makes an argument for considering the growing capacities of the nineteenth-century state to extract revenues from commercial sources; on the sale of degrees, see Xu Dalin 1950.

[7]For an assembling of figures on silver/copper ratios and an analysis of the economic problems the silver deflation caused, see Peng Zeyi 1983:24–71.

sistance was already a problem, as were rent resistance and struggles over food.[8] Our view of official responses to these small-scale conflicts is often obscured by the looming presence of the Taiping rebels and the state's response.

Major tax resistance incidents took place in several Middle Yangzi counties both before and during the Taiping Rebellion. Hubei conflicts were largely in Wuchang prefecture, including 1842 disturbances in Chongyang and 1853 incidents in Tongshan, Tongcheng, and Jiayu, as well as Guangji in Huangzhou prefecture. Hunan tax resistance took place in Leiyang (1844) and Anhua (1853–54). Expensive silver and unstable harvests set the stage for these conflicts. In Hunan, the two counties where tax resistance broke out were particularly vulnerable to subsistence insecurities and relied on sales of cloth (Leiyang) and tea (Anhua) to secure grain purchases. Tax resistance was not, however, a simple and direct response to these difficulties. People protested specifically the excess tax collections (*foushou*) that resulted when common people paid their silver-denominated taxes in copper, receiving a less favorable exchange rate than gentry households did (Kojima 1978:96–103; Otsuki 1983:563–67).

From Philip Kuhn (1970) we learn that officials in the Middle Yangzi region combined with local elites to forge local militia that defended communities and regional armies that pursued and ultimately defeated the rebel forces. The militarization process and taxation were organizationally connected in two distinct ways. First, Kuhn shows how the militia unit (*tuan*) could become the organizational instrument for tax collection, a move he claims helped to postpone tax resistance because the militia unit was better able to resist official demands than individual households (1970:99–100). He also gives an example of a *lang* (league) in southwest China that managed tax collection without government interference; indeed, it became recognized as a kind of *baojia* unit, and like the militia, formed a buffer between local people and officials with their tax demands (1970:127–29). Kuhn's so-called "orthodox" organizations engage in tax collection as part of the militarization process. Their actions help to prevent rather than promote tax resistance.

The second linkage that Kuhn draws between militarization and taxes is the outbreak of armed resistance by South China "lodges" (*tang*), in many respects the "heterodox" analogue to the militias (1970:170–71). Kuhn's discussion of taxation and tax resistance fits well within his larger arguments about orthodox and heterodox organizations. Tax resistance, an action challenging orthodox authorities, is organized by heterodox groups.

Kojima Shinji, a leading Japanese specialist on the Taiping, finds examples of tax resistance that cross the divide between Kuhn's orthodox and heterodox organizations. It is the very forces of order, the leaders of the militia (*tuanlian*) and militia-like units (*mintuan, lianzhuang hui*), that also engage in tax resistance. Kojima offers examples from Hunan and mentions other cases from Henan, Shan-

---

[8]On Hunan food riots, see R. B. Wong 1982; on rent resistance and food riots in the Middle Yangzi region, see Kojima 1978:117–31.

dong, and Zhejiang studied by other scholars (Kojima 1978:96–103). That militia leaders engaged in tax resistance reveals the difficulty of making sharp distinctions between orthodox and heterodox, a problem that only a flexible approach can solve. In some cases, such as Anhua, a tax protest led by a militia leader may have protected the local community against outside resource extraction much as the militia was expected to defend the people against outside threats of physical violence (Kojima 1978:102). The difference, of course, matters; the threats come from the government and the rebels respectively.

Militia units themselves could become organizational vehicles for protest. In Shandong, as we shall see, tax resistance became part of a much larger endeavor to replace local governments. Whether militia-based tax collection turned into tax resistance depended less on militia actions than on official reactions. Officials often stigmatized militia-based tax collection as resistance because it threatened their authority. In other cases, the militia–official relationship permitted militia-based tax collection without friction.

The proper forms of participation in tax collection by resident landlords and lower-degree holders also became an issue in tax resistance. Kojima argues that many of the events were led by resident landlords holding *jiansheng* or *xiucai* degrees. The documents show that "rich households" were involved in Leiyang and "rich households known for their good works" (*youming xingshan de fuhu*) in Chongyang; elsewhere, lower-level degree holders were the leaders. These people were hardly rebels seeking to use violence to overthrow the state. They opposed certain official actions, much as their ancestors had. Unlike the leaders of the eighteenth-century cases, however, those of the nineteenth-century episodes were often seeking a larger direct role in the tax collection process. Nineteenth-century tax resistance therefore reflects the sometimes uneasy expansion of elite participation in local government affairs. To the degree that elites displaced officials in tax collection without being integrated into the administrative apparatus, local government was undermined. Yet, at the same time, elite abilities to collect taxes compensated for the limitations of formal government. The complex role of elites in tax collection remained contested during the postrebellion Restoration period and beyond. Tax resistance in the mid-nineteenth century began to signal basic uncertainties about the bases of state authority and control.

Tax resistance also tells us about social relations. Shigeta Atsushi, for instance, on the basis of evidence from two Hunan counties, argues that tax resistance is the type of conflict likely to emerge in economically less advanced areas where resident landlords and lower-level gentry live among the people. In economically more prosperous locales where landlords are nonresident, conflicts between landlords and tenants dominate; resistance centers on payments of rental deposits and the rates of rent collection (Shigeta 1975:66–81). Shigeta's basic point is useful—the small-scale conflicts typical of a locale can expose characteristics of the area's social structure. Rent resistance reflects class-based antagonisms, while tax resistance evokes the community's shared opposition to outsider demands. Class and community offer two different social axes along which small-scale collective action can be organized. But gross differences in social structure by themselves are a crude indicator of which forms of collective action are likely; the sharp contrasts between areas of tax and rent resistance that Shigeta finds in Hunan are not typical of other parts of the empire. Moreover, different kinds of small conflicts can also be linked. For instance, Anhua tax resistance, as pointed out most clearly in Kojima's work, is linked to struggles over food (Kojima 1978:117–22). Particular features of local social organization can make some kinds of small-scale collective action more likely than others, but certain forms, including tax resistance and conflicts over food, can emerge in a variety of social settings. Spatial variations exist, but tax resistance is not completely determined by particular features of local social structures.

Mid-nineteenth-century small-scale protests were more frequent and concentrated than eighteenth-century examples. Not surprisingly, where political authority has weakened, protests often increase, but not simply for the obvious reason that the government is vulnerable. Weak government also fails to play its role as an adjudicator or mediator of disputes. Does this mean that the multiplication of conflicts equals large-scale rebellion? Kojima, for one, believes so. He goes beyond linkages among small-scale conflicts to argue for a relationship between small-scale conflicts and the Taiping rebellion more generally. The clearest relationship he demonstrates is one mediated by the state—the state's weakness is reflected by both the Taiping armies' successes and the outbreaks of small-scale conflicts. There is in fact little, at least in the Middle Yangzi region, in the way of direct relationships between tax resistance and rebellion. In the Lower Yangzi, however, we'll see that a more direct relationship is possible.

Jiangnan

Jiangnan was facing change and crisis in the mid-nineteenth century. Merchants, sailors, and smugglers moved about in response to the trade possibilities created by the foreign presence. They were joined by the Taiping rebels who swept down the Yangzi and stormed the cities and towns of Jiangnan. Tax resistance was part of the unsettled scene in which these larger events took place. As Kathryn Bernhardt's research has shown, tax resistance occurred in two waves, a long and relatively gentle wave between 1840 and 1846 followed by a shorter, sharper wave in 1853 (Bernhardt 1992:55–83). These events in the lower Yangzi shared a number of features with tax resistance elsewhere. Economic hardships spread through the region with the silver deflation and consequent fall of cotton and wheat prices. In this highly commercialized economy, the burdens of taxation were exacerbated by the weak demand for cash crops and handicraft goods. But economic hardship itself was only part of the backdrop. Resistance was often triggered by perceived injustices. Thus, when Suzhou peasants working government lands paid taxes at a rate above that used in nearby Taicang, they protested.[9]

---

[9]Two brothers led the resistance when tribute boat sailors came to press collection of back "rents"—in essence, taxes used to defray expenses of tribute boat sailors (Bernhardt 1992:56–57).

The maintenance of distinctions among households for tax collection purposes caused resistance in a number of Jiangnan cases. In Changshu and Zhaowen counties a distinction between "big households" (*dahu*) and "little households" (*xiaohu*) meant that the latter had incentives to have their payments made by "big households" at more favorable rates. This practice of proxy remittance (*baolan*) cut into government revenues, which in turn meant that officials raised the conversion rate between silver and copper to compensate for lost revenues. This reinforced the already strong incentives to avoid taxation at the "little household" rate. James Polachek captures the problem clearly:

> Once a certain critical level of disparity between privileged and nonprivileged rate-payers was reached, for whatever reason, a self-sustained snowballing effect could be expected to appear before long. The wider the gap between *ta-hu* [*dahu*] and *hsiao-hu* [*xiaohu*] commutation rates, the more irresistible became the logic of proxy remittance (*pao-lan*) [*baolan*] of the tribute rice obligation through indigent junior gentrymen. But the more land that went into the *ta-hu* [*dahu*] registry, the greater the share that had to be absorbed by the remaining *hsiao-hu* [*xiaohu*] rate-payers. Thus the process perpetuated itself. (Polachek 1975:220)

These collection difficulties persuaded officials to eliminate the distinction between large and small households. Indeed, proxy remittance was not in fact sanctioned by officials who searched, often in vain, for effective alternative means of tax collection. A decision to halt proxy remittance was implemented in Changshu but not in Zhaowen. As a result there was no rioting in Changshu, but considerable violence in Zhaowen (Bernhardt 1992:58–59).

A related distinction among taxpaying households was practiced in the Ningbo region. The so-called "red" method of direct payment to officials by individual households was followed by wealthier families who placed their tax payments in red envelopes; the contrasting "white" method of collection by runners sent out to the countryside was used by all other households. The silver/copper rate for the rich using the "red" method was 2,000 *wen*/tael, while the others using the "white" method paid 3,000 *wen*/tael; in other words, their burden was 50 percent higher. This inequity, in combination with excess collections, stimulated resistance (Sasaki 1963:189–99).

As events, these tax resistance actions with their issues of equitable tax burdens look similar to instances recorded in the previous century. But they posed a larger challenge, in part because they were linked to other forms of conflict. In Zhaowen, for instance, tax resistance at the end of 1845 was followed by rent resistance in 1846. The tax resistance was spearheaded by a first protest of some forty households from an area near the town of Meilizhen. The rent resistance actions were concentrated in other market towns in the eastern part of the county (Bernhardt 1992:58). The Zhaowen conditions form a contrast to those in Hunan, where different forms of collective action were associated with variations in social structures across counties. The Zhaowen case suggests that the kinds of organizations and networks in local areas matter more than general features of social stratification.

The Zhaowen case also points out that the density of small-scale collective actions posed serious challenges to authorities. More serious yet, tax resistance in Jiangnan, again unlike upstream examples from the Middle Yangzi region, became tied directly to larger challenges. In Jiading, a certain Zhou Lichun, a tax functionary (*dibao*), led people in a revolt against paying back taxes; Zhou represented people who asked for continued tax relief because of poor harvests. After his initial successes, Zhou faced arrest and punishment by officials. Rather than accept such an outcome, he linked up with the Small Swords Society and attacked Jiading with the intention of overthrowing the local authorities. The secret society's involvement separates the Jiading case from eighteenth-century examples of tax resistance and provides the key to escalation from tax resistance to armed struggle (Perry 1985:85–100; Bernhardt 1992:69–73).

The emergence of secret societies was intimately tied to changes in Jiangnan society brought on by foreign impact. As Elizabeth Perry has argued, "In a variety of ways then, we can trace the impact of the treaty port setting on the genesis and character of the Small Swords: cash crop areas affected by the foreign intrusion launched the initial tax resistance; opium smuggling provided the link between rural and urban protest; merchant guilds spearheaded the formation of rebel militia; and foreign ideas influenced Small Sword ideology and symbolism" (Perry 1985:98). Tax resistance became part of the changing social setting of Jiangnan society, even as it remained rooted in older issues.

The solutions proposed by leading reformers, like the problems themselves, followed patterns outlined in earlier centuries. In 1853 Feng Guifen made abolishing the distinction between big and little households a central aspect of his tax reform proposals (Usui 1986). Restoration reforms were certainly limited and, as James Polachek has shown, bounded by factional networks of officials and gentry, but in their goals such policies tied the state to venerable social concerns even as politics were changing (Polachek 1975). Statesmen and elites aimed to defuse discontent over tax issues based on household self-interest, the community's welfare, and the state's desire to sustain a stable relationship with local society.

Shandong

Tax resistance was more widespread in the northern province of Shandong than in central and eastern provinces along the Yangzi River. Incidents took place in each of Shandong's twelve prefectures in the 1850s and 1860s (Kanbe 1972:78). Poor harvests, expensive silver, and excess tax collections played roles as they did in other parts of the empire. But in contrast to other provinces, Shandong featured militia playing a prominent role as instigators of resistance (Perry 1985:101). Indeed, terms like "militia bandits" (*tuanfei*) and "black militia" (*heituan*), in contrast to "white militia" (*baituan*), signal the political flexibility of the militia and the ambiguity of their actions. The militias' need for funding and inability to work out bases of support with local officials helps to explain the widespread occurrence of tax resistance in Shandong.

The large numbers of relatively poor peasants with small holdings also contributed to resistance possibilities. From rare nineteenth-century landownership data Kanbe Teruo has ascertained that places in Shandong where tax resistance took place had a large number of individuals who owned all their land or who owned some land and rented additional plots (Kanbe 1972:77–85). These Shandong peasants with small holdings were especially vulnerable to changes in the tax burden. Even if the burden were in some absolute sense light, their small margin for economic success and security could be wiped out by a higher tax rate.

As in the Lower Yangzi, tax resistance in Shandong could become part of a larger, direct challenge to local authorities. Perry has presented the case of one Liu Depei, a lower-degree holder who first organized a protest against grain tribute collections and then organized a militia force with gentry support. Liu took his militia and engaged official authorities in a sequence of skirmishes as he sought to take over the management of taxation and administration of justice in Zichuan county (Perry 1985:100–108; Yokoyama 1972:261–64). Liu Depei's first step was a protest against tax collection rates. This act did not challenge the officials' authority to collect taxes; it only argued against then-current collection practices. But the uncertain role of local officials in Shandong and the gentry's willingness to move against the authorities permitted Liu to take further steps. Liu's formation of a militia unit created a military challenge to complement his fiscal challenge to local authorities. When he temporarily took over judicial functions in Zichuan, he had captured the basics of local governance—taxation, military, and justice. This move from mere tax resistance to an explicit assault on local government alerts us to the shift from eighteenth-century to nineteenth-century possibilities.

Nineteenth-Century Tax Resistance in Late Imperial Perspective

As specific small-scale events, tax resistance incidents in the nineteenth century sometimes look very much like those common in the eighteenth century. The same kinds of motivations often prompted protests over official collection procedures—people came together to oppose inequities of tax apportionment or to protest rates of collection because of harvest shortfalls. But the political meaning of these protests was transformed as the mid-nineteenth-century government faced more conflicts of all types. Tax resistance became simply one dimension of a more general challenge to state control and power.

The linkage between tax resistance and larger conflicts prompted Hamashima Atsutoshi to remark on the "revolutionary" character of nineteenth-century tax resistance compared to the more "traditional" character of late Ming tax resistance which he argues was aimed at securing more equitable taxation (Hamashima 1982:527–39). This argument stresses important organizational and contextual changes, the ways people organized to express commitments to equitable tax assessment, and opportunities to engage in other forms of collective action. But the nomenclature of "traditional" and "revolutionary" obscures the contingent relationships between tax resistance and large-scale collective action. In the examples we reviewed, different kinds of relationships between tax resistance and rebellions can be seen. In Hunan, the Taiping movement is analytically distinct from the tax resistance events that take place in the province. In Jiangsu, however, the leader of a tax resistance action chose to link up with the Small Swords to embark on a larger challenge to local authorities. In Shandong, protest leaders who first engaged in tax resistance then went on to lead a larger rebellion. Some large-scale collective actions grew out of small-scale conflicts, while others simply supplied a context for small-scale actions. Events like tax resistance improve our understanding of rebellion by delineating a range of possible relations between small-scale and large-scale protests.

But if tax resistance did not become "revolutionary" in the nineteenth century, it did indicate significant political changes. Eighteenth-century tax resistance pitted local communities against a state perceived as an outside force. In the nineteenth century, the state–community axis of protest split in several directions. At stake in nineteenth-century tax resistance was control over the extraction of additional resources among groups organized more effectively than eighteenth-century protesters. This nineteenth-century competition over resource mobilization fueled by military needs brought elites, secret societies, and local officials into confrontation, creating difficulties more serious than those faced by eighteenth-century officials. The later period's tax resistance reveals the state's dual vulnerability to elites and rebels. Limitations on the late imperial state's formal bureaucratic capacities had always required some reliance on elites to shoulder political responsibilities, but tax collection by elites was never really sanctioned, let alone encouraged, as was elite participation in welfare (granaries and famine relief) and educational–ideological activities (schools, village compacts).

In the nineteenth century, militia and secret societies became involved in tax resistance. Their organizational capacities gave the tax resistance event a more durable presence. These actions became simply one act in larger dramas. Militia often strove to reorganize tax collection, while secret societies rejected local government more generally and attempted to replace the authorities. The relationship of militia to tax resistance was doubly contingent. First, militia in Kanbe's picture of Shandong could engage in tax resistance, while those in the Hunan examples of Kuhn took over tax collection without resistance. Second, tax resistance could be mounted by the militia's antagonists, secret societies, as easily as by the militia themselves, as happened in Hunan and Jiangsu. Nineteenth-century officials faced hard choices between permitting elites a larger de facto role in tax collection and suffering insufficient resources. These difficulties were superceded for a time by the dangers posed by rebels bent upon displacing local governments. But while rebels could be defeated by military force, the state's problematic relationship with elites lasted into the twentieth century.

Changes in the organization of tax resistance transformed its political significance. Tax collection and local authority generally were transformed by the late
Qing and Republican expansion of the elite's paragovernmental activities. While
many participants in tax resistance events remained the same, as did the immediate issues, the relations among participants changed further as China entered the
twentieth century.

Revolution, State Making, and Political Change

New taxes were a basic component of the reform policies initiated by late Qing
officials. Tax resistance was a common reaction to these impositions in the years
preceding the 1911 Revolution (Hsieh 1974:131). Postimperial governments
continued to raise additional revenues with new surtaxes and miscellaneous taxes. Scholars have yet to reach a consensus on the real economic impact of these
taxes; some believe increases in productivity absorbed any potential shock of rising real taxes, while others remain convinced that peasants must have been seriously harassed by new taxes. Whatever the real economic burden of the taxes,
peasant response to additional levies at least is clearcut—protests against taxes became the most common form of popular conflict in Republican China. New taxes were often unacceptable because they had no precedent; their implementation
often violated old expectations—failures to adjust collections according to harvest
conditions and perceived inequalities in the distribution of the tax burden continued to provoke opposition. Distrust of government investigators even meant
that people opposed proposals that officials claimed would make tax burdens more
equitable (Bianco 1986:280–85).

Twentieth-century tax resistance continued to represent criticisms of collection practices. But much else had clearly changed over the previous two hundred
years. By the twentieth century the blurred distinction between local officials and
local elites was paralleled by a growing ambiguity over who had authority to decide basic issues like taxation. The locale's desire to free itself from extraction by
outsiders increased as the revenue needs of expanding government offices became
more salient. Twentieth-century tax resistance expressed the tense ambiguities of
expanded efforts at resource mobilization amidst growing uncertainties over the
bases of political authority and social order in the Chinese countryside. This apparent trend of growing conflict led Yokoyama Suguru (1955) to view tax resistance as a sign of growing contradictions pushing society toward revolution.

A closer look at tax resistance precludes easy acceptance of such a view. Tax resistance events exhibit no clear and simple set of social relations and thus give no
clear indication of increasingly strained social relations; indeed, typical cases pitted landowning peasants, often under lower-level gentry leadership, against local
officials. There was little class-conflict angle at all to the events. Nor is it clear that
local conflicts always gave rise to widespread dissent. Kobayashi Kazumi, for instance, stresses the ideological differences between rebellion and revolution, on
one side, and rent and tax resistance, on the other (Kobayashi 1973). As we have

seen, there were structurally contingent relations between large and small-scale actions. Although some groups that engaged in tax resistance in the nineteenth century then went on to challenge state authority, others did not. Moreover, twentieth-century tax resistance remained a reactive form of conflict. The effort to limit the government's extractive demands on local society worked from an impulse that was implicitly anarchist; insofar as the government was defined by its demands for monies and men, popular sentiment favored as little government as possible. These sentiments do not inspire people to remake society; they can be coopted by a revolutionary vision but have no necessary and obvious role to play in radical social change.

The Republican period was not characterized by European-like state making in which a centralizing government expands its bureaucratic capacities at the expense of local and regional authorities. Instead, the expansion of certain capacities at central, provincial, and local levels of government accompanied a decline in bureaucratic integration and coordination. Different levels of government enjoyed shifting degrees of autonomy from each other; the central government was by no means stronger and more effective than it had been two centuries earlier.

Tax resistance was a sign of the uncertainty that plagued Republican China. From above came countless proclamations, orders, and plans generally devoid of any plan for implementation. From below came hostility and opposition to any local efforts to implement new policies. Elites and commoners in rural society pursued two basic strategies to limit the impact of local government initiatives. First, they strove to keep the local government out of the villages. Building on nineteenth-century traditions of organizing local militia, twentieth-century people mobilized to repel local government advances. Tax resistance was an important dimension of this larger rejection of local government (Perry 1980:163, 166, 205). Second, the radical alternative to keeping the government out was taking it over. The expansion of local elite participation in increasingly formal, if not always bureaucratic, forms of governance transformed government offices into an arena for competition. Thus, when people in Changle, south of Fuzhou, disliked the new opium tax, they replaced local functionaries with their own representatives (Bianco 1986:297–99).

There is no question that officials were *attempting* to expand the government's reach into local society. It is equally clear that popular mobilization could take place outside official efforts.[10] Tax resistance exemplifies the antagonistic relationship between community mobilization and official extraction. But twentieth-century tax resistance has another dimension that complicates the picture. Neither the ideology nor the organizational bases of tax resistance appear to have changed greatly between the nineteenth and twentieth centuries, but the targets of attack became more numerous. From Roxann Prazniak (1981) we learn that tax resis-

---

[10]Elizabeth Perry (1984) made this point a central theme in an essay on Chinese collective action. Perry suggests that the two processes of expanding local government and popular mobilization were competitive.

tance in early twentieth-century Shandong included a clear anti-elite component, the result of the local elites' expanded role in governmental affairs. Complementing this theme is Kathryn Bernhardt's argument that rent resistance struggles in Jiangnan acquired an antistate element after officials became more involved with rent collection (Bernhardt 1992:189–224). Together these arguments suggest that previously distinct types of small-scale collective action were becoming more similar as their targets became the same. The problems of rule were becoming sharper as officials and elites found themselves the common focus for popular opposition. Elites could be found participating in the expansion of local government, as well as leading popular mobilization. The transformation of tax resistance events from isolated small-scale conflicts into phenomena easily linked to other conflicts, both small and large, is evidence of the Qing empire's political decline. Twentieth-century tax resistance required new solutions.

Chinese and European Experiences of Tax Resistance

Tax resistance in China and Europe shared important basic features. People joined together to oppose tax collections which violated their sense of what was equitable and just. Opposition to taxes was rooted in beliefs about how the political order should function. Protestors affirmed a legitimate role for the holders of state power by rejecting unacceptable behavior and stating their expectations for a return to earlier practices. Tax resistance was thus a popular defense of political authority according to rules that protestors believed the state failed to follow.

Taxation has drawn attention as an indicator of postimperial Chinese state-building efforts, seen by some scholars as somewhat similar to European state making several centuries earlier. Chinese tax resistance resembled that in seventeenth-century France, where so much of the correspondence to and from Paris centered on tax collection and its problems. More generally, Republican China with its seemingly constant military skirmishes whetting warlord appetites for steadily increasing resources bears a measure of similarity to war-torn early modern Europe. Insofar as European national state making took shape amidst the extraction of resources to field armies, it is little wonder that some scholars have seen parallels in twentieth-century China. The actions of crowds usually appear focused and limited in their objectives; the kind of rational behavior first analyzed by George Rudé and Charles Tilly in European crowds is also present in China (Rudé 1964, 1974; C. Tilly 1975). Moreover, a common form of Chinese tax resistance pits the community against officials; in such cases we may witness popular notions of justice of a sort parallel to the sensibilities evoked by E. P. Thompson's (1971) moral economy of the English crowd.

Participants in Chinese and European tax resistance both had notions of what was acceptable taxation by the government and aimed to enforce through protests appropriate levels of extraction. Where numerous people were liable for taxes but tax resistance was rare, either state claims were viewed as legitimate, as appears true for the English case, or claims were effectively channeled by local social groups to deflect possibilities for protest, as appears to have happened in South China. In both Europe and China, the spatial incidence of tax resistance varied according to local social structures and the ways in which state taxation affected different groups in society.

The protestors themselves had similar features in China and Europe. At both ends of Eurasia protestors opposed state claims that they deemed inappropriate. But the larger historical contexts for tax resistance were crucially different. Centralizing European states, compared to the Chinese central government, possessed very weak taxation powers. Feudal rule provided few useful strategies for increasing central government revenues as modern European state making got under way. Strapped for funds and limited in their capacities to extract additional revenues, European governments turned to a range of other techniques, including taking out loans and developing public credit mechanisms, confiscating properties, and selling offices or royal assets. Tax resistance in general opposed *new* claims put on people by centralizing governments. China had a tradition of tax resistance predating nineteenth-century rebellion and twentieth-century revolution. In that tradition tax resistance was usually a small-scale conflict that set limits on effective and acceptable state extraction, limits within which the state usually functioned without conflict.

Studies of Chinese and European tax resistance stress the two analytically distinct axes of "class" and "community." In a debate familiar to historians of France, the Russian scholar Boris Porchnev has argued most strongly for the class basis of tax protests. Roland Mousnier led the rebuttal of Porchnev's position, stressing vertical ties among people engaged in actions not against each other but against the outside forces of the expanding state. In contrast to Marxist interpretations which often announce the progressive aspects of protests as well as their historical limitations, Mousnier and others who attacked Marxist analyses stressed the context, contingency, and complexity of events. Thus Mousnier found that tax resistance was often tied to new exactions levied to meet the demands of war; he saw such exactions as a product of particular circumstances rather than as part of a more general process of warfare and fiscal extraction that created states.[11]

The multiple meanings and possible significance of tax resistance cases cannot be exhausted by the Marxist scheme, yet basic realities of interest expressed by "class" are too easily obscured by a panoramic survey of features large and small in tax resistance events. For instance, the tax resistance of peasants in the Boulonnais in 1662 had less to do with their payment of the *dons voluntaires* than with the exemptions granted to nobility and *fermiers* (Bernard 1975:172). A kind of "class" interest is expressed which parallels nineteenth-century Chinese anger over

---

[11]See Woloch 1970 for convenient presentations of both Mousnier and Porchnev's arguments as well as those of other scholars. Tax resistance events could involve defense of municipal privileges by elites as artisans opposed new levies; these combined in the 1630s in Amiens with fears of inadequate urban food supplies and the threat of plague to create multiple uncertainties (Gallet 1975).

preferential rates of collections for rich and privileged households. Structural similarities are real as well as the bases for perceived injustices.

There is no reason to submit to an extreme view of tax resistance exclusively as class-based or solely as pitting members of a locale against the central government. Realities lie along the whole space defined by the class and community axes: some actions neatly represent class, others community, but most represent a combination, a variety of links that are closer to either class or community. In Chinese tax resistance, we can see the shifting character of this collective action from a community-based activity to a class-based one as the elites became more closely and clearly aligned with local government.

In Europe, two institutional groups had good reasons to defend their privileges and powers against centralizing states. Towns were the locus of considerable tax resistance, as in the case of a new tax levied on finished fabrics in Amiens, France, which led to tax protests in defense of municipal independence in 1636. Nobles, too, organized through their *parlements* to protect and promote their authority against the Crown's desires to expand its power, like the *parlement* of Provence which opposed the Crown's establishment of *élus* (Gallet 1975; Pillorget 1975). Taxation was either a community issue or an issue of provincial authority versus central power. The center generally won after 1650, but not without negotiating and compromising with other interests. As the Industrial Revolution and its associated economic changes dramatically raised output and made mobilizing larger revenues an easier project, new explanations of legitimate taxation dissolved earlier motivations for tax resistance. Collective tax resistance turned out to be a rearguard effort against the advance of national states. As collective tax resistance faded from the European picture, it became more common in China.

The trajectory to increased tax resistance in postimperial China began with the collapse of the government's long-standing authority to collect routine agrarian taxes according to an ideology stressing light taxation and equitable distribution of tax burdens. Adjusting tax levies to meet harvest conditions had been an expected part of routine tax collection. Eighteenth-century tax resistance was based on arguments over tax equity and appropriateness to harvest conditions. These disputes were part of a routine effort by the state to extract revenues in a manner deemed acceptable by commoners and elites alike.

In the nineteenth century, expanding state revenue needs stimulated increased sales of degrees, the formation of new capacities to tax commerce, and new forms of government borrowing. Nineteenth-century tax resistance included events in which there was intense competition to control taxation among organized contenders for power, including militias, secret societies, local elites, and local officials. Whereas centralizing European states expanded their capacities to penetrate local societies, we find in China a shift from a centralized state facing community-based tax resistance in the eighteenth century to a multiplication of groups that challenged and redefined the dimensions of state power through their tax resistance actions in the nineteenth and twentieth centuries. The expansion of twentieth-century taxation in agrarian areas resulted from a combination of initiatives, beginning with the Qing central government's mandate to raise additional taxes for its new policies including schools and police and ending with both local and provincial impositions decided without central government directives.

Increased taxation multiplied the levies, most of which were made without any ideological defense of their legitimacy. People did not consider the new types of schooling or the foreign indemnities to be projects from which they gained any benefit. As protests against new levies not deemed acceptable, twentieth-century Chinese tax resistance more closely resembled early modern European cases than late imperial Chinese ones. The persistent increase of exactions without any attempt at legitimation was, for China, a twentieth-century phenomenon. The target was usually a local government that was collecting taxes on its own authority, on behalf of a provincial (or warlord) leader, or as an agent of the national state. In some cases, protesters were organized groups seeking to collect taxes themselves and thus to acquire political power. Twentieth-century tax resistance, therefore, illustrates the uncertain development of state power in China. Though the expansion of a formal state presence in the countryside is clear, who would control what kind of state power was fuzzy at best. In comparative terms, the contrast of the rearguard quality of European cases with the forward-looking struggle of the Chinese cases reminds us that tax resistance events were not components of a single process of social and political change.

In Europe, tax resistance accompanied the initial expansion of centralized state power. Protestors won and lost various battles in different countries. The most startling victory came during the French Revolution, when the Crown's inability to gain agreement on tax collection and financing its debt led to representative government control over tax assessments. Similar changes took place during the American Revolution. In contrast to the clearly defined role tax resistance played in Western state making, tax resistance in China went from being part of an ongoing set of eighteenth-century negotiations to set routine collections at agreeable rates to becoming a mark of nineteenth-century competition among different levels of government and organized contenders for power to gain the capacities to extract revenues. The post-Taiping Qing state's successful resolution of these problems was short-lived; in the first several decades of the twentieth century postimperial governments again struggled to create an acceptable division of taxation authority and responsibility among different levels of government. The uncertainties over taxation and frequent tax resistance of the postimperial period were symptomatic of larger political instabilities that made possible radical political change.

11

REVOLUTIONS

For small-scale collective actions, similar events can be embedded in different large-scale structures from which they take on some of their meanings and significance. People pursuing their common interests achieve similar immediate results from parallel forms of protest, but their actions may become parts of distinct trajectories of political and economic change. What happens when we turn to large-scale collective actions? Are the distinctions drawn for grain seizures and tax resistance likely to apply to the complex processes of revolution? There are good reasons to be sceptical.

Most social science scholarship on revolutions has gone into creating taxonomies of revolution that stress similarities. Differences among revolutions are explained within the same categories of analysis as the similarities. Theda Skocpol, for instance, in her highly regarded work (1979) on the French, Russian, and Chinese revolutions considers these three revolutions to form a group that can be explained by a set of common features. She identifies structural similarities that distinguish these three countries from those in which radical upheavals did not take place. She argues that two factors led to social revolution. First, all three countries were in crisis—their states were unable to meet growing international military competition in a world being remade by capitalism. Second, all faced peasant revolts which they could not suppress. For contrast, Skocpol cites cases lacking either state crisis (Japan and Prussia) or peasant revolts (England and Germany). She then moves on to consider the different outcomes to the three social revolutions—a "modern state edifice" in France, a "dictatorial party-state" in Russia, and a "mass-mobilizing party-state" in China. In each case an emerging elite created its own administrative and military organizations; guided by distinctive political ideologies, these elites produced new forms of political order to rule societies in which social hierarchies and structures had been remade. In all three countries a more centralized and bureaucratic state emerged.

Skocpol's account identifies similarities as well as differences in the states that emerged from revolutionary processes in France, Russia, and China; the strength of her analysis lies in its ability to account for similarities among these revolutions and the differences between them and cases where revolution did not occur. All three cases exemplify a forward movement in the building of modern states. Yet the kinds of states that they built had only certain features in common. How do we account for the differences?

In this chapter I compare the French and Chinese revolutions using the categories of challenges, capacities, claims, and commitments I developed above. I am interested in looking more closely at the reasons for state breakdown preceding the Chinese and French revolutions and at the type of state that was created out of the revolutionary situation that emerged in each case. Having established similarities and differences, I look at each revolution from the vantage point of the other in order to highlight their distinctive features. Finally, I consider how the analysis of revolution set forth in this chapter relates to recent social science literature on revolution and to the historiographies of the French and Chinese revolutions.

State Crisis and State Making

Challenges

Both the French monarchy and the Qing dynasty faced multiple problems. For the French, perhaps the fundamental challenge was a fiscal crisis—how to pay for the various wars in which the government had engaged, wars that defined a basic component of France's relations with foreign powers. The deliberations over how to pay for them involved the government in complex negotiations with France's elites. These negotiations took place within an institutional framework of representation and discussion that offered elites an arena within which their expression of concerns about the monarchy's drift into despotism could directly affect the possibilities contemplated for resolving the fiscal crises facing the government. The challenge facing the French monarchy was not the absolute paucity of funds or the poverty of the society from which revenues were to be raised. Instead, what crippled the government was the absence of mechanisms on which elites as well as officials agreed for choosing among strategies for raising revenues.

The late Qing dynasty also faced fiscal problems, especially in the wake of the Sino-Japanese War and the Boxer Rebellion. But in large measure the court developed instruments to raise the necessary funds; a combination of increased taxation and loans created the resources necessary to meet the fiscal obligations incurred through China's increasing contacts with foreigners. Chinese elites could not limit government fiscal strategies in the manner or to the degree possible in France. Instead, the primary challenge that faced the late Qing dynasty was how to create new institutions of rule and new policies suited to the challenges of transforming the state into a Western-style government. As this task was being met, the even greater challenge of relating these new institutions to the pre-existing bureaucracy of rule loomed large.

Louis XVI encountered no similar bureaucratic challenges when he ascended in 1774. The French monarchy had created the bureaucratic infrastructure for expanding its territorial administration and building a national army. Of course, the spatial and organizational scales of these challenges were significantly smaller than those China confronted. Ruling an agrarian empire was bureaucratically a far greater challenge than ruling even a large European country like France. Although similar in some ways, the most important challenges facing the late Qing government and Louis XVI's government were in fact different. Not surprisingly, therefore, the kinds of solutions attempted and achieved also differed. Neither the French monarchy nor the Qing dynasty successfully met their challenges. Both were replaced by new states.

Some of the new challenges of the postrevolutionary states were also broadly similar: to achieve centralized control over government administration; to promote economic development to achieve wealth and power; and to create societies responsive to state demands. By the nineteenth century, all successful states, including France, had developed strategies to deal with other states, and these strategies often entailed more effective domestic centralization. By the mid-nineteenth century, it was clear that governments could promote industrialization through specific policies; by the late nineteenth century it was believed that governments needed strong economies to compete in the modern world. But the Chinese and French states carried problems and possibilities from their own particular pasts. For the postimperial Chinese state, meeting the challenges of economic development and social change proved difficult to achieve across what had been an agrarian empire with its own state-making traditions and strategies. For France, the challenge of consolidating state institutions according to ideas of popular sovereignty vexed political leaders, social activists, and common people for many decades after the initial collapse of the French monarchy.

Capacities

Over the course of the seventeenth and eighteenth centuries the French state had expanded many important capacities—tax, judiciary, bureaucratic, and military. The state-making process in France had created a far stronger state in the 1780s than had existed in the 1580s or 1680s. The Revolution expanded these capacities even further. In particular, the central state raised additional taxes and mobilized young men to serve in the army. Indirect taxes on consumers rose far more than direct taxes on land. Despite opposition to both conscription and higher taxes, the Napoleonic state was able to increase its extractive capacities. New forms of parliamentary representation built on ideas expressed during the Revolution also developed, with universal male suffrage proclaimed in the Second Republic founded in 1848. French leaders met the challenge of crafting new capacities of government. Larger bureaucracies with expanded personnel and new forms of central government penetration of locales meant that the French state created new capacities to meet the challenges of postrevolutionary government.

The situation in China was quite different. In the half-century from 1900 to 1950 the Chinese expanded governmental capacities in some areas but not others. The New Policies of 1905 included new ministries of commerce and education as well as a reconstituted fiscal bureaucracy, but institutional integration proved difficult to achieve. In particular, the new armies of the late Qing operated independently and outside central government control, raising the possibility of their acting against the government, as they eventually did in 1911. After the 1911 Revolution, the basic challenge to postimperial regimes lay in creating and stabilizing an alternative structure of rule. While Yuan Shikai reasserted a degree of control over the country, the success of the central state proved short-lived. From 1916 to 1949 China was subject to competing and usually separate regimes. Beneath the Nationalist regime's claim to territorial rule between 1927 and 1937, provincial warlords continued to rule some areas with large degrees of independence despite their nominal allegiance to the central government. There were general increases in extractive capacities coupled with mixed success at educational initiatives and the formation of police forces. Coercive and extractive controls increased; material controls, at least of the welfare variety, declined further; and new ideological methods of control were attempted with uneven results. The continued lack of vertical bureaucratic integration meant that a unitary state no longer existed.

From the vantage point of the country as a whole, multiple sovereignty created what analysts often call a "revolutionary situation." The presence of more than one group claiming autonomous control over part of the domestic scene meant that some major changes in political institutions and ideologies became possible. These included revolutionary changes in social structure and in the organization and purposes of political power. But a revolutionary outcome was by no means the most obvious, let alone the only, possibility in the several decades after 1911. At least as likely was China's continued inability to overcome the fragmented political situation that rendered the former agrarian empire vulnerable to both domestic fighting and foreign intervention.

Where the French Revolution proved to mark a transition between political regimes with even greater state capacities, the 1911 Revolution in China threatened an end to rule by a vertically integrated bureaucracy. The expansion of state capacities on multiple levels without a coherent and integrated bureaucracy to replace the one that had existed in Qing times created a far less certain path of state building. Revolution was to be a far more protracted process in China and one without a guaranteed outcome.

Claims

Participants in the French Revolution dramatically expanded the bases for legitimation of political rule from the behavior of monarchs or select elites to the people more broadly defined. The new French citizens could make claims on their governments to honor personal freedoms and political liberties. The formation of assemblies during the Revolution and in succeeding decades of the nineteenth century built a republican tradition shared by a broad spectrum of people. At one end were forces of social order, skeptical of the broad masses but adamant about developing institutions of representation. At the other extreme were the politicized common people, committed to organized social movements to press their claims against the government through demonstrations, elections, rallies, and political associations.

The 1911 Chinese Revolution did not institutionalize effective claims to popular sovereignty. Chinese assemblies never succeeded in imposing on the government constraints or claims like those the French representative assemblies achieved. Chinese claims on post-1911 governments did little to improve the institutionalized voice of Chinese elites or common people, but social movements did emerge that made substantive rather than procedural claims on the government. The largest early social movement was the May 4th movement, which opposed Chinese acceptance of the Treaty of Versailles in 1919 because it reassigned German leaseholds in China to the Japanese, an infringement of Chinese sovereignty. The pushing of claims in China did less to establish procedures for a representative democracy than it did to express substantive demands or make general critiques of those in power. This proved true not only during the protracted revolutionary situation of the first half of the twentieth century, but in social movements as different as the Cultural Revolution (1966–69) and the Democracy Movement beginning in the mid-1970s.

The institutionalization of claims in the French case, including most importantly claims to participation in representative political processes, contrasts sharply with the absence of effective claim-making mechanisms during the Chinese Revolution. When claims were made in China, they were more likely to be substantive rather than procedural, to be claims on what leaders do rather than claims about how decisions should be made or who is to make them. These contrasts were expressed as different commitments in the two revolutionary ideologies. France's republican legacy of revolution celebrates the principle of popular sovereignty as a commitment institutionalized in representative government in the nineteenth century through fits and starts. In China, the Communist Party claims to represent the people and to act in the name of the people. The basic political concepts of these two revolutions and their state-building implications have therefore been crucially different.

Commitments

The late Qing government adopted new commitments learned from Western countries, especially to forge wealth and power. For the government to be strong, society had to be rich. These new priorities did not always consciously replace Confucian commitments to rural social order and agrarian prosperity. But in practice, government resources were shifted away from projects to sustain the agrarian economy in poorer areas to activities addressing foreign-inspired issues of wealth and power. In the postimperial period, localized expressions of commitments to rural social order were made amidst a more general forsaking of government support for stabilizing local society. The increase in tax resistance reflects this general condition. The local exceptions of commitments to rural order took the form of competing strategies to reorder agrarian society. Most familiar were Liang Shuming's strategies for revitalizing agrarian communities. But unlike many gentry leaders of earlier centuries who accommodated themselves to state initiatives to promote local order, Liang labored to remain independent of government involvement. Nationalist government President Jiang Jieshi aspired to coopt Liang's initiative and turn it into a model to be emulated elsewhere (Alitto 1979). James Yen's rural reconstruction effort expanded the dimensions of "local" by embracing American money, research methodologies, and social visions of rural development. Operating largely outside official channels, Yen's project redefined the dimensions and content of social activism beyond the formula applied in late imperial times. Less influenced by Western models for developing the countryside, Mao Zedong and the Communists focused on organizing opposition to the government (taxes) and elites (rents) during the late 1920s and the 1930s. In their base areas of the late 1930s and the 1940s they became the local governments imposing taxes and regulating rent collections.

In France, the revolutionary process heightened popular expectations for government action to affirm official commitments to alleviate subsistence troubles and taxation hardships. Elites could express their grievances through the *cahiers de doléances*. The idea of promoting interests through different forms of representation depended on the assumption that the state was committed to recognizing the expression of people's interests, whether or not it agreed with them. While this was true of French government in the 1780s regarding elite interests, the commitments to the population more generally were expressed not in terms of representation but mainly in the form of paternalistic welfare efforts. The emergence of the *sans culottes*, a popular movement by no means composed solely of working-class individuals, who demanded direct participation in government rather than representation signaled a shift in boundaries of what was politically possible. The government's commitment to engage and involve popular social movements in the creation of governmental institutions was an important component of the revolutionary process in France.

The CCP (Chinese Communist Party) made a commitment to mobilizing peasants in Yanan more directly and intensely than had ever been seen before. But this logic of the "mass line" became a way for the Party to assert more complete control over peasants by broadening the communications flow between Party and people as a mobilization method. Missing from Yanan "democracy" were any autonomous claims of the peasants akin to those of the *sans culottes*, who had inserted their own opinions into political decision making.

The Chinese Revolution in French Perspective

The collapse of the Qing dynasty in 1911 created a major political crisis in China. The creation of a new government outside the ideological and institutional framework of the Qing state was a staggering task that required nearly four decades. At first glance, this seems dramatically different from France, where an effective central government replaced the fallen monarchy in just a few years. But upon closer reflection, important similarities can also be discerned. Nineteenth-century France witnessed several governmental forms—monarchy, republic, and empire—while no "revolution" marked the transitions among these forms, the uncertainty about the nature of central government reminds us that the French Revolution did not usher in an era of political stability. The basic difference in the Chinese instability was the absence of national unity. Between 1912 and 1949, there was only one decade, 1927–37, when any government could even claim nominal control over China as a whole.[1] Even during the one decade of Nationalist rule the government was weak in several ways. First, Nationalist leaders in their capital of Nanjing could not create a bureaucratic government to penetrate into rural areas throughout the country; second, the Nationalist government faced pressures from foreign governments; third, urban elites and urban people more generally challenged the government to be stronger internationally and more effective domestically than it was. China as an agrarian empire had always been a challenge to rule. Exacerbating those challenges was the late nineteenth and early twentieth-century development of new kinds of cities with new kinds of economic and social elites who clamored for an institutionalized political voice. The difficulty of conceiving a form of rule for both rural China and a new kind of urban China meant that postimperial forms of rule had to include principles and policies not imagined in late imperial times. This combination of circumstances naturally made effective central state rule extremely difficult to achieve.

The four decades following the collapse of the Qing dynasty formed an extended period of multiple sovereignty in which there was no effective national government with a vertically integrated bureaucratic administration. Further uncertainty arose because some contenders did not aim to rule the entire country but only a certain part of it, threatening the country with segmentation, a different sort of "multiple sovereignty" more akin to the multistate system in Europe. Within this overall social context, political and social activists with fundamentally different beliefs entered the countryside. The range included Liang Shuming, with a Confucian vision of social order; James Yen's Western-influenced liberal-minded reforms; and Mao Zedong's restructuring of agrarian social relations. Despite the inspiration of radically different ideologies, there was an agreement to address the social, economic, and political problems of agrarian China. Unsettled political conditions created opportunities for different programs to compete for

---

[1] The whole did not include some of the Inner Asian parts of the Qing empire and Tibet.

support in agrarian China. To be successful, these efforts had to respond to economic and social issues of immediate material concern to peasants. None of these competing strategies for creating rural social order was integrated vertically within a bureaucratic structure of rule similar to that of late imperial times. The various more general efforts at state rebuilding, within which the Chinese revolution took place, engaged competing elites in mobilizing people to address crises shared by either different classes or the nation conceived more generally, a process John Fitzgerald has termed "awakening China" (1996).

Within this setting, Chinese Communist notions of "democracy" were developed. "Democracy" was a mobilizational phenomenon bringing peasants into new Party-led organizations allowing peasants to play a real role in local politics in place of elites. The so-called "mass line," a flow of communication and ideas from and to the masses, makes sense only because the Party assumes that peasants have a common orientation. There is no institutionally defined division to provide peasants with an autonomous organization or expression of their opinions, but rather a flow of communication and a downward movement of control. The "mass line" idea brought peasants into politics without giving them much space to make their own claims on the Party. This local level of engagement did not include any institutional framework for peasants to make their concerns known to higher levels of government independently of the local Party cadres.

French experiences do not offer a reasonable guide for the ideas about "democracy" that emerged as Communist pockets of political control were developed in the 1930s and 1940s. Nor were the rejections of monarchy very similar in the two cases. The choice and creation of political forms in the Chinese Revolution included the easy dismissal of Yuan Shikai's 1916 attempt to reestablish a monarchy. This attempt was seen as a laughable anachronistic exercise. When viewed in light of nineteenth-century French experiments with constitutional monarchy after the French Revolution it is no longer clear why the Chinese case is so easily dismissed. Part of the answer has to do with the availability of models from which to choose a form of government. Another part has to do with the specific context of Chinese politics, in which monarchy was intimately associated with the Chinese government's failures in preceding years. The failures before 1911 to establish a constitutional monarchy made imagining any form of monarchy more difficult in later years. The puppet regime of Manchukuo put the last Manchu emperor back on the throne, but this gesture had perhaps less to do with Chinese patterns of emperorship than with Japanese ones, which accorded the emperor symbolic and ritual roles only.

If monarchy was difficult to imagine in China, it was unclear what "republic" meant. Certainly the Chinese did not stress "liberty, equality, and fraternity." There was no strong push for social justice. Political participation by elites had only limited success against administrative leaders who desired bureaucratic power unfettered by representative bodies. While French leaders may have been little more enthusiastic about enfranchising people, they repeatedly agreed to parliamentary bodies. But we exaggerate the differences between China and France if we fail to recognize both the accomplishments of the Chinese provincial assemblies and the limitations of the French parliaments. While Chinese assemblies failed to forge an institutionally accepted role, there were efforts in the first three decades of the twentieth century to argue for assemblies. In France, parliamentary institutions enjoyed a mixed record under Napoleon and through the Second Republic and Second Empire; only in the 1870s under the Third Republic was a parliamentary democracy achieved. The differences between the Chinese and French cases emerge clearly only after a protracted history. Parliamentary institutions were of limited importance in the decades-long Chinese Revolution, but they did not develop smoothly or swiftly in France, either. Representative democracy did nevertheless develop in France, while it has not yet done so in China.

Lacking in the Chinese Revolution were some of the targets of the French Revolution. In particular, there were no institutional or social equivalents to nobles and clergy in Chinese society. There was not, therefore, the same impetus to redefine legal statuses that led to the concept of citizen in France. Complementing the new category of citizen was the collective category of *patrie* or nation. Between the two, citizen and nation replaced a society composed of orders—the monarchy, clergy, and nobility, in particular, all lost their previous positions. China had little sense of "citizen" in the first half of the twentieth century, while "nationalism" prompted both provincial and national initiatives by Chinese officials and politicians seeking reforms. Chinese ideas of building a nation out of smaller territorial and kin units contrasted with the European idea of displacing such allegiances with the nation.

Comparing the Chinese Revolution with the French Revolution reveals ways in which the Chinese experience differed from the French. The French Revolution included a set of social changes that transformed the basic categories within which people were organized. From a society of orders emerged a society of classes, with a new political significance assigned to the individual. The citizen became a key actor in discussions of democracy and nation. The Chinese Revolution lacked these clusters of social and political change. Not surprisingly, therefore, the political meanings and institutional manifestations of terms such as "democracy" were different. Considering the Chinese Revolution according to the standards of the French Revolution reminds us just how inadequate the categories of change in the French case are for explaining changes in China. The symmetric exercise of thinking about the French Revolution from a Chinese perspective yields another set of insights.

The French Revolution in Chinese Perspective

It is difficult to imagine the French Revolution without the organization of elites into estates and a monarch with limited abilities to mobilize revenues independently of elites. Estates with specific political claims gave rise to two changes during the Revolution—the elaboration of rights associated with individuals as citizens and the development of a society of classes. From the institutional and ideological resources of old-regime France was assembled a revolutionary new government. It first had to overcome the challenges unmet by the old regime, then to create more effective capacities. With new claims and new commitments, the governments succeeding the old regime constructed a different kind of state. But these changes were historically bounded. The French Revolution was institutionally and ideologically a European transformation. Consider several limitations that are highlighted by comparison with the Chinese Revolution.

Peasants figured centrally in the Chinese Revolution. The consolidation of a foundation for social order depended on creating a viable set of social relations in the countryside. Chinese Communists spent nearly two decades before 1949 in this arena of action developing their policies of rule. Party power was intimately associated with organizing rural society. Peasants in the French Revolution reacted against the government, its policies, and its failures to meet customary expectations. They were not organized by an outside force and assigned a central role in shaping the outcome of the Revolution. Peasant rights to land were affirmed by the Revolution, but their political role changed little as a result. A more active role for the peasantry developed only a half-century later, when the countryside mobilized during the fall of the July monarchy and founding of the Second Republic. Rural collective action in 1846 and 1847 followed the traditions of earlier protests during subsistence crises. Groups engaged in food riots similar to those of the Revolutionary period and before. But in 1848 and 1849 rural people began to take advantage of a much broader range of activist options. When the Second Republic proclaimed universal manhood suffrage, rural people became active in elections; many voiced their opposition to new indirect taxes by voting for Louis-Napoléon. Peasants also joined political clubs and participated in debates waged in the popular press. Rural political mobilization frightened some of the powerful, who maneuvered to change electoral qualifications to disenfranchise roughly one-third of the electorate. The defenders of the Social and Democratic Republic were forced into clandestine political opposition. While in some areas republicanism was the concern of urban workers and artisans of small towns, it was a more broadly shared political commitment in other areas, involving rural people as well as urban. When Louis-Napoléon executed his military coup d'état on 2 December 1851, republican resistance spread across much of the country.

Specialists have disagreed over how to interpret rural participation in social protests. Edward Berenson, Theodore Margadant, John Merriman, and Charles Tilly have all argued for a politically informed activism diffused from urban centers into the countryside (C. Tilly 1972b; Merriman 1978; Margadant 1979; Berenson 1984). For them, peasants came to understand and defend principles of democracy. In contrast, Eugen Weber has argued that mid-century peasant protests were archaic forms of violence rooted in local circumstances (Weber 1991:137–88). Weber's rejection of mid-century rural protests as "modern" is supported by Peter Jones and A. Corbin. Jones (1981) sees political divisions in the Southern Massif Central area as determined by religious, family, and geographical divisions; Corbin (1975) sees southwestern responses to Paris as communalist and not democratic. In part, the differences of interpretation hinge on the kinds of evidence assembled or selected, but these differences need not be mutually exclusive. Republican opposition to the destruction of the Second Republic may also have reinforced local disputes and divisions (McPhee 1992). Even if compromise among different interpretations is not achieved, the range of roles identified by these alternatives fails to include the kinds of roles played by peasants in the Chinese Revolution. Chinese peasants were more central actors in the conflicts that counted. At the same time, Chinese peasants were more closely organized and strongly controlled by outside political forces than was the case in France.

In the Chinese Revolution, the contest for political control was conducted in villages. The Communist Party's strategies for governing developed out of their efforts at ruling a remote and poor region far from the concentrations of wealth, culture, and power found in cities. The first challenge was to create effective local order. Success at this project gave revolutionaries an opportunity to compete for power across a broader area. Organized as a highly disciplined, vertically integrated party, revolutionaries had a strong structural base on which to build a new government. The Chinese Revolution was many decades in the making, but once the Communist Party seized power, the development of a new government proceeded swiftly. Amidst policy changes of sometimes dramatic dimensions, the state re-created a unitary state for which constructing a social order that would encompass an agrarian society remained a primary task. In contrast, the French Revolution was centered in Paris, where competing factions mobilized forces and forged rationales of authority and rule. The provinces did not all support the policies pushed by Paris, but the center asserted its capacity to control the country against a spate of provincial resistance efforts in the 1790s, most famously in the Vendée. During the nineteenth century, political disagreements had, on occasion, strong regional as well as class dimensions, but the center's ability to assert authority was never completely broken.

In France, the political issues of the pre-1870 period centered on the roles that different interests would play and on the organization of different parts of the government and their powers and responsibilities. The construction of a central government with capacities to rule the country and a set of social interests with institutionalized methods of expressing themselves to the government was a structural given. In China the political issues preceding 1949 concerned relations among different levels of government. Social interests were likely to be expressed by efforts to *avoid* government rather than efforts to create voices in government. The gap between governor and governed remained much larger in China, while the boundaries between state and society (carefully drawn in France, as in many other European countries) remained vaguely marked.

The French state that emerged from revolution also lacked the central role in economic affairs that the Chinese state adopted. The government founded in 1949 asserted degrees of control over both industrial development and the agrarian economy that are inconceivable in the French case. In part the differences reflect the temporal distance between the early nineteenth and mid–twentieth centuries. But the spatial differences are even more important. Chinese traditions of political economy of the late imperial and postimperial periods came together to promote a set of state policies to direct the industrial and agrarian economies. Postrevolutionary French governments did not aspire to the range of economic policies and types of social penetration that were expected in post-1949 China. Despite these many differences, the historiographies of the French and Chinese revolutions have followed similar paths.

France: A Continuing Revolution of Interpretation

As all students of European history know, Karl Marx, more than any of the other great nineteenth- and early twentieth-century social theorists, created an analytical vocabulary and a conceptual scheme to explain violent challenges in state power. As all students of Chinese history realize, this scheme has been extended to the study of twentieth-century history with mixed results. In his grand vision of European historical change Marx located political crises against a dramatic story of economic and social progress in which power changed hands as classes rose and fell in economic centrality and social prominence. In the historiographies of both the Chinese and French revolutions, we can see the application of Marxist categories of analysis followed by successive revisions and rejections. At the core of Marxist and many non-Marxist analyses has been attention to the mobilization of social groups, their expression of political interests, and the nature of government responses. In the historiography of the 1960s and 1970s, collective actors were central to the drama of political contention. Their social backgrounds and economic interests shaped their behavior and conditioned their interactions with others. The struggle for political power was a struggle among socially and economically defined groups anxious to push their interests. Revolution in both China and France marked success for some of these groups and defeat for others.

In the French case, explanations that portrayed a bourgeoisie seeking to translate its growing economic presence into political power, culminating in destruction of the monarchy in 1789, turned out to be vulnerable to multiple empirical challenges. One important cluster of findings centered on the interpenetration of the nobility and the bourgeoisie in the eighteenth century. On the eve of the Revolution, a quarter to a third of all noble families had received their titles within the past fifty years (Sutherland 1986:19); at least some successful bourgeois families were becoming ennobled. Moreover, nobles increasingly took up commercial activities, behaving much as nontitled entrepreneurs would (Forster 1980; Dewald 1987); at least some noble families were succeeding economically through investments in trade, agriculture, and real estate.

This interpenetration of the nobility and bourgeoisie meant that their shared intellectual and cultural spaces overlapped, creating a common sphere within which they could agree and disagree about political issues and social change; there was no specifically "bourgeois" or "noble" position on society and politics. Both titled and nontitled people of wealth sought to purchase land and establish a grand lifestyle in the countryside. They created regional alliances against the central state within their shared intellectual and social spaces.

If class conflict is insufficient to explain the revolutionary process, contemporaries saw the basic outcome of the Revolution as the displacement of the monarchy and aristocracy by the bourgeoisie. Nineteenth-century observers generally believed that the French Revolution was a bourgeois revolution that would result in the middle class becoming increasingly important in politics and society. Nineteenth-century analysts placed the French Revolution within a larger historical framework, recognizing its roots in the Enlightenment and among independent medieval burghers (Hobsbawm 1990:1–31). The democratic institutions established under the Third Republic originated nearly a century earlier during the French Revolution. Although certainly rooted initially within a French context marked by long-term continuities, the Revolution also represented a significant shift that broadened the goals, settings, and commitments of political leaders. The French Revolution promoted in a passionate and pointed form principles of political authority that in the nineteenth century were translated fully or in part into new institutions of government in France, other parts of Europe, and the Americas. An inspiration to people in Europe and the Americas, the French Revolution had significant impact beyond French borders. The ideologies invented by the French had meaning for other Europeans and in European colonies in the Americas.

Considering the French Revolution principally in terms of its intellectual content has been a major focus since the 1980s. François Furet (1981) has led the way in refocusing attention to the political culture of the old regime within which the ideology crystallizing in the Revolution became possible. Building on French political texts highlighting the notion of undivided sovereignty, Furet sees the French Revolution as a moment in political thought. A focus on discourse examines how participants and later analysts could, in their own ways, "invent" the French Revolution. Stressing elite intellectuals and political culture, this vein of scholarship rarely addresses major social groups, popular culture, economic change, or socioeconomic crises. Virtually missing is the *Annales* tradition with its rich and varied efforts to capture the social changes, demographic movements, economic fluctuations, and crowd dynamics that set the stage for the events that triggered the Revolution.

French historians have addressed many of the institutional problems and possibilities as well as their settings within larger social and economic contexts. The state, elites, and common people were grappling to solve serious problems in the decades preceding the French Revolution. Nothing in the analysis of political culture and ideology directly denies this. The government did have serious fiscal problems. Elites were unsure of how best to meet the government's demands for resources. Common people suffered anxieties about grain prices and taxes. Given these conditions, different "solutions" to fiscal crisis and popular anxieties could be imagined. The ones that were forged in the 1780s and 1790s became a revolution.

Specific elements in French political culture offered the materials from which a revolutionary ideology could be fashioned. The French Revolution was distinctly a phenomenon embedded in French history. Institutionally, as well as ideologically, the structures and sentiments of the French Revolution were historically particular. The particular constellation of categories within which individuals came to understand their problems and their options defined the range of possible solutions to their crises. The importance of political culture doesn't deny that a fiscal crisis was at hand or that fears of food riots spread through the land. Rather it takes these as givens which on their own cannot "cause" the construction of any particular set of political arguments. Ideologies in general offer guidance on how to conceive relationships among sets of issues. Ideologies assign value and offer interpretations of what is worth doing and why. Revolutionary ideologies do all this and more. They promise a new way to solve current problems that carries with its solutions hopes for a better society. Thus large-scale collective actions can differ from small-scale actions that in general do not mount a fundamental challenge against rulers.

French revolutionaries recognized both popular unrest and fiscal crisis; they believed themselves to be addressing those issues as well as creating principles for a new kind of government. Revolutionary thought afforded a new way to "read" the meaning of small-scale conflicts. Antiseigneurial attacks, for example, could take on new meanings when the goal was no longer to constrain seigneurs to act according to custom but rather became a rejection of seigneurial authority in principle. French political culture provided resources with which to fashion new understandings of small-scale conflicts and to see in them significance for larger challenges. At the same time, people's commitments to older forms of local struggle, be these contests over food or over taxes, gave them a frame of reference within which to understand what revolutionaries were about. For revolutionaries, as leaders of a complex social movement of political protest, one of the key challenges is to create a taxonomy of meanings for people's multiple reasons to support a large-scale assault on the government. French revolutionary leaders succeeded at this challenge by drawing upon culturally generated symbolic resources to fashion an ideology that persuaded enough people in an adequate number of ways to support dramatic changes. But the French Revolution was certainly far more than a series of new and persuasive understandings of political order.

The revolutionary situation included the failure of extant political institutions and the formation of popular social movements. The combination created fundamental political uncertainties in the early 1790s leading to efforts at asserting ever-stronger central control. Political factionalism at the center made competition for control a bloody battle. A troubling gap opened between the stirring moral principles of revolutionary ideology and the sordid violence of leaders seeking to consolidate power as a means of asserting order more broadly. The realities of the Terror came swiftly, while the hopes for a democratic republic were nurtured over the nineteenth century amidst the different political formats of republic, monarchy, and empire, achieving a fuller measure of implementation with the Third Republic founded in 1871.

Recent scholarship on the French Revolution has considered the legacy of 1789 as much as analyzed the revolutionary events themselves. Some of the leading voices have spoken ambivalently about revolution, its violent excesses, and its legacy for modern society. In studies of the Chinese Communist movement we can find many similar intellectual trends: (1) a movement away from simple class labels to identify collective actors, their interests, and their actions to a closer reconstruction of the actual processes of Communist efforts at making revolution; (2) a concern with ideologies and representations of revolutionary process; and (3) a questioning of the revolution's positive achievements and legacies with a particular concern for the violence not only of the pre-1949 period but in the decades thereafter. Traveling a somewhat different path of historiography, recent scholarship on the Chinese Revolution ends up posing some of the same questions about revolution as those raised in studies of the French Revolution.

China: A Continuing Revolution

The Communist movement had been initially geared to address the urban challenge of creating a new kind of political order. Chinese Communists in the early 1920s expected to make their mark in China's largest cities by leading the nascent proletariat. But the Nationalist success in driving them out of the cities of necessity shifted the focus of Communist concerns to rural society and its problems. As Elizabeth Perry's (1980) work has shown, the Communist movement in the Huaibei region of North China attempted a variety of strategies for working with local groups, ultimately opting for the mobilization of the peasantry into new kinds of groups distinct from earlier rebel organizations. Perry's contrast of rebels and revolutionaries points out some of the basic changes made by Communist organizers to transcend the limits of nineteenth-century rebels and bandits. Part of the challenge to Communists was how to take over small-scale conflicts and make them part of their larger movement. Peasant efforts to assert claims to social order came through tax resistance and to a lesser degree grain seizures. Communists promoted policies to create more land security for peasants and to reduce the ill effects of rent and tax levies. The Communists conceived themselves as a radical alternative to exploitive and evil officials and landlords. Their narrative of revolution anticipated a new type of government serving working-class and peasant interests. Little ideological attention went to explaining how this government could integrate urban and rural areas. Even less went to persuading people that its rule should extend over the entire country. The Communists, like the Nationalists they battled, could assume the integration of China conceptually, even if creating integration institutionally was a difficult challenge.

The Communists first succeeded in rebuilding local social order. The challenge of national unification was initially a military challenge. Once the Nationalists were defeated, the Communists created a new government, a unitary state with bureaucratic power penetrating the countryside and quite separately organizing the cities. They elaborated a new ideology based on Marxist-inspired categories of classes, class struggle, and vanguard Party leadership. They deployed these categories to explain both their successes at gaining power and their agenda for further social change and political development.

How persuasive were Communist explanations of their own efforts? Ralph Thaxton (1983) has suggested that North China peasants in Communist base areas experienced a reaffirmation of their traditional expectations of government. Their world was, in his terms, "turned right side up" by the Communist movement. Subsequent scholarship has challenged Thaxton's argument and his evidence to suggest that there is little reason to believe Chinese peasants followed the kind of moral economy he ascribed to them in which the community aimed to create collective security (Chen and Benton 1986). While Thaxton's version of moral economy has been criticized, the more basic idea that peasants experienced the Revolution as a set of improved opportunities to achieve customary expectations about the good life still stands. One important difference between this revolution and the French Revolution lies in the arena of gender relations and family life. For poor male Chinese peasants, the Revolution promised the possibility of owning land and thus acquiring the economic security to make marriage more likely (Stacey 1983). Peasants and party shared at least an overlapping set of goals through the land reform period. But the Communists certainly intended more. How then did peasants perceive Communist policies and efforts? David Apter and Tony Saich, in their 1994 study of revolutionary discourse, stress the theoretical principles supporting collective action. They seek to explain how and why Mao was a persuasive visionary, how he and other Communists created commitments binding Party and people with a force beyond that easily explained by rational, individual concepts of self-interest. Apter and Saich suggest that some people became persuaded by Communist explanations of their revolution, but did such people include many peasants? How many of what kinds of people bought into China's revolutionary discourse has not yet been established. It is important to estimate these numbers if, as Sidney Tarrow (1994) has argued, it is important for revolutionaries to create a logic for collective action that transcends personal calculations of benefit and cost. Tarrow argues persuasively that the problem for social movements is not to gain participants according to their perceptions of individual gains and losses, but rather to create social meaning and purpose for group actions. This is especially true for revolutionary movements that may require sustained sacrifices before victory is achieved. While the Communists may have succeeded in persuading people of their visions of social change during a revolutionary struggle, they appear to have been decidedly less successful in sustaining social commitment to large-scale movements of social change during the collectivization drives of the 1950s. Certainly this is the story that Edward Friedman, Paul Pickowicz, and Mark Selden (1991) tell when they condemn collectivization for the traumas and hardships it caused. If their analysis can be generalized, peasants may not have bought into some larger social logic beyond their own calculation of gains and losses. The Communist Party may have sought to achieve a new revolutionary logic and simply failed. Philip Huang (1995) goes further, postulating a significant gap between official representations of land reform and the realities of social change, a gap that only grew larger during the Cultural Revolution. Drawing on Jack and Sulamith Potter's (1990) characterization of the Cultural Revolution as a kind of religious revitalization movement, Huang argues that Cultural Revolution mass actions were not interest group activities. Once again we are alerted to how the logic of social movements diverge from the rational calculus of benefits and costs apparent at the level of individual actions and small-scale collective actions.

Within both the Chinese Revolution and the People's Republic there has been a tension between rational interest based on decision making and large-scale collective movements. Chinese revolutionaries, dedicated to transforming rural social structures, moved beyond immediate peasant self-interests but failed to create an ideological justification for these changes that could satisfy many peasants for long periods of time. Having few means to express their dissatisfaction openly, peasants appeared to go along with collectivization, but the rapid rise of areal productivity after decollectivization suggests that peasants immediately began to work much harder when taken out of a collective farming situation. Both passive resistance to collectivized agriculture and active support for household farming were expressed at the individual and household levels. No extensive social movements developed in the countryside to challenge state policies or power because the government's coercive reserves made it difficult to contemplate such actions.

If we consider rural protests and violence, we find some important changes from earlier practices that reflect the successes of the revolution. But we can also discover evidence of opposition to the state that resonates with pre-1949 concerns. Elizabeth Perry's research on rural violence in the 1950s shows that many cases of conflict were instigated by former elites who had been dispossessed economically and politically by land reform and cooperativization. In contrast, she finds that rural violence in the 1980s was far more likely to involve competition among community or kin groups over land and water rights; rural cadres even led protests against other local groups.[2] The central state's difficulty in maintaining local social order indicates the structural fragility of its rule over a vast rural population. Another significant indication the problems faced by late imperial and Republican governments continue is tax resistance, not just silent and clever maneuvering to reduce real burdens, but the large-scale and open mobilization of large numbers of peasants. With major changes in social organization and political institutions, the precise character of tax resistance events does not mirror exactly the forms and features of earlier cases, but the protests do document the

---

[2]Perry also finds that religious components are important features of rural protests. She also finds instances of people who persuade peasants that they are new emperors who will overthrow the Communist state (1985a, 1985b).

state's continued difficulties in creating defensible patterns of taxation despite having made a revolution in 1949.[3]

In cities, more "modern" forms of protest have become common. A Chinese government report states that more than 6,000 strikes took place in 1993 alone (Link 1994). For us to account for the wide repertoire of collective action forms in China the arc of change described by European experiences of contention is not enough. It does not prepare us for the simultaneous presence of tax resistance, community-based battles over land and water, and strikes. China's trajectory of political and economic changes presently includes patterns of protest that took place sequentially in European history.

More salient in the global press has been China's Democracy Movement. Posters and demonstrations to promote democracy occurred in China's largest cities during the 1970s and 1980s, culminating in the Spring 1989 protests. The Democracy Movement in China is the kind of social movement one would expect in a country with a strong state and a weak society, in particular a society short on autonomous social organizations with well-defined spheres of activity apart from the state and lacking in effective routine means for people to make claims on the state.

The Democracy Movement of the 1970s and 1980s posed serious challenges to the state's institutions and ideology. The product of urban China and of a decades-long tradition of political protest, the calls for "democracy" can be neither easily accepted nor lightly dismissed by the state because its revolution contains an acknowledgement of "democratic" principles. Yet the Democracy Movement represented a fundamental challenge to a unitary state unwilling to recognize either greater popular participation in political decision making or greater autonomy for social and cultural activities outside strictly governmental operations. As a challenge to a bureaucratic mode of decision making and rationality, the Democracy Movement complemented the erosion of bureaucratic political authority caused by some of the economic reforms. The consequence of this erosion was the emergence of personal ties and connections as political links to a market economy. The Democracy Movement therefore challenged the corruption of a system of political economy in which certain well-placed individuals benefit most from economic reform.

Ironically, the concerns of the Democracy Movement with official corruption, in particular personal profit making through political position, resemble in substance and form the concerns of Mao Zedong as he surveyed the conditions of Chinese state and society in the 1960s. Mao chose to resist what he saw as a trend toward increasing bureaucratization and a widening gap between common people and the officials above them. His strategy was to mobilize people, first young people and then workers, into a mass movement to challenge authorities.

---

[3]For studies that put post-Mao Chinese tax resistance into a broader context of rural disputes, see O'Brien and Li 1995, Li and O'Brien 1996. Opposition to taxes is especially common in areas with no township or village industries, where peasants consequently must meet increased local taxes primarily from agricultural production (Bernstein forthcoming).

The violence and horrors of the Cultural Revolution are a part of the nightmare that both proponents of democracy and their foes wish to avoid in the future.

The Cultural Revolution was the last of Mao's mass movements to mobilize people through a disruption of daily life to make extraordinary efforts in response to normative appeals about what was necessary, just, and correct. These movements were intense and temporary; they could not be transformed into routinized patterns of conventional behavior. But Mao did have a notion of permanent revolution which he offered in the late 1950s. His extension of mass movements from those aimed at increased production or social change to political criticism meant campaigns could mobilize people to challenge as well as to follow authority. Mao's logic of campaigns formed a counterweight to bureaucratization and the institutionalization of power in a modern state. Within this dialectical relationship there was no obvious synthesis to move state–society relations to a new plateau. This became the goal of the Democracy Movement. The challenge remains to propose institutional changes that reconfigure the distribution of power within the state and between state and society.

There is a complex relationship between the process of centralized state building and the articulation and pursuit of political ideals in all revolutions. In the French case, nineteenth-century struggles for popular participation in democratic politics promised by revolutionary rhetoric struggled against the power of successive central governments. In China, Communists had begun in the 1930s to mobilize peasants into political activity on a broader and more continuous basis than any previous political leadership had done. By the 1940s the idea of a "mass line" in which the people participated actively in the formulation and implementation of Party policies empowered peasants to a degree unprecedented in Chinese history. But this dynamic was qualified after 1949 by centralized state building seeking to establish firmer control over agrarian China. In the French and Chinese revolutions, a tension between state making and popular political participation was present from the beginning, but the ideological and institutional resources available to states and social groups differed significantly. These issues have attracted less attention in recent studies than the subject of revolutionary violence.

Revolution and Modernization

Scholars have become disenchanted with the Chinese and French revolutions. In the Chinese case, doubts about the benefits that the Revolution brought to peasants, the putative prime beneficiaries, have been exacerbated by laments over the senseless destruction of the Cultural Revolution. The "Revolution" leading to the establishment of the People's Republic in 1949 is made responsible for the future excesses and lunacies of people acting seventeen to twenty years later. This logic of blame takes a long-run view of revolution and sees a tragedy of needless suffering that obstructed social change and economic development. With such a perspective it becomes difficult to see much that is positive in the Revolution, despite its reduction of inequality and exploitation. If the horrors of the Cultural Revolution were foretold by the dynamics of the Revolution, then little positive value remains in the Chinese Revolution.

The assessment of the French Revolution is more mixed, since the republican legacy that inspired both elite forces of order and popular movements of change during the nineteenth century offers a positive counterweight for the memory of violence. The Terror, the violence visited upon not only the King but many of the revolutionaries themselves, was a high price indeed for revolutionary change. This critique works better if the horrors of the Terror are seen as integral and necessary features of the Revolution (Furet 1989). The balance against the Revolution tips further if republican ideas could have developed and flourished without the violence endemic to the French Revolution. Since democratic institutions developed in both England and the United States without the kinds of violence permeating the 1790s in France, the idea of republicanism without the violence of the French Revolution is plausible. The triumph of parliamentary democracy in the Third Republic at the end of protracted struggle makes the necessity of the French Revolution seem less obvious. The same line of reasoning, however, raises the question whether the republican vision of 1789 necessarily led to the Terror of 1792 and 1793.

It is difficult to draw necessary causal links from the outbreak of the Revolution to the Terror. At most, the possibilities for a Terror were created during the early years of the Revolution, when an ideological space for it was created. The larger social question prompted by reevaluations of the Terror and the Revolution more generally concern the role of crowds, those urban masses who initially brought their own claims and challenges to the state but then lost their autonomous and representative qualities as they became an audience for the government under the Terror (Lucas 1988).

The Chinese Revolution's "Terror" did not occur during the process that established the People's Republic. No urban crowds pushed the government toward revolutionary violence until some seventeen years later, when the Cultural Revolution raised serious questions about the role of crowds and violence in Chinese politics. But China lacked the positive counterweight of a republican tradition to balance the negative assessment of revolution. Moreover, the Cultural Revolution's persistence in the living memories of millions of Chinese has created an emotional urgency to the search for an acceptable place in the nation's collective memory for that social trauma. The violence of the Cultural Revolution calls into question the identity of Chinese in a way that the more distant Terror does not for the French.

Beyond the critique of revolutionary violence, there is a critique of the Chinese Revolution's economic costs and failures. In fact, the French Revolution was costly, but since France's economy continued to develop in the nineteenth century, an economic critique of the revolution is not usually made. For China, the critique of socialist policies in the countryside implicitly assumes that a market alternative would have been better, and that such reforms would have transformed the countryside. Recall that life expectancies in the 1930s hovered in the low 30s, while they reached the high 60s in the 1980s, largely as a result of successes that preceded the economic reforms. Can we therefore be sure that if the post-1978 reforms had not taken place, the commercialization of the 1930s would have been superior to the collectivization of the 1950s? Did the political economy of the day handle the 1920–21 North China famine any more successfully than the far larger disasters of the late 1950s? These are not easy questions, but they matter, because they speak to our expectations of revolutions in general and the Chinese Revolution in particular.

The economic failings currently attributed to the socialist revolutions represent a shift from earlier, more positive assessments of economic development. Whatever the political unpleasantness of the socialist revolutions, Western scholarship once generally argued that rapid economic advances were secured through centralized planning, which made possible the mobilization of social savings to be invested by the state in the creation of a modern industrial infrastructure. Discussing the Soviet Union, Alec Nove wrote, "Yet the success of the Soviet Union, albeit by totalitarian and economically inefficient methods, in making of itself the world's second industrial and military power is indisputable" (Nove 1969:378). In the 1950s the Chinese state succeeded in building a heavy industry base with impressive annual growth rates. While there were certainly policy failings and serious economic disruptions both during the Great Leap Forward and the Cultural Revolution, analysts also noted that the economy continued to grow. Moreover, the country was avoiding some of the serious social problems of other African, Asian, and Latin American countries—uncontrolled urban population growth with thousands upon thousands of unemployed people squatting in urban shacks, widespread poverty in rural areas, and societies marked by sharp disparities of wealth between rich and poor.

Since 1980 these earlier assessments have largely been superceded by a growing chorus of voices singing the praises of reform economics, both within and outside China. After overseeing the dismantling of collective agriculture in the countryside, the central government began to promote wide-ranging industrial reforms. As a result, China has begun to produce a growing array of consumer and producer goods for both international markets and domestic consumption. Staggering rates of growth make China one of the more attractive investment opportunities for international corporations.

Scholars previously expected the Revolution to achieve both political and economic changes, but now observers deny its contributions in either sphere. Lurking behind this denial is a reaffirmation of a liberal myth of political and economic change in Western Europe that is used as a standard for evaluating changes in China. By "liberal myth" I mean a vision of capitalism and democracy developing hand in hand to create a triumph at once political and economic. This myth envisions a happy union of capitalist economy and democratic polity that has been challenged even for England, the home of this vision. The myth ignores both the antagonisms toward capitalism expressed by what J. G. A. Pocock (1985) has called "civic republicanism" and the tension that C. B. MacPherson's "possessive individualism" (1962) poses to democratic politics.

The rejection of revolution as a violent tragedy interrupting the more cheerful storyline of economic development and expanding political participation ill equips us for discovering the ways in which revolutions are embedded in distinctive state-building trajectories that in turn determine forms of economic change. French concerns about private property and civil law mirrored concerns in other European countries and laid the bases for nineteenth-century French economic development. The Chinese desire to follow a Soviet model of heavy industrial growth under a planned economy obviously defined the basic parameters of economic development in 1950s China. The French Revolution addressed a series of issues particular to European, if not specifically French, situations, including political representation of elites, the role of the Christian churches, and changing economic and social roles of aristocracies, peasants, bourgeoisies, and workers. The Chinese Revolution addressed issues such as creating institutional and ideological bases for agrarian social order, integrating the former agrarian empire, and aligning rural–urban relations. Revolutions were not necessary to address these distinctive clusters of issues. Other European countries confronted the French issues without revolution. The Chinese could have seen alternative states emerge from the revolutionary situation that did not aspire to revolutionary social transformation. With or without revolutions, France and China faced different state-building challenges.

Most previous comparative analyses of revolution have emphasized the traits revolutions share, pointing out features common to both processes and outcomes. In my view, similarities are most salient for situations and processes; outcomes are far less similar. States that emerge from revolution may share less with other revolutionary states than they do with their own predecessors and with states that did not experience revolutions. Nineteenth-century France has more institutional and ideological similarities to other European cases than to twentieth-century China. The challenges of ruling revolutionary China were more similar in many ways to those of ruling late imperial and postimperial China than they were to ruling revolutionary France or Russia. Revolutionary outcomes are defined by a range of distinctly bounded and culturally specific possibilities. The nineteenth-century vacillation between republican and monarchical forms of government makes ideological and institutional sense in light of the French past. The post-1949 reconstruction of a unitary state anxious to assert its authority over both lower levels of government and society reproduces assumptions about government in Chinese history. These observations do not mean, of course, that either the nineteenth-century French or the post-1949 Chinese governments mindlessly continued past practices. They do, however, indicate the different ranges of possibility that exist in each case.

Looking at revolutions as unusual cases of similar phenomena is an exercise with recognized limitations. Revolutions like the French, Russian, and Chinese are obviously rare events. Most states and societies never experience this type of crisis and upheaval. Not surprisingly, the few that do share important structural similarities. But with so few cases of great revolutions, it is difficult to know how to relate these cataclysmic events to political transformations more generally.

One person who has attempted to place revolutionary political change within a broader context is Charles Tilly (1993). Tilly argues for multiple types of European revolutions associated with circumstances that change over time. He begins by distinguishing between revolutionary situations—those sets of circumstances under which "revolution" is a possibility—and revolutionary outcomes—instances in which basic political change has followed from a revolutionary situation. Revolutionary situations often share structural characteristics such as a growing gap between what states demand of those subjects who are best able to resist and what these subjects consider acceptable, a perceived threat to organized or collective identities by state intentions and actions, and the appearance of challengers to state authority. Tilly offers a fivefold taxonomy of revolutionary situations: (1) communal; (2) patron–client; (3) dynastic revolutionary; (4) national revolutionary; and (5) class coalitions.[4] His framework expands the number of cases of revolutionary situations beyond the previously paradigmatic cases of successful revolution. His strategy is to normalize revolutions amidst a more general analysis of politics and so improve our grasp of the systematic variations among political structures and activities making for revolutions and other forms of political action. Tilly thus poses a new structuralist alternative to earlier efforts in this tradition. By locating great revolutions within a wider spectrum of political conflicts, Tilly helps us to appreciate the multiple possibilities for violence and contention present in different settings.

The analysis in this chapter is intended to supply some of the variations Tilly has requested. Where Tilly's taxonomy expands the number of cases of temporally limited events, my assessment of just two cases expands the temporal depth of evaluation to construct alternative frameworks from which to view revolutionary change. Such an approach should move us from a "praise and blame" approach to revolution and back to the more basic and difficult task of explaining long-term dynamics of historical change. Like small-scale collective actions and protests, moments of large-scale violence and political uncertainty are embedded in historical structures and processes that define different ranges of possible outcomes to particular revolutionary situations. To understand revolutions and their significance, attention to their general similarities may matter less than establishing the reasons for their differences.

---

[4]His communal cases include protests by small groups like guilds or communities; he offers as an example the German peasant revolts of 1525 in which villages demanded religious and political autonomy. His patron–client cases refer to instances when elites lead popular resistance to state authority such as the Cossack rebellions against Polish control between 1591 and 1734. The third category of dynastic revolutionary situations includes challenges that groups (especially nobles) pose to ruling houses, like the Orangist seizure of Dutch towns in 1672. In the fourth type of national revolutionary situations, political entrepreneurs speak on behalf of populations who claim common origins or traditions and want their own rulers; for instance, Albania's struggle against the Ottoman Empire (1830–35). Finally, class coalitions mark those revolutionary situations in which two or more social classes organize to challenge those in positions of power, such as the largely unsuccessful revolutions of 1848 (Tilly 1993).

12

COMPARATIVE HISTORY
AND SOCIAL THEORY

The development of capitalism and the formation of national states are two long-term processes of historical change responsible for many of the most salient features of the modern world. Since these processes began in Europe, earlier generations of scholars considered the construction of the modern world to have been at base a European project. More recent scholarship has rebelled against such naked self-importance. Some scholars argue for successful political resistance and for the construction of social identities and cultural meanings outside the framework of possibilities defined by European categories. Others have proposed dynamics of change outside Europe that parallel or mesh with those within Europe. In the Chinese case, these efforts to assert separate identities and parallel dynamics of change reproduce intellectual strategies of late nineteenth and early twentieth-century Chinese scholars whose efforts were deemed a forced exercise in the 1950s and 1960s (Levenson 1968). That judgment may have been too simplistic if more recent efforts of the same kind are to be given credence. Yet scholarship arguing primarily for similarities and parallels ultimately fails to satisfy us, because we know that the political and economic trajectories of European countries and China differ dramatically.

I have argued in this book that some parallels between Chinese and European historical dynamics of change are more persuasive than others. In economics, discussions of the shared material limitations of preindustrial settings and the dynamics of commercial expansion both seem to me useful guides to a common world of natural possibilities before the Industrial Revolution. Parallels of a political and social nature seem to me more complex. We can discern some common elements to processes of state formation and transformation, but differences are at least as salient. Comparisons of the sorts made in this book encourage a closer look at common assumptions about similarities and differences between Chinese

277

and European dynamics of historical change. Some comparisons highlight possible similarities between Chinese and European dynamics of preindustrial economic change and qualify assumptions that a broad set of special European characteristics explains commercial expansion leading to the Industrial Revolution. Others stress the relevance of differences to understanding the distinctive arcs of state formation and transformation. Together these comparisons remind us that historical dynamics in China and Europe combine shared elements with distinctive ones to form multiple trajectories of change.

Economic Change

One important theme in research on seventeenth- and eighteenth-century European economic history has been the discovery of economic growth dynamics that precede the Industrial Revolution, a phenomenon which has consequently lost its position as a watershed event. A process of gradual economic growth is seen to start a century or more before the development of factory textiles and the subsequent use of coal and production of steel. The Industrial Revolution did not suddenly raise economic growth rates; instead, these had already begun to rise gradually at an earlier date. Europe's development of markets, rural industries, and commercial agriculture all seem to lead to the Industrial Revolution, which becomes an important installment in a much longer narrative of economic change.

Putting early modern European economic changes into a line of growth that goes through the Industrial Revolution to the establishment of economic superiority in the nineteenth century can easily lead to the assumption that none of these changes occurred elsewhere. But, as I argued in Part I, China and Europe shared important similarities of preindustrial economic expansion based on Smithian dynamics. These included increased rural industries, more productive agricultures, and expanded commercial networks.

These similarities disrupt a simple contrast between European economic dynamism and Chinese material stagnation. We can see that common factors were at work before the Industrial Revolution and that the mere presence of these factors cannot explain the Industrial Revolution. The comparative perspective reveals an element of contingency that reflects the incompleteness of our explanations of European patterns of economic change.

Generally speaking, explanations can be incomplete for several reasons. We may lack adequate knowledge of a situation, so we categorize it as one of a class of situations about which we know more. Sometimes this works: the similarities of Chinese and European forms of protests over food and taxes, for example, support their classification as small-scale events of a similar sort. Studies of revolution, too, conventionally seek the shared traits that allow us to predict similar outcomes. Revolutions, however, are much more complex and protracted events than small conflicts like grain seizures or tax resistance. While a kind of explanation is achieved by classifying a situation as a "revolution," understanding the case may still be limited, because processes of revolution contain multiple phenomena and the relationships among them are uncertain. For example, the way a fiscal crisis is met affects official relations among levels of government and with various domestic elites and foreign powers. Such linkages, themselves at best *probable,* add to our uncertainty about the outcomes of complex processes. The concessions officials make in return for fiscal support or foreign loans are difficult to pinpoint before the fact, although these concessions in turn affect later sequences of events. In short, our predictions of outcomes in complex situations need not turn out to be true; in fact, the least likely of several outcomes may in fact obtain. When we seek to fix on one result as the only possible outcome we invoke a form of historical determinism that goes beyond the simple explanation of a set of events. Just because such and such did happen does not mean it was "destined" to happen.

Historical determinism is especially problematic in discussing moments of dramatic change. Such moments are extremely rare, and our abilities to explain them correspondingly weak. In economics, the Industrial Revolution is one such moment. Much effort has gone into downplaying the rupture caused by the Industrial Revolution. But the world of material possibilities was dramatically altered between 1780 and 1880. No previous century witnessed such changes. I have suggested that the clustering of a group of macroinventions in a brief period of time created the material possibilities for industrialization. But only the initially contingent fit between the institutions of capitalism and the technologies of industrialization made possible the pattern of economic change that unfolded in nineteenth-century Europe, a pattern that broke free of the world of limited material growth analyzed by the classical economists. If we accept these contingencies, we can also accept more easily the prior presence of similar dynamics of economic expansion which on their own could not drive either the Chinese or European economies into a world of vastly greater material wealth. This argument about economic change suggests that the presence in China of some dynamics of expansion similar to those in Europe makes likely a set of contingent rather than causal connections between commercial development and industrial breakthroughs.

With the Industrial Revolution, economic possibilities became available. Analyses of economic change after the Industrial Revolution usually either advocate that countries follow the path taken by successful developers or argue that the possibilities for economic change in any specific area are largely dictated by the position this area comes to play in a world economy dominated by Europeans. In general, the former type of analysis is used to explain successes, while the latter is applied to economic failures. Together they remind us of the different paths countries take toward a common economic goal such as industrialization in which the roles of governments, financial networks, firm organization, and much more all vary. Economic development has always been geographically uneven: Eastern Europe remains far poorer than Western Europe; even within Western Europe, the centers of greatest success shifted between 1500 and 1800, from the Mediterranean to the Dutch Republic to England.

The powerful dynamics of economic change that made the modern economic world have yet to create uniformity. Even when people consciously aim for certain economic results, they do not always succeed, because the processes creating economic change outrun the human capacity to control them. Realistic social theory must develop a tolerance for these limitations without forsaking all efforts to order and explain economic change. This book poses claims about Chinese and European paths of economic change that will surely be refined, if not revised, by future research. Its value, however, lies in stimulating alternative explanations for the similarities and differences in Chinese and European patterns of economic change. At a minimum, we should no longer privilege European patterns as a set of norms against which to locate Chinese failures.

One implication of the arguments I'm making about economic change is that they can be thought of as modular, that is, as discrete clusters of change. If we separate the cluster of major technological innovations from the dynamics of commercial expansion and the political economies of capitalism and agrarian empire, we can then see how the Industrial Revolution "module" fits into Chinese and European settings. The differences in Chinese and European political economy tell us about larger dimensions of state transformation—what governments think is important, what they attempt to achieve, how they define challenges and capacities, the kinds of commitments they make as well as the kinds of claims they face. The Chinese state aimed for and to some degree achieved its goal of static efficiency; that is, spreading the best techniques available across a vast area. This goal made sense within a world of limited possibilities. Europeans, in contrast, sought competition and growth. Though they didn't anticipate the possibilities that came with the Industrial Revolution, their attitudes helped them to develop systems to exploit those possibilities more swiftly and effectively than could happen in China.

The Industrial Revolution fit within European economic institutions more effectively than Chinese ones. But despite the differences, industrialization did take place in early twentieth-century China. Even if the spatial dynamics of economic change in China remain unclear, the political economy within which twentieth-century Chinese economic development took place is visibly different from that of industrializing Europe. Thus multiple formats can yield comparable economic results.

Economic productivity, repeatedly expanded by technological changes since the Industrial Revolution, has created a promise of material prosperity unimaginable even two centuries ago. More recently we have discovered that industrialization also poses the threat of ecological disaster. Economic hopes and fears have become increasingly global as awareness of the connections among economic activity in distinct places has become more acute—markets for information, raw materials, labor, capital and products have all become more integrated. Models and strategies for economic success travel around the globe as the regional economies of the world become more interconnected.

Despite a global convention of taking Europe as the center of development of the modern economic world, Europe's leading role has been exaggerated both spatially and temporally. The development of extensive commerce in the sixteenth and seventeenth centuries was only partially a European phenomenon. The subsequent advantages of industrial capitalism were limited to parts of Europe and North America for a few decades before the industrial transformation of Asia began. By the 1950s, parts of Asia—Japan, Jiangnan, and Northeast China—were all in the same economic league as the more developed parts of Western Europe and North America and therefore ahead of Eastern Europe and South America.

While the world remains unevenly developed economically, it is generally agreed that the expansion of material wealth has been largely a positive development. Most criticisms of materialist excess and anxieties over ecological balances take for granted certain advantages of an industrialized economic system even as they lament and rail against features they find problematic or dangerous. General agreement about the direction of economic change and its basic advantages confirms that at least in this realm people across cultures associate quality of life with material security and abundance. The multiple dynamics of economic change since industrialization all point in a single direction of increased productivity and greater material wealth. This is a shared condition of modernity. The situation in politics is different.

State Making and Unmaking

European state formation is embedded in a particular combination of institutions and ideologies quite distinct from the combination of institutions and ideologies that make possible the reproduction and transformation of agrarian empire in China. In early modern Europe two major challenges faced would-be central government rulers. Externally, they competed with other would-be state makers often by engaging in wars; domestically, centralizing governments negotiated with distinct and delimited elite groups which developed their claims on the state as the state expanded its capacities to extract resources and make war. European states made few commitments to their subjects; instead the dynamic of elite claim-making became generalized as the ideologies and institutions of liberties and representation were shared by larger numbers of people. Throughout this process, the expansion of state power was accompanied by increasingly clear separation of the state realm from civil society.

In late imperial China, the state also faced major challenges. Externally the government aimed to enhance its stature and security vis à vis the nomadic and seminomadic peoples to the north and the smaller sedentary societies to the southwest and across the seas. The empire projected a Sinocentric world order that rulers of other peoples tolerated for one of three reasons: (1) they were too weak militarily to challenge this order; (2) they gained material and symbolic benefits from the tribute system; or (3) they were little affected by the Chinese empire's pretensions to world order. Domestically, the government faced more daunting challenges centered on the construction and routine maintenance of social order under state control. The Chinese state developed the bureaucratic capacities to create a unitary form of government, in which a hierarchy of officials was responsible for implementing the state's agenda for domestic order. The success of official labors depended on the efforts and resources of elites who shared their social sensibilities. Officials and elites jointly made commitments to the common people, expressing their ability and willingness to create and maintain material and moral institutions of social order that in turn provided them with the means for social control. Unlike their European counterparts, neither elites nor common people in China enjoyed institutionalized positions of autonomous power from which they could place claims on the state as a counterweight to its continued expansion. But neither did the Chinese state expand its power at the expense of elites, but rather worked in concert with them.

To compare state-making experiences I argue that the standards we apply must be ultimately derived from some set of empirical experiences. We cannot entirely escape judging Asian state making by European standards because there is no metatheoretical ground on which to base our comparisons. Instead, we must achieve symmetry by looking at Europe from a Chinese perspective. If we do, a distinctive set of absences and commonalities emerges, not at all the same as the ones highlighted in looking at China from a European perspective.

The payoffs of symmetric perspectives are several. We recognize relativism without abandoning comparison entirely. In fact, we can make *more* comparisons this way. Neither China nor Europe becomes more general or particular than the other. Symmetric perspectives allow us to recognize that there are many state formation and transformation possibilities.

When we compare concrete capacities to accomplish particular tasks, we discover that the late imperial Chinese state sometimes outperformed early modern European states. European states lacked the ability to expand the taxation of their agrarian populations, because elite claims on the land kept governments from establishing major new claims of their own. Nor could European governments enumerate their subject populations. Finally, before the nineteenth century no European state could imagine an attempt to shape social opinion and cultural practices. The Chinese had routinely taxed its people in an organized bureaucratic fashion since the third century B.C.E. Population registration and enumerations also began two millennia ago; by the eighteenth century population records were kept by the government throughout the empire, while in Europe only the Church recorded demographic data. The highly institutionalized religions of Europe also took care of defining an orthodoxy of belief that was within the province of state power and responsibility in China.

When examined according to the same criteria, the Chinese state engaged in certain activities before European states did. The standard strategy for addressing the anomaly thus created is to argue that the Chinese case lacks an important feature of the European case that allows the latter to be considered "modern." For instance, China's late imperial bureaucracy is often said to lack the standards of expertise and rule-governed behavior demanded (ideally) in Western settings. An implicit equation of European and modern takes place in these critiques of Chinese practices and facilitates the identification of Chinese practices as "tradition-al" or "premodern." Differences no doubt exist, but they may be better labeled simply as "Chinese" and "European" than traditional and modern that imply par-ticular dynamics of historical change. Otherwise, we limit unnecessarily our abil-ities to account for dynamics of political change.

In Europe, the separation of state and society, the elaboration of functionally distinct and institutionally independent levels of government, the construction of organizations within society, and the formation of representational theories of government grew from an initial situation in which centralizing rulers sought to expand capacities and negotiated with elites to do so. This basic relationship between rulers and elites as well as its political and social institutionalization did not appear in China. There officials and elites shared common commitments to domestic order that produced a continuum between state and society, limited in-stitutionalization of distinct groups within society, and reinforced political pref-erences for a vertically integrated unitary state with a fractal vision of rule that could survive the collapse of central government power. To think that only one of these dynamics leads to "modern" state–society relations makes sense only if one completely displaces the other at some point in time. But, while we are often encouraged to think that such displacement did take place in twentieth-century China, a mere increase in the number of Western-style institutions will not initi-ate a Western dynamic as long as earlier dynamics of state formation and trans-formation remain relevant.

Before 1800 we can reasonably view the political agendas of China and Europe as independent—there were analytical similarities and modest points of contact, but rulers at either end of Eurasia conceived of their roles using culturally sepa-rate and distinct vocabularies.[1] Over the course of the nineteenth and twentieth centuries, this ceased to be true. European categories and conventions reached China as they did other parts of the world. This book argues that the important differences in political agendas that developed before intense contact continued to matter in the nineteenth century and in postimperial times even though they are doubly obscured: by the modern Western inclination to see only distorted im-ages of Europe in countries with separate pasts; and by new Chinese vocabularies that assign newness to concerns that in fact stretch back centuries. If we fail to take seriously the characteristics of late imperial state–society relations, we limit our abilities to explain postimperial state transformation in China.

A final reason to be more cautious about holding up the results of European state making as the norm against which to understand Chinese or other situations

---

[1]One could argue that before 1800, Chinese influences on Europe were greater than European influ-ences on China. The Enlightenment embrace of Chinese political institutions, which included recog-nition of the moral sensibilities that engaged Chinese rulers in welfare activities, could even be considered part of the background for nineteenth-century European ideas about state welfare concerns. Thus stress on the relative lack of pre-1800 contact between China and Europe tends to discount the ways in which China may have influenced Europe before the more familiar period of Western influence on China.

is the implicit assumption that state making is complete. The current reconfiguration of state power within Europe is redefining levels and relations of power and authority, transforming a system of competing states into a single more integrated state structure. One might almost say, from a Chinese perspective, that Europe is finally achieving a modest measure of unity that weakly reflects the kind of integration that has been basic to Chinese state formation for millennia. Such a comparison may be limited, but is taking Chinese integration as the norm against which to measure more modest European achievements in this regard that much less sensible than taking European state making as the norm for Chinese political successes and failures?

At the same time, the current reconfiguration of relations among center, province, and locale in China may transform what was once a unitary state with a fractal vision of rule, in both its Confucian and Communist formulations, into an institutionally differentiated state structure with clearer divisions of power, responsibility, and authority at different levels of government. Is the Chinese or the European situation more "modern" than the other? Although both changes may represent elements of convergence, we should expect that political changes in China and Europe will remain distinct.

Social Protest and Political Change

Social protests, which reflect political and economic struggles, also contribute to our senses of historical change. Remarkably similar types of popular protest took place in early modern Europe and late imperial China. Events like grain seizures and tax resistance occurred when authorities violated expectations held by protestors. The immediate interests of protestors were the same—to secure more and cheaper food and lower taxes. Popular expectations were grounded in material interests that seem reasonably similar across different cultures. As the material conditions under which these events took place changed, they became more or less common. Charles Tilly has outlined the general pattern of changing forms of social protest in France from reactive forms including grain seizures and tax resistance to proactive ones like strikes and demonstrations.[2] For Tilly and scholars of European protest who have followed his lead, protest "modernized" as state, society, and economy all did likewise.

Tilly's initial taxonomy has stood up well through time. And when we extend it across space it offers some guidance as well. In China, strikes, demonstrations, and boycotts all became forms of popular protest in twentieth-century cities. But other forms of protest continued into the twentieth century, with tax resistance by peasants an issue even in the 1990s. We could interpret these persistent con-

---

[2]C. Tilly 1972a and 1972b lay out the relationship between changing forms of collective action and extensive social change. In a more recent statement Tilly contrasts the "parochial and patronized" forms of collective action typical of the period between 1650 and 1850 with the "national and autonomous" forms of the period 1850 to 1980 (Tilly 1986:380–404).

flicts as signs of China's rather halting and incomplete forward movement. Certainly grain seizures continue to make sense under conditions of food scarcity. For tax resistance, the logic is less clear. Tax resistance did not prove to be a rearguard action against a centralizing state able to negotiate with elites and agree upon institutional bases of taxation authority. The issue of what is forward movement is less clear for politics than it is for economics.

The differences in the significance and meaning of small-scale conflicts reflects in part ideologies of rule that assign these conflicts greater or lesser centrality to politics. In China, grain seizures signaled an awkward failure for a government that put subsistence issues high on its list of indicators of successful rule. A well-fed population was a clear sign of virtuous and effective rule. To make its rule morally acceptable, a Chinese government had to create and implement strategies to ensure subsistence security. Not that all dynasties routinely succeeded at this goal, but the ideal was certainly affirmed and even expanded over time. Chinese tax policy was heavily shaped by issues of equity and equality. Both the absolute size of levies and the fairness of their distribution were central. Efforts at tax reform routinely sought to equalize burdens and simplify collections.

European protests do not seem to have been embedded so centrally in ideologies of rule. In fact, they emerged just as the twin processes of capitalist development and state formation disrupted previous economic and political patterns. New ideologies were constructed to promote commerce and the authority of centralizing states. Subsistence issues and tax equity did not figure prominently in these discourses.

Although the immediate structural contexts for small-scale protests like food riots and tax resistance were similar, the processes of economic and political change within which these events took place were different in significant ways. Each small-scale event is a module with many shared characteristics, an element in a specific type of political economy and a distinct dynamic of state formation and transformation. In the differences we can see how similar problems and issues acquire different meanings and end in distinct solutions determined by alternative combinations of material and ideological changes.

When we turn to revolutions, we again discover similarities and differences. Most of the similarities concern structural and contextual crises that make plausible dramatic political change. The differences are products of the distinctive arcs of political transformation within which violent change takes place. Revolutions embrace material changes and the construction of new world views. Social structures and sentiments are both contested in such situations, but revolutions nonetheless remain bounded by path-dependent patterns of change. Putting revolutions back into their respective historical trajectories may encourage us to reduce our expectations as to what revolutions can achieve and therefore mitigate our disappointment over their failures and limitations.

As recently as the 1970s, few analysts, either Western or Chinese would have predicted how important issues of taxation and resistance to taxes would become. The development of Euro-American welfare states seemed obvious. When we reviewed the early modern era, we spoke of tax resistance as one form of collective protest that marked popular resistance to the expansion of state power. Tax resistance disappeared from the European scene as states consolidated their powers and incorporated, in some places, representative power in setting taxes. Our narratives of state building didn't lead us to expect the decline of the welfare state that is proceeding apace in numerous Euro-American settings. In the United States, this initiative has been spearheaded by a kind of tax resistance that would have been unimaginable in old-regime Europe: political movements persuading voters to favor limits on certain types of taxes. As welfare states in North America and Europe are being dismantled, the powers and responsibilities of different levels of government are being renegotiated. No one seeks to defend government as it has been practiced; few seem to be able to articulate in substantive terms what they believe government can do well and should be doing.

From a very different starting point, the government of the People's Republic of China has also been facing contraction and scaling down of its activities. One of the basic issues that has exercised Chinese leaders since the 1980s has been fiscal reforms; we discover the central government's real structural weakness as it negotiates to draw resources from provinces and locales where the expansion of political capacities to extract revenues has accompanied the development of the economy. Locales and provinces are pitted against both the center eager for more revenues and enterprises that are seeking to avoid taxation as much as they can. The changing balance between central and local tax bases has significant implications for the future Chinese state.[3]

Structural uncertainties about the roles of different levels of government as well as the overall role of government in society affect China as they do the United States. Issues of taxation matter to both, but tax resistance in China remains very different from what we see in the United States. While the Chinese economic reforms have reduced the roles of the state and the Party in a wide number of social and economic activities, increased popular participation in governmental decision making through representative government has not accompanied these changes. Popular engagement in politics to influence government policies has therefore continued to be expressed in part through protests. The leaders of the Chinese revolution, who transformed agrarian social relations, continue to face the challenges of taxing rural society without provoking protests. A particularly dramatic example involved some ten thousand peasants in Renshou County, Sichuan who, armed with clubs and scythes, protested new grain taxes in a confrontation with officials (Link 1994:32).

Once we set about explaining the operations of the socialist state in China with little, if any, attention to the processes of state formation that had preceded it. We were confident that a rupture of the magnitude that occurred in 1949 made knowledge of earlier history unnecessary, a convenient assumption since much

---

[3]For a review of fiscal changes, see Wang Shaoguang 1994. He draws some suggestive (and debatable) historical contrasts that resonate with dynastic cycle theory.

then remained unstudied. The persistence of tax resistance in China today suggests that peasants still oppose the state in ways and for reasons their ancestors would have understood. But will this continue in the future? Institutional structures may change further to make such protests unlikely. But for the moment at least, the changing horizons of tax resistance in Chinese history don't promise future peasant collective actions radically divorced from past practices. Euro-American welfare states are contracting their range of responsibilities, and the Chinese socialist state is reducing its range of activities. But wherever these processes are leading, they do not yet appear to be converging toward a common end.

Combining Comparisons and Connections

Western ideas made it possible for late nineteenth and twentieth-century Chinese intellectuals to imagine new futures. Problems and possibilities most easily expressed in Western categories gained salience—most of them, not surprisingly, concerned relations with foreigners. Reaction to studies of China's "response" to the West has highlighted scholarship on pre-nineteenth-century Chinese dynamics of change. But how to combine in the late twentieth century those native dynamics predating China's nineteenth-century "response" with the new challenges intimately connected to foreign relations has been confusing to participants and later observers alike. Few intellectuals in the first half of the twentieth century were aware of any positive dynamics of change in Chinese history before the nineteenth century that were not analogues to Western phenomena. But while China might claim certain parallels, society more generally lacked the overall European dynamics of change. Social Darwinism gave Chinese intellectuals the opportunity to imagine China's evolution into a stronger and more dynamic country. Failure to do so could spell fatal destruction. Most scholarly studies focused on pre-1949 China have followed participants' predilections for confronting China in terms of an adapted Western discourse.

Problems on an earlier agenda for late imperial rule were not always easily expressed in new discourses. But the old problems were unmistakably present. Creating social order and economic security in the countryside was a goal for those intellectuals and political leaders still inspired by a Confucian rhetoric of social possibilities as well as for Western liberal reformers and radical Communist revolutionaries. The degree to which these issues could be addressed with some degree of independence from the new agenda of urban and foreign issues indicates the difficulties of combining urban and rural issues. In our conventional presentations of twentieth-century history we speak of China's "modern" problems, created by contacts with the West, and its "traditional" problems that predate such contact. But if we adopt the vantage point of 1935 for a moment, both sets of problems were part of the contemporary situation. The fact that the origins of one set were farther back in time than the other doesn't alter the pressing urgency of both in 1935. Many of the challenges of moving forward concerned linking urban treaty ports politically and economically to the rest of China. Although urban industrial growth had already transformed the Shanghai region and the Northeast, a basic question in 1935 was the integration of China's economy. Politically, developing a strategy for rebuilding or replacing the bureaucratic integration of rural China posed an immediate challenge. Local government had been penetrating the rural scene more deeply since the late Qing, but the integration of this local government into a bureaucratic hierarchy proved difficult before 1949.

State formation and economic development in China, as in Europe, remain tied to earlier structural dynamics of change. Institutional patterns and habits of mind can indeed be changed, but, however much people declare their intent to break radically with the past, they rarely achieve a thorough rupture. The connections among institutional practices as well as individual norms of behavior are culturally constructed. People face similar material problems or possibilities, but the ways in which they perceive them and respond to them are distinctive. These contrasts are often obscured, at least to outside observers, by the similarities among different situations created by different models for political and economic organization that make change appear to follow well-established paths.

Such practices are responsible for the deterministic readings of social change that characterize one stream of social theory. The stream has two distinct currents which battle each other, but both flow in a single direction. First are the developmentalists, who believe in clear patterns of change; whether these are democratic institutions or market economies, they make a better political or economic system possible. Second are the system theorists, who see opportunities as defined less by the models the advanced world offers the less developed countries than by the constraints imposed by the system of states and the international economy; only certain roles are available to states and their economies, and these are defined by the distribution of power and wealth in the world. Both perspectives have clear merit, but by themselves or even together they remain incomplete, because they limit the range of possible processes that give rise to historical changes.

The implicit, if not always explicit, expectations that historical trajectories of advanced and less developed countries will either converge or be defined systemically fail to account for obvious historical parallels such as when people struggled against comparable material problems and met some of the same political and economic challenges—tax resistance and food protests, for instance, cannot be explained by either convergence or systemic links. Nor can either group explain why, as people's lives become more connected, they do not necessarily become either more similar or mutually dependent. Social theory must take seriously the task of moving beyond failed teleologies rooted in nineteenth-century visions to a reasoned consideration of the multiple paths into and out of the present.

Types of Historical Analyses

Each generation writes its own history, in part because it exists at a distinct moment. New retrospective analyses are necessary in each new generation. The choice of end points often heavily influences the choice of the beginning points from which a causal chain unfolds. If we instead begin at a point in time and consider the possibilities stretching forward we can introduce contingency and openness, basic features of prospective analysis. Some scholars claim that they aren't interested in what might have happened, only in what did occur. But unless one understands what else could have happened, neither the reasons for nor the significance of what did happen can be identified with confidence.

Prospective and retrospective analyses can be joined together and to some degree are necessarily related. A hybrid explanation aims to account for possibilities as well as what actually happened. But even if prospective and retrospective analyses are analytically linked, they are asymmetric exercises. Prospective analyses lack the degree of certainty and closure that retrospective analyses enjoy. They frame the universe of possibilities within which the world we wish to explain and understand came into being.

Certain problems can only be treated retrospectively. For instance, the role of technological change in pre-twentieth-century economic history is an instance in which scholars can offer explanations of specific technological changes retrospectively but cannot predict what changes will take place where and with what impact. In other instances, a retrospective analysis of a complex phenomenon will prove a poor guide to finding similar changes elsewhere. For example, explaining how a particular revolution took place doesn't really tell you much about how to predict the outcomes of future ones. Finally, retrospective and prospective analyses can fit together in different ways. Prospective explanations of when and where to expect people to protest food-supply problems and taxation issues may become parts of larger retrospective analyses of revolutionary situations. These latter analyses must account for the very different sets of events that accompany grain seizures and tax resistance and lead to different political outcomes.

Sorting out how prospective and retrospective analyses fit together promises to sharpen our abilities to create more general social theory. Theory becomes more general as it is applied to an ever-larger number of different scenarios; this is, for example, the aspiration of rational choice theory which searches for law-like regularities. General theory may also seek to explain linkages among different situations. Nineteenth-century social theory was understandably focused on explaining patterns of European social change. It achieved one level of generality by claiming to explain a long stretch of complex historical dynamics in Europe. It generally ignored consideration of historical change outside of Europe, believing that other times and places lacked the dynamics of change found in Europe and hence were stagnant. After the initial accomplishment of explaining European patterns of historical change, some twentieth-century social theorists elaborated on these nineteenth-century foundations to explain other parts of the world in terms of their connections to the West. Now we recognize that such social theory's relevance to historical dynamics elsewhere is limited, especially in instances that predate major Western contact. Social theory in the twenty-first century will have to incorporate far richer and more complex sets of historical experiences.

Thinking how to phrase the most basic questions about patterns of historical change with a sense of multiple possibilities liberates us from false teleologies of preordained ends. We can aim to account effectively for specific modules, some of which are present in more than one set of historical dynamics. But when we place these modules in sequences of historical change, we have to consider what dynamics explain their similarities and dissimilarities. Prospective analyses take a set of circumstances as given and project them forward. To say that the future is not predetermined is not to say that all scenarios are equally probable. Knowing that certain factors are present in one situation but not in another should alert us to the likelihood that future changes will also be different. In politics, for instance, we may expect Chinese commitments to social welfare to continue to be different from those of the West, where the "welfare state" is a twentieth-century phenomenon. But our expectation is tempered by the radical displacement of a Confucian discourse by a Communist one and the latter's subsequent crisis which makes tracking these possibilities difficult.

In the realm of contemporary economics, the possibilities are clearer, because we can associate different policy packages with different outcomes, given certain initial conditions. But if we imagine China's economic future in 1750, for example, it is difficult to see any radical rupture in the economic system, although Europe, of course, did experience such a rupture. Retrospective readings can "explain" the changes without predicting that they would necessarily occur.

Recognizing the difference between prospective and retrospective analyses is basic to escaping teleological social theory while still believing that various pasts are explainable. We can move from thinking about how social theory can order diverse historical experiences to a sense of possible futures, not necessary conclusions by any means but not senseless or random ones either. With prospective and retrospective analyses we can take a final look at the problem of making comparisons. The economic comparisons in this book employ a prospective analysis and argue that the divergence of European and Chinese paths is hard to predict, though each path can be explained retrospectively. In addition, the initial divergence caused by the Industrial Revolution has not been sustained, because the technologies of economic development can travel to new settings and become successful despite the absence of many of the political, social, and cultural contexts present in European cases.

In my political comparisons I explore two basically different trajectories within which limited similarities can be found. Using explicit norms to predict change establishes the relevance of counterfactuals. By comparing two alternative predictive schemes, we can eliminate the dangers of explaining what didn't happen from one perspective only. State formation and transformation include both parallel and connected elements, but the combination of the two incompletely determines the trajectories of political change. The openness of possibilities is bounded by the repertoire of ideological and institutional resources that officials and elites can bring to politics.

Finally, this book examines types of social protest. Small-scale collective actions are limited sequences for which prospective analyses can yield clear similarities—the results have similar causes. Once these small events are framed by larger structures, we can see that there are different state-making dynamics and political economies within which the same sorts of small-scale protests can be located. When we shift from these small-scale protests to the larger narratives of revolution, we find that structural models give good prospective explanations of how revolutionary situations come into being but are inadequate to predict the character of revolutionary outcomes which are embedded within a set of possibilities constructed by state formation and transformation processes and quite separate from the crises of the moment.

Becoming Modern

How well ideas and practices travel across cultures is crucial to explicating similarity and difference in an increasingly interconnected world. Some ideas travel with virtually no cultural baggage. Most obvious are sciences like mathematics or physics. But even Western classical music travels well, for it has generated no distinctly Asian response or adaptation; the cultural sensibilities it represents can be generalized. In contrast, some cultural practices travel, then become embedded in their new contexts and acquire meanings different from those in their country of origin. Japanese baseball is an obvious case of adapting an American pastime to make a Japanese game. The sense of team spirit, individual sacrifice, discipline, and shame are all distinctly Japanese. Political ideas and institutions also represent a case of complex transmission. The import of foreign ideas is enmeshed with the reproduction and transformation of native ideas. Foreign ideas and institutions may completely displace native ones in some cases but not in others. The domestication of foreign political practices can vary tremendously. Tracking the dynamics of these variations demands a recognition of domestic political sensibilities and their reproduction and transformation over time.

Francis Fukuyama's *End of History and the Last Man* delivers a stirring victory speech for liberal democracy and capitalist markets guaranteed to warm the hearts of any and all believers in the superiority of the American system. Fukuyama grounds his arguments in a Hegelian view of history's movement. The fundamental point about Fukuyama's sense of historical change is that the West became modern through a historical process and now the rest of the world is converging upon this state as the common and ultimate end of history. But the dynamics leading non–West European and non–North American parts of the world to this point have, it appears, nothing to do with their own histories, but everything to do with Europe's.

A similar denial of history outside Europe as a guide to modern historical change and social theory is made by Anthony Giddens, a very different type of social theorist, most explicitly in *The Consequences of Modernity*, in which moder-

nity is distinguished from the ways of life preceding it by some key discontinuities—the pace and size of change and the character of modern institutions. Giddens proceeds to critique elements in the great traditions of Western social theory
and to advance his own alternative centered on the separation of time and space,
relocation of social practices in different places, and the reflexive character of social knowledge. The history that appears in Giddens's account of modernity is European history driven by the familiar processes of the development of capitalism
and state formation. He sees the creation of a modern world as the globalization
of these processes begun in the West. "In terms of institutional clustering, two
distinct organisational complexes are of particular significance in the development
of modernity: the nation-state and systematic capitalist production . . . Is modernity distinctively a Western project in terms of the ways of life fostered by these
two great transformative agencies? To this query, the blunt answer must be 'yes'"
(1990:174–75). Giddens's view of the prospects for modernity and postmoder-
nity grow out of his very Western trajectory. His "utopian realism" includes:
emancipatory politics (politics of inequality), politicization of the global, life politics (politics of self-actualization), and politicization of the local. His roles for social movements are: ecological movements (counterculture), peace movements,
free speech/democratic movements, and labor movements. Giddens's general
traits of modernity advance us beyond the great social theorists of the late nineteenth and early twentieth centuries. But grand as this project is, becoming modern must include the possibility of following trajectories of change shaped by the
development of capitalism and nation-states but in no complete and ultimate sense
defined by these movements alone.

The denial of history obviously stakes out a temporal claim about the irrelevance of historical processes. But it is also a spatial claim about the irrelevance of
variations across the globe. To many scholars, the construction of modernity is a
universal project neither historically nor culturally specific, despite its temporal
and spatial origins in Europe. Some features of the contemporary world lend support to this view of historical change. Strategies to gain control of the material
world through science and technology as well as decisions about economic organization and planning are all drawn out of a common repertoire of possibilities
constantly being enlarged by experiments in different parts of the world. Yet we
can exaggerate the degree to which such commonalities have emerged only since
European processes of state formation and capitalist development spread Western
power across the globe. As many specialists know, we may ignore how China, for
instance, was also changing before Western contact. Smithian dynamics of economic expansion are an important example addressed in this book. Less obviously, Chinese and European political practices exhibit parallels that predate the
introduction of Western political institutions and ideologies into Asia. The parallels are less obvious because the late imperial Chinese practices of seeking domestic order and integration through moral and material strategies of control predate
European state efforts at similar tasks. The existence of parallels points to com-

mon directions of historical change, but their limitations also remind us of historical differences.

Many of the themes in this book highlight the specificity of Chinese and European dynamics of economic and political change. The plurality of historical pasts makes more likely the persistence of multiple, open, and contingent futures. Because large-scale and long-term historical change is path-dependent, we can gain a measure of control over what types of changes are more or less probable. We reduce our abilities to predict if we insist that history no longer matters and that places like China are simply being propelled by the universal dynamics of political and economic change historically generated out of European experiences. When we break long sequences of change into smaller units, we can find comparable units of activity in earlier periods of Chinese and European history. We can make prospective explanations of particular events such as small-scale conflicts. More long-term prospective explanations reveal difficulties—predicting European economic successes turns out to be more problematic than we expected when we recognize the parallels with Chinese economic conditions before the Industrial Revolution. Large-scale and long-term changes are often specific and therefore are better explained retrospectively. The challenge of anticipating future changes from any point in time lies in combining prospective explanations of limited phenomena with a sense of path-dependent possibilities afforded by reviewing retrospective explanations of long-term changes.

China and Europe have been shaped by historical processes both similar and different, both shared and solitary. Capitalism and European state formation are important processes in explaining the arc of Western historical change. They also matter to a larger world. But they cannot substitute for other dynamics of political and economic change that owe their meaning to historically distinct processes of change. Knowing this should encourage us to formulate better social theory and carry out better historical research.

Like many others dissatisfied with the historically and culturally specific teleologies of historical change based on nineteenth-century social theory, I am arguing that we should exceed the limitations of historical explanations derived from European experiences. Postmodern anxieties expressed in literary criticism and cultural studies are real. They identify and at times celebrate the indeterminancy and multiplicity of social meanings that challenge any simple reading of present, past or future. But unlike many whose postmodern rejection of the modernist project accepts extreme relativism without, it seems to me, a capacity to compare or a commitment to explain diversity, I am arguing for the importance of continued efforts to expand the capacities of social theory through a more systematic grounding in multiple historical experiences. Difference deserves to be explained. The vantage point of Western theory and experience is inadequate but not irrelevant to this project. Complemented by explanations of other kinds of experience and by efforts to compare the results of different historical experiences, we can hope to create historically grounded and culturally realistic social theory.

Particular cultural pasts may become increasingly irrelevant in the future. But this will be completely so only when all societies and cultures choose from the same set of alternatives to address the same problems. As long as situations are different, then the historical trajectories carrying different societies into the present and future will differ.

Examining the Chinese and European trajectories of historical change confirms the presence of multiple paths with important common features. The challenge of advancing historical knowledge lies in reducing the number of our theoretical assumptions about how change should take place universally and expanding the number of historically supported propositions that go into our explanations of social change. The challenge of advancing social theory lies in sifting through the particulars of different historical experiences to discover what in fact can claim greater general significance. The danger of confronting so much diversity is that we will lose a belief in our ability to create order, discover patterns of variation amidst variety, and explain change. But if we fail to face the rich range of possibilities, we will diminish our capacities to explain multiple pasts. Lacking such faith to expand our knowledge we may become less able to create desirable futures.

REFERENCES

Abel, Wilhelm. 1980. *Agricultural Fluctuations in Europe from the Thirteenth to the Twentieth Century,* trans. Olive Ordish. Methuen.

Alford, Robert, and Roger Friedland. 1985. *Powers of Theory: Capitalism, the State and Democracy.* Cambridge University Press.

Alitto, Guy. 1979. *The Last Confucian: Liang Shu-ming and the Chinese Dilemma of Modernity.* University of California Press.

Amano Monotsuke. 1953. *Chūgoku nōgyō no sho mondai* (Problems of Chinese agriculture). 2 vols. Gipoto.

Anagnost, Ann. Forthcoming. "Constructing the Civilized Community." In Ted Huters, R. Bin Wong, and Pauline Yu, eds., *Culture and State in Chinese History: Conventions, Conflicts, and Accommodations.* Stanford University Press.

Anderson, Benedict. 1991. *Imagined Communities.* 2d ed. Verso.

Anderson, Eugene. 1988. *The Food of China.* Yale University Press.

Anderson, Perry. 1974. *Lineages of the Absolutist State.* New Left Books.

——. 1992. *A Zone of Engagement.* Verso.

Appleby, Andrew. 1969. "Grain Prices and Subsistence Crises in England and France. 1590–1740." *Journal of Economic History* 29.4:864–87.

——. 1978. *Famine in Tudor and Stuart England.* Stanford University Press.

Appleby, Joyce. 1992. *Liberalism and Republicanism in the Historical Imagination.* Harvard University Press.

Apter, David, and Tony Saich. 1994. *Revolutionary Discourse in Mao's Republic.* Harvard University Press.

Ardant, Gabriel. 1975. "Financial Policy and Economic Infrastructure of Modern States and Nations." In Charles Tilly, ed., *The Formation of National States in Western Europe.* Princeton University Press.

Badie, Bertrand. 1987. *Les Deux Etats: Pouvoir et société en Occident et en terre d'Islam.* Fayard.

Badie, Bertrand, and Pierre Birnbaum. 1983. *The Sociology of the State.* Trans. Arthur Goldhammer. University of Chicago Press.

Baehrel, René. 1961. *Une Croissance: La Basse-Provence rurale, de la fin du seizième siècle à 1789.* S.E.V.P.E.N.

Balasz, Etienne. 1964. *Chinese Civilization and Bureaucracy: Variations on a Theme.* Yale University Press.

Barmé, Geremie, and Linda Jaivin, eds. 1992. *New Ghosts, Old Dreams: Chinese Rebel Voices.* Random House.

Bartlett, Beatrice S. 1991. *Monarchs and Ministers: The Grand Council in Mid-Ch'ing China, 1723–1820*. University of California Press.

Beik, William. 1985. *Absolutism and Society in Seventeenth-Century France*. Cambridge University Press.

Bendix, Reinhard. 1964. *Nation-Building and Citizenship*. Wiley.

——. 1978. *Kings or People: Power and the Mandate to Rule*. University of California Press.

Bercé, Yves. 1990. *History of Peasant Revolts: The Social Origins of Rebellion in Early Modern France*. Cornell University Press.

Berenson, Edward. 1984. *Populist Religion and Left-Wing Politics in France, 1830–1852*. Princeton University Press.

Berg, Maxine. 1986. *The Age of Manufactures, 1700–1820*. Oxford University Press.

Berg, Maxine, and Pat Hudson. 1992. "Rehabilitating the Industrial Revolution." *Economic History Review* 45.1:24–50.

Berg, Maxine, Pat Hudson, and Michael Sonenscher. 1983. *Manufacture in Town and Country before the Factory*. Cambridge University Press.

Berman, Howard. 1983. *Law and Revolution: The Formation of the Western Legal Tradition*. Harvard University Press.

Bernard, Leon. 1975. "French Society and Popular Uprisings under Louis XIV." In Raymond F. Kierstead, ed. *State and Society in Seventeenth-Century France*. New Viewpoints.

Bernhardt, Kathryn. 1992. *Rents, Taxes, and Peasant Resistance: The Lower Yangzi Region, 1840–1950*. Stanford University Press.

Bernstein, Thomas. Forthcoming. "Incorporating Group Interests into National Policy: The Case of Farmers during China's Reform Era." In Roderick MacFarquhar and Merle Goldman, eds., *The Non-Economic Impact of China's Economic Reforms*. Harvard University Press.

Bianco, Lucien. 1986. "Peasant Movements." In John Fairbank and Albert Feuerwerker, eds., *Cambridge History of China*, 13:270–328. Cambridge University Press.

——. 1991. "Two Different Kinds of 'Food Riots': Kiangshu, 910 and 1932." *Jindai Zhongguoshi yanjiu tongxun* 11:33–49.

Birch, Cyril. 1958. *Stories from a Ming Collection*. Grove Press.

Blaug, Mark. 1985. *Economic Theory in Retrospect*. Cambridge University Press.

Bloch, Marc. 1961. *Feudal Society*. Trans. L. A. Manyon. 2 vols. University of Chicago Press.

Blockmans, Wim P. 1994. "Voracious States and Obstructing Cities: An Aspect of State Formation in Preindustrial Europe." In Charles Tilly and Wim P. Blockmans, eds., *Cities and the Rise of States in Europe, A.D. 1000–1800*. Westview Press.

Blum, Jerome. 1978. *The End of the Old Order in Rural Europe*. Princeton University Press.

Bohr, Paul Richard. 1972. *Famine in China and the Missionary: Timothy Richard as Relief Administrator and Advocate of National Reform*. Harvard University East Asian Research Center.

Bois, Guy. 1984. *The Crisis of Feudalism*. Cambridge University Press.

Bongaarts, John, and Mead Cain. 1980. *Demographic Responses to Famine.* Population Council.

Boserup, Ester. 1981. *Population and Technological Change: A Study of Long-Term Trends.* University of Chicago Press.

Bossy, John. 1985. *Christianity in the West, 1400–1700.* Oxford University Press.

Brady, Thomas A. 1991. "The Rise of Merchant Empires, 1400–1700: A European Counterpoint." In James D. Tracy, ed., *The Political Economy of Merchant Empires.* Cambridge University Press.

Brandt, Loren. 1989. *Commercialization and Agricultural Development: Central and Eastern China, 1870–1939.* Cambridge University Press.

Braudel, Fernand. 1977. *Afterthoughts on Material Civilization and Capitalism.* Johns Hopkins University Press.

——. 1981. *The Structures of Everyday Life.* Trans. Sian Reynolds. Harper & Row.

——. 1982. *The Wheels of Commerce.* Trans. Sian Reynolds. Harper & Row.

——. 1984. *The Perspective of the World.* Trans. Sian Reynolds. Harper & Row.

Braun, Rudolph. 1978. "Early Industrialization and Demographic Change in the Canton of Zurich." In Charles Tilly, ed., *Historical Studies of Changing Fertility.* Princeton University Press.

Bray, Francesca. 1986. *The Rice Economies: Technology and Development in Asian Societies.* Basil Blackwell.

Brook, Timothy. 1990. "Family Continuity and Cultural Hegemony: The Gentry of Ningbo, 1368–1911." In Joseph Esherick and Mary Rankin, eds., *Chinese Local Elites and Patterns of Dominance.* University of California Press.

——. 1993. *Praying for Power: Buddhism and the Formation of Gentry Society in Late Ming China.* Harvard University Press.

Bythell, Duncan. 1978. *The Sweated Trades: Outwork in the Nineteenth Century.* Batsford Academic.

Carmichael, Ann G. 1985. "Infection, Hidden Hunger, and History." In Robert I. Rotberg and Theodore Rabb, eds., *The Impact of Changing Production and Consumption Patterns on Society.* Cambridge University Press.

Caton, Hiram. 1985. "The Preindustrial Economics of Adam Smith." *Journal of Economic History* 45.4:833–53.

Chafee, John W. 1993. "The Historian as Critic: Li Hsin-ch'uan and the Dilemmas of Statecraft in Southern Sung China." In Robert P. Hymes and Conrad Schirokauer, eds., *Ordering the World: Approaches to State and Society in Sung Dynasty China,* 310–35. University of California Press.

Chandler, Alfred D., Jr. 1977. *The Visible Hand: The Managerial Revolution in American Business.* Harvard University Press.

Chandler, Alfred D., Jr., et al. 1990. "*Scale and Scope:* A Review Colloquium." *Business History Review* 64:690–735.

Chao Kang. 1975. "The Growth of a Modern Cotton Textile Industry and Competition with Handicrafts." In Dwight H. Perkins, ed., *China's Modern Economy in Historical Perspective.* Stanford University Press.

——. 1977. *The Development of Cotton Textile Production in China.* Harvard University Press.

——. 1983. *The Economic Development of Manchuria: The Rise of a Frontier Economy.* University of Michigan Center for Chinese Studies.

——. 1986. *Man and Land in Chinese History.* Stanford University Press.

Charbonneau, Hubert, and André LaRose, eds. 1979. *The Great Mortalities: Methodological Studies of Demographic Crises in the Past.* Ordina Editions.

Chen Feng. 1988. *Qingdai yanzheng yu yanshui* (Qing dynasty salt administration and salt taxes). Zhongzhou guji chubanshe.

Chen Hongmou. 1763. *Peiyuan oucungao.*

Ch'en, Jerome. 1979. *The Military–Gentry Coalition: China under the Warlords.* University of Toronto–York University Joint Centre on Modern East Asia.

Chen Liangxue and Zuo Rongchu. 1988. "Qingdai qianqi kemin yiken yu Shaanxi de kaifa" (Early Qing dynasty immigrants, land clearance, and the development of Shaanxi). *Shaanxi shida xuebao* 1988.1:82–89.

Chen Xuewen. 1989. *Zhongguo fengjian wanqi de shangpin jingji* (China's late feudal commercial economy). Hunan renmin chubanshe.

Chen Yung-fa and Gregor Benton. 1986. *Moral Economy and the Chinese Revolution: A Critique.* Anthropological-Sociological Centre, University of Amsterdam.

Chen Zhaolun. N.d. "Jin tun wuyi mijia shu" (Prohibiting hoarding has no benefit for rice prices). In He Changling, ed., *Huangchao jingshi wenbian* 40.18a–b.

Ch'uan Han-sheng and Richard Kraus. 1975. *Mid-Ch'ing Rice Markets and Trade.* Harvard University Council on East Asian Studies.

Cipolla, Carlo. 1980. *Before the Industrial Revolution: European Society and Economy, 1000–1700.* 2d ed. Norton.

——. ed. 1972–74. *The Fontana Economic History of Europe.* Vols 1–4. Fontana Books.

Clark, Gregory. 1987. "Why Isn't the Whole World Developed? Lessons from the Cotton Mills." *Journal of Economic History* 47.1:141–73.

Clarkson, L. A. 1985. *Proto-Industrialization: The First Phase of Industrialization?* Macmillan.

Clunas, Craig. 1991. *Superfluous Things: Material Culture and Social Status in Early Modern China.* Polity Press.

Coale, Ansley. 1984. "Fertility in Prerevolutionary China: In Defense of a Reassessment." *Population and Development Review* 10.3:471–80.

Cohen, Myron. 1991. "Being Chinese: The Peripheralization of Traditional Identity." *Daedalus,* Spring, 113–34.

Coleman, D. C. 1983. "Proto-Industrialization: A Concept Too Many." *Economic History Review* 36.3 (August): 435–48.

Corbin, Alain. 1975. *Archaisme et modernité en Limousin au XIX siècle, 1845–1880.* M. Rivière.

Da Qing huidian shi (Collected statutes and regulations of the Qing dynasty). 1899 ed.

Dai Angang. 1985. "Jindai Zhongguo xinshi nongken qiye shulue" (Modern Chinese agricultural reclamation companies). *Zhongguo nongshi* 1985.1:14–21.

Davis, Natalie Zemon. 1975. *Society and Culture in Early Modern France: Eight Essays.* Stanford University Press.

De Bary, William. 1991. *The Trouble with Confucianism.* Harvard University Press.

——. 1993. *Waiting for the Dawn: A Plan for the Prince.* A translation of Huang Zongxi's *Mingyi daifang lu,* with introduction. Columbia University Press.

Deng Gang. 1993. *Development versus Stagnation: Technological Continuity and Agricultural Progress in Pre-Modern China.* Greenwood Press.

Deng Xianhe. 1851. "Lun huangzheng" (On famine relief). *Hunan wenzheng* (A Hunan literary collection). *Guochao wen* 29.23a–24b.

Dennerline, Jerry. 1975. "Fiscal Reform and Local Control: The Gentry Bureaucratic Alliance Survives the Conquest." In Frederic Wakeman and Carolyn Grant, eds., *Local Control and Conflict in Late Imperial China.* University of California Press.

Dernberger, Robert. 1975. "The Role of the Foreigner in China's Economic Development." In Dwight Perkins, ed., *China's Modern Economy in Historical Perspective.* Stanford University Press.

Dessert, Daniel. 1984. *Argent, pouvoir et société au grand siècle.* Fayard.

Dewald, Jonathan. 1987. *Pont St-Pierre, 1398–1789: Lordship, Community, and Capitalism in Early Modern France.* University of California Press.

Dore, Ronald. 1987. *Taking Japan Seriously: A Confucian Perspective on Leading Economic Issues.* Stanford University Press.

Downing, Brian. 1992. *The Military Revolution and Political Change: Origins of Democracy and Autocracy in Early Modern Europe.* Princeton University Press.

Doyle, William. 1992. *The Old European Order, 1660–1800.* 2d ed. Oxford University Press.

Duan Benluo and Zhang Qifu. 1986. *Suzhou shougongye shi* (A history of Suzhou handicraft industries). Jiangsu guji chubanshe.

Duara, Prasenjit. 1987. "State Involution: A Study of Local Finances in North China, 1911–1935." *Comparative Studies in Society and History* 29.1:132–61.

——. 1988a. *Culture, Power, and the State.* Stanford: Stanford University Press.

——. 1988b. "Superscribing Symbols: the Myth of Guandi, Chinese God of War." *Journal of Asian Studies* 47.4:778–95.

——. 1995. *Rescuing History from the Nation.* University of Chicago Press.

Dunstan, Helen. 1997. *Conflicting Counsels to Confuse the Age: A Documentary Study of Political Economy in Qing China, 1644–1840.* University of Michigan Center for China Studies.

Dutton, Michael R. 1992. *Policing and Punishment in China.* Cambridge University Press.

——. 1995. "Dreaming of Better Times: "Repetition with a Difference" and Community Policing in China." *Positions* 3.2:415–47.

Dyson, Kenneth. 1980. *The State Tradition in Western Europe.* Martin Robertson.

Ebrey, Patricia. 1978. *The Aristocratic Families of Early Imperial China: A Case Study of the Po-ling Ts'ui Family.* Cambridge University Press.

Elvin, Mark. 1969. "The Gentry Democracy in Chinese Shanghai, 1905–1914." In Jack Gray, ed., *Modern China's Search for a Political Form*. Oxford University Press.

———. 1973. *The Pattern of the Chinese Past*. Stanford University Press.

Esherick, Joseph. 1991. Review of Loren Brandt 1989. *Journal of Economic History* 51.2:501–3.

Esherick, Joseph, and Mary Rankin, eds. 1990. *Chinese Local Elites and Patterns of Dominance*. University of California Press.

Everitt, Alan. 1967. "The Marketing of Agricultural Produce." In Joan Thirsk, ed., *The Agrarian History of England and Wales*, 8 vols., 4:466–592. Cambridge University Press.

Fairbank, John K. 1978. "Introduction: The Old Order." In Fairbank, ed., *Cambridge History of China*, vol. 10. Cambridge University Press.

Fan Shuzhi. 1990. *Ming Qing Jiangnan shizhen tanwei* (An investigation of Ming Qing Jiangnan towns). Fudan daxue chubanshe.

Fang Guancheng. 1753. *Jifu yicang tu* (Maps of charity granaries in Zhili). Taibei: Chengwen chubanshe, 1969.

Fang Xing. 1979. "Qingdai Shaanxi diqu zibenzhuyi mengya xingshuai tiaojian de tansuo" (an investigation of the conditions for the rise and fall of incipient capitalism in Qing dynasty Shaanxi). *Jingji yanjiu* 1979.12:59–66.

Faure, David. 1994. *China and Capitalism: Business Enterprise in Modern China*. Hong Kong University of Science and Technology, Division of Humanities.

Fei Hsiao-tung. 1953. *China's Gentry: Essays in Rural–Urban Relations*. University of Chicago Press.

Feng Guifen. N.d. "Fu zongfa yi" (On lineages), *Huangchao jingshi wenxubian* 55:5b–6b.

Feuerwerker, Albert. 1984. "The State and Economy in Late Imperial China." *Theory and Society* 13:297–326.

———. 1990. "An Old Question Revisited: Was the Glass Half-Full or Half-Empty for China's Agriculture before 1949?" *Peasant Studies* 17.3:207–16.

———. 1992. "Presidential Address: Questions about China's Early Modern Economic History That I Wish I Could Answer." *Journal of Asian Studies* 51.4:757–69.

Fincher, John. 1981. *Chinese Democracy*. Australian National University Press.

Fletcher, Joseph, Jr. 1978. "The Heyday of the Ch'ing Order in Mongolia, Sinkiang, and Tibet." In John K. Fairbank, ed., *The Cambridge History of China*, 10:351–408. Cambridge University Press.

———. 1979. "A Brief History of the Chinese Northwestern Frontier." In M. E. Alonso, ed., *China's Inner Asian Frontier: Photographs of the Wulsin Expedition to Northwest China in 1923*. Peabody Museum.

———. 1979–80. "Turco-Mongolian Monarchic Tradition in the Ottoman Empire." In Ihor, Ševčenko and Frank E. Sysyn, eds., *Eucharisterion: Essays Presented to Omeljan Pritsak*. Harvard University Ukrainian Research Institute.

———. 1986. "The Mongols: Ecological and Social Perspectives." *Harvard Journal of Asiatic Studies* 46:11–50.

Flinn, Michael W. 1981. *The European Demographic System, 1500–1820.* Johns Hopkins University Press.

Forster, Robert. 1980. *Merchants, Landlords, Magistrates: The Depont Family in Eighteenth-Century France.* Johns Hopkins University Press.

Freedman, Maurice. 1966. *Chinese Lineage and Society: Fukien and Kwangtung.* Athlone Press.

Friedman, Edward. 1994. "Reconstructing China's National Identity: A Southern Alternative to Mao-Era Anti-Imperialist Nationalism." *Journal of Asian Studies* 53.1:67–91.

Friedman, Edward, Paul Pickowicz, and Mark Selden. 1991. *Chinese Village, Socialist State.* Yale University Press.

Fu Yiling. 1941. "Ming Qing shidai Fujian de qiangmi fengchao" (Grain seizures in Fujian during the Ming Qing period). *Fujian wenhua* 1.2:7–13.

———. 1956. *Ming Qing shidai shangren ji shangye ziben* (Merchants and merchant capital in the Ming-Qing period). Renmin chubanshe.

———. 1982. "Qingdai zhongye Chuan Shaan Hu sansheng bianqu shougongye xingtai ji qi lishi yiyi" (The nature and significance of mid-Qing handicraft industry in the border region of Sichuan, Shaanxi, and Hubei). In Fu Yiling, *Ming Qing shehui jingjishi lunwenji* (Collected essays on Ming-Qing social and economic history). Renmin chubanshe.

Fudan daxue lishi xi and Guoji jiaoliu bangongshi, eds. 1991. *Rujia sixiang yu weilai shehui* (Confucian thought and future society). Shanghai renmin chubanshe.

Fuji Hiroshi. 1953–54. "Shin'an shōnin no kenkyū" (A study of the Xin'an merchants). *Tōō gakuhō* 36.1:1–44; 2:32–60; 3:65–118; 4:115–45.

Fukuyama, Francis. 1992. *The End of History and the Last Man.* Macmillan.

Furber, Holden. 1976. *Rival Empires of Trade in the Orient, 1600–1800; Europe and the World in the Age of Expansion.* Vol. 2. University of Minnesota Press.

Furet, François. 1981. *Interpreting the French Revolution.* Trans. Elborg Forster. Cambridge University Press.

———. 1989. "Terror." In François Furet and Mona Ozouf, eds., *A Critical Dictionary of the French Revolution,* trans. Arthur Goldhammer. Harvard University Press.

Gallet, J. 1975. "Research on the Popular Movements at Amiens in 1635 and 1636." In Raymond F. Kierstead, ed., *State and Society in Seventeenth-Century France.* New Viewpoints.

Gaojin. 1775. "Qing haiqiang hemian jianzhong shu" (A proposal to grow both grain and cotton in seacoast areas). In He Changling, ed., *Huangchao jingshi wenbian* 37.6a–7b.

Geertz, Clifford. 1963. *Agricultural Involution: The Process of Ecological Change in Indonesia.* University of California Press.

Gellner, Ernest. 1983. *Nations and Nationalism.* Cornell University Press.

Gernet, Jacques. 1972/1982. *Le monde chinois.* Armand Colin. Trans. J. R. Foster as *A History of Chinese Civilization.* Cambridge University Press.

Gershenkron, Alexander. 1962. *Economic Backwardness in Historical Perspective*. Harvard University Press.

Giddens, Anthony. 1990. *The Consequences of Modernity*. Stanford University Press.

Gleick, James. 1987. *Chaos: Making a New Science*. Penguin.

Goldstone, Jack A. 1990. *Revolution and Rebellion in the Early Modern World*. University of California Press.

——. 1996. "Gender, Work, and Culture: Why the Industrial Revolution Came Early to England but Late to China." *Sociological Perspectives* 39.1:1–21.

Goodman, Bryna. 1995. *Native Place, City, and Nation: Regional Networks and Identities in Shanghai, 1853–1937*. University of California Press.

Goody, Jack, Joan Thirsk, and E. P. Thompson, eds. 1976. *Family and Inheritance: Rural Society in Western Europe, 1200–1800*. Cambridge University Press.

Grantham, George, and Mary MacKinnon, eds. 1994. *Labour Market Evolution: The Economic History of Market Integration, Wage Flexibility, and the Employment Relation*. Routledge.

Gras, N. S. B. 1915. *The Evolution of the English Corn Market from the Twelfth to the Eighteenth Century*. Harvard University Press.

Grove, Linda, and Christian Daniels, eds. 1984. *State and Society in China: Japanese Perspectives on Ming-Qing Social and Economic History*. University of Tokyo Press.

Guenée, Bernard. 1985. *States and Rulers in Later Medieval Europe*. Trans. Juliet Vale. Basil Blackwell.

Gullickson, Gay L. 1986. *The Spinners and Weavers of Auffay: Rural Industry and the Sexual Division of Labor in a French Village, 1750–1850*. Cambridge University Press.

Guo Yanjing, ed. 1989. *Tianjin gudai chengshi fazhanshi* (The premodern development of Tianjin). Tianjin guji chubanshe.

Habermas, Jürgen. 1989. *The Structural Transformation of the Public Sphere*. Trans. Thomas Burger. MIT Press.

Habib, Irfan. 1969. "Potentialities of Capitalist Development in the Economy of Mughal India." *Journal of Economic History* 29.1:32–78.

Hajnal, John. 1982. "Two Kinds of Preindustrial Household Formation System." *Population and Development Review* 8 (September): 449–93.

Hall, John A. 1985. *Powers and Liberties: The Causes and Consequences of the Rise of the West*. Basil Blackwell.

——. 1993. "Nationalisms: Classified and Explained." *Daedalus* 122.3:1–28.

Hall, John W. 1965. "Changing Conceptions of the Modernization of Japan." In Marius Jansen, ed., *Changing Japanese Attitudes toward Modernization*. Princeton University Press.

Hamashima Atsutoshi. 1982. *Mindai Kōnan nōson shakai no kenkyū* (Rural society in Jiangnan during the Ming dynasty). Tokyo University Press.

Hamashita Takeshi. 1989. *Chūgoku kindai keizaishi kenkyū*. University of Tokyo Institute of Oriental Culture.

Handlin, Joanna. 1983. *Action in Late Ming Thought*. University of California Press.

Harrell, Stevan. 1987. "On the Holes in Chinese Genealogies." *Late Imperial China* 8.2:53–79.

Hartwell, Robert. 1982. "Demographic, Political, and Social Transformations of China, 750–1550." *Harvard Journal of Asiatic Studies* 42.2:365–442.

Hayami Akira. 1989. "Kinsei Nihon no keizai hatten to Industrious Revolution" (The economic development of modern Japan and the Industrious Revolution). In Hayami Akira, Saito Osamu, and Sugiyama Shinya, eds., *Tokugawa shaikai kara no tembō*. Tobunkan.

Henry, Louis. 1956. *Anciennes Familles génévoises*. Presses Universitaires de France.

Hevia, James. 1995. *Cherishing Men from Afar*. Duke University Press.

Hinton, Harold. 1956. *The Grain Tribute System, 1845–1911*. Harvard University East Asian Research Center.

Hirschman, Albert O. 1977. *The Passions and the Interests: Political Arguments for Capitalism before Its Triumph*. Princeton University Press.

Ho Ping-ti. 1959. *Studies on the Population of China, 1368–1953*. Harvard University Press.

Hobsbawm, Eric. 1990. *Echoes of the Marseillaise: Two Centuries Look Back on the French Revolution*. Rutgers University Press.

Hoffman, Philip T., and Kathryn Norberg. 1994. *Fiscal Crises, Liberty, and Representative Government, 1450–1789*. Stanford University Press.

Hoffman, Philip T., Gilles Postel-Vinay, and Jean-Laurent Rosenthal. 1992. "Private Credit Markets in Paris, 1690–1840." *Journal of Economic History* 52.2:293–306.

Hohenberg, Paul, and Lynn Lees. 1985. *The Making of Urban Europe, 1000–1950*. Harvard University Press.

Hollingsworth, T. H. 1965. "A Demographic Study of the British Ducal Families." In D. V. Glass and D. E. C. Eversley, eds., *Population in History*. Edward Arnold.

Hong Huanchun. 1983. "Ming Qing fengjian zhuanzhi zhengquan dui zibenzhuyi mengya de zuai" (Obstacles to the development of nascent capitalism posed by the feudal autocracy of the Ming and Qing dynasties). In Nanjing daxue lishi xi Ming Qing shi yanjiu shi, ed., *Zhongguo ziben zhuyi mengya wenti lunwenji*. Jiangsu renmin chubanshe.

Hoshi Ayao. 1971. *Daiunga: Chūgoku no soun* (The Grand Canal: China's grain tribute). Kondo shuppansha.

———. 1985. *Chūgoku shakai fukushi seisatsu shi no kenkyū—Shindai no shinsaiso o chushin ni* (A history of social welfare policies in China with special reference to the relief granary system under the Qing). Kokusho Kankokai.

———. 1988. *Chūgoku no shakai fukushi no rekishi* (A history of China's social welfare). Yamagawa shuppansha.

Hou Chi-ming. 1965. *Foreign Investment and Economic Development in China, 1840–1937*. Harvard University Press.

Hsiao Kung-chuan. 1960. *Rural China: Imperial Control in the Nineteenth Century*. University of Washington Press.

Hsieh, Winston. 1974. "Peasant Insurrection and the Marketing Hierarchy in the Canton Delta, 1911." In Mark Elvin and G. William Skinner, eds., *The Chinese City between Two Worlds*. Stanford University Press.

Hsu Cho-yun. 1965. *Ancient China in Transition: An Analysis of Social Mobility, 722–222* B.C. Stanford University Press.

Huang Liuhong. 1984 [1694]. *A Complete Handbook of Happiness and Benevolence*. Trans. Djang Chu. University of Arizona Press.

Huang Miantang. 1990. "Qingdai nongtian de danwei mianji chanliang kaobian" (Qing dynasty land productivity). *Wenshizhe* 1990.3:27–38.

Huang, Philip. 1985. *The Peasant Economy and Social Change in North China*. Stanford University Press.

——. 1990. *The Peasant Family and Rural Development in the Yangzi Delta, 1350–1988*. Stanford University Press.

——. 1995. "Rural Class Struggle in the Chinese Revolution." *Modern China* 21.1:105–43.

Huang, Ray. 1974. *Taxation and Governmental Finance in Sixteenth-Century Ming China*. Cambridge University Press.

——. 1981. *1587, A Year of No Significance: The Ming Dynasty in Decline*. Yale University Press.

Huang Yiping and Zhang Min. 1988. "Jindai zaoqi nongye kenzhi gongsi jianlun" (Agricultural reclamation companies in the modern period). *Huadong shifan daxue xuebao*. 1988.3:65–72.

Igarashi Shoichi. 1979. *Chūgoku kinsei kyōikushi no kenkyū* (Research on modern Chinese educational history). Kokusho kankokai.

Institute of Pacific Relations, ed. 1938. *Agrarian China*. University of Chicago Press.

Jeannin, Pierre. 1972. *Merchants of the Sixteenth Century*. Trans. Paul Fittingoff. Harper & Row.

——. 1980. "La proto-industrialisation: Développement ou impasse?" *Annales: Economies, Sociétés, Civilisations* 35.1:52–65.

Johnson, Chalmers. 1962. *Peasant Nationalism and Communist Power: The Emergence of Revolutionary China*. Stanford University Press.

Johnson, David. 1977. *The Medieval Chinese Oligarchy*. Westview Press.

Jones, E. L. 1981. *The European Miracle: Environments, Economies and Geopolitics in the History of Europe and Asia*. Cambridge University Press.

——. 1988. *Growth Recurring: Economic Change in World History*. Clarendon Press.

Jones, Peter. 1981. *The 1848 Revolutions*. Longmans.

Jones, Susan Mann, and Philip Kuhn. 1978. "Dynastic Decline and the Roots of Rebellion." In John Fairbank, ed., *The Cambridge History of China*, 10:107–62. Cambridge University Press.

Kanbe Teruo. 1972. "Shindai goki Santōshō ni okeru danhi to nōson mondai" (The *tuanfei* in late Qing Shandong and village problems). *Shirin* 55.4:61–98.

Kanbur, R., and J. McIntosh. 1989. "Dual Economies." In John Eatwell, Murray Milgate, and Peter Newman, eds. *Economic Development: The New Palgrave*, 114–21. Norton.

Kaplan, Steven. 1976. *Bread, Politics, and Political Economy in the Reign of Louis XV.* 2 vols. Martinus Nijhoff.

Katayama Tsuyoshi. 1982a. "Shinmatsu Kantō sho Shuko deruta no toko to sore o meguru sho mondai" (Some problems concerning the *tujia* charts in the Pearl River Delta in Guangdong province during the late Qing period: Land taxes, household registers, and lineages). *Shigaku zasshi* 91.4:42–81.

———. 1982b. "Shindai Kantōsho Shuko deruta no toko ni tsuite" (The *tujia* system in the Pearl River Delta area of Guangdong province during the Qing period: Land taxes, household registers, and lineages). *Tōyō gakuhō* 63.3–4:1–34.

———. 1984. "Shinmatsu Kantō sho Shuko deruta ni okeru tokosei no shu mujun to sono kaikaku" (Contradictions and their reform in the *tujia* system in the Pearl River Delta of Guangdong in the late Qing). *Chūgoku kindaishi* 4:1–48.

Kaye, Lincoln. 1994. "Against the Grain: A Maoist Village Puts Capitalism to Shame." *Far Eastern Economic Review* 157 (17 November): 32–33.

Kishimoto, Mio. 1984. "The Kangxi Depression and Early Qing Local Markets." *Modern China* 10.2:227–55.

Knodel, John. 1988. *Demographic Behavior in the Past.* Cambridge University Press.

Kobayashi Kazumi. 1973. "Kōso, kōryō tōsō no kanata—Kasō seikatsusha no omoi to seijiteki shūkyōteki jiritsu no michi." *Shisō* 2:228–47. Trans. Cynthia Brokaw and Timothy Brook as "The Other Side of Rent and Tax Resistance Struggles: Ideology and the Road to Rebellion," in Linda Grove and Christian Daniels, eds., *State and Society in China: Japanese Perspectives on Ming-Qing Social and Economic History.* University of Tokyo Press, 1984.

Kojima Shinji. 1978. *Taihei tenkoku kakumei no rekishi to shisō* (The history and thought of the Taiping revolution). Yamamoto Shoten.

Kriedte, Peter, Hans Medick, and Jurgen Schlumbohm. 1981. *Industrialization before Industrialization.* Trans. Beate Schempp. Cambridge University Press.

Kuhn, Philip. 1970. *Rebellion and Its Enemies in Late Imperial China.* Harvard University Press.

———. 1975. "Local Self-Government under the Republic: Problems of Control, Autonomy, and Mobilization." In Frederic Wakeman, Jr., and Carolyn Grant, eds., *Conflict and Control in Late Imperial China.* University of California Press.

———. 1986. "The Development of Local Government." In John K. Fairbank and Albert Feuerwerker, eds., *The Cambridge History of China*, 13:329–69. Cambridge University Press.

Kuznets, Simon. 1966. *Modern Economic Growth: Rate, Structure, and Spread.* Yale University Press.

Kwan Man Bun. 1990. "The Merchant World of Tianjin: Society and Economy of a Chinese City." Ph.D. dissertation, Stanford University.

Labrousse, Ernest. 1990. *La Crise de l'économie française à la fin de l'Ancien Régime et au debut de la Révolution.* 2d ed. Presses Universitaires de France.

Landes, David. 1969. *The Unbound Prometheus: Technological Change and Industrial Development in Western Europe from 1750 to the Present.* Cambridge University Press.

Lang Qingxiao. 1937. *Zhongguo minshi shi* (A history of Chinese food supplies). Shangwu chubanshe.

Lardy, Nicholas. 1978. *Economic Growth and Distribution in China.* Cambridge University Press.

Lary, Diana. 1996. "The Tomb of the King of Nanyue—The Contemporary Agenda of History: Scholarship and Identity." *Modern China* 22.1:3–27.

Lavely, William R., and R. Bin Wong. 1991. "Population and Resources in Modern China: A Comparative Approach." Paper presented at the Annual Meeting of the Association for Asian Studies, New Orleans.

——. 1992. "Family Division and Mobility in North China." *Comparative Studies in Society and History* 34, no. 3: 439–63.

Lee, James, and Cameron Campbell. 1997. *Fate and Fortune in Rural China: Social Stratification and Population Behavior in Liaoning, 1774–1873.* Cambridge University Press.

Lee, James, Wang Feng, and Cameron Campbell. 1994. "Infant and Child Mortality among Qing Nobility: Implications of Two Kinds of Positive Checks," *Population Studies* 48:395–411.

Lee, James, and Jon Gjerde. 1986. "Comparative Household Morphology in China, Norway and the United States." *Continuity and Change* 1, no. 1: 89–112.

Lee, James, and R. Bin Wong. 1991. "Population Movements in Qing China and Their Linguistic Legacy." In William S-Y. Wang, ed., *Languages and Dialects of China.* Journal of Chinese Linguistics Monograph Series.

LeFebvre, George. 1973. *The Great Fear of 1789,* trans. Joan White. Vintage.

Le Roy Ladurie, Emmanuel. 1976. *The Peasants of Languedoc.* Trans. John Day. University of Illinois Press.

Leung, Angela. 1994. "Elementary Education in the Lower Yangtze Region in the Seventeenth and Eighteenth Centuries." In Benjamin A. Elman and Alexander Woodside, eds., *Education and Society in Late Imperial China, 1600–1900.* University of California Press.

Levenson, Joseph. 1968. *Confucian China and Its Modern Fate: A Trilogy.* University of California Press.

Levine, David. 1977. *Family Formation in an Age of Nascent Capitalism.* Academic Press.

——. 1983. "Proto-Industrialization and Demographic Upheaval." In Leslie Page Moch and Gary D. Stark, eds., *Essays on the Family and Historical Change.* Texas A&M University Press.

——. 1987. *Reproducing Families.* Cambridge University Press.

Lewis, W. Arthur. 1954. "Economic Development with Unlimited Supplies of Labour." *Manchester School* 22.2:139–91.

Li Bozhong. 1984a. "Ming Qing shiqi Jiangnan shuidao shengchan jiyue chengdu de tigao—Ming Qing Jiangnan nongye jingji fazhan tedian tantao zhi yi" (The rise in paddy productivity in Ming-Qing period Jiangnan: A study of the economic development of Ming-Qing period Jiangnan agriculture). *Zhongguo nongshi* 1984.1:24–37.

——. 1984b. "Ming Qing Jiangnan gongnong ye shengchan zhong de ranliao wenti" (Fuel problems in Jiangnan industry and agriculture during the Ming and Qing dynasties). *Zhongguo shehui jingjishi yanjiu* 1984.4:34–49.

——. Forthcoming. *Agricultural Development in the Yangzi Delta, 1600–1850.* Trans. R. Bin Wong. Macmillan.

Li Hua. 1986. "Qingdai Shandong shangren shulue" (Qing dynasty Shandong merchants). *Pingjun xuekan* 3.2:133–60.

Li Jinming. 1990. *Mingdai haiwai maoyishi* (A history of Ming dynasty maritime trade). Zhongguo shehui kexue chubanshe.

Li Lianjiang and Kevin J. O'Brien. 1996. "Villagers and Popular Resistance in Contemporary China." *Modern China* 22.1:28–61.

Li Sanmou. 1990. *Ming Qing caijing shi xintan* (A new study of Ming and Qing economic and fiscal history). Shanxi jingji chubanshe.

Li Wenzhi. 1955. *Zhongguo jindai nongye shi ziliao* (Sources on modern Chinese agricultural history). Sanlian.

——. 1981. "Lun Zhongguo dizhu jingjizhi yu nongye zibenzhuyi mengya" (On the Chinese landlord economy and agrarian sprouts of capitalism). *Zhongguo shehui kexue* 7:143–60.

Li Wenzhi, Wei Jinyu, and Jing Junjian. 1983. *Ming Qing shiqi de nongye zibenzhuyi mengya wenti* (The problem of incipient capitalism in agriculture during the Ming-Qing period). Zhongguo shebui kexue chubanshe.

Lieberthal, Kenneth, and Michel Oksenberg. 1988. *Policy Making in China: Leaders, Structures, and Process.* Princeton University Press.

Lin Renchuan. 1987. *Mingmo Qingchu siren haishang maoyi* (Late Ming and early Qing private sea trade). Huadong shifan daxue chubanshe.

Lin Yong and Wang Xi. 1991. *Qingdai xibei minzu maoyi shi* (A history of Qing dynasty northwestern trade). Zhongyang minzu xueyuan chubanshe.

Lindert, Peter. 1986. "English Population, Wages and Prices: 1541–1913." In Robert I. Rotberg and Theodore K. Rabb, eds., *Population and Economy.* Cambridge University.

Link, Perry. 1994. "The Old Man's New China." *New York Review of Books,* June 9, 31–36.

Link, Perry, Richard Madsen, and Paul Pickowicz, eds. 1989. *Unofficial China.* Westview Press.

Little, Daniel. 1992. Review of Brandt 1989. *Economic Development and Cultural Change* 40.2:425–32.

Liu Kexiang. 1988. "1895–1927 nian tongshang kouan fujin he tielu yanxian diqu de nongchanpin shangpinhua" (Agricultural commercialization near treaty ports and railroads between 1895 and 1927). *Jingji yanjiusuo jikan,* no. 11, 1–105.

Liu Shiji. 1987. *Ming Qing shidai Jiangnan shizhen yanjiu* (Studies of Ming and Qing dynasty Jiangnan market towns). Zhongguo shehui kexue chubanshe.

Liu, Tessie P. 1994. *The Weavers's Knot: The Contradictions of Class Struggle and Family Solidarity in Western France, 1750–1914.* Cornell University Press.

Liu Ts'ui-jung. 1985. "The Demography of Two Chinese Clans in Hsiao-shan, Chekiang, 1650–1850." In Susan B. Hanley and Arthur P. Wolf, eds., *Family and Population in East Asian History*. Stanford University Press.

———. 1992. *Ming Qing shiqi jiazu renkou yu shehui jingji bianqian* (Lineage population and socioeconomic changes in the Ming-Qing period). 2 vols. Academia Sinica Institute of Economics.

Liu Yongcheng. 1982. *Qingdai qianqi nongye zibenzhuyi mengya chutan* (A preliminary discussion of incipient capitalism in early Qing agriculture). Fujian renmin chubanshe.

Livi-Bacci, Massimo. 1985. "The Nutrition-Mortality Link in Past Times: A Comment." In Robert I. Rotberg and Theodore Rabb, eds., *The Impact of Changing Production and Consumption Patterns on Society*. Cambridge University Press.

Lopez, Robert. 1971. *The Commercial Revolution of the Middle Ages, 950–1350*. Prentice-Hall.

Lucas, Colin. 1988. "The Crowd and Politics." In Colin Lucas, ed., *The French Revolution and the Creation of Modern Political Culture*, 2:259–85. Pergamon.

Luo Yixing. 1985. "Ming Qing shiqi Foshan yetieye yanjiu" (Foshan iron industry during the Ming-Qing period). In Guangdong lishi xuehui, ed., *Ming Qing Guangdong shehui jingji xingtai yanjiu*, 75–116. Guangdong renmin chubanshe.

Luo Yudong. 1936. *Zhongguo lijin shi* (The history of the *likin* in China). Commercial Press.

Ma Daying. 1983. *Handai caizheng shi* (Han dynasty fiscal history). Zhongguo caizheng jingji chubanshe.

Ma Ruheng and Ma Dazheng. 1990. *Qingdai bianjiang kaifa yanjiu* (Studies of the Qing development of border areas). Zhongguo shehui kexue chubanshe.

MacPherson, C. B. 1962. *The Political Theory of Possessive Individualism*. Clarendon Press.

Mair, Victor. 1985. "Language and Ideology in the Written Popularizations of the Sacred Edict." In David Johnson, Andrew Nathan, and Evelyn Rawski, eds., *Popular Culture in Late Imperial China*. University of California Press.

Malthus, Thomas. 1976. *An Essay on the Principle of Population*. Norton.

Mann, Susan. 1987. *Local Merchants and the Chinese Bureaucracy, 1750–1950*. Stanford University Press.

———. 1992. "Household Handicrafts and State Policy in Qing Times." In Jane Kate Leonard and John R. Watt, eds., *To Achieve Wealth and Security: The Qing Imperial State and the Economy, 1644–1911*. Cornell University East Asia Program.

Margadant, Ted. 1979. *French Peasants in Revolt: The Insurrection of 1851*. Princeton University Press.

Matsuda Yoshiro. 1988. "Shindai goki Kanto Kanshufu no soku to santo" (Late Qing Guangzhou treasuries and benevolent halls). *Tōyō gakuhō* 69.1–2:27–57.

Matsumoto Yoshimi. 1977. *Chūgoku sonraku seido no shi teki kenkyū* (Historical studies on China's village government). Iwanami.

McCord, Edward. 1993. *The Power of the Gun: The Emergence of Modern Chinese Warlordism*. University of California Press.

McPhee, Peter. 1992. *The Politics of Rural Life: Political Mobilization in the French Countryside, 1846–1852*. Clarendon Press.

Meguro Katsuhiko. 1971. "Sekko Kikoken Oshi gisō ni tsuite" (The Ying family charitable estate in Yongkang county, Zhejiang). *Shūkan Tōyōgaku* 26:22–46.

Mendels, Franklin. 1972. "Proto-Industrialization: The First Phase of the Industrialization Process." *Journal of Economic History* 32.1:241–61.

———. 1980. "Seasons and Regions in Agriculture and Industry during the Process of Industrialization." In Sidney Pollard, ed., *Region und Industrialisierung: Studien zur Rollen der Region in der Wirtschaftsgeschichte der letzten zwei jahrhunderte*. Vandenhoeck & Ruprecht.

———. 1984. "Des industries rurales à la protoindustrialisation: Historique d'un changement de perspective." *Annales: Economies, Sociétés, Civilisations* 39 (September–October):977–1008.

Merriman, John. 1978. *The Agony of the Republic: The Repression of the Left in Revolutionary France, 1848–1851*. Yale University Press.

Migdal, Joel. 1988. *Strong Societies and Weak States: State–Society Relations and State Capabilities in the Third World*. Princeton University Press.

Min Tu-ki. 1989. *National Polity and Local Power: The Transformation of Late Imperial China*. Ed. Philip Kuhn and Timothy Brook. Harvard University Council on East Asian Studies.

Min Zongdian. 1984. "Song Ming Qing shiqi Taihu diqu shuidao mou chanliang de tantao" (Rice paddy productivity in the Lake Tai area during the Song, Ming, and Qing dynasties). *Zhongguo nongshi* 1984.3:37–52.

Miskimin, Harry A. 1969. *The Economy of Early Renaissance Europe, 1300–1460*. Prentice-Hall.

———. 1977. *the Economy of Later Renaissance Europe, 1460–1600*. Cambridge University Press.

Mizoguchi Yūzō. 1980. "Chūgoku ni okeru ko, shi gainen no tenkai" (The evolution of the concepts of "public" and "private" in China). *shisō* 669:19–38.

———. 1991. *Chūgoku no shisō*. Hōsō daigaku.

Mokyr, Joel. 1990. *The Lever of Riches*. Oxford University Press.

Mori Masao. 1969. "Jūroku-juhachi seiki ni okeru kōsei to jinushi denko kankei" (Famine relief and landlord-tenant relations from the sixteenth to eighteenth centuries). *Tōyōshi kenkyū* 27.4:69–111.

———. 1975–76. "Nihon no Min-Shin jidaishi kenkyū ni okeru kyōshinron ni tsuite" [Theories of the gentry in Japanese studies of Ming-Qing history]. 3 parts. *Rekishi hyōron*, no. 308, 40–60; no. 312, 74–84; no. 314, 113–28.

———. 1980. "The Gentry in the Ming." *Acta Asiatica* 38:31–53.

Moriceau, Jean-Marc. 1994. *Les Fermiers de l'Ile-de-France*. Fayard.

Morishima, Michio. 1981. *Why Has Japan 'Succeeded'?* Cambridge University Press.

Morita Akira. 1981. "Shindai 'goto' sei saiko" (Reexamination of the *yitu* system in the Qing era). *Tōyō Gakuhō* 62.3–4:1–35.

Mousnier, Roland. 1979. *The Institutions of France under Absolute Monarchy, 1598–1789*. University of Chicago Press.

Najita, Tetsuo. 1987. *Visions of Virtue in Tokugawa Japan: The Kaitokudo Merchant Academy of Osaka*. University of Chicago.

Nanjing daxue lishi xi Ming Qing shi yanjiu shi, ed. 1981. *Ming Qing ziben zhuyi mengya yanjiu lunwen ji* (Essays on sprouts of capitalism in the Ming and Qing dynasties). Shanghai renmin chubanshe.

——. 1983. *Zhongguo ziben zhuyi mengya wenti lunwen ji* (Essays on the problem of the sprouts of capitalism). Jiangsu renmin chubanshe.

Nanjing tushuguan tecangbu and Jiangsu sheng shehui kexue yuan jingji shi keti zu, eds. 1987. *Jiangsu sheng gongye diaocha tongji ziliao (1927–1937)* (Statistical materials on Jiangsu province industry [1927–1937]). Nanjing gongxue yuan chubanshe.

Nathan, Andrew. 1985. *Chinese Democracy*. Knopf.

Neizheng bu tongjichu. 1938. *Cangku tongji* (Granary statistics). N.p.

Nishijima Sadao. 1966/1984. "Chūgoku shoki mengyō no keisei to sono kōzō." In *Chugoku keizaishi kenkyū*. Trans. Linda Grove as "The Formation of the Early Chinese Cotton Industry," in Linda Grove and Christian Daniels, eds., *State and Society in China*. University of Tokyo Press.

North, Douglass C. 1981. *Structure and Change in Economic History*. Norton.

——. 1990. *Institutions, Institutional Change, and Economic Performance*. Cambridge University Press.

North, Douglass C., Terry L. Anderson, and Peter J. Hill. 1983. *Growth and Welfare in the American Past: A New Economic History*. 3d ed. Prentice-Hall.

O'Brien, Kevin J., and Lianjiang Li. 1995. "The Politics of Lodging Complaints in Rural China." *China Quarterly*, no. 143, 756–83.

Ogawa Yoshiko. 1958. "Shindai ni okeru gigaku setsuritsu no kiban" (The basis for the establishment of Qing dynasty charity schools). In *Kinsei Chūgoku kyōikushi kenkyū*. Kokutosha.

Ogilvie, Sheilagh C. 1996. "Social Institutions and Proto-Industrialization." In Sheilagh C. Ogilvie and Markus Cerman, eds., *European Proto-Industrialization*. Cambridge University Press.

Oglivie, Sheilagh C., and Markus Cerman. 1996. "Proto-Industrialization, Economic Development and Social Change in Early Modern Europe." In Sheilagh C. Ogilvie and Markus Cerman, eds., *European Proto-Industrialization*. Cambridge University Press.

Oi, Jean. 1992. "Fiscal Reform and the Economic Foundations of Local State Corporatism in China." *World Politics*, October, 99–126.

——. 1995. "The Role of the Local State in China's Transitional Economy." *China Quarterly* 144:1132–49.

Otsuki Yushi. 1983. "Chūgoku minshū hanran shiron" (The history of popular disturbances in China). In Seinen Chugoku kenkyusha kaigi, ed., *Zoku Chūgoku minshū hanran no sekai*. Kyuko shoin.

Outhwaite, R. B. 1978. "Food Crises in Early Modern England: Patterns of Public Response." In Michael Flinn, ed., *Proceedings of the Seventh International Economic History Congress*, 2:367–74. Edinburgh University Press.

Palat, Ravi Arvind. 1995. "Historical Transformations in Agrarian Systems Based on Wet-Rice Cultivation: Toward an Alternative Model of Social Change." In Philip McMichael, ed. *Food and Agrarian Orders in the World Economy*. Greenwood Press.

Pan Ming-te. 1994. "The Rural Credit Market and Peasant Economy in China (1600–1949)," Ph.D. dissertation, University of California, Irvine.

Parker, Geoffrey. 1988. *The Military Revolution: Military Innovation and the Rise of the West*. Cambridge University Press.

Parrish, William, and Martin K. Whyte. 1978. *Village and Family in Contemporary China*. University of Chicago Press.

Parry, J. H. 1966. *The Establishment of European Hegemony, 1415–1715: Trade and Exploration in the Age of the Renaissance*. 3d ed. Harper & Row.

Parsons, Talcott. 1966. *Societies: Evolutionary and Comparative Perspectives*. Prentice-Hall.

Peng Yuxin. 1990. *Qingdai tudi kaikenshi* (A history of Qing dynasty land clearance). Nongye chubanshe.

Peng Zeyi. 1983. *Shijiu shiji houban qi de Zhongguo caizheng yu jingji* (Chinese fiscal administration and economy in the second half of the nineteenth century). Renmin chubanshe.

Perkins, Dwight. 1969. *Agricultural Development in China, 1368–1968*. Aldine.

———, ed. 1975. *China's Modern Economy in Historical Perspective*. Harvard University Press.

Perlin, Frank. 1983. "Proto-Industrialization and Pre-Colonial South Asia." *Past and Present* 98:30–95.

Perry, Elizabeth. 1980. *Rebels and Revolutionaries in North China, 1845–1945*. Stanford University Press.

———. 1984. "Collective Violence in China, 1880–1980." *Theory and Society* 13.3:427–54.

———. 1985a. "Tax Revolt in Late Qing China: The Small Swords Society of Shanghai and Liu Depei of Shandong." *Late Imperial China* 6.1:83–111.

———. 1985b. "Rural Collective Violence: The Fruits of Recent Reforms." In Elizabeth J. Perry and Christine Wong, eds., *The Political Economy of Reform in Post-Mao China*. Harvard University Council on East Asian Studies.

Pillorget, René. 1975. "The Cascaveoux: The Insurrection at Aix in the Autumn of 1630." In Raymond F. Kierstead, ed., *State and Society in Seventeenth-Century France*. New Viewpoints.

Pocock, J. G. A. 1985. *Virtue, Commerce, and History: Essays on Political Thought and History, Chiefly in the Eighteenth Century*. Cambridge University Press.

Poggi, Gianfranco. 1978. *The Development of the Modern State*. Stanford University Press.

Polachek, James. 1975. "Gentry Hegemony: Soochow in the T'ung-chih Restoration." In Frederic Wakeman, Jr., and Carolyn Grant, eds., *Conflict and Control in Late Imperial China*. University of California Press.

Pollard, Sidney. 1981. *Peaceful Conquest: The Industrialization of Europe, 1760–1970*. Oxford University Press.

Pomeranz, Kenneth. 1991. "Water to Iron, Widows to Warlords: The Handan Rain Shrine in Chinese History." *Late Imperial China* 12.1:62–100.

——. 1993. *From Core to Hinterland: State, Society, and Economy in Inland North China, 1900–1937*. University of California Press.

——. Forthcoming. "Protecting Goddess, Dangerous Woman: Power, Gender, and Pluralism in the Cult of the Goddess of Taishan." In Theodore Huters, R. Bin Wong, and Pauline Yu, eds., *Culture and State in Chinese History: Conventions, Critiques, and Accommodations*. Stanford University Press.

Post, John D. 1977. *The Last Great Subsistence Crisis in the Western World*. Johns Hopkins University Press.

Postel-Vinay, Gilles. 1994. "The Disintegration of Traditional Labour Markets in France: From Agriculture and Industry to Agriculture or Industry." In George Grantham and Mary MacKinnon, eds., *Labour Market Evolution: The Economic History of Market Integration, Wage Flexibility, and the Employment Relation*, 64–83. Routledge.

Potter, Sulamith Heins, and Jack M. Potter. 1990. *China's Peasants: The Anthropology of a Revolution*. Cambridge University Press.

Prazniak, Roxann. 1981. "Community and Protest in Rural China: Tax Resistance and County-Village Politics on the Eve of the 1911 Revolution." Ph.D. dissertation, University of California, Davis.

Pye, Lucian W. 1971. *Warlord Politics: Conflict and Coalition in the Modernization of Republican China*. Praeger.

——. 1985. *Asian Power and Politics*. Harvard University Press.

Rankin, Mary. 1986. *Elite Activism and Political Transformation in China: Zhejiang Province, 1865–1911*. Stanford University Press.

——. 1990. "The Origins of a Chinese Public Sphere: Local Elites and Community Affairs in the Late-Imperial Period." *Etudes Chinoises* 9.2:13–60.

Rawski, Evelyn Sakakida. 1972. *Agricultural Change and the Peasant Economy of South China*. Harvard University Press.

——. 1996. "Presidential Address: Reenvisioning the Qing: The Significance of the Qing Period in Chinese History." *Journal of Asian Studies* 55.4:829–50.

Rawski, Thomas G. 1989. *Economic Growth in Prewar China*. University of California Press.

Rawski, Thomas G., and Lillian M. Li. 1992. *Chinese History in Economic Perspective*. University of California Press.

Rosenthal, Jean-Laurent. 1993. "Credit Markets and Economic Change in Southeastern France, 1630–1788." *Explorations in Economic History* 30.2:129–57.

Rossabi, Morris, ed. 1983. *China among Equals: The Middle Kingdom and Its Neighbors, 10th–14th Centuries*. University of California Press.

Rowe, William. 1984. *Hankow: Commerce and Society in a Chinese City, 1796–1889*. Stanford University Press.

——. 1989. *Hankow: Conflict and Community in a Chinese City, 1796–1895*. Stanford University Press.

——. 1990. "The Public Sphere in Modern China." *Modern China* 16.3:309–29.

——. 1994. "Education and Empire in Southwest China: Ch'en Hung-mou in Yunnan, 1733–1738." In Benjamin A. Elman and Alexander Woodside, eds., *Education and Society in Late Imperial China, 1600–1900*. University of California Press.

Rudé, George. 1964. *The Crowd in History, 1730–1848*. John Wiley.

——. 1974. *Paris and London in the Eighteenth Century*. Fontana.

Sabel, Charles, and Jonathan Zeitlin. 1985. "Historical Alternatives to Mass Production: Politics, Markets, and Technology in Nineteenth-Century Industrialization." *Past and Present* 108:133–76.

Saito Osamu. 1985. *Puroto kogyōka no jidai* (The age of proto-industrialization). Nihon Hyōronsha.

Sasaki Masaya. 1963. "Kanpo ninen Ginken no koryo bōdō" (The tax resistance uprising in Yin county in 1852). In *Kindai Chūgoku kenkyū* (Studies on modern China) 5:185–299. University of Tokyo.

Schofield, Roger. 1989. "Family Structure, Demographic Behavior, and Economic Growth." In John Walter and Roger Schofield, eds., *Famine, Disease, and the Social Order in Early Modern Society*. Cambridge University Press.

Schoppa, R. Keith. 1982. *Chinese Elites and Political Change: Zhejiang Province in the Early Twentieth Century*. Harvard University Press.

Schulmbohm, Jurgen. 1996. "'Proto-Industrialization' as a Research Strategy and a historical period—A Balance Sheet." In Sheilagh C. Ogilvie and Markus Cerman, eds., *European Proto-Industrialization*. Cambridge University Press.

Schurmann, Franz. 1968. *Ideology and Organization in Communist China*. 2d ed. University of California Press.

Scott, James. 1976. *The Moral Economy of the Peasant: Rebellion and Subsistence in Southeast Asia*. Yale University Press.

——. 1985. *Weapons of the Weak: Everyday Forms of Peasant Resistance*. Yale University Press.

Scranton, Philip. 1991. "Diversity in Diversity: Flexible Production and American Industrialization, 1880–1930." *Business History Review* 65:27–90.

Scrimshaw, Nevin S. 1985. "Functional Consequences of Malnutrition for Human Populations: A Comment." In Robert I. Rotberg and Theodore K. Rabb, eds., *Hunger and History: The Impact of Changing Food Production and Consumption Patterns on Society*. Cambridge University Press.

Searle, Eleanor. 1988. *Predatory Kinship and the Creation of Norman Power*. University of California Press.

Sen, Amartya. 1981. *Poverty and Famines: An Essay on Entitlement and Deprivation*. Oxford University Press.

Shen Guanghui. 1985. *Zhongguo gudai duiwai maoyi shi* (A history of ancient Chinese foreign trade). Guangdong renmin chubanshe.

Shiba Yoshinobu. 1968/1970. *Sōdai shogyoshi kenkyū*. Kazama Shobo. Abridged trans. by Mark Elvin as *Commerce and Society in Sung China*. University of Michigan Center for Chinese Studies.

Shigeta Atsushi. 1975. *Shindai shakai keizaishi kenkyū* (Studies of Qing social and economic history). Iwanami.

——. 1984. "The Origins and Structure of Gentry Rule." In Linda Grove and Christian Daniels, eds., *State and Society in China*. University of Tokyo Press.

Shimizu Morimitsu. 1951. *Chūgoku kyōson shakai ron* (On Chinese village society). Iwanami.

Shuili bu Huanghe shuili weiyuanhui, ed. 1984. *Huanghe shuili shi shuyao* (A brief history of Yellow River water management). Shuili dianli chubanshe.

Simon, Julian L. 1985. "The Effects of Population on Nutrition and Economic Well-being." In Robert I. Rotberg and Theodore K. Rabb, eds., *Hunger and History: The Impact of Changing Food Production and Consumption Patterns on Society*. Cambridge University Press.

Skinner, G. William. 1964–65. "Marketing and Social Structure in Rural China." *Journal of Asian Studies* 24.1:3–43; 2:195–228; 3:363–99.

——, ed. 1977. *The City in Late Imperial China*. Stanford University Press.

Skinner, G. William, and Edwin Winckler. 1969. "Compliance Succession in Rural Communist China: A Cyclical Theory." In Amitai Etzioni, ed., *A Sociological Reader on Complex organizations*. Holt, Rinehart & Winston.

Skocpol, Theda. 1979. *States and Social Revolutions*. Cambridge University Press.

Smith, Adam. 1937. *The Wealth of Nations*. Random House.

Smith, Paul J. 1991. *Taxing Heaven's Storehouse: Horses, Bureaucrats, and the Destruction of the Sichuan Tea Industry, 1024–1224*. Harvard University Council on East Asian Studies.

Smith, Richard M. 1981. "Fertility, Economy, and Household Formation in England over Three Centuries." *Population and Development Review* 7:595–622.

Snooks, Graeme Donald. 1994. "New Perspectives on the Industrial Revolution." In Snooks, ed., *Was the Industrial Revolution Necessary?* Routledge.

Snow, Edgar. 1969. *Red Star over China*. Grove Press.

Solinger, Dorothy. 1984. *Chinese Business under Socialism*. University of California Press.

——. 1996. "Despite Decentralization: Disadvantages, Dependence, and Ongoing Central Power in the Inland—The Case of Wuhan." *China Quarterly* 145:1–34.

——. Forthcoming. *Contesting Citizenship: Peasant Migrants, the State, and the Logic of the Market in Urban China*. University of California Press.

Stackey, Judith. 1983. *Patriarchy and Socialist Revolution in China*. University of California Press.

Stone, Lawrence. 1979. *The Family, Sex, and Marriage in England, 1500–1800*. Harper & Row.

Strand, David. 1991. "An Early Republican Perspective on the Traditional Bases of Civil Society and Public Sphere in China." Paper prepared for the American–European Symposium on State and Society in East Asian Traditions.

Strayer, Joseph. 1970. *On the Medieval Origins of the Modern State*. Princeton University Press.

Su Xiaokang and Wang Luxiang. 1991. *Deathsong of the River: A Reader's Guide to the Chinese TV Series Heshang*. Trans. Richard W. Bodman and Pin P. Wan, Cornell University East Asia Program.

Sun Yat-sen. N.d. *The Principle of Nationalism*. Trans. Frank W. Price. Chinese Cultural Service.

Sutherland, Donald. 1986. *France, 1789–1815: Revolution and Counter-Revolution*. Oxford University Press.

Sutton, Donald. 1980. *Provincial Militarism and the Chinese Republic: The Yunnan Army, 1905–1925*. University of Michigan Press.

Suzuki Chusei. 1952. *Shincho chukishi kenkyū* (Studies of mid-Qing history). Aichi University.

———. 1958. "Shinmatsu no zaisei to kanryo no seikaku" (Late Qing fiscal administration and the character of officials). In *Kindai Chūgoku kenkyū* 2:190–281.

Taga Akigoro. 1960. "Kindai Chugoku ni okeru zokujuku no seikaku" (The lineage school in modern China). *Kindai Chūgoku kenkyū* (University of Tokyo). no. 4, 207–54.

Tan Zuogang. 1986. "Qingdai Shaannan diqu de yimin, nongye kenzhi yu ziran huanjing de ehua" (Qing dynasty southern Shaanxi immigrants, agricultural land clearance and the degradation of the natural environment). *Zhongguo nongshi* 4:1–10.

Tanaka Masatoshi. 1973/1984. "Rural Handicraft in Jiangnan in the Sixteenth and Seventeenth Centuries." Trans. Linda Grove. In Linda Grove and Christian Daniels, eds., *State and Society in China*. University of Tokyo Press.

Tang Sen and Li Longqian. 1985. "Ming Qing Guangdong jingji zuowu de zhongzhi ji qi yiyi" (The planting of cash crops in Ming-Qing Guangdong and their significance). In Guangdong lishi xuehui, ed., *Ming Qing Guangdong shehui jingji xingtai yanjiu*, 1–21. Guangdong renmin chubanshe.

Tarrow, Sidney. 1994. *Power in Movement: Social Movements, Collective Action, and Politics*. Cambridge University Press.

Tawney, R. H. 1966. *Land and Labor in China*. Beacon Press.

Taylor, Carl E. 1985. "Synergy among Mass Infections, Famines, and Poverty." In Robert I. Rotberg and Theodore K. Rabb, eds., *Hunger and History: The Impact of Changing Food Production and Consumption Patterns on Society*. Cambridge University Press.

Telford, Ted A. 1990. "Patching the Holes in Chinese Genealogies: Mortality in the Lineage Population of Tongcheng County, 1300–1800." *Late Imperial China* 11.2:116–36.

Terada Takanobu. 1972. *Sansei shōnin no kenkyū* (An analysis of Shanxi merchants). Dohosha.

Thompson, E. P. 1971. "The Moral Economy of the English Crowd in the Eighteenth Century." *Past and Present* 50:76–136.

Thompson, I. A. A. 1994. "Castile: Polity, Fiscality, and Fiscal Crisis." In Philip T. Hoffman and Kathryn Norbert, eds., *Fiscal Crises, Liberty, and Representative Government, 1450–1789*. Stanford University Press.

Thompson, Roger. 1988. "Statecraft and Self-Government: Competing Visions of Community and State in Late Imperial China." Modern China 14.2:188–221.

———. 1995. *China's Local Councils in the Age of Constitutional Reform, 1898–1911.* Harvard University Council on East Asian Studies.

Tian Jujian and Song Yuanqiang, eds. 1987. *Zhongguo zibenzhuyi mengya* (Chinese sprouts of capitalism). Bashu shushe.

Tilly, Charles. 1972a. "The Modernization of Political Conflict in France." In Edward B. Harvey, ed., *Perspectives on Modernization: Essays in Memory of Ian Weinberg.* University of Toronto Press.

———. 1972b. "How Protest Modernized in France." In William Aydelotte, Allan Bogue, and Robert Fogel, eds., *The Dimensions of Quantitative Research in History.* Princeton University Press.

———. 1978. "Migration in Modern European History." In William H. McNeill, ed., *Human Migration: Patterns, Implications, Policies.* Indiana University Press.

———. 1983. "Flows of Capital and Forms of Industry in Europe, 1500–1900." *Theory and society* 12 (January):123–43.

———. 1984. "Demographic Origins of the European Proletariat." In David Levine, ed., *Proletarianization and Family History.* Academic Press.

———. 1986. *The Contentious French: Four Centuries of Popular Struggle.* Harvard University Press.

———. 1990. *Coercion, Capital and European States, A.D. 990–1990.* Basil Blackwell.

———. 1993. *European Revolutions, 1492–1992.* Basil Blackwell.

———, ed. 1975. *The Formation of National States in Western Europe.* Princeton University Press.

Tilly, Louise. 1971. "The Food Riot as a Form of Political Conflict in France." *Journal of Interdisciplinary History* 2:23–57.

Tocqueville, Alexis de. 1960. *Democracy in America.* Knopf.

Tracy, James, ed. 1990. *The Rise of Merchant Empires: Long-Distance Trade in the Early Modern World.* Cambridge University Press.

———, ed. 1991. *The Political Economy of Merchant Empires.* Cambridge University Press.

Tsurumi Naohiro. 1984. "Rural Control in the Ming Dynasty." In Linda Grove and Christian Daniels, eds., *State and Society in China.* University of Tokyo Press.

Underdown, Anthony. 1987. *Revel, Riot, and Rebellion: Popular Politics and Culture in England, 1603–1600.* Oxford University Press.

Usher, A. P. 1913. *The History of the Grain Trade in France.* Harvard University Press.

Usui Sachiko. 1986. "Tosei yon (1865) nen Kōsei sho ni okeru 'fushui gaige'" (Tax reform in Jiangnan, 1865). *Tōyōshi kenkyū* 45.2:104–29.

Vandenbroeke, Christian. 1996. "Proto-Industry in Flanders: A Critical Review." In Sheilagh C. Ogilvie and Markus Cerman, eds., *European Proto-Industrialization.* Cambridge University Press.

Vardi, Lianna. 1993. *The Land and the Loom: Peasants and Profit in Northern France, 1680–1800.* Duke University Press.

Vries, Jan de. 1984. *European Urbanization*. Harvard University Press.

——. 1993. "Between Purchasing Power and the World of Goods: Understanding the Household Economy in Early Modern Europe." In John Brewer and Roy Porter, eds., *Consumption and the World of Goods*. Routledge.

——. 1994. "The Industrial Revolution and the Industrious Revolution." *Journal of Economic History* 54.2:249–70.

Wada Sei. 1939. *Shina chiho jiji hattatsu shi* (A history of the development of local self-government in China). Kyuko shoin.

Wagner, Donald B. 1985. *Dabeishan: Traditional Chinese Iron-Production Techniques Practised in Southern Henan in the Twentieth Century*. Curzon Press.

Wakeman, Frederic, and Carolyn Grant, eds. 1975. *Conflict and Control in Late Imperial China*. University of California Press.

Walder, Andrew. 1995. "China's Transitional Economy: Interpreting Its Significance." *China Quarterly* 144:963–79.

Waldron, Arthur. 1995. *From War to Nationalism: China's Turning Point, 1924–1925*. Cambridge University Press.

Wallerstein, Immanuel. 1980. *The Modern World System: Mercantilism and the Consolidation of the European World Economy, 1600–1750*. Academic Press.

——. 1984. *The Politics of the World Economy*. Cambridge University Press.

Wallis, John. 1984. "The Birth of the Old Federalism: Financing the New Deal, 1932–1940." *Journal of Economic History* 44.1:139–59.

Wang Feng, James Lee, and Cameron Campbell. 1995. "Marital Fertility Control among the Qing Nobility: Implications of Two Types of Preventive Checks." *Population Studies* 49:383–400.

Wang Shaoguang. 1994. "Central–Local Fiscal Politics in China." In Jia Hao and Lin Zhimin, eds., *Changing Central–Local Relations in China: Reform and State Capacity*. Westview Press.

Wang Xilong. 1990. *Qingdai xibei tuntian yanjiu* (Studies of Qing dynasty northwestern land colonies). Lanzhou daxue chubanshe.

Wang Yeh-chien. 1973. *Land Taxation in Imperial China, 1750–1911*. Harvard University Press.

Wang Yuchuan, Liu Zhongri, Guo Songyi, and Lin Yongkui. 1991. *Zhongguo tunken shi* (A history of Chinese land clearance). Vol. 3. Nongye chubanshe.

Watson, James L. 1985. "Standardizing the Gods: The Promotion of T'ien Hou ("Empress of Heaven") along the South China Coast, 960–1960." In David Johnson, Andrew J. Nathan, and Evelyn S. Rawski, eds., *Popular Culture in Late Imperial China*. University of California Press.

Webber, Carolyn, and Aaron Wildavsky. 1986. *A History of Taxation and Expenditure in the Western World*. Simon & Schuster.

Weber, Eugene. 1991. *My France*. Harvard University Press.

Wei Guangqi. 1986. "Qingdai houqi zhongyang jiquan caizheng tizhi di wajie" (The collapse of the fiscal system of central authority in the late Qing). *Jindaishi yanjiu* 1:207–30.

Will, Pierre-Etienne. 1990. *Bureaucracy and Famine in Eighteenth-Century China*. Trans. Elborg Forster. Stanford University Press.

Will, Pierre-Etienne, and R. Bin Wong. 1991. *Nourish the People: The State Civilian Granary System in China, 1650–1850*. Ann Arbor: University of Michigan Center for Chinese Studies.

Wittfogel, Karl. 1957. *Oriental Despotism: A Comparative Study of Total Power*. Yale University Press.

Wolf, Arthur. 1974. "Gods, Ghosts, and Ancestors." In *Religion and Ritual in Chinese Society*. Stanford University Press.

———. 1984. "Fertility in Prerevolutionary Rural China." *Population and Development Review* 10.3:443–70.

Woloch, Isser, ed. 1970. *The Peasantry and the Old Regime: Conditions and Protests*. Holt, Rinehart & Winston.

Wong, Christine P. W. 1991. "Central-Local Relations in an Era of Fiscal Decline: The Paradox of Fiscal Decentralization in Post-Mao China." *China Quarterly*, no. 128, 691–715.

Wong, Christine, Christopher Heady, and Wing T. Woo. 1995. *Fiscal Management and Economic Reform in the People's Republic of China*. Oxford University Press.

Wong, R. Bin. 1982. "Food Riots in the Qing Dynasty" *Journal of Asian Studies* 41.4:767–88.

———. 1992. "Chinese Economic History and Development: A Note on the Myers-Huang Exchange." *Journal of Asian Studies* 51.3:600–611.

———. 1993. "Great Expectations: The 'Public Sphere' and the Search for Modern Times in Chinese History." *Chūgoku shigaku* 3:7–50.

Wong, R. Bin, and Peter C. Perdue. 1983. "Famine's Foes in Ch'ing China." *Harvard Journal of Asiatic Studies* 43 (June): 291–332.

Woodside, Alexander. 1990. "State, Scholars, and Orthodoxy: The Ch'ing Academies, 1736–1839." In K. C. Liu, ed., *Orthodoxy in Late Imperial China*. University of California Press.

World Bank. 1990. *China: Revenue Mobilization and Tax Policy*. World Bank.

Wright, Tim. 1984. *Coal Mining in China's Economy and Society 1895–1937*. Cambridge University Press.

Wrigley, E. A. 1988. *Continuity, Chance and Change: The Character of the Industrial Revolution in England*. Cambridge University Press.

———. 1989. "The Limits to Growth: Malthus and the Classical Economists." In Michael S. Teitelbaum and Jay M. Winter, eds., *Population and Resources in Western Intellectual Traditions*. Cambridge University Press.

Wrigley, E. A., and R. S. Schofield. 1981. *The Population History of England, 1541–1871*. Edward Arnold.

Wu Chengming and Xu Dixin. 1985. *Zhongguo zibenzhuyi fazhan shi* (A history of the development of Chinese capitalism). Vol. 1: *Zhongguo zibenzhuyi de mengya* (Incipient Chinese capitalism). Renmin chubanshe.

Xiao Zhenghong. 1988. "Qingdai Shaannan zhongzhiye de shengshuai ji qi yuanyin" (Changes in Qing dynasty southern Shaanxi cropping patterns). *Zhongguo nongshi* 1988.4:69–84.

Xu Dalin. 1950. *Qingdai juanna zhidu* (The system of purchasing offices by contributions during the Qing period). Yanjing University Press.

Xu Hong. 1972. *Qingdai Lianghuai yanchang de yanjiu* (Studies of the Lianghuai salt yards in the Qing period). Jiaxin shuini gongsi.

Xu Tan. 1986. "Ming Qing shiqi de Linqing shangye" (Linqing commerce in the Ming Qing period). *Zhongguo jingjishi yanjiu*. 1986.2:135–57.

Yamana Hirofumi. 1980. "Shinmatsu Kōnan no giso ni tsuite" (Late Qing charity estates in the Jiangnan area). *Tōyō gakuhō* 62.1–2:99–131.

Yan Zhongping, ed. 1989. *Zhongguo jindai jingjishi, 1840–1894* (Modern Chinese economic history, 1840–1894). Vols. 1 and 2. Renmin chubanshe.

Yang Guozhen. 1988. *Ming Qing tudi qiyue wenshu yanjiu* (Studies of Ming-Qing period land contracts). Renmin chubanshe.

Yang Xifu. 1748. "Chenming migui zhi you shu" (A report on the reasons for high rice prices). In He Changling, ed., *Huangchao jingshi wenbian*, 39.21a–25b.

Yasuba Yasukichi and Saito Osamu, eds. 1983. *Puroto kogyokaki no keizai to shakai* (The economy and society of the proto-industrialization period). Nihon keizai shinbunsha.

Yokoyama Suguru. 1955. "Chūgoku ni okeru nōmin undo no ichi keitai" (One form of the peasant movement in China: The tax resistance movement before the Taiping Rebellion). *Hiroshima daigaku bungakubu kiyo* (Bulletin of the Faculty of Letters. Hiroshima University) 7:311–49.

———. 1972. *Chūgoku kindaika no keizai kōzō* (The economic structure of China's modernization). Aki Shobo.

Yu Yingshi. 1987. *Zhongguo jinshe zongjiao lunli yu shangren jingshen* (Modern Chinese religious ethics and merchant spirit). Lianjing chuban shiye gongsi.

Yuan Senpo. 1991. *Kang Yong Qian jingying yu kaifa beijiang* (Managing and developing the northern border region in the Kangxi, Yongzheng, and Qianlong reigns). Zhongguo shehui kexue chubanshe.

Zelin, Madeleine. 1984. *The Magistrate's Tael: Rationalizing Fiscal Reform in Eighteenth-Century Ch'ing China.* University of California Press.

Zhang Guohui. 1986. "Lun Zhongguo zibenzhuyi xiandai qiye chansheng de lishi tiaojian" (On the historical conditions for the emergence of modern industry in Chinese capitalism). *Zhongguo shehui kexue.* 1986.3:139–51.

Zhang Haipeng and Zhang Haiying. 1993. *Zhongguo shi da shangbang* (China's ten large merchant groups). Huangshan shushe.

Zhang Jianmin. 1987. "Qingdai Xiang E xishanqu de jingji kaifa ji qi yingxiang" (The economic expansion of the western mountain region of Qing dynasty Hunan and Jiangxi and its influence). *Zhongguo shehui jingjishi yanjiu* 1987.4:19–23.

Zhang Wengui, Tao Guangliang, Dai Juanping, and Ke Xiaodan. 1988. *Zhongguo shangye dili* (China's commercial geography). Zhongguo caizheng jingji chubanshe.

Zhang Wenmin, Zhang Zhuoyuan, and Wu Jinglian. 1979. *Jianguo yilai shehuizhuyi shangpin shengchan he jiazhi guilu lunwen xuan* (A collection of articles on socialist commodity production and the law of value). 2 vols. Shanghai renmin chubanshe.

Zheng Changgan. 1989. *Ming Qing nongcun shangpin jingji* (Ming Qing agrarian commercial economy). Zhongguo renmin daxue chubanshe.

Zhongguo renmin daxue, ed. 1979. *Kang Yong Qian shiqi zhengxiang renmin fankang douzheng ziliao* (Sources on popular protests and struggles in the Kangxi, Yongzheng, and Qianlong reigns). Zhonghua shuju.

——, ed. 1983. *Qingdai de kuangye* (Qing dynasty mining). 2 vols. Zhonghua shuju.

Zhou Bodi. 1981. *Zhongguo caizheng shi* (A history of Chinese fiscal policies). Shanghai renmin chubanshe.

Zhu Cishou. 1990. *Zhongguo xiandai gongyeshi* (A history of contemporary Chinese industry). Chongqing chubanshe.

Zhu Yong. 1987. *Qingdai zongzufa yanjiu* (Studies of lineages during the Qing dynasty). Hunan jiaoyu chubanshe.

Zito, Angela. 1987. "Filiality, Hegemony, and City God Cults in Late Imperial China." *Modern China* 13.3:333–71.

INDEX

Anderson, Benedict, 175
Appleby, Andrew, 218n, 220
Apter, David, 268

Badie, Bertrand, 81n
Baojia: mutual surveillance, 100, 118–19, 167, 239
Bendix, Reinhard, 93
Berenson, Edward, 262
Berg, Maxine, 61
Berman, Harold, 87n
Bernhardt, Kathryn, 241, 248
Bianco, Lucien, 228
Blaug, Mark, 22
Bloch, Marc, 106–7n
Brady, Thomas, 85
Brandt, Loren, 22n, 66n
Braudel, Fernand, 50–51, 146, 149, 150, 204
Bray, Francesca, 46

Capitalism, 27; Chinese "incipient," 4, 40; commercial, 50–51, 57–58, 138, 146, 147, 149, 150, 227; and democracy as liberal myth, 273; distinctions from commerce more generally, 50–51, 146, 150, 204–5; global and Chinese reforms, 189–90; industrial, 56–58, 62, 149–50; managerial, 57; two kinds of, 52; as universal endpoint for historical development, 204–5
Catholic Church, 87, 97n, 106
Challenges, capacities, claims, and commitments, 82–83, 202, 280; in early modern Europe, 94; late 20th-century Chinese, 201; 19th-century Chinese, 156–57
Chandler, Alfred, 57
Chao Kang, 27, 42n, 60
Chen Hongmou, 115, 118n
Chinese Communist Party: explanation of

revolution, 267–68; persuasiveness of visions of social change, 267–68; strategies for governing before 1949, 263, 267
Chinese cultural identity, 166–77
Chinese economic change: cash cropping, 17, 19, 37; foreign impact, 21–22; handicrafts, 17, 19, 37; land distribution, 135–36; post-1949 agrarian, 67–68; regional cycles, 19–21, 49; regional variations, 19. *See also* Industrialization
Chinese fiscal practices, 90, 94–95, 102, 117, 129–35; commercial revenues, 133; "contributions" (*juan*), 90, 132–33; and militarization in 19th century, 239; 19th-century, 120n, 155–56, 238n; post-1978, 193–94; problems in 1980s, 286; proxy remittance (*baolan*), 242; and social welfare, 77; 20th-century, 167
Chinese grain seizures, 213–14, 216, 241
Chinese political economy: achieving static efficiencies, 149, 280; agrarian since 1949, 183–85; anxieties about luxury, 136, 138, 145; attitudes toward private grain trade in Qing dynasty, 214–15; contrast of late imperial and reform-era agrarian policies, 186; debates on post-1978 reforms, 185; economic reforms and unitary state, 187–89; emperor and officials promoting agricultural production, 143; end to institutional separation of industry and agriculture after 1978, 185; foreign trade, 137, 147; granaries in Qing dynasty, 160n, 215; industrialization policies, 182, 190; land distribution, 135; late imperial, 135–39; mercantilism, 147n; mining policies, 136n; movements of grain in Qing dynasty, 215; 19th-century industrialization, 151; post-1949 parallels to earlier practices, 181–82; Qing vs. post-1949, 183–84, 190; in reform era, 193–94;

Porchnev, Boris, 106–7n, 249
Potter, Jack, 269
Potter, Sulamith Heins, 269
Prazniak, Roxann, 247–48
Prospective analyses, 289, 293
Proto-industrialization. *See* Rural industry
Public sphere: in China, 112–13, 116,
    122–26, 164–66, 191–92; in Europe,
    112, 125, 126
Pye, Lucian, 194n

Rankin, Mary, 112–13, 165
Rawski, Evelyn, 173n
Rawski, Thomas, 60, 64, 65, 66n
Relations among levels of government: in
    China, 124–25, 162–63, 171–72, 191,
    193, 201, 256, 284; and Chinese agri-
    cultural policy after 1949, 183; and Chi-
    nese industrialization in 1950s, 183; in
    Europe, 109–10, 284; parallels between
    late 20th-century Chinese and Euro-
    pean, 205–6; and taxation in reform-era
    China, 187, 286; vertical integration of
    Chinese bureaucracy in late imperial and
    contemporary times, 192
Retrospective analyses, 104, 154, 288–89, 293
Revolution: Chinese vs. French, 259,
    262–63, 267, 274; critique of revolu-
    tionary violence, 271–72; and explaining
    long-term historical change, 275, 285;
    limitations of explanations of, 274; and
    political ideals, 270; and political partici-
    pation, 271; and state making, 253, 270,
    271. *See also* Chinese Revolution and
    Cultural Revolution; French Revolution
Ricardo, David, 9, 22, 142
River Elegy, 180–81
Roman empire, 75
Rowe, William, 6n, 112, 115, 163, 165
Rudé, George, 218n, 221, 248
Rural industry, 18–19; Chinese, 37–38, 68;
    and Chinese agriculture since 1978,
    186; and Chinese social mobility, 45–46;
    Chinese township and village industries
    (TVE), 184–85; collective ownership in
    China, 186; and demographic change,
    34–38; economic and political signifi-
    cance in China since 1978, 189; Euro-
    pean, 34–37; European proto-
    industrialization, 34, 36–43, 47, 60;
    and European social mobility, 43–45;
    labor absorption, 180n, 186n; Nanjie

case, 186–87; and Smithian dynamics,
    38

Saich, Tony, 268
Saito Osamu, 46
Schoppa, Keith, 113n
Selden, Mark, 268
Sen, Amartya, 221n
Shigeta Atsushi, 112, 240–41
Skinner, G. William, 34n, 91n, 112, 198–99
Skocpol, Theda, 253
Smith, Adam, 14, 16, 17, 22, 24, 141; and
    technological change, 55
Smithian dynamics of growth, 27, 29, 32, 42,
    59; vs. capitalism, 51; in China, 17–19,
    21, 62; in Europe, 16, 50, 56; and rural
    industry, 38
Social movements. *See* Social protests
Social order: Chinese vs. European strategies
    for, 118–19; urban vs. rural, 159, 166,
    174–79, 201–2. *See also* Chinese social
    order; European social order
Social protests: Chinese vs. European, 270;
    decline in study of, 208; difficulties com-
    paring revolutions, 207–8; meanings of,
    285; as popular engagement in politics,
    286; in post-1949 China, 269–70;
    small-scale, 207, 285; small-scale vs.
    large-scale, 241, 243–45, 247, 266
Social structures: changes during revolution,
    261; in China vs. Europe, 52; Chinese
    class differentiation, 45–46; and Chinese
    tax resistance, 240–41, 246, 249; Euro-
    pean class differentiation, 45n, 47; Euro-
    pean proletarianization, 43–44
Social theory: alternative to postmodern cri-
    tique, 293; Chinese Marxist, 14; class in
    Chinese and European history, 106–7;
    combining comparisons and connec-
    tions, 287–88; contingent connections
    between economic and political change,
    205; dangers of increased historical
    knowledge, 294; defining modern,
    291–92; denial of history outside of Eu-
    rope, 291–92; equating Western and
    modern, Chinese and traditional, 6, 158,
    202–4, 282–83; explaining differences,
    7, 78–79; and explanations of social
    protests, 291; grounding in expanded
    historical experiences, 293; historical
    change as modular, 280, 290; historical
    determinism, 279; importance of study

of historical change, 208; incomplete explanations, 278–79; limitations of developmental and system theories, 288; moving beyond failed teleologies, 288; native categories, 5; role of non-Western experiences, 6, 103–4; symmetric perspectives, 93, 282; in the 21st century, 289. *See also* Historical change

Solinger, Dorothy, 188

State capacities, Chinese vs. European, 282. *See also* Chinese state capacities; European state capacities

State challenges: Chinese vs. European, 281; French vs. Chinese, 255. *See also* Chinese state challenges; European state challenges

State commitments, Chinese vs. French, 257–58. *See also* Chinese state commitments; European state commitments

State formation and transformation: approaches to 20th-century changes, 179; comparing China and Europe, 80–82, 101–3, 198–200; comparing Chinese and European spatial scales, 198–99, 281–82; comparing early modern Europe and Republican China, 168–69; comparing Warring States China and early modern Europe, 75–76; early modern Europe in Chinese perspective, 101; general categories of analysis, 82–83; as incomplete processes, 206, 284, 287; and Mongols, 79–80; multiple paths, 202–3; political strength and weakness, 83, 91

State-economy relations: Chinese foreign trade, 147; Chinese policy options, 136–37; Chinese promotion of agriculture, 139; Chinese visions of social stability and prosperity, 139; European foreign trade, 140–41; European state role in development of grain trade, 218–20; misunderstanding role of the state, 128–29; post-1949 Chinese, 181–90; views of Chinese cases, 127–28; views of European cases, 127–28

Stone, Lawrence, 124

Strand, David, 164–65

Strayer, Joseph, 86

Subsistence crises: in China, 25–26, 157; in Europe, 17, 26

Sun Yat-sen, 174–75

Tanaka Masatoshi, 40

Tarrow, Sidney, 268

Tawney, R. H., 64

Tax resistance: and American and French revolutions, 234; in China and Europe, 231, 248–49, 286–87; class and community dimensions of, 249–50. *See also* Chinese tax resistance; European tax resistance

Technological change, 47, 53–58; in China, 54–55

Telford, Ted, 26

Thaxton, Ralph, 268

Thompson, E. P., 142, 218n, 219, 220, 248

Tilly, Charles, 39–40, 43, 73, 85, 93, 198–99, 216, 248, 262, 275, 284

Tilly, Louise, 219

Tocqueville, Alexis de, 110–11

Township and village industries (TVE), 184–85). *See* Rural industry

Unitary state, 169–70, 187–88, 190, 193–94, 256; Communist construction of, 268; conditions for success, 201; Confucianism and communism as ideologies for, 196; Democracy Movement's challenge to, 270; and fractal agendas, 196; in the 20th century, 200

Usher, A. P., 217–18

Vardi, Liana, 43–44

Vries, Jan de, 30, 31, 145n

Waldron, Arthur, 169

Wallerstein, Immanuel, 128n, 162

Wang Shaoguang, 286n

Weber, Eugene, 262

Weber, Max, 4, 15

William, Rowe, 112–13

Woodside, Alexander, 116

World systems theory, 150

Wrigley, E. A., 50–52, 63, 149

Xiangyue, 117, 192

Yokoyama Suguru, 246

Yu Ying-shih, 15

Yuan Shikai, 169, 260

Zelin, Madeleine, 134n